Hermeneutical Theology
and the Imperative of Public Ethics

Missional Church, Public Theology, World Christianity

Stephen Bevans, Paul S. Chung, Veli-Matti Kärkkäinen
and Craig L. Nessan, Series Editors

IN THE MIDST OF globalization there is crisis as well as opportunity. A model of God's mission is of special significance for ecclesiology and public theology when explored in diverse perspectives and frameworks in the postcolonial context of World Christianity. In the face of the new, complex global civilization characterized by the Second Axial Age, the theology of mission, missional ecclesiology, and public ethics endeavor to provide a larger framework for missiology. It does so in interaction with our social, multicultural, political, economic, and intercivilizational situation. These fields create ways to refurbish mission as constructive theology in critical and creative engagement with cultural anthropology, world religions, prophetic theology, postcolonial hermeneutics, and contextual theologies of World Christianity. Such endeavors play a critical role in generating theological, missional, social-ethical alternatives to the reality of Empire—a reality characterized by civilizational conflict, and by the complex system of a colonized lifeworld that is embedded within practices of greed, dominion, and ecological devastation. This series—Missional Church, Public Theology, World Christianity—invites scholars to promote alternative church practices for life-enhancing culture and for evangelization as telling the truth in the public sphere, especially in solidarity with those on the margins and in ecological stewardship for the lifeworld.

Hermeneutical Theology
and the
Imperative of Public Ethics

Confessing Christ in Post-Colonial World Christianity

PAUL S. CHUNG

Foreword by
CRAIG L. NESSAN

☙PICKWICK *Publications* • Eugene, Oregon

HERMENEUTICAL THEOLOGY AND THE IMPERATIVE OF PUBLIC ETHICS
Confessing Christ in Post-Colonial World Christianity

Missional Church, Public Theology, World Christianity 2

Copyright © 2013 Paul S. Chung. All rights reserved. Except for brief quotations in critical publications or reviews, no part of this book may be reproduced in any manner without prior written permission from the publisher. Write: Permissions, Wipf and Stock Publishers, 199 W. 8th Ave., Suite 3, Eugene, OR 97401.

Pickwick Publications
An Imprint of Wipf and Stock Publishers
199 W. 8th Ave., Suite 3
Eugene, OR 97401

www.wipfandstock.com

ISBN 13: 978-1-61097-502-5

Cataloguing-in-Publication data:

Chung, Paul S.

Hermeneutical theology and the imperative of public ethics : confessing Christ in post-colonial world Christianity / Paul S. Chung ; foreword by Craig L. Nessan.

xxxviii + 388 pp. ; 23 cm. Includes bibliographical references and indices.

ISBN 13: 978-1-61097-502-5

Missional Church, Public Theology, World Christianity 2

1. Missions—Theory. 2. Christianity and culture. 3. Postcolonialism. I. Nessan, Craig L. II. Title. III. Series.

BT78 .C496 2013

Manufactured in the U.S.A.

New Revised Standard Version Bible, copyright 1989, Division of Christian Education of the National Council of the Churches of Christ in the United States of America. Used by permission. All rights reserved.

Dedicated to Rev. Dr. Craig L. Nessan, a confessional, public ethicist and practitioner of shalom church in solidarity with a theology of *massa perditionis* on the globe

Contents

Foreword by Craig L. Nessan | ix
Preface | xiii
Introduction | xxiii

I. Reformation Theology, Public Ethics, and God's Mission | 1

1 Martin Luther: Public Ethics and the Discipleship of God's Mission | 3

2 John Calvin: Mission and Evangelism | 20

3 Hermeneutics of the Word-Event in the Jewish-Christian Context | 37

4 Georg F. Vicedom and God's Mission in a Larger Framework | 56

II. God's Mission, Public Ethics, and Israel: Karl Barth Revisited | 73

5 Theology of Reconciliation: God's Mission and Missional Church | 75

6 Hermeneutics of God's Mission and Prophetic *Diakonia* | 93

7 Theological-Political Ethics and the Discipleship of God's Mission | 114

8 God's Mission and Israel in the Jewish-Christian Context | 133

III. Public Ethical Theology and a Transformative Construal of the World | 153

9 Public Theology and the Discipleship of God's Mission | 155

10 Christian Social Ethics and Public Theology | 164

11 Ethical Hermeneutics, Discourse Ethics, Moral Plurality | 174

12 Moral Deliberation, Sociocultural Embeddedness, and Emancipation | 184

IV. Theological Ethics and Missional Implication | 195

13 Ethics in Integrative Framework: Duty and Virtue | 197

14 Theocentric Ethics, Theonomy, and Method of Correlation | 214

15 Narrative Theology and a Community of Character | 232

16 Biblical Realism and a Global Public Theology | 250

V. Postcolonial Public Theology and World Christianity | 271

17 Postcolonial Public Theology: Hermeneutical Reorientation and Comparative Ethics | 275

18 Dietrich Bonhoeffer and Comparative Religious Ethics: Minjung and Confucian Ethics | 291

19 Karl Barth: Religion, Pluralism, and World Christianity | 312

Excursus: A Dialogue with Karl Barth and Beyond | 329

20 Eschatology, Political Ethics, and Liberation | 341

Epilogue | 353

Bibliography | 369

Index | 385

Foreword

To encounter Paul Chung, as person or author, is to be drawn into theological conversation that is deep, expansive, and alive. At the center of this conversation is conviction about the centrality of the Triune God, who encompasses all space and time and who captivates our attention as the central reality of all life. Chung's writings vibrate with passion about the God who continues to speak to us today, who claims our allegiance, and who challenges us to confess that the world as we have conceived it until now is much too small. The book in your hands, *Hermeneutical Theology and the Imperative of Public Ethics: Confessing Christ in Post-Colonial World Christianity*, builds upon the formidable body of work that precedes it. The voice of Chung has burst upon the theological landscape over the last decade in a series of publications that demand our attention for their theological breadth, interreligious engagement, and prophetic power.

Paul Chung was born in Korea and the soul of East Asian thought is embodied in his writings in creative dialogue with the Western theological tradition. Because he knows acutely the social and economic conditions under which the subaltern-*minjung* suffer in their struggle for survival, Chung insists that the *massa perditionis*, wherever they endure, be taken seriously as subjects who must be heard and heeded in the practice of theology. He does so not only out of his personal commitment but for the sake of Jesus Christ, who himself became incarnate in the form of a humble servant, born of the peasant girl, Mary, and crucified in solidarity with all the excluded ones of this world.

Chung's theological contribution encompasses creative interreligious hermeneutics, as in this book Confucian ethics, Pure Land Buddhism, and the Hindu/Jain thought of Gandhi are brought into lively exchange with Western theology and philosophy. Such Eastern sources of wisdom are incorporated with a spirit of humility and appreciative inquiry for their constructive contributions to the pursuit of deeper understanding within the horizon of Christian theology. Of particular interest in this work are the interpretations not only of Paul Tillich but especially Karl Barth, whose reflections on world religions disclose surprising openness to insights from Asian thought.

Especially in light of his conversation with East Asian thought and other contemporary currents across the globe, Chung's theological stance is thoroughly post-colonial in perspective. He locates contemporary theology necessarily at the end of Christendom and its concomitant history of colonial imperialism. He is particularly conversant with Latin American liberation theology and its emphatic post-colonial critique of Western theology for its failures to generate emancipating praxis in solidarity with those on the underside of history, the poor and wretched of the earth.

Foundational for Chung's project are the figures of Luther and Calvin. The first two orienting chapters of this book are devoted to Luther on public ethics and the discipleship of God's mission and Calvin on mission and evangelism. Central to Luther's theology is the Word-event in Jesus Christ which becomes the organizing center for Chung's own hermeneutics of the Word-event. God as Word-event activates ever anew the *viva vox evangelii* as God-in-dialogue with the world. God as Word-event is never tame, however, insofar as God disrupts our expectations wherever God chooses to utter an irregular voice in the world (cf. Barth). Through the Word-event who is Jesus Christ, God draws all humanity into an inclusive dialogue, embracing as subjects in the conversation especially those whom the world has forgotten. Calvin's theology of the Holy Spirit in a parallel way provides activating presence to the church's mission and evangelizing.

Paul Chung engaged in graduate education in Germany and Switzerland, thus his theological and ethical perspective is deeply conversant with the major figures of continental theology from the 19th and 20th centuries. Karl Barth and Dietrich Bonhoeffer are central interlocutors in this theological conversation, especially as their thought has been transposed by Friedrich-Wilhelm Marquardt and Helmut Gollwitzer. Chung has made substantial contributions to the interpretation of both Barth and Bonhoeffer in earlier books and essays, and here draws imaginatively upon their works for the project of constructing a public ethical theology. This book builds upon Chung's original construal of Barth's theology in its socio-historical context as against the "Barthians" and proposes an astute interpretation of the Bonhoeffer legacy for a socially engaged ethics in our time.

As Chung interprets the work of other major theologians (including Schleiermacher, Ritschl, Moltmann, and Pannenberg) and theological ethicists (including Reinhold Niebuhr, H. Richard Niebuhr, Gustafson, and Hauerwas), he applies razor sharp precision in analyzing both the lasting contributions and limitations of each. His interpretations are always insightful and provocative in retrieving a usable theology for the challenges of the present. The reader is also introduced to the less familiar, yet especially significant voices of Vicedom, Marquardt, and Gollwitzer, whose work revivified Protestant theology in the post-World War II context. Marquardt, in particular, is decisive for Chung's insistence on respecting God's covenant with the Jews as binding also for all Christian theology after the Holocaust.

Chung's comparative hermeneutical method draws from the Great Tradition of the Christian faith (particularly as reformulated by Luther and Calvin and as interpreted by recent theologians), embraces major claims of Great World Religions, and takes seriously the communicative rationality of other academic disciplines, all in the service of constructing a socially-engaged public ethical theology. He defines ethics "as the theory of the conduct of human life, in which ethical questions become life questions and thereby construct meaning. Thus ethics considers concrete life situations that generate moral reflection upon particular issues, which are intertwined with the institutional life of families, schools, churches, social and public institutions, and the state. Given this, public ethical theology relates a discipleship of God's mission to life situations and develops theological, moral reflection in a broader horizon of diversity, plurality, and difference."

Finally, Paul Chung engages as a teaching theologian and professor in the North American context. This means he brings both his interreligious breadth and theological command into conversation with currents of North American theology, such as the themes of missional church or the idolatries of capitalist economy. He brings a unique voice to this work, grounded in his distinctive linguistic-emancipatory paradigm and oriented toward an archeological rewriting of the Christian tradition. Always daring to speak with boldness (*parrhesia!*) and in solidarity with the suffering ones according to the theology of the cross (*theologia crucis*), Chung advocates for a prophetic *diakonia*. Resisting all forms of totalizing discourse that fracture human identities according to gender, ethnicity, culture, or language, this book imagines, invites, and invokes the arrival of God's kingdom of shalom, encompassing peace, social justice, and the integrity of creation.

We listen again to the author's own voice as we enter into the conversations generated by this book: "I utilize a notion of public ethical theology by reconfiguring a hermeneutical theology of speech-event and God's economy in light of Christ's resurrection in solidarity with those who are fragile, vulnerable, and poor. All the while, I incorporate history and social location as affecting human moral consciousness and reasoning for the sake of the fusion of horizons between biblical narrative and social discourse of the Other in the world. Public ethical theology remains an undercurrent in refurbishing discipleship of God's mission through God's economy in light of God's speech-event in the reconciled world, while standing in expectation of the coming of the kingdom of God."

I am grateful to count Paul Chung not only as my colleague and theological companion, but as my friend. For the theological conversations that have been, for the conversation generated by this book, and for the eternal conversations yet to come, I give God thanks and praise.

Craig L. Nessan
Wartburg Theological Seminary
Dubuque, Iowa

Preface

THE THEOLOGICAL DISCOURSE OF "God's mission and the missional church conversation" is facing a challenge today from those who are variously interpreting God's mission as inculturation or solidarity with the subaltern in postcolonial World Christianity. Likewise, public theology, which emphasizes ethical guidance in the social, cultural, political, and economic spheres, attempts to reconfigure God's mission as a public, ethical discourse in engagement with the social sciences, philosophical hermeneutics, cultural anthropology, and world religions. Public theology brings a discourse of God's mission and the missional church home into the church's realm of responsibility for and engagement with society in multicultural surroundings.

The purpose of this book is to articulate and present public ethical theology and a discipleship of God's mission in a constructive, hermeneutical manner, confessing Jesus Christ in postcolonial World Christianity. If God's mission is comprehended in the Trinitarian sense, it must be seen and interpreted in the salvific activity of God's economy in relation with the sphere of political economy. Thus, God's mission as God's economy in the universal horizon of God's act of speech underlies the understanding of the discipleship of God's mission as solidarity, recognition, and emancipation in expectation of the coming kingdom of God. This perspective, which has been underdeveloped in a theological discourse of God's mission and in the missional church conversation, becomes a catalyst in the project of constructing public ethical theology in relation to discipleship of God's mission engaging in postcolonial challenges and experiences of World Christianity.

The public ethical approach to God's mission and the missional church learns from cultural anthropology to better formulate a linguistic, cultural, and emancipatory understanding of God's mission as translation in the act of interpretation in the experience of the world and to contextualize the relationship between gospel and culture, at home and abroad. In short, anthropology, in the proper sense, is the systematic study of cultural others[1] in comparison to hermeneutics as studies of the self in dialogue with the other. The hermeneutical self encounters the anthropological other in studies of public ethical theology and the discipleship of God's mission in postcolonial formation and the World Christianity perspective.

World Christianity radically breaks from the Enlightenment framework, which has been and is still influential in Western Christianity. In the context of World Christianity, the theology of *missio Dei* is reconceptualized as the translation of biblical narrative, which emphasizes the human experience of God's Word in one's own linguistic-cultural life setting. Scholars in the circle of World Christianity warn that colonial annexation and subjugation has displaced native and indigenous cultures and languages under Christendom. Indigenizing the faith calls for the decolonization of Western Christianity and theology. Inculturation and emancipation come together in the project of postcolonial World Christianity.

GOD'S MISSION AND WORD-EVENT IN THE AFTERMATH OF COLONIALISM

God's mission as translation within the perspective of World Christianity brings us home to the hermeneutical-ethical endeavor of decolonization through a confluence of multiple horizons between different cultural and linguistic worldviews for the sake of the inculturation of biblical narratives or hybridity. A hermeneutical-emancipatory theology based on word-event or speech-event, according to which God comes to us in the Word of God—thereby in the Torah and in the life, death, and resurrection of Jesus Christ—undergirds a reframing of biblical narrative in terms of understanding, translation, interpretation, and transformation in varying cultural contexts. Here, the relation between Christ and culture cannot be typologized in a way of occasional and static interaction (H. R. Niebuhr), but must be reinterpreted in the dynamic interaction or fusion of horizons between gospel and culture in an eschatologically open-ended manner.

1. Adams, *Philosophical Roots of Anthropology*, 1.

This perspective, drawing upon Christ's reconciliation with the world, develops a theological discourse of God's mission as word-event imbued with God's act of speech. This takes place by way of a hermeneutical-ethical path of approximation in an open-ended manner: meaning-appropriation from scripture, language, and history, while maintaining critical distance from, or a deconstructive strategy toward oppressive legacies in the Christian past (hermeneutics of suspicion and refusal). A final step is undertaken to recover a new horizon of meaning in the reconstruction of a self-renewed identity in the presence of the Other. In this hermeneutical-emancipatory circle I take seriously anthropological studies of culture and society as internally diverse, always changing, and affected by social discourse and hegemonic power.

This aspect becomes an arbiter in shaping and characterizing publicly oriented ethical theology in the act of interpretation and discipleship of God's mission in solidarity with those who are fragile, vulnerable, and victimized, underpinning its constructive and integrative theological direction in the experience of, while learning from, postcolonial World Christianity.[2]

A sociolinguistic theory helps a theological theory of language to better understand the mutual influences between culture and language that shape and influence moral theory in ethical life settings. A focus on language and culture in mutual interaction articulates contextual issues like ethnic stratification, gender, social inequality, and political representation to be related to social judgments of language and dialects, multilingual societies, and language contact.[3]

There is no single method available for hermeneutically informed and publically guided ethical theology for a pluralistic world. Conceptualizing a coherent, dialogical, and hospitable vision, systematic/constructive theology seeks a consistent, balanced understanding of Christian truth and faith in light of Christian (biblical and historical) tradition. It engages in the context of social contemporary thought, culture, living faith, and God's mission, and interprets God's economy in light of God's act of speech concerning the coming of kingdom of God.[4]

In appreciating the coherent, balanced, and hospitable vision, I further attempt to present a postcolonial horizon of God's mission as

2. Chung, *Public Theology in an Age of World Christianity*, 1–7.

3. Eade, *Courtroom Talk and Neocolonial Control*; Howell and Paris, *Cultural Anthropology*, 53.

4. Kärkäinnen, *Christ and Reconciliation*, 15.

speech-event in an archeological reasoning in which God is understood as the Subject of speech in the otherness of the Other, the infinite horizon of word-event in the life of Israel, the Noahide universal covenant as culminated in the life, death, and resurrection of Jesus Christ, and the communication of the Holy Spirit for all. This perspective sharpens the biblical symbol of creation in the triadic sense—original creation, ongoing creation, and the new creation—in light of Christ's *diakonia* of reconciliation underlying a linguistic-creational-emancipatory approach to public ethical theology, God's mission, and World Christianity.

We recognize in the biblical symbol of creation a complex unity between diverse structural patterns of life and events, and the dynamic interaction between natural and social, cultural process.[5] If the gospel, defined as the living word-event, implies God's self-communication in Christ to the reconciled world in an ongoing manner, public ethical theology retains its constructive character and hermeneutical-emancipatory horizon in the experience of the multiple horizons of the world and different languages, by reinterpreting and translating the biblical narrative in different times, places, and cultures. This constructive aspect drives studies of God's mission in terms of a "hermeneutical conversation" with, ethical responsibility for, and solidarity with people of other cultures and faiths, in the act of empathic listening.

PUBLIC ETHICAL EPISTEMOLOGY AND HERMENEUTICAL CONVERSATION

"Hermeneutical" logic consists of the affirmative appropriation of biblical narrative for the communication of God's salvific-economic drama to the world, while it also distances itself from the unfortunate chapter of Christian mission linked to colonialism in the past and takes into account both the postcolonial challenge and World Christianity. In terms of archeologically deciphering history and tradition, and also critical distance and deconstructive embrace, a public ethical theology seeks to acquire a new meaning of God's mission and discipleship in engagement with the others, even as it is imbued with the audacious willingness to appreciate the others and renew one's identity through them.

---

5. Schweiker, *Theological Ethics and Global Dynamics*, 33.

Furthermore, it entails a cultural-discourse framework, as it involves understanding history as the history of effect, and contemporary social location as a helpful corrective to history from the top down. Such an aspect rearticulates the irregular side of history through the lens of archeology concerning social-cultural biography and topography of those who are marginalized and discarded on the underside of history. It pursues a thick description of the gospel in different life settings, regarding the interplay between history as effect and culture as social process and system. In the history of God's mission, culture and cultural diversity will not be eradicated but redeemed, since these belong to God's blessing in the eschatological context (Rev 21:24).

Driven by God's Word as a living and emancipatory speech-event, a public ethical theology begins with understanding the biblical narrative and then seeks to translate the divine narrative of the salvific drama in the experience of the world and to communicate it to people in the public sphere. This is why the Word of God as word-event (living voice of God) occupies the central pivot in the studies of public theology, mission, and its postcolonial hermeneutical direction.

A public ethical project concerning God's mission and the missional church in hermeneutical framework contains a constructive character and methodology in terms of conceptualizing a logical, coherent, open-ended step in approximation to the subject matter of God's speech-event in the sense of *viva vox evangelii*. That is, (1) construction of Trinitarian mission in light of God's act of speech, God-in-dialogue, by embracing the church and the world through God's word-in-action and in the sense of *creatio continua*; (2) appreciation of the Christian confessional tradition, classical theology and texts, and church history as sites of missional learning; (3) a deconstructive critique of limitations, setback, and backwardness within the tradition of Christian mission in its oppressive and colonial manner while undergirding a critical analysis of the interplay between knowledge, power, and interest, and considering gender, ethnicity, race, and dominion in the social-cultural-material formation of a given society; (4) a thick description of the biblical narrative engaging in God's speech act, which embraces texuality and the social world while listening to social biography and narrative in the life of the others; (5) reconstructing a new horizon of meaning in terms of fusion of horizons between biblical narrative and worldly life connection underlying dialogue, translation, interpretation, and renewal in open-ended manner which is eschatologically driven; (6) articulation of God's mission through God's economy in the threefold sense concerning hermeneutical relation between the kingdom of the gospel, the kingdom of creation (reconciliation), and the kingdom of glory; and (7) ethical discipleship concerning God's mission in salvaging the lifeworld of God's reconciled creation from the reality of the unredeemed world—that is, the system of lordless powers. An ethical commitment should be taken in empathic listening to those who are fragile and vulnerable by way of prophetic *diakonia* in light of the grace of justification, reconciliation, and public discipleship.

A project of public ethical theology in relation to discipleship of God's mission, first of all, is biblically grounded, integrative, and in relationship with other theological disciplines. It helps missional theology to stand in public ethical orientation to the coming of the kingdom of God. Public ethical theology brings missional theology in interaction with culture, moral ethos, diverse religious worldviews, and social-economic and political backgrounds concerning those who receive the gospel about Jesus's message of the kingdom of God.

Externally, the public ethical project of God's mission in hermeneutical-emancipatory construction correlates with non-theological methods, which are involved in the study of cultural anthropology, sociology of religion, comparative religious studies, philosophical hermeneutics, and political economy. Faithful living and ethical discipleship receive their impulse from the grace of God in Christ's *diakonia* of reconciliation to the world, just as water flows from a fountain. Christian identity, as the graced missional self, lives in the conviction that it is in the presence of God and is ethically accountable in solidarity with others. Thus, the ethical self sharpens the missional self.

A public ethical theology is biblically-exegetically grounded, historically related, culturally-contextually sensitive and thick, hermeneutically deliberate, and eschatologically-liberatively driven in approximation to God who constitutes the infinite horizon of speech-event. It is also oriented toward enhancing the integrity of life in creation and solidarity with those on margins. This approach in hermeneutical and epistemological framework is sharply differentiated from an approach to integrative theology which apologetically defends the classical doctrine as universally relevant and permanently valid.[6] Such an apologetic and doctrinal ap-

---

6. Lewis and Demarest, *Integrative Theology*, 1:7–10.

proach is performed in negligence of hermeneutical-ethical engagement with the living word of God in different contexts, and thus it undermines mutual learning in dialogue with the others.

Given my project of public ethical theology and the discipleship of God's mission in postcolonial World Christianity, the introductory chapter is an attempt to hermeneutically mediate a relationship between public theology and a discourse of God's mission while also incorporating a postcolonial discourse embedded within World Christianity to public ethical theology and discipleship of God's mission. This introduction seeks to refresh and develop the conceptual clarity and transparency in relation to God's mission via God's economy in terms of word-event underlying ethical discipleship oriented toward the coming of the kingdom of God

Part I includes a public ethical reading of Reformation theology and its missional contribution while expanding its horizon toward the experience of World Christianity. This reading strategy entails a study of Martin Luther's and John Calvin's contributions to public ethical theology and the discipleship of God's mission. This study seeks to uphold an ecumenical theology of God's mission in our own context. Then I shall examine the theology of word-event in the Jewish-Christian context and Georg Vicedom's contribution to God's mission and World Christianity.

Part II explores Barth's contribution to God's mission in the Trinitarian framework, and in light of reconciliation, as I deal with public-political ethics and Jewish-Christian relationship. I shall revisit Karl Barth's contribution toward God's mission, the missional church, and World Christianity, which has been under-investigated in the North American study of Barth. Barth's theology of God's mission shall be explored in regard to theological hermeneutics, its political-prophetic ethics, and Christ's reconciliation.

Part III is a study of public ethical theology and the discipleship of God's mission by relating such discourse to practical and transformative construal of the world. I seek to benchmark a notion of God's mission against God's economy and solidarity in light of God's act of speech through the church and in the otherness of the Other. A public ethical theology and its characterization can be delineated in a broader horizon in terms of method, framework, and epistemology concerning God's mission in terms of political economy and the pace of creation.

Troeltsch's Christian social ethics will come into critical focus. A public ethical theology in an interdisciplinary framework extends moral deliberation and ethical approach to race, gender, and inequality in terms of social, cultural life connection and emancipation. A black theology and feminist approach to sexuality, difference, and inequality shall also be included in this regard.

Part IV is a study exploring theology and ethics in diverse models for missional implication. Theological ethics and their different perspectives will be mapped in view of their public and missional implication and relevance. Insofar as theological ethics aims at engaging socially with mundane issues, ethical deliberation remains substantial. Schleiermacher's contribution to ethical theology lies in articulating his ethics in an integrative framework and focusing on the relationship between duty and virtue. This aspect finds its expression in Schleiermacher-inspired [post-] modern ethics in its theocentric framework and human experience, notably in the case of James M. Gustafson in relation to Paul Tillich. Gustafson runs counter to Stanley Hauerwas's narrative theology of Jesus's gospel in light of God's kingdom and ethics of character. Reinhold Niebuhr's ethics of biblical realism and Max Stackhouse's public theology chart a socially engaged form of public theology.

Part V is a study of public ethical theology in a postcolonial formation and religious pluralism in the broader horizon of World Christianity, underpinning public-ethical hermeneutics in interreligious engagement and comparative theology. David Tracy's hermeneutics of recognition in interreligious context and William Schweiker's hermeneutical reorientation to responsibility and moral reasoning in ethically pluralistic context provide an insight toward the postcolonial public theology concerning God's creation, reconciliation, and eschatology in a linguistic-creational-emancipatory framework.

To stimulate God's mission in the postcolonial horizon of World Christianity, I choose two theologians—Dietrich Bonhoeffer and Karl Barth for reinterpreting their theological insights and legacy into underscoring public ethical theology correlated with postcolonial orientation in the experience of World Christianity. My reading strategy concerning these two theologians is a path less travelled so far. The Excursus entails my critical-constructive dialogue with Karl Barth for the breakthrough toward postcolonial public theology.

Along with Barth and Bonhoeffer, a study of the eschatological foundation for ethics of discipleship and liberation can be undertaken in the Western context of political theology as well as in the Latin American context of liberation theology. Configuring a post-Barthian course, a postcolonial contour is given to the development of liberation theology for the next generation.

The epilogue is a study of postcolonial public theology and the ethics of solidarity in approach to Trinitarian theology, an emancipatory theology of speech event, eschatology, and translation in the postcolonial context of World Christianity.

In completing a study of God's mission and public ethics, I extend my gratitude to Charlie Collier, editor at Wipf & Stock Publishers who generously has accepted my project for publication in promotion of academic studies of Missional Church, Public Theology, and World Christianity. I appreciate Prof. Dr. Craig L. Nessan who has written the foreword as encouragement and solidarity for a postcolonial project of God's mission and the imperative of public ethics in confession of Jesus Christ in the midst of World Christianity.

My assistants Timothy Maybee and Nicholas Huseby must be thanked for their careful proofreading. I would also like to thank the following for giving permission in using selected texts: from the work of *Martin Luther's Basic Theological Writings*, ed. Timothy F. Lull, with permission from Fortress Press, 1989; from the work of Karl Barth, *Church Dogmatics* I/1, II/2, IV/3.1. IV/3.2., eds. Geoffrey W. Bromiley and T. F. Torrance, first paperback edition, 2004, with permission from T. & T. Clark and the Continuum International Publishing Group. Chapter 8, "God's Mission and Israel in Jewish-Christian Context," revises "Karl Barth Regarding Election and Israel: For Jewish-Christian Mutuality in Interreligious Context," *Journal of Reformed Theology* 4/1 (2010) 23–41. The Bible quotations and references are based on the New Revised Standard Version.

Introduction

IN THE FACE OF the new and complex global civilization, this book intertwines the missional church conversation, public theology, and postcolonial World Christianity to provide a larger framework to employ public theology and the discipleship of God's mission in an interdisciplinary manner. This framework interacts with our social, multicultural, political, economic, and intercivilizational situation.

This introduction is an attempt to hermeneutically mediate public theology with God's mission and the missional church conversation in postcolonial World Christianity for developing a public ethical theology and discipleship of God's mission. Such an endeavor will lay a life-enhancing and justice-sensitive foundation for a public theology in promotion of an ethics of discipleship and solidarity concerning the coming of God's kingdom. First, I shall examine diverse models of public theology such as Stackhouse's neo-orthodox model, a liberative model, and David Tracy's revisionist correlation model in relation to the prophetic congregation study.

THE NEO-ORTHODOX AND LIBERATIVE MODELS

Public theology is best understood as the theological-philosophical endeavor to provide a broader framework to facilitate the church's engagement with social and cultural issues, in American multiculturalized society in particular. It is also helpful to advance a concept of global civil society at large. Max Stackhouse argues that theology and theological ethics remain core disciplines in undertaking "the critical examination, refinement, and guidance of religious conviction and social-ethical orientations" in the public sphere.[1]

Stackhouse proposes a public theology built on the Christian notion of stewardship involved in interpretation of public life and articulated in public discourse, including an understanding of the political, economic structure of modern life. Stewardship (translation of the biblical Greek *oikonomia*) is defined in terms of the whole inhabited world. This definition affirms that the structures of civilization under the guidance of God have brought a new interdependence in the life of the globe. Along this line Stackhouse finds social democratization or social democracy to be consonant with the Christian notion of political and economic issues. His major concept of stewardship plays as arbiter mediating a public theology with a social perspective on political economics.[2]

Since the Enlightenment, religion, ethics, moral values, and meaning have tended to relegate themselves to the private, personal, and subjective spheres of life. These elements are removed from the public, social, and objective manifestations of life. Running counter to such a dichotomy, Stackhouse advocates for public theology, arguing against the fact that God is one thing and mammon another. For one thing Christians are called to provide the world with its salvation. For another, Christian theology offers guidance to the structures and policies of public life in ethical character.[3] Having considered this, Stackhouse finds scripture, tradition, reason, and experience as guides for the construction of public theology in constant interaction with social human sciences in an ecumenical, global, interreligious, and pluralistic age.[4]

Insofar as tradition is accepted as a criterion of validity in a public theology, it is to be interpreted through the prisms of Scripture, reason, and experience.[5] Stackhouse remains within the confines of neo-orthodox theology, especially under the influence of Reinhold Niebuhr.[6] One of the important marks of neo-orthodox public theology lies in its emphasis on the relation between the Word of God and God's economic stewardship,

1. Stackhouse, *Globalization and Grace*, 80.
2. Stackhouse, *Public Theology and Political Economy*, xii.
3. Ibid., x–xi.
4. Ibid., 1–15.
5. Ibid., 8.
6. Ibid., 29.

which a faith community is called to clarify, defend, and propagate in public discourse. We also are to embody the word of God in social and institutional life, while contextualizing it in the complexities of modern political economies.[7]

In contrast to public theology in a neo-orthodox fashion, however, public theology in a liberative and feminist perspective takes interest in advancing a theological discourse that deals with a wide public arena. It challenges the boundaries of separating religious community from secular spheres.[8] This public theology seeks to incorporate distinctive insights into the building of a deliberate and democratic civil society for its direction. It circumvents the institutionalized structure of injustice and engages in curbing violence within the public sphere. This public theology addresses a concern for the quality of our communal lives as a social whole and it undergirds an emancipatory project for justice, fairness, and solidarity in the struggle for racial and cultural justice, gender and class equality, multireligious recognition, and peace within the civil society.[9]

A sociological concept of civil society plays an important role in connecting theological discourse with sociopolitical analysis and cultural imagination.[10] Gaining an important profile in constructing theology as publicly accountable discourse, public theology finds its unique place in upholding non-partisan and open theological research along with natural science, social-critical science, and other religions.[11]

THE REVISIONIST CORRELATION MODEL

David Tracy's revisionist model is best described as proposing public theology in terms of the correlation between Christian theology and philosophical reflection. Seen in his basic argument of correlational revisionist theology, the self-referent as a subject of the revisionist model is committed to a contemporary revisionist notion of the beliefs, values, and faith of an authentic secularity (a non-theistic and anti-Christian

7. Ibid., 34.
8. Valentin, *Mapping Public Theology*, 85; Cady, *Religion, Theology, and American Life*.
9. Valentin, *Mapping Public Theology*, 87.
10. Ibid., 83.
11. Ibid., 86; Kaufman, *In Face of Mystery*.

secularism). It also deals with a revisionist understanding of the beliefs, values, and faith of an authentic Christianity (as an anti-secular, religious supernaturalism).[12]

For the praxis of a revisionist theory, Tracy pays attention to political theology and liberation theology in their reinterpretation of the classical Hegelian-Marxist notion of praxis. These two forms of political and liberation theology have managed to retrieve the social and political dimension against the individualism of transcendental theology (seen in Johannes Metz's critique of Karl Rahner). These theologies also retrieve Jewish and Christian eschatological meanings in the field of social, political and religious liberation. These are seen in Jűrgen Moltmann's critique of the existentialism of Rudolf Bultmann and the "Kierkegaardian" Barth.[13]

Distancing himself from the existential individualism in the neo-orthodox model, Tracy incorporates eschatological theologies of praxis and their achievements into his model of revisionist theology of praxis. On the other hand, in distinction from eschatological theologies, Tracy advocates the critical theory or philosophy for the full demands of praxis, that is, "our ineluctable commitment to the ultimate meaningfulness of every struggle against oppression and for social justice and agapeic love."[14]

Such a perspective leads Tracy to appreciate critical social theory in the work of Jürgen Habermas. The chief distinguishing characteristic of both the revisionist theology and critical social theory entails the central demand for continually refining critical theory in a genuine sense. This aspect seeks to universally apply to all experience and all symbol-systems.[15]

Related to a critical social theory, a revisionist theology as practical public theology assumes a form of philosophical reflection which embraces the meanings manifested in our common human experience and in the Christian tradition, as well. This critical-theoretical aspect of the constructive theological model, expanding scientific empirical data, critical social analyses, and ethical analysis, retains the hermeneutical aspect in the reinterpretation of societal and projective limit-possibilities as revealed in the Christian symbols.

---

12. Tracy, *Blessed Rage for Order*, 33.
13. Ibid., 243.
14. Ibid., 245.
15. Ibid., 246.

In his heuristic alliance between critical social theory and philosophical hermeneutics, Tracy values Habermas's theory of communicative action while not leaving the sure ground of hermeneutical reflection. Tracy's proposal clarifies the nature of public theology as fundamental, hermeneutical, systematic, and practical in terms of the revised correlational method.[16]

Tracy identifies three publics which are relevant to public theology, society, the academy, and the church. A public theology seeks to make the structure and logic of the argument explicit. It presents arguments available to all rational persons. Finally, it demonstrates that the theological position is grounded in some form of general philosophical arguments rather than based on the theological logic of Christian faith.[17]

PUBLIC THEOLOGY AND PROPHETIC CONGREGATION

It is essential to seek a common language or common ground for public discourse in a pluralistic society with competing values and judgments about the good life. The public church can be credible in a religiously pluralist context. As we have already seen, public theologians advocate for the public sphere and language as the background for shaping and sharpening theological or ecclesial language to be more amenable to public, secular, and ethical issues. They challenge a narrow minded spectrum of missional theology, providing what is important in public matters. They strive to mediate the differences between theology and philosophy or other scientific disciplines for the sake of openness and commonality.

When they speak of the Trinitarian theology, they are concerned with the freedom of the triune God who speaks to the church through diverse ways and in multiple manners. Here friendly and open dialogue remains central in the public theological endeavor and struggle with public, ethical, and non-theological matters.

In a Jewish-Christian context, the God of Israel (YHWH) is valued and a commonality between biblical monotheism and the Christian Trinity is emphasized. Tracy insists that "the central religious affirmation of Judaism, Christianity, and Islam will be the classic *shema Yisrael* of

---

16. Tracy, "Theology, Critical Social Theory," in Browning and Fiorenza, eds., *Habermas, Modernity, and Public Theology*, 25–26.

17. Tracy and Cobb, *Talking About God*, 9; Tracy, *Analogical Imagination*, 64.

Deuteronomy 6:4–5."[18] Thus Christian monotheism is best described as a Trinitarian monotheism.[19] George Lindbeck, convinced of St Paul's theology of Israel in Romans 11, stresses that Israel is the tree and the church is an engrafted branch.[20] God's covenant with the Jews is irrevocable and unconditional. This biblical perspective delivers the missional church from the ecclesial triumphalism following from its expropriation.[21]

Missional church based on God's mission and the New Testament's great command (Matt 28:19) must be a form of pubic witness in dialogue with the Jewish community regarding God's one covenant of solidarity into which Jesus Christ grafts the church as an alien guest through his death and resurrection.

Furthermore, Habermas and his socio-critical theory remain influential by helping theologians to investigate the significance of communicative theory and action for developing public church and theology in the communicative framework of civil society and deliberate democracy. A communicative understanding and rationality becomes a significant arbiter for shaping the public nature and character of Christian faith. Christian community cannot be dissociated with true public life in a civil society which is led and constituted by open conversation, plural discourses.[22]

Public theology in a sociological communicative framework integrates the socio–critical theory of the lifeworld and attempts to call for the prophetic vocation of missional congregations for the sake of public companions. Here, congregations are understood as primal and productive centers of theological imagination in which a critical theology of vocation undergirds a model of church as servant. A critical theology of vocation argues that everyone participates in God's public, acknowledging social places and institutions as God's creative work or God's companions. Here a concept of civil society is preferred as the location for the congregational vocation of public companionship.

Thus congregations are conceptualized as places of encounter between individual-personal and civil-public life. Congregation as the community of public vocation can be seen in light of the communicatively

---

18. Frymer-Kensky et al., *Christianity in Jewish Terms*, 79.
19. Ibid., 83.
20. Ibid., 108.
21. Ibid., 110.
22. Browning and Fiorenza, eds., *Habermas, Modernity, and Public Theology*, 1–5.

prophetic public companion. They bring a compassionate commitment and moral contribution to other civil institutions while contesting the systematic colonization of the lifeworld.[23]

GOD'S MISSION AND THE MISSIONAL CHURCH CONVERSATION

Public theology in a sociological communicative framework shares a common interest in God's mission and the missional church conversation with those committed to relating and reconceptualizing God's mission in regard to congregational study in North American society. It is certain that the concept of God's mission has assumed its post-colonial character. Early in the twentieth century many critiques were raised against the missionary-colonialist enterprise. The fierce reactions to colonialism were heard in the context of "younger churches" in Africa and Asia and the growth of indigenous nationalist and anti-colonial movements made the missionary enterprise suspect.

In the 1930s Karl Barth was already a catalyst in paving the way to God's mission in the Trinitarian framework. The Barthian sending model, built on Trinitarian sending and election, marks theological progress in undergirding ecumenical development about God's mission, overcoming the anthropocentric and ecclesiocentric model of mission which was previously under suspicion of the political charge of colonialism. Given this, the fundamental statement of the Willingen Conference reads: "The mission is not only obedience to a word of the Lord, . . . it is participation in the sending of the Son, in the *missio Dei*, with the inclusive aim of establishing the lordship of Christ over the whole redeemed creation."[24]

With his reflection on the Willingen Conference, George Vicedom propagated a notion of God's mission through his seminal book *Mission of God* in which he comprehends the mission of the triune God in a special and a general framework in accordance with the Lutheran model of two kingdoms. Both the church's mission and the church are defined as instruments of God through which God carries out God's mission.[25]

On the other hand, Barth's notion of a sending triune God was accepted and mediated into undergirding the missional church conversa-

23. Simpson, *Critical Social Theory*, 141–44.
24. Vicedom, *Mission of God*, 5.
25. Ibid., 5–6.

tion through the writings of Leslie Newbigin who underpins the term "the missionary God." However, it is open to debate whether Barth himself coined the terminology of God as "a missionary God."[26]

At any rate, Newbigin's legacy is succeeded and developed in terms of the missional church conversation. Newbigin is an important mentor for the project of the Gospel and Our Culture Network through his development of a Trinitarian-ecclesiological approach to mission. Within the context of the missional literature, this approach has demonstrated a theological, congregational, and spiritual response to the decline of Christian religion in the United States. Addressing the individualistic and private manner of American religious behavior, the missional church movement proposes missional and congregational ecclesiology by emphasizing what it means for the church to be a part of the *missio Dei* in the world.[27]

Theology of *Missio Dei* also became foundational for David Bosch's notion of transforming mission and for the Gospel and Our Culture Network within the reformed, Baptist, and ecumenical framework. Bosch noticed that Barth was the decisive Protestant missiologist in his generation. According to Bosch's evaluation, Barth in his *Church Dogmatics* develops the missional dimension of his ecclesiology.[28]

According to Guder, the missional reorientation of theology under the rubric of a missionary God and the church as a "sent people" redefines an understanding of the Trinity. In light of this Trinitarian model of sending (following the lead of Barth and Bosch), the church is seen as the instrument of God's mission. According to Guder, the term "missional" refers to the essential nature and vocation of the church. A missional ecclesiology is biblical, historical, contextual, eschatological, and practical.[29]

Developing the legacy of Karl Barth in the American context, several scholars have developed a transforming model of covenant and law in terms of the sending character of God (Augustine, Karl Barth, and Karl Rahner) as well as the social doctrine of the Trinity (John Zizioulas, J. Moltmann, Miroslav Volf, and Catherine LaCugna). Moltmann's participatory model based on a shared *perichoresis* between God and creation

---

26. Van Gelder and Zscheile, *Missional Church in Perspective*, 26–27. See Flett, *Witness of God*, 196–239.

27. Guder, ed., *Missional Church*, 1–17.

28. Bosch, *Transforming Mission*, 373.

29 Guder, ed., *Missional Church*, 11.

comes to the fore.[30] In a missional theology of creation and culture, a model of participation in the Trinitarian sense is comprehended in a qualified manner focusing on the incarnation of Christ, who is the ultimate key as the meeting point between God, humanity, and the world.[31]

Furthermore, God's mission is comprehended as God's ongoing activity in the world related to the reign (kingdom) of God to which Jesus's message and practice of the reign of God remains central.[32] However, there is some complexity in dealing with the relationship between God's mission as work of redemption (specialized) and God's mission in relation to all creation (generalized) for further discussion of theology of *missio Dei*. During the 1960s J. C. Hoekendijk, a Dutch missiologist, already raised a controversial version of God's mission in a way of establishing shalom on earth in a universal and generalizing manner. Thus the leitmotif in Christian mission is that God intends to redeem the whole creation.[33]

GOD'S MISSION AND WORLD CHRISTIANITY

In the circle of the missional church conversation, globalization is taken seriously as leading to multiple ethnic cultures in pluralist society which is characteristic of increased mobility, the socioeconomic and racial transition of communities, and diversity and racial tradition among those living together in the neighborhoods of North America.[34]

Attention is given to cultural diversity and hybridity in a networked world, while acknowledging cultural and religious pluralism in the twenty-first-century landscape of the U.S context, as in many societies. Globalizing civilization has strikingly caused a deterritorialization of culture, making it a hybrid, relational complex fused within cultures. It entails de-Europeanizing American Christianity, thus the *missio Dei* is ahead of the church's mission moving far beyond the control of the church.[35] It is important to consider the challenge of World Christianity in terms of the hermeneutics of difference and appreciation of many stories

30. Van Gelder and Zscheile, *Missional Church in Perspective*, 112.
31. Ibid., 139.
32. Ibid., 47.
33. Hoekendijk, *Church Inside Out*, 19–20.
34. Gruder, ed., *Missional Church*, 43, 45.
35. Van Gelder and Zscheile, *Missional Church in Perspective*, 128, 131.

in which God's mission is presented to be more amenable to multicultural engagement through hospitality and reciprocity.[36]

In view of the globalized context of World Christianity, Stephen Bevan and Roger Schroeder have made a substantial contribution to proposing an interactive model which takes seriously the worldliness of God's mission in terms of their approach for the sake of the constants of God's grace in the world of nature. They are engaged with the painful history of colonial mission in terms of self-renewal and reconstruction of one's identity in appreciation of others. For instance, their study of the mission of Las Casas in Spanish colonialism as liberation in solidarity with the indigenous people and Matteo Ricci's mission as inculturation in Chinese Confucian context (including Robert de Nobili and Alexandre de Rhodes) remains an inspiration for theologians of World Christianity to further develop God's mission in terms of prophetic justice, dialogue, and a hermeneutics of appreciation.[37] This interactive model finds its further inspiration and becomes sharpened in a World Christianity model of the *missio Dei* as emancipation and translation in a postcolonial relief.

In the rise of World Christianity much has been said about the indigenization of the Christian narrative. Being 'transcultural' means indigenous discovery of the biblical narrative and vernacular interpretation of it.[38] Furthermore, Postcolonial theologians denounce Christian concepts of the church's mission as imperial expansion of the idea of white Christian Europe or America. Postcolonial theory takes issue with the cultural and economic legacy and aftermath of colonialism which continue in previously colonized countries. It takes issue with ongoing relationships of the political system, economic exchange, and elitists' cultural hegemony and education between former colonies and colonizers. Postcolonial theory helps to identify a hidden regime of power and dominion and guide a new strategy of resistance in counter hegemony against the neocolonial reality in the aftermath of colonialism.

---

36. Ibid., 132.
37. Bevans and Schroeder, *Constants in Context*, 176–95.
38. Sanneh, *Disciples of All Nations*, 27.

POSTCOLONIAL RECONSTRUCTION OF MISSION BEYOND EMPIRE

As already stated, scholars of World Christianity argue that the biblical narrative must be interpreted through a plurality of models of inculturation through acknowledging various local idioms and practices. The translatability of Scripture into different languages and the indigenous naming of God in different religious contexts becomes a watershed for recognizing and promoting the indigenous contribution to God's mission as translation in an age of post-western Christianity.

Similarly, Postcolonialists take interest in denouncing neo-colonial discourse and hegemony structure embedded within the abuse of power, developing a reading strategy in confrontation with the Western discourse of Orientalism in its representation of the non-Western. They propose a methodology of suspicion, refusal, and deconstruction concerning any presentation and argument about the truth entrapped with a colonialist discourse of representation, hegemony and dominion.

A postcolonial reconstruction of God's mission is biblically grounded on Jesus's narration of remembrance which is connected with the place of those who are fragile, vulnerable, and victimized. A strategy of rewiring history in not-forgetting the place of those on the margin entails an important task for postcolonial mission concerning an unfortunate espousal between mission and the barbarism of colonialism. A postcolonial mission is interrogated by the question "can the subaltern speak?" and attempts to create a larger space for the subaltern to speak for themselves.

Postcolonial missional theologians, such as Jonathan Ingleby, take issue with the Empire in terms of a consistent biblical theme. The Empire has its appointed task. In a biography of Rudyard Kipling, we read about the imperial mission to the American nation: "Take Up The White Man's Burden" for the colonization of the Philippines.[39] White European nations had an imperial responsibility for colonial intervention.

Michael Hardt and Antonio Negri in their book *Empire* are welcomed in the circle of postcolonial deconstructive theology, because it reveals that the new imperial order controls its subjects. By using the ideology of mass communications, proponents of Empire are critical of the linguistic mechanism of generating a global imagery and reality. An imperial system and culture of Empire is noticed by interventions related

---

39. Ingleby, *Beyond Empire*, 32.

to the cultural or communications field and to the financial market as well as the use of military force.

To overcome the structure of the legitimation of hegemony under Empire, Ingleby advocates a prophetic tradition of the scriptures and other prophetic voices in religion and politics. A new biblical exegesis, which focuses on the Old Testament, the Apocalyptic writing in the gospels and Paul's letters, is introduced to promote anti-imperialist or postcolonial theology and mission beyond Empire.[40]

A postcolonial notion of resistance is characterized by interpolation, mimicry, archeology and magic realism, palimpsest, and representation. These concepts provide practical epistemologies for the church to propose a postcolonial theology and mission in public places. According to the basic principle of interpolation, the colonized uses the cultural capital of the imperial system to dismantle it. Lamin Sanneh's model of translation is a commentary on interpolation. Translation relies upon local wisdom and language, transferring power away from the center. The notion of interpolation corrects some shortcomings of Edward Said's logic of Orientalism. Said posits too passive a role for the colonized, undermining the power of religious classics in the colonized. A discourse of representation is written off. This refers to the hermeneutical malnutrition visible in Said's colonial study of Orientalism. We need to differentiate the Western misrepresentation from the indigenous' own re-presentation of their discourse, tradition, history, and culture.

According to Ingleby, a postcolonial notion of re-presentation can be done within the project of rewriting history. A postcolonial passion for rewriting or re-presenting history calls for a new hermeneutical strategy for deciphering the irregular side buried on the underside of history through archeological methodology. This aspect in quest for history has nothing to do with a nostalgic journey back to the colonized past, a general concept critically spread in the postcolonial deconstructive circle influenced by the anti-historical semiology of Derrida.

Cutting through a social reality of binary opposition in the previous colonial era, an archeology is undertaken to unearth history. A contemporary use of traditional material derived from local sources, written or oral, calls into question the assumptions of Western rational narrative. A postcolonial hermeneutics in an archeological sense requires a herme-

---

40. Ibid., 29.

neutical audacity to reinterpret the traditional story or texts for engendering a new, fresh, extraordinary meaning for the sake of a fusion of horizons between the present and the past which aims at reconstructing the project of the future.

The idea of a palimpsest was simply a piece of manuscript on which the previous entry had been replaced by another. Colonialism may have written itself on a place, for instance, through maps and boundaries, through choosing names and ways of representation. But no inscription is indelible. Missionaries originally wrote their version of the gospel under their cultural, linguistic biases. Subsequently, those who inhabit the place need to re-write their cultural story on the place in question, proposing a meaning of the Gospel in a different context.

An idea of mimicry originates in mimic persons. The colonial authorities needed them as intermediaries to serve the interest of the colonizer by mediating and interpreting between the colonial authority and the colonized. This mimic person is indigenous in blood and color, while Western in taste, in opinions, in morals, and in intellect.[41] Mimicry is not necessarily a deliberate strategy, rather a reminder to those in authority to use people. A policy of mimicry has consequence. Nonetheless, I am less convinced of the psychological notion of mimicry because of its unhealthy political consequence on the relationship between semi-periphery country and periphery country. The colonial rule and its politics of dominion could be exercised in the sense of political mimicry on the part of the previously colonized against the neighboring weaker countries.

PUBLIC THEOLOGY AND DISCIPLESHIP OF GOD'S MISSION

In the investigation of public theology and discipleship of God's mission in a postcolonial and constructive framework, I interchangeably use the term "word-event" with "speech-event" in the sense of God's act of speech transpiring in intertextuality between the biblical text and social world, especially in the otherness of the other: the subaltern-minjung.

If God's mission in the world stands in dialogical relationship with God's mission of grace in the gospel in expectation of the coming of God's kingdom, the *regnum naturae* (kingdom of nature) is the reflection of *regnum gloriae* (kingdom of glory). There is a deep interaction

---

41. Ibid., 51.

between the world of gospel and the *regnum naturae* in light of the future glory of God.[42]

If God comes to us as word-event, God's word is expressed through human language. The word 'God' brings to utterance the mystery of reality, becoming the most pure possibility of language for us to be open to God and the reality of the world. The problem of language is closely interwoven with the question of God. In a situation in which words are spoken, communicative links with our fellow people are associated with the utterance. Utterance in language would not be possible without the possibility of participation and exchange in the shared subjectivity, interdependence of social reality, and in the experience of the world.[43]

Critically appreciating the hermeneutical theology of word-event, I maintain that to "construct" means to "pile up," "build," or "put together," conveying creative imagery to place things together, fashioning a meaningful arrangement and a semblance of order out of chaos.[44]

Public theology in a constructive manner requires a continual process of interpretation that constructs new visions of Christian faith and practice in the context of contemporary cultural challenges and flux. It is certain that liberationists make a substantial contribution to denouncing the power structure and oppression underneath Christian discourse and institutionalized discourse. Their theological method is driven by a particular human experience of liberation in the preferential option for the poor. The social-historical experience of liberation and solidarity with the poor are central in the liberationist definition of theology as critical reflection on Christian praxis in light of the Word of God.

"Faith in search of understanding" has shaped systematic-dogmatic theology in terms of Christian faith. Simple answers to the meaning of faith in the public sphere are not easy to find with an awareness of the complexity, multiplicity, and indeterminacy in our time. If faith seeks understanding, faith and understanding come together in a linguistic, comprehensive circle, rather than expressing a one-sided fideism. If faith is a gift of the Holy Spirit and grasped by the living word-event of God who loves in freedom and embodiment, the word of God as word-event guides and shapes a linguistic configuration between faith and understanding

---

42. Iwand, *Nachgelassene Werke: Glauben und Wissen*, 1:290.
43. Ebeling, *Introduction to Language*, 56.
44. Hodgson, *Winds of the Spirit*, 39.

for underlying God's mission through God's economy in the experience and renewal of world.

In comprehending language of faith as language of dialogue with the world, God is the One who provides the place of life arrangements enhancing integrity of life and developing fullness of life underlying God's mission as God's *oikonomia*. This perspective takes issue with economic issues in terms of the correlation between God's mission and God's *oikonomia*. God's *oikos* becomes a conceptual tool in the church's practice in dealing with how God and economy are correlated in the political economic context. The gospel has a logic coming from the Logos, Jesus Christ, who has come to us through Israel. God's household is constituted by *diakonia* which helps formulate how to promote and engage the Christian praxis and discipleship following in the economic work of God in the public realm.[45]

In the Christian faith connected with the economy of God, we observe that God's righteousness (Isa 24:16) articulates God as the One who does steadfast love, justice, righteousness on earth (Jer 9:24; Ps 15:1–2), creating and liberating life out of the power of nothingness. Torah includes God's economy and grace because it is guidance for the life of righteousness and equality in God's household, favoring the weaker members of society based on the ethos of the exodus. (Exod 22:21–24; Deut 24:17–18). The Covenant code (Exod 20:22—23:33), the Deuteronomic Code (Deut 12–26), and the Holiness Code (Lev 17–26) demonstrate God's economic concern in protecting the endangered livelihood of the weak, the fragile, and the vulnerable. Likewise, Jesus as circumcised deacon (Rom 15:8) continues to embody God's economy in his sociobiographical solidarity with public sinners and tax collectors–ochlos–minjung and in his identity with the hungry, the thirsty, a stranger, the naked, the sick, and a prisoner—thereby "one of the least of these who are members of my family" (Matt 25: 40). Jesus's mission for the kingdom of God is expressed well in the prophetic spirit (Luke 4:18–19).

This aspect becomes the driving force for me to public-ethically comprehend God's mission through God's economy in terms of God's act of speech concerning Christian eschatology: in terms of double listening (to the Word in the churchly life and to God's irregular voice in the world) and archeological rewriting of the irregular side or underside of

---

45. Meeks, *God the Economist*, 45.

history. Archeological strategy is inseparably connected with a project of social narrative through the material formation of labor, capital, and marketing as well as social discourse based on the interplay between knowledge and power. An interpretative circulation in this regard can be summarized: self-exposure to the Other, creative appropriation of the meaning of Christian narrative (evangelization/witness), critical distance from the limitations in the past of Christian mission (for instance, espousal between mission and colonialism), self-renewal, reconstruction of Christian public identity in recognition of and learning from the Other, and attending to the place of language as social and cultural discourse built on the interplay between religious knowledge and the institutionalized power system.

This perspective sharpens the church's public activity of evangelization and God's mission in the horizon of God's kingdom by claiming prophetic awareness and solidarity in relation to the world-economy and Empire. Theological discourse of God's mission and missional church conversation expands and enriches its horizon as it advances and engages in postcolonial challenge and in the voice of World Christianity in an interdisciplinary framework, especially from the perspective of public theology and ethics of discipleship. This perspective underlines the study of Reformation, public ethics, and God's mission in Part I.

Reformation Theology, Public Ethics, and God's Mission

1

Martin Luther

Public Ethics and the Discipleship of God's Mission

THERE HAVE BEEN STRIKINGLY critical remarks about Lutheran ethics. Ernst Troeltsch critiques Luther for failing to attain comprehensive sociological influence and significance because of his vocational ethic, which views the secular institution as the divinely appointed means for perfecting Christian morality.[1] On the other hand, others charge Luther with ignoring the missionary duty of the church. Bosch, for instance, accuses Luther's teaching on justification of paralyzing any missionary effort because it overemphasizes God's initiative and is preoccupied with human depravity. Such a perspective propels a pessimistic view of humanity "as mere pawns on a chessboard."[2] Given this critique of Luther, I shall undertake a study exploring Luther's contribution to public ethics and discipleship of God's mission by heeding diverse dimensions of his theology.

GOD'S MISSION IN TRINITARIAN FRAMEWORK AND THE MISSIONAL CHURCH

Barthian grounding of mission as God's sending has become a theological principle in an ecumenical context by inspiring Barth's followers to advance God's mission in the Trinitarian framework. Luther's Trinitarian

1. Gayhart, *Ethics of Ernst Troeltsch*, 195–96.
2. Bosch, *Transforming Mission*, 242.

thinking is reluctant to conflate God *in self* (the immanent Trinity) with God *for us* (the economic Trinity). God *in self* belongs to God's majesty and mystery while God *for us* in the world brings us to respect the freedom and majesty of God *in self*.

The doctrine of the Trinity embedded within the gospel becomes the sum of the gospel of justification, because the triune God is the God who reveals God's self in the gospel of Jesus Christ through the Holy Spirit. Thus, Luther defines God as the "glowing oven full of love,"[3] which underlines an active horizon of the Word of God. The Word of God is active and emancipatory because God is love. The triune God who is revealed as the glowing oven full of love is the One who speaks in terms of *opus alienum* (God's strange work), *nomos* (law), and *opus proprium* (the gospel).

According to Luther, Jesus Christ opens to us "the most profound depths of his fatherly heart and his pure, unutterable love."[4] Thus, Luther's concept of *theologia crucis* (theology of the cross) provides an insight into qualifying and characterizing the mission of the triune God. Conformity to Christ characterizes our discipleship and participation in Christ's ministry and mission for God's reign in the world. Trinitarian mission is grounded in Luther's basic conviction that "the Father gives us all creation, Christ all his works, the Holy Spirit all his gifts."[5]

Having considered this, God sent the church into the world and it exists for the sake of the world, because the church is the assembly of saints that occurs through the Word and the sacraments in the presence of the Holy Spirit. The Spirit is the One "who effects faith where and when it pleases God in those who hear the gospel, . . . not on account of our own merits but on account of Christ."[6]

The church as the assembly of saints has essentially a missional character and public responsibility. Luther elaborates his missional ecclesiology in terms of the third article: the Holy Spirit. Our existence is made holy by the Holy Spirit and by the Word. We become holy in the community of saints through the forgiveness of sins, and we are in hope of the resurrection of the body, and the life everlasting. The word *ecclesia*, rendered

---

3. See Gollwitzer, "Zur Einheit von Gesetz und Evangelium," in Gollwitzer, *Auch das Denken darf dienen*, 1:156.

4. Luther, "Large Catechism," in Kolb and Wengert, eds., *Book of Concord* (=BC), 439–50.

5. Ibid., 440.

6. "Augsburg Confession," art. 5, in Kolb and Wengert, eds., BC, 41.

in English to mean "church," properly means an assembly rather than a consecrated house or building. The word *church* really means a common assembly, "a holy Christian people." Furthermore, the church is defined as "the mother that begets and bears every Christian through the Word of God, which the Holy Spirit reveals and proclaims, through which he illuminates and inflames hearts so that they grasp and accept it, cling to it, and persevere in it."[7] So we see the missional church, in proclamation of the Word and the effectiveness of the Spirit, is grounded in Trinitarian activity for the world.

The classic doctrine of appropriation entails the possibility of bringing the triune God toward a language-event because we can call God in terms of Creator, Redeemer, and Sanctifier. God's life in *perichoresis* (the mutual relatedness of the Triune God as inhering in God's self-permeation without confusion) is inseparably connected with a hermeneutical process of defining the name of God (assigning to one person that which is common to all). The Augustinian rule becomes meaningful in a linguistically innovative manner: *opera trinitatis ad extra sunt indivisa* (the external works of the Trinity are indivisible). This rule does not necessarily mean for Luther the immutability and unrelatedness of the divine being in relation to the world.

LINGUISTIC FEATURING OF THE TRINITY AND THE MISSION OF WORD-EVENT

In Luther's exposition of John's Prologue, God is the Word speaking in, with, and to God's self. God's being is the subject of speaking because the Word of God as the force of communication enables communication within God's self and for the world. This perspective undergirds Luther's notion of gospel as *viva vox Dei*. God is living, effective, life-giving, forgiving, and emancipating in the gospel, since God's Trinitarian being is comprehended in the internal structure of speech-event in terms of promise, dialogue, and communication. "God of himself speaks his word so that the godhead follows the word and remains with its nature in the word and is there in its essence."[8]

---

7. Luther, "Large Catechism," in Kolb and Wengert, eds., BC, 436.
8. Cited in Bayer, *Luther's Theology*, 340n47.

In contrast to the Greek *logos*, the *Word* or incarnation in Christian tradition is pure event by affirming that the Word became flesh. The theological idea of incarnation emphasizes the unity between God the Father and God the Son whose Trinitarian mystery is conceived of in the phenomenon of language. John's Prologue describes the sending of the Son and the mystery of the incarnation by way of the Word.

Luther demonstrates a linguistic understanding of the gospel as the living voice of God (*viva vox evangelii*) and this Word is ever new in proclamation. The gospel already points to the multiplicity of its proclamation, so that the meaning of the Word is closely connected with the event of proclamation. God's act of speech is not only present in the ecclesial sphere, but is also working in the world of creation. Insofar as God binds God's Word to us through the Spirit, we can believe in God. Faith grounded in the grace of Jesus Christ is the event in which God comes to us in the presence of the Spirit.[9]

The Word explicating itself in the multiplicity of words brings out the character of language as event. According to Gadamer, "being an event is a characteristic belonging to the meaning itself."[10] In light of God's speech-event, Luther presents in his *Smalcald Articles* "the mutual conversation and consolation of brothers and sisters"[11] as an objective and necessary form of the gospel (what I call the fifth form of the gospel) coupled with preaching, the sacraments, and the office of the keys. God's speech-event points to an open event involved in the communicative sphere of daily human life. Luther conceptualizes a notion of the mutual conversation and consolation of brothers and sisters according to Matt 18:20. Luther's theology of proclamation in light of the word-event contains a dynamic, relational notion of God's involvement in the human communicative sphere. This aspect characterizes the Hebrew orientation in Luther's thought. We read in 1 Sam 23:42, "The Lord is witness between you and me forever . . . The Lord shall be between me and you, and between my descendants and your descendants, forever."

Luther defines and determines the Word of God by its effect. Here, the full historicity of the speech and action of God is adequate in the sense of Hebrews 1:1. "God spoke to our ancestors in many and various

---

9. Iwand, "Theologie als Beruf," in *Glauben und Wissen*, 243.

10. Gadamer, *Truth and Method*, 427.

11. Luther, "Smalcald Articles," in Kolb and Wengert, eds., BC, 319.

ways by the prophets." The Word of God in Jesus Christ must be comprehended in God's act of speech throughout all the ages in their plural horizons of effect.

Luther's fifth form of the gospel is appropriate for the historical effect of God's word in action or word-event. God's speech-event is not merely fixed or conceptualized in an abstract manner, but takes place in an ongoing and open-ended manner. God's word can be understood interpersonally, having an authority in *mutual conversation*. The *consolation of brothers and sisters* explains mutual conversation in terms of a supplementary characteristic of God's Word.[12] Luther heeds the dialogical presence of God in Jesus Christ by the Spirit, expressing the comforting and pastoral aspect of the gospel. Luther is portrayed as a theologian of dialogue and colloquium in the interpersonal and public sphere, listening attentively to God's Word as event in the sense of the *Dabar* (God's Word-in-action) and *Logos*.

As previously stated, the word-event is embodied in the gospel, which is the living voice of God. Scripture as a witness to the Word of God sets forth Christ; it is "what urges Christ." Jesus Christ as the heart of Scripture, which is called the "canon within the canon," qualifies the law-gospel hermeneutics pertaining to proclamation. A theology of proclamation is foundational for a missional theology in terms of God's promise and evangelization as word-event.

THE MISSION OF THE WORD-EVENT AND INTERPRETATION

The Spirit was actually poured out at Pentecost, including the gift of speech and understanding across ethnic boundaries. With the gift of speech people of every nation can understand each other. If understanding becomes possible in a hermeneutical sense through language, the Word of God in the presence of the Holy Spirit opens up and brings human existence to an encounter with the reality of God's speech to us. The character of the gospel as *pro nobis* (for us) is grounded in God's *promissio* (promise) underlying God's *missio*.

A concept of *viva vox evangelii* (the living voice of the gospel) puts a priority of the spoken word (God's Saying; *Dabar* in Hebrew) in relation

---

12. Marquardt, *Von Elend und Heimsuchung der Theologie*, 160–61.

to the written word (the Scripture). Theology is thus for the proclamation of the Word of God through the dynamism of law and gospel, living and effective in us and emancipating our life.[13]

Luther's heuristic distinction between God's incomprehensibleness and God's self-disclosure in the gospel can be missionally refurbished in the linguistic comprehensive circle for the sake of articulating God's mission of grace as word-event in conversation with God's ongoing activity in the world of creation, that is, the life horizon of the first function of the law.

Given this, Luther was interested in establishing the necessity of an interpretation to be undertaken in a new and fresh light by listening to the word of Scripture. This is in contrast to a normative interpretation previously fixed over the Scripture. The interpretation of the Word of God is necessary in different times and places because Luther was convinced that the gospel is not merely written word, but a living voice of God. The living voice of God encounters us in our midst and here and now (Heb 4:12–13; 1 Cor 1:18; Isa 55:11). Driven by God's acts of speaking, Luther relates God's word to a real thing or action (*verbum reale*). God's being is in God's word-in-deed, that is, speaking is doing, thus the word is the deed.[14]

Interpretation establishes the claim of the Scripture to be the Word of God. This perspective provides an important hermeneutical resource for refining mission as interpretation or translation. Mission is not imposition of certain words or statements from Scripture mechanically and unilaterally to people of other cultures who receive the gospel. Even the same word can be spoken differently to another context, having multiple meanings. Mission as an interpretation of biblical narrative sharpens God's mission as translation which is seen obviously in the postcolonial World Christianity today.

JUSTIFICATION AND JUSTICE

Luther's teaching of justification is of a dialectical character by incorporating a forensic element from without into an effective and transformative moment of the happy exchange. The living Christ in the presence of Word and Spirit is the driving force for our justification and renewal, making the grace of justification complete and dynamic.

---

13. Ebeling, "Word of God and Hermeneutics," in Ebeling, *Word and Faith*, 78–110.

14. Marquardt, *Das christliche Bekentnis*, 1:141–45.

In speaking of Luther's public ethical theology, it is important to review Moltmann's position in his theology of hope, in connection with Hans J. Iwand's interpretation of Luther's teaching of justification. According to Iwand, God justifies human beings by grace while human beings acknowledge God's justice by confessing their sins. In this reciprocal event, not only the sinner but also God is given the right. The event of justification is the promise of an all-inclusive setting to right on God's part. Given this, Moltmann argues that the teaching of the *justificatio impii* (justification of the impious) comes to terms with the eschatological horizon of the *resurrectio mortuorum* (resurrection of the dead) and the *creatio ex nihil* (creation from nothing).[15]

SPIRITUAL FORMATION AND *DIAKONIA* IN THE HAPPY EXCHANGE

For Luther, Christ shares his attributes and grace with the believers in terms of happy exchange. This participation model upholds our spiritual formation and discipleship in terms of *theologia crucis* (theology of the cross) and in conformity to Jesus Christ for the sake of *diakonia* (service) of those in need.[16]

According to Luther, the soul and Christ are coupled together in a marriage in the incomparable grace of faith (according to Eph 5:31–32). The soul may possess and glory in everything that Christ has (his grace, life, and salvation). Likewise, Christ makes his own everything that belongs to the soul (its sin, death, and damnation). Christ and the soul become one flesh. The gift of faith dwelling in our hearts is the source and substance of all our righteousness. In this light, Luther states that we are a chosen race, God's own people, and a royal priesthood.[17]

Considering Christian freedom coupled with his reflection on happy exchange, Luther maintains that a Christian is a perfectly free lord of all, subject to none while he or she is a perfectly dutiful servant of all, subject to all.[18] As the rule for the life of Christians, we should devote all our

15. Moltmann, *Theology of Hope*, 207.
16. Peura, "Gott und Mensch in der Unio," in Repo und Vinke, eds., *Unio*, 44.
17. Luther, "Freedom of Christian (1520)," in Lull and Russell, eds., *Luther's Basic Writings*, 398.
18. Ibid., 393.

works to the welfare of others. We serve the neighbors through voluntary benevolence and doing good works to them.[19] Luther amplifies this view by stating that the Christian must become a second Christ to fellows, since the Christian lives in Christ through faith.[20] Spiritual formation and social justice get along with the framework of the grace of justification which underlines a public ethical orientation. The grace of justification coupled with the living Christ in union with us in Word and sacrament emphasizes the service of those who are fragile, vulnerable and economically weaker. We observe an ethical dimension of the Lord's Supper and public justice expressed in Luther's prophetic statement:

> "Here your heart must go out in love and learn that this is a sacrament of love. As love and support are given you, you in turn must render love and support to Christ in his needy ones. You must feel with sorrow all the dishonor done to Christ in his Holy Word, all the misery of Christendom, all the unjust suffering of the innocent, with which the world is everywhere filled to overflowing. You must fight [resist], work, pray, and—if you cannot do more—have heartfelt sympathy."[21]

Eucharistic theology entails a prophetic notion in anamnestic reason concerning the reality of mass suffering of the innocent victims in the world, which shapes a public ethical horizon of Luther. Furthermore, Luther argues that the justified person proceeds to the active life of discipleship for service.[22] An integrative perspective on the grace of justification *extra nos* in the embrace of the model of happy exchange needs to be interpreted in the direction of Christ's *diakonia*, his cross-formed leadership, and genuine lordship in regard to humility (Phil 2:6–11).

The old symbol of happy exchange, a Christian spirituality which justified the freedom of the church in the medieval time is valid for the unity of every Christian with Christ in terms of freedom, *diakonia*, and emancipation. Christ as freedom-speaking Word of God is the place of freedom which determines the true art of *diakonia* and emancipation. The freedom of faith is responsible for the social deed. "Free out of faith"

---

19. Ibid., 405.
20. Ibid., 408.
21. Luther, "The Blessed Sacrament of the Holy and True Body and Blood of Christ (1519)," in Timothy F. Lull, ed., *Martin Luther's Basic Theological Writings*, 247.
22. Gollwitzer, *Krummes Holz*, 313.

remains the emancipating responsibility for society which is fundamental for public ethical theology.[23]

LUTHER AND THE SOCIO-ECONOMIC PROBLEM

According to Troeltsch, Luther's vocational ethic lacks an impulse toward social reform which was the major deficiency of Lutheran ethics. Lutheran theology failed to engender a unified Christian social ethic, because it sanctioned the secular institutions as the divinely appointed realms for exercising and perfecting Christian morality.[24] Similarly, Max Weber characterizes Lutheran vocational ethic and critique of usury, or interest rate, as definitely backward from a capitalist standpoint. Luther is regarded as the one who is not able "to establish a new or in any way fundamental connection between worldly activity and religious principles."[25] However, Luther perceives the economic reality and its injustice in the time of early capitalism. Luther's own insight into God's economy against mammon expresses the social-critical and prophetic line and trajectory which is biblically grounded and in confession to God. Luther's teaching of justification becomes the driving force for him to cope with the begging of mendicant monks, sharply critiquing the issue of usury.[26] Luther strives to perceive the coercive system of early capitalism in terms of a metaphor of devouring capital, taking a stance in solidarity with the poor.

According to Luther, the trust and faith of the heart alone make both God and an idol. Those who believe in God and have everything needed (money and property), but have no care for anyone else, have mammon as a god; it is money and property on which they set their whole hearts. "This is the most common idol on earth."[27] Idolatry is primarily a matter of the heart rather than merely a matter of erecting an image and praying to it. Luther advances his theological critique of mammon concerning the Seventh Commandment ("You are not to steal").

Luther defines stealing in a broader spectrum occurring at the individual and at the socioeconomic level within the market system: "taking

23. Ebeling, *Lutherstudien* 1:321–24, 329.
24. Gayhart, *Ethics of Ernst Troeltsch*, 195–96.
25. Weber, *Protestant Ethic*, 85.
26. Linbeck, *Beyond Charity*.
27. Luther, "Large Catechism," in Kolb and Wengert, eds., BC, 387.

advantage of someone in the market, . . . in short, wherever business is transacted and money is exchanged for goods or service."[28] Thievery is the most common craft and the largest guild on earth. These people are called armchair bandits and highway robbers. They sit in the seats of power and are known as great lords and honorable citizens, while robbing and stealing under the cloak of legality. This economic reality, which is stamped by misusing the market in an arbitrary, defiant, and arrogant way, causes the poor to be defrauded every day. New burdens and higher prices are imposed upon their lives.[29] As Luther continues, "And it continues to rise, devour and fetter us; . . . So anyone who has a hundred florins . . . earns an annual forty, which means devouring a peasant or city-dweller . . . . If he has a hundred thousand, which must be the case with big businessmen, he earns an annual forty thousand, which means devouring a great, rich prince in one year . . . . In that way a robber can sit comfortably at home and in ten years swallow up the whole world."[30]

Luther's texts on the problem of interest (usury) are connected with the emerging international monopolist trading and banking companies (Fugger, Wesler, etc.) and their capital accumulation. The power of these companies was far reaching; Charles V depended on the Fuggers. Luther admonishes the community of faith to speak out against this social evil and violence, having an influence on the Protestant church.

Given this, the ethical issue in the economic field becomes for Luther a confessional problem in the sense of *status confessionis*. Public ethical theology and the discipleship of God's mission find their concrete expression in Luther's confession of God's economy against the structure of mammon. In the *Large Catechism* Luther critiques mammon as a system of totality. In such a system people want to be god of the whole world through mammon and to be worshipped as god.[31] This aspect runs counter to Troeltsch's argument, according to which the Lutheran ethic fails to critique and shape the social environment because of its loose and careless acceptance of existing social conditions and values.[32]

---

28. Ibid., 416.

29. Ibid., 417–18.

30. Luther, *Admonition to the Clergy*, cited in Duchrow, *Alternatives to Global Capitalism*, 219.

31. Duchrow, *Global Economy*, 176.

32. Troeltsch, *Social Teaching*, 2:1000.

Luther sharply critiques the devouring capital system and the process of capital concentration and accumulation. He was aware of the Christian character of early capitalism in reference to colonialism in America. The concept of greed is in contradiction to faith in God. In a biblical, prophetic passion, Luther challenges the church to promote the responsibility of faith for the sake of the worldly and economic realm, based on positive change and renewal.[33]

For Luther, *Deum justificare*, which means giving God justice, actually expresses the justification of God according to a grace of justification; it embraces the justification of God in social and public life.[34] Therefore, Luther's witness to the gospel of justification has striking public, ethical, and missional relevance in respect to God's mission and discipleship in the economic realm. Such a contribution can be obviously seen in the Lutheran World Federation's documents and its critical engagement with economic globalization[35] in ecumenical collaboration with Reformed Christians.

GOD'S UNIVERSAL REIGN AND *THEOLOGIA CRUCIS*

In the *Heidelberg Disputation* Luther sharply articulates his *theologia crucis* in contrast to the scholastic notion of *theologia gloriae* (theology of glory). The hiddenness of God is conceptualized in Christ's suffering.[36] In Luther's early state, the hidden God was existentially connected with his concept of *Anfechtungen*. The knowledge of God given in Jesus Christ does not supplement a general knowledge of God, but it is the beginning of all true knowledge of God. "We know of no God excepting only the incarnate and human God (*Deus incarnates, Deus humanus*)."[37]

Luther distinguishes the God of majesty from the crucified God, the triune God as such (the immanent Trinity) from the incarnated God (the economic Trinity). Luther does not make *theologia crucis* into a piety that

---

33. Fabiunke, *Luther als Nationalöknom*, 193–230; Rieth, *"Habsucht" bei Luther*, 220–21.

34. Iwand, *Righteousness of Faith*, 21.

35. Lutheran World Federation (=LWF), "Call to Participate in Transforming Economic Globalization."

36. Lohse, *Luther's Theology*, 216.

37. Ebeling, *Luther*, 235.

venerates and even reduces God in its own small quarter. *Theologia crucis* must be seen in connection with the God who is withdrawn from us.

In *On the Bondage of the Will*, Luther entitles the omnipotent God who is withdrawn from us the *Deus absconditus*, in contrast to *Deus revelatus*, which is preached and announced. God is wholly incomprehensible and inaccessible, as St. Paul exclaims (Rom 11:33).[38] Reserving Divine majesty only for God's self, Luther maintains that "God must therefore be left to himself in his own majesty."[39] We have something to do with God insofar as God is set forth in God's Word. God hidden in God's majesty works life, death, and all in all, keeping God's self to be free over all things.[40] However, "Jesus, the crucified, allows us to believe in God as omnipotent in impotence, and only in this way makes God really God for us at all."[41]

Luther's argument against Erasmus is to guard against a speculation of the divine will. God hides God's self from human speculation. God's being for us can be understood by envisaging God's unfathomable being in God's self as the *terminus a quo* (initial impulse). God's being for us as the miracle of grace is revealed in the gospel and grounded in God's freedom.[42] The justified becomes a collaborator with God, as seen in St. Paul's teaching in the Corinthians (1 Cor 3:9). The human being remains passive in the grace of justification, while he or she is called to be a collaborator with God in the public ethical and missional field.[43]

GOD'S REIGN AND PUBLIC DISCIPLESHIP

Luther's teaching of God's universal reign based on two kingdoms (or better, strategies) has undergone misunderstanding, debate, controversy, and renewal. Troeltsch argues that Lutheranism has always represented the principle of patriarchalism and conservatism, opposing the modern

---

38. In Rupp and Watson, eds., *Luther and Erasmus*, 330.
39. Ibid., 201.
40. Ibid.
41. Ebeling, *Luther*, 241.
42. Gollwitzer, *Existence of God*, 221.
43. *On the Bondage of the Will*, in Rupp and Watson, eds., *Luther and Erasmus*, 287–88.

development of the State.⁴⁴ During the period of National Socialism in Germany, neo-Lutherans represented a notion of creation as ordered by God, which was central to nineteenth century German Lutheranism. It paved the way for support of the state as an autonomous order of creation which later claimed a naturalistic law unto the state itself. The independent autonomy of worldly life and the cultural meaning of the state were fixed. Apart from the grace of Jesus Christ, the Lutheran idea of general revelation in creation was idolized blindly in favor of Nazi racist ideology. Indeed, Karl Barth became keenly critical of Lutheran quietism based on a model of the two kingdoms, which creates a space for German paganism because of the fixing of creation as an autonomous order independent of the gospel. Barth's "No" to Nazism in the Confessing Church is clearly expressed in the first article of the Barmen Declaration (May 29–31, 1934): Jesus Christ is the one Word of God.

Against the Barmen Declaration, Werner Elert and Paul Althaus at Erlangen University issued the *Ansbach Counsel*, deeming the Barmen Declaration inappropriate in its critique of German renewal under the direction of National Socialism.

However, Luther's teaching of God's universal reign based on a dialectical relationship between law and gospel runs counter to a Neo-Lutheran dualist reading of the independent orders of creation. Actually, Luther comprehends three life arrangements (political realm, economic sphere, and church) within the kingdom of nature, by dynamically relating the subject matter of the gospel (kingdom of Christ) to the public realm.

Like a prophetic view of economic justice, Luther argues that the political state belongs to God. In defending the freedom of the gospel, Luther challenged those who attempted to misuse his theology of justification and economic justice ideologically to promote a theology of revolution. However, Luther seeks another political form of church struggle against the violence of the state. He argues, "For the princes and 'big shots' find it quite intolerable that the whole world should be criticized if only they themselves are exempted from this criticism. But they must certainly be criticized too and anyone entrusted with the office of preaching owes it to them to point out where they act unjustly and do wrong, even if they protest that such criticism of rulers will lead to rebellion."⁴⁵ The preacher and the politician

---

44. Troeltsch, *Social Teaching*, 2:573.
45. Cited in Duchrow, *Alternatives to Global Capitalism*, 216.

must listen to the living word of God which upholds the new world of God in contrast to political and economic powers and dominion.[46]

MISSION AND *CREATIO CONTINUA*

The church is called to announce the Good News for all, thereby participating in God's ongoing work in the creation. The basis of God's universal reign as the hiddenness of God plays as a realistic criterion against a Catholic or Calvinistic attempt to establish the world as a theocracy in light of a christocentric universal lordship. In confrontation with Zwingli and his followers, Luther develops his notion of the right hand of God in terms of the almighty power of God working even in the midst of the tiniest leaf of a tree. For Luther, all creatures are understood as God's masks (*larva Dei*). God the Creator, penetrating into the created world and filling the cosmos, preserves creation in a hidden and mysterious way. God's ongoing act of new creation implies divine power itself preserving the creation and being present in its innermost and outermost aspects.

In Luther's understanding of faith and creation, a lively faith comes along with the praise of God's beauty and glory in the world. Comprehending all creatures as tools or masks in the service of God's working, Luther contends that God hides God's activity under them, while remaining free to give to all in the ongoing activity. God through God's word gives effective authority to rulers, and thus preserves the effectiveness of the structure that orders human life. A new understanding of the natural and the worldly realm can be undertaken in God's ongoing work of new creation. The article of creation is the article of faith, because faith in God's creation means faith in the triune God. Faith and justification interact with our stewardship of all creatures.

Luther retains a marvelous sense of the aesthetic dimension of the creation: "the wonderful and most lovely music [comes] from the harmony of the motions that are in the celestial spheres."[47] We are summoned to listen carefully to the beautiful music of God which comes from the creation. God's work faithfully and trustfully takes place in the realm of the creation. "For the word of the Lord is trustful, and what he promises,

---

46. For a detailed analysis of Luther's model of two kingdoms in this direction, see Chung et al., *Liberating Lutheran Theology*, 138–39.

47. LW 1:126.

he certainly keeps" (Ps 33). Creation is the sphere of dialogue and communication which transpires between God and the creatures. "Day to day pours forth speech, and night to night declares knowledge"(Ps 19:2). Luther's theology of word-event correlates with God's act of speech in the sense of *creatio continua*.

According to Luther, God's work of creation is a speaking work, making itself understandable. *Creatio continua* (continuing creation) implies God's act of speech or speech-event for its own sake. Through the effective word of address, God's trustfulness can be heard in the world, because it is a pledge and promise. God's *promissio* is not only the fundamental category in regard to the sacraments and the sermon, but also in view of the realm of creation.[48]

Seeing the creation as a communicative sphere, Luther conceives of the world as text, readable and understandable. Luther's linguistic renovation embraces the church and creation in light of God's act of speech, and it remains the arbiter for upholding public theology and the discipleship of God's mission in the field of stewardship of creation.

THEOLOGY OF GRACE AND RECOGNITION OF THE OTHER

Luther provides a hermeneutical way of speaking of God in both an all-embracing and inclusive manner, and yet with a radical and particularist tone. Luther's teaching of justification is to be seen in light of God's universal reign, and this aspect retains an inclusive horizon in his commentary on 1 Timothy and his reflection on Jesus' descent into hell. For Luther, through God preached all people will be saved (1 Tim 2:4), as God comes to all with the word of salvation.[49] In openness to the world, Luther does not hesitate to consider that pagan authority is a model which demonstrates what the task of secular authority is better than the Christian state does. God is a gentle and rich Lord who is willing to grant a great deal of riches, dominions, reason, wisdom, and languages. God gives the kingdoms to the godless. In comparison with pagan authority, Luther argues that Christians rather become mere children, fools, and beggars.

---

48. Bayer, *Luther's Theology*, 102.
49. *On the Bondage of the Will*, in *Luther and Erasmus*, 202.

Given this, Luther does not hesitate to praise the Turkish state while demonstrating a critique of Christian authorities without reservation.[50]

Luther's sensitivity to others is expressed in his reflection on the irregular grace of God through the Other. It is of special significance to observe Luther's comment on Ishmael: "For the expulsion does not mean that Ishmael should be utterly excluded from the kingdom of God . . . The descendants of Ishmael also joined the church of Abraham and became heirs of the promise, not by reason of a right, but because of irregular grace."[51]

Here, I am convinced of the hermeneutical notion of the fusion of horizons between the meaning of the gospel and God's irregular voice in the creation for the thick description of the biblical narrative as we engage in dialogue with people of other faiths, acknowledging their wisdom, language, and spiritual relationship with the ultimate truth.[52] In the hermeneutical-historical perspective, human existence is thoroughly historical or embedded in the world because we can never escape our historical linguistic context, or lifeworld. Grounded in the world, tradition, and a language, we can anticipate experiencing a fusion of horizon between our own and another's. In such a hermeneutical conversation with the Other, a new meaning emerges, helping dialogue partners to each understand both traditions better. In an encounter of different horizons interpretation is open-ended and dynamic toward the future.[53]

According to Luther, "it is not said, therefore, that God desires to convert everyone. St. Paul only declares of the Gospel that it is a cry, which he causes to go out over everyone. It is supposed to be pure blessing."[54] Announcing the gospel is

> just as if one throws a stone into the water. It makes waves and circles or wheels around itself, and the waves roll always farther outward . . . The waves continue forward. So it is with preaching.[55]

---

50. Ebeling, *Luther*, 189.

51. LW 4:42–44.

52. Chung, *Luther and Buddhism*.

53. Gadamer, *Truth and Method*, 306–7.

54. Stolle, *Luther Texts on Mission*, 29. According to Lutheran confessional theology, "[c]onversion to God is the work of God the Holy Spirit alone." See Formula of Concord, BC 561.

55. Stolle, *Luther Texts on Mission*, 24.

Our proclamation or witness is undertaken as gratitude for the grace of God to serve the initiative of the Holy Spirit. Luther's theology of conversion is uniquely seen in light of the grace of justification *extra nos*, while acknowledging the people of other cultures. Our mission witnesses that God's promise comes to us as God's mission in the gospel of Jesus Christ, affirming the dignity of people of other cultures and religions under God's universal reign. Mission is an endeavor to communicate and translate the glad tidings of Jesus Christ as the living voice of God in its universal message for all in different times and locations.

2

John Calvin

Mission and Evangelism

It is a constructive task to hermeneutically retrieve John Calvin's (1509–1564) thought in matters of mission and evangelism in light of his teaching of the Holy Spirit. A controversial person, Calvin has been accused of being an unevangelistic theologian and unconcerned about mission. Furthermore, Calvin's teaching on predestination is critiqued as the theological bulwark opposing evangelistic passion and fervor. A doctrine of divine election makes all missionary and evangelistic activity futile and meaningless.

Having considered this negative picture, a study of Calvin and his teaching of the Holy Spirit is definitively needed to discover the undercurrent of mission and evangelism in his thought, an undercurrent which has been forgotten and sidestepped in the history of Calvin studies. My basic argument can be found in a hermeneutical strategy of appreciating Calvin as a preeminent theologian of the Holy Spirit, which supports Calvin's intensified zeal for mission, evangelism, and public discipleship. A close examination of Calvin's theological framework and its historical context would help us to contextualize John Calvin as a missional theologian committed to the spread of the gospel in undertaking public discipleship. This aspect is still amenable to the ecumenical and global context in our own time.

CALVIN'S CONCERN ABOUT MISSION IN HISTORICAL CONTEXT

The scattered condition of Protestantism was worsened by the intense efforts of the Roman Church to eradicate the Protestant movement. Protestant churches were struggling not only for their identity but also for their very survival. Calvin himself had to leave France for his personal safety and found his career in Geneva as one of the great reformers. He wrote the first edition of the *Institutes* (1536) in response to the ill treatment of French Protestants, bearing a strong appeal to King Francis.[1]

Calvin's thought related to how to develop church organization, conceptualize Reformed theology, and train ministers to the new church body. Such an aspect also entailed evangelical efforts to spread the Reformation understanding of the gospel and the church. Calvin's primary interest can be seen in building a theological foundation in the context of the Reformation and in establishing the church at home. He was not keen on direct intervention in overseas foreign mission. Actually, foreign mission was restricted by most European governments. However, Calvin's ministry to the refugees from France and others can be seen as his evangelical endeavor and commitment to the ministry of the gospel and public discipleship.

CALVIN AND FRENCH CALVINISM

Calvin and the Genevan Consistory properly trained missionaries to send back to France, while Calvin himself was deeply involved in political and religious affairs in France through pastoral letters, advice, and admonitions. The notorious *Chambre Ardente* was set up in France from 1547 onwards, which helped the civil authorities deal directly with heretics, arresting Protestant martyrs.[2] It resulted in the extraordinary civil inquisition, trying to destroy all Protestant groups and associations. Five young students who trained themselves as preachers in Lausanne and worked in France were placed under arrest and sentenced to be burned alive in May, 1553. Nevertheless, in September 1555, a congregation in Paris was set up by a pastor sent from Geneva and according to the Geneva

---

1. McNeill, *History and Character of Calvinism*, 243.
2. Wallace, *Calvin*, 157.

church patterns, included a pastor, elders, and deacons. On May 25, 1559, representatives of about fifty churches met each other and organized a General Synod of the Reformed Church in Saint-Germain-des-Pres, which is called petite Geneve.[3] The December 1559 martyrdom of Anne Du Bourg, who was executed in Paris as a young student, played a decisive role in deepening the political resistance of French Calvinists for the sake of the gospel. According to Hans Scholl, this incident refers to the fact that righteous and integral politics, good politics, means repentance.[4]

During this period of persecution Calvin stood in deep solidarity with these French Calvinists. His later correspondence was full of diplomatic advice and pastoral concern and it was addressed to members of the French upper nobility, many of whom adopted the Reformed faith. The history of French Calvinism is seen as a history of martyrdom. History shows that Calvin was enraptured by missions, far from being disengaged from it.

By 1562, religious wars had broken out in France and Calvin's concern about mission to France constitutes a powerful chapter of witnessing to the gospel of Jesus Christ. In the context of persecuted Protestants in France, Calvin's theological and personal engagement with the core value of the gospel can become a great example for understanding him as a committed missional theologian for the sake of the gospel and public responsibility.

Deacons were socially engaged in helping the needy and poor in the city of Geneva, which was filled with refugees for the sake of the freedom of faith. Protestant refugees from all over Europe fled to Geneva. They came not merely for safety, but also to learn the doctrines of the Reformation from Calvin so they could return home to spread the gospel. Geneva was a dynamic center of missionary concern and activity for those who were sent forth in the service of Jesus Christ in the world. Geneva had become a center for refuges and a missionary hub throughout Europe.

CALVIN AND FOREIGN MISSION

In April 1555 the *Register of the Company of Pastors in Geneva* refers to ministers who were sent abroad on missions to France and Piedmont.[5] Hundreds of men were sent out, reaching Italy, Germany, Scotland,

---

3. Brandenburg, *Hugenotten*, 33.
4. Scholl, *Reformation und Politik*, 102.
5. Wallace, *Calvin*, 156.

England, and practically covering France. Geneva, under Calvin's direction, served as the heart of the Reformation in Europe, pumping out the lifeblood of trained ministers into all areas.

In addition to the extensive work in Europe, one group of Genevan missionaries was sent to Brazil. The *Register* simply states that two pastors, Pierre Richer and Guillaume Charterier were sent from Geneva in August 25, 1556, to act as chaplains to a group from the Reformed Church for the work of mission and evangelism in Brazil. The ministers were sent in response to a request from Admiral Gaspard de Coligny, a Huguenot leader, who was interested in the founding of a colony in South America for Huguenots. In 1555 he brought about the expedition of Nicholas Durand de Villegagnon to Rio de Janeiro. Upon the leader's request to Coligny for divines from Geneva, Calvin and his colleagues sent out fourteen young men to the colony. Among them were Richer and Chartier, the first Protestant ministers to cross the Atlantic.

They were to serve as chaplains for a group of Protestants who were going to Brazil to establish a colony, and they would have the opportunity to instruct the natives in the gospel. French Protestant emigrants might settle there for the freedom of faith, free from persecution while evangelizing the South American Indians. However, the whole effort was a tragic failure. The Governor of the colony betrayed his trust in Protestantism, killing some of them and forcing the others back home.[6] "Abortive though this excursion proved to be," "it testifies strikingly to the far-reaching vision which Calvin and the Church in Geneva had of their missionary task."[7]

UNION WITH CHRIST:
SPIRITUAL FORMATION AND MISSIONAL LEADERSHIP

Appreciating Calvin's contribution to mission and evangelization, it is important to consider the historical development of Calvin's doctrine of predestination. In the *Institutes* of 1559 Calvin explores the teaching of eternal election (*Inst.* III.xxi) in the context of Christ's benefit in the secret working of the Holy Spirit. This aspect provides us with an insight approaching Calvin's theology of election in terms of union with Christ imbued with the working of the Holy Spirit.

6. McNeil, *History and Character of Calvinism*, 331.
7. Wallace, *Calvin*, 160.

William Bouwsma, in his biography of Calvin, argues that an interpretation of Calvin as a systematic thinker would be an anachronism because systematic thinkers in the sixteenth century were not considered significant. Thomas Aquinas represented a philosopher, a rationalist, and a schoolman in the high Scholastic tradition. However, a rhetorician and humanist was primed to celebrate and welcome the paradoxes and mystery underlined at the heart of existence.[8] The Scholastic side of Calvin tends toward static orthodoxy, craving for intelligibility, order, and certainty. All the while, the rhetorical and humanist side is concerned about the primacy of experience and practice over theory. In later Calvinist development, the philosophical and systematic side of Calvin prevailed, while unfortunately undermining the rhetorical and humanistic qualities in Calvin's own thought.[9]

Driven by Bouwsma's insight, I am interested in reinterpreting a spiritual side of Calvin as a theologian of the Holy Spirit, especially in terms of his theological acumen of the union with Christ. The notion of union with Christ facilitates our understanding of election in a christological-pneumatological framework. In parallel with the union with Christ, Calvin refers to the basis and ground of our election in Christ alone. Thus Calvin refrains from human attempts to seek and clarify predestination outside Christ (*Inst.* III.xxiv.4). In fact, God has chosen us in Christ before the foundation of the world. Our election in Christ takes place *extra nos*, that is, without recourse to human righteousness or merits (*Inst.* III.xxii.3). Christ *extra nos*, who is the basis and mirror of our election, refers to Calvin's radical understanding of election as God's grace by pointing to the soteriological horizon of Jesus Christ.

In Calvin's terminology, the union with Christ is of a distinctively christological character because we are united to God by Christ, that is, we are so engrafted into Christ by faith while Christ joins us to God.[10] In the Trinitarian sense Calvin holds that the Father is the One who sends the Son, Christ, in whom we are engrafted while the Spirit is the communicator of Christ for the Christian life by justifying and sanctifying us. If we embrace communion with Christ, we come to enjoy Christ and all of his benefits for us (*Inst.* III.i.1). The grace of justification and sanctifica-

---

8. Bouwsma, *John Calvin*, 231.
9. Ibid., 234.
10. Tamburello, *Union with Christ*, 93.

tion, faith and morality are seen by Calvin in light of this engrafting into Christ. Insofar as we accept Christ by faith, being implanted into his body through Word and sacrament, the residence of Christ transpires in our hearts, in a mystical union (in French, *union sacrée*) (III.xi.10).

Having considered Calvin's train of thought, Karl Barth maintains that the *unio cum Christo* is the central and dominating concept in Calvin's definition of the gift and fruit of the Lord's Supper, which differentiates Calvin from Zwingli. With incomprehensible mystery we grow up to be one body with Christ by becoming one with Him. Consequently, what is ours is His and His is ours. Barth holds that the concept of union with Christ has a comprehensive and basic significance in a much wider theological context for Calvin. What distinguishes Calvin from Luther, according to Barth, is that the union with Christ is primarily and comprehensively the sanctification of the person. As Christ lives in us, He rules us by His Spirit in directing our actions. Within this framework, the union with Christ is also the grace of justification as the presupposition of Christ's Lordship. Against Osiander, Calvin points out that the proper being of Christ does not become ours. Rather by the power of His Spirit Christ gives us a share in His life—thereby a share in all that He has received of the Father.

In the *Institutes* of 1559 Calvin makes union with Christ become the common denominator under which to arrange his whole doctrine of the appropriation of the salvation which is achieved and revealed in Christ. Under the influence of the *Institutes* of 1559 the Reformed theology of the sixteenth and seventeenth centuries opened its whole doctrine of the appropriation of salvation in terms of the special and basic doctrine of *instititio* or *insertio in Christum*. Thus Reformed theology acknowledged vividly that the vocation of the elect consists essentially in this concept of union with Christ.[11]

Furthermore, Calvin, in exegeting Ephesians 4:11, holds that of the offices listed only pastors and teachers are ordinary officers of the church, and to these he adds elders and deacons (*Inst.* IV.iii.4–9). There is no limit set to the command to "go, preach the gospel to every creature" (Mark 16:15), but the whole earth is assigned to the gospel to bring into obedience to Christ. By spreading the gospel, the apostles may raise up the kingdom of Christ everywhere (*Inst.* IV.iii.4).

---

11. Barth, *Church Dogmatics*, 4/3.2:551–54.

In his ecclesiology, the pastoral and missional dimension can be expressed in congregational leadership characterized by the mutual confession, admonition, correction, consolation, and edification in the lives of lay people. Like Luther's concern about mutual conversation and consolation of brothers and sisters, Calvin expresses his notion of mutuality among believers. We should lay our infirmities on one another's breasts, to receive spiritual counsel, mutual compassion, and mutual consolation (*Inst.* III. iv.6). Calvin's ecclesiology, seen in light of Christ-union and mutual compassion and consolation, provides an important place of spiritual formation and missional leadership for missional theology.[12]

Calvin's theology of the union with Christ contributes to shaping congregational vocation in terms of spiritual formation, service, discipleship, and leadership. Missional vocation, spiritual formation, and leadership look to the grace of union with Christ through faith. The diverse gifts of the Holy Spirit guide missional leadership in undertaking spiritual formation. The process of vocation is spiritually and socially engaged, as the Holy Spirit has called us through the gospel, enlightened us by the gifts of the Spirit, and sanctified us in the true faith. In this regard spiritual formation and leadership cultivation fosters community in faith and the equipping of God's people to live into the world with a missional sense of Christian vocation and discipleship. In the missional faith journey, spirituality is grounded in our union with Christ in word and sacrament through the power of the Holy Spirit. Missional leadership as cultivation is the ongoing work grounded in the soil of the congregation, forming the environment for the people of God to discern what the Spirit is doing among people as a community.[13]

THE HOLY SPIRIT: CREATION AND PREDESTINATION

It was Karl Barth who initiated a paradigm shift from an ecclesiocentric notion of mission toward God's mission in a Trinitarian-predestinarian framework. For Barth, Calvin's notion of God's election provides a theological basis for conceptualizing God's mission within the Trinitarian life, which is "built upon the solid rock of God's election."[14] It is certain that it

---

12. Chung, *Spirit of God Transforming Life*, 137.
13. Chung, *Reclaiming Mission as Constructive Theology*, 173–74.
14. Thomas, ed., *Classic Texts in Mission and World Christianity*, 105.

would be difficult to properly understand the theology of God's mission without appropriating Calvin's notion of predestination.

To be more articulate about Calvin's theology of the Holy Spirit and predestination, it is imperative to examine his theology of the Spirit, first of all, in matters of creation. Then we come to look at the teaching of election in the universal horizon of the Spirit.

For Calvin, the Holy Spirit as *spiritus creator* is conceptualized in the threefold way: universal life, human life, and the regenerated life of the believers. There is a distinction between the cosmic but hidden power (*arcana Dei virtus*), the general, indiscriminate bestowal of various gifts upon all human beings, and the particular regenerating work of the Spirit.[15] Calvin's reflection on the cosmic and universal dimension of the Spirit undergirds God's concern about the preservation of creation within the mission of the Spirit. This refers to a continuous action of God in the realm of creatures until the Last Day (*Inst.* I.xiv.20).

Calvin's praise of the beauty of creation becomes tremendously striking. The created world is the "most beautiful theatre" that "endows each with its own nature, assigned functions, appointed places, and stations" (*Inst.* I.xiv.20). Calvin contends that the universe is a book, theatre, or mirror because God appears in the garment of creation (*Inst.* I.v.1). All living creatures could be witnesses and messengers of divine glory to us for God's service and honor. "For the little singing birds sang of God, the animals acclaimed him, the elements feared and the mountains resounded with him, the river and springs threw glances toward him, the grasses and the flowers smiled."[16]

Calvin's theology of creation within the cosmic and universal horizon of the Holy Spirit facilitates our understanding of God's mission for the integrity of life in creation. The Holy Spirit as the *fons vitae* (the well of life) is life-giver so that all creatures are aflame with the glory of the Lord, full of the wonderful hymn of creation.[17]

---

15. Krusche, *Das Wirken des Heiligen Geistes nach Calvin*, 14.
16. Cited in Santmire, *Travail of Nature*, 128.
17. Moltmann, *Spirit of Life*, 134.

PREDESTINATION AND EVANGELIZATION

As previously stated, Calvin's teaching of election within the context of union with Christ is concerned about the gospel, which should be preached to all. Proclamation of the gospel results in the salvation of the elect, while hardening the non-elect. In addition to the positive side of election in Jesus Christ, there is a negative side (reprobation). "God adopts some to hope of life, and sentences others to eternal death" (III. xxi.5). According to Calvin, God, by God's just and irreprehensible but incomprehensible judgment, has blocked the door of life to those who God has given over to damnation (*Inst*. III. xxi.7). However, Calvin expresses his negative view on the ground of his own *empirical facts and experiences*. The certainty of empirical facts remains an obstacle in conceptualizing and developing a theology of God's eternal decree in a constantly christological manner. Barth argues that Calvin tends to justify his teaching of predestination in the Puritan context, in which certain works of faith and existence should "give direct confirmation of faith and indirect confirmation of election."[18]

Nonetheless, Calvin does not imply a practical syllogism concerning election. In speaking of latter signs (*signa posteriora*: *Inst*. III. xxiv. 4), Calvin does not mean our election-producing praxis, but solely in Christ *extra nos*. Thus Francois Wendel holds that a notion of a practical syllogism providing the manifest proof of our election and our salvation is contrary to authentic Calvinist thought.[19] This perspective brings Weber's sociology of Calvinism and the spirit of capitalism to have more careful conversation with Calvin's own theology of election and economic justice, which shall be investigated later in more detail concerning mission and economic justice.

Calvin did not limit the announcement of the gospel only to those considered to be elect. He definitely encouraged Christians to be involved in evangelism. Evangelism befits us to desire all people to be saved. The result of this proper desire should make us try to invite everyone to faith in Christ. By the preaching of the gospel under the power of the Holy Spirit, God had chosen to save people. Conversion to God becomes possible under the power of the Spirit.

Calvin expresses the dialectical tension which is inherent in the relationship between the universality of God's election and its particularity

---

18. Barth, *Church Dogmatics*, 2/2:113.

19. Wendel, *Calvin*, 276–77. See further Niesel, *Theology of Calvin*, 169–81; *Inst*. III. xiv.18.19.

in a historical and empirical setting: "God is said to have ordained from eternity those whom he wills to embrace in love, and those upon whom he wills to vent his wrath. Yet he announces salvation to *all men indiscriminately*" (*Inst.* III.xxiv.17, italics added).

Seen in light of Calvin's notion of the secret impulse of the Spirit (*arcano Dei instinctu*), Calvin expresses this mysterious work among the life of the reprobate. "The reprobate are sometimes affected by almost the same feeling as the elect . . . This does not at all hinder that lower working of the Spirit from taking its course even in the reprobate . . . The reprobate are justly said to believe that God is merciful toward them" (*Inst.* III.ii.11). The truth of predestination does not lie in denying the possibility of salvation among the reprobate. Calvin's genuine concern becomes obvious in witnessing to the sovereign initiative of God in Christ through the work of the Spirit for the salvation of all. Given this, a theology of election becomes a catalyst for the church to engage in God's mission and evangelism.[20]

Calvin strongly supported the idea of mission. In other words, the Great Commission was not fulfilled and completed by the apostles and, consequently, this mission is still the responsibility of Christians. In commenting on 1 Tim 2:4, Calvin says "there is no people and no rank in the world that is excluded from salvation; because God wishes that the gospel should be proclaimed to all without exception."[21] Gospel is the power of God for salvation to everyone who believes (Rom 1:16). Thus all those whom the gospel addresses are invited to the hope of eternal life. Missional duty should be solicitous and do our endeavor for the salvation of all through our godly prayers.[22]

Calvin has no intention to suppress the inclusive nature of the gospel imbued with the universal horizon of the Holy Spirit. According to Calvin, God desires foreign nations to hear the gospel and to be included in salvation through Jesus Christ. Calvin's predestination serves as the theological acumen of Christian mission to awaken the elected Christian to be faithful to God's activity even among the reprobates in the sense of *arcana virtus Dei*.

In this light, it is important to examine Calvin's notion of the *sensus divinitatis* and the *conscientia* as a natural endowment of human beings

---

20. Chung, *Christian Spirituality and Ethical Life*, 76.
21. Calvin, *Commentaries on I and II Timothy*, 54–55.
22. Ibid., 55.

which are undestroyable by sin. The *sensus divinitatis* (sometimes referred to as *semen religionis*) and the *conscientia* needs to be seen in light of the hiddenness and efficacy of the Holy Spirit rather than functioning as a point of contact with redeeming grace.

The Holy Spirit does not destroy life in creation, but brings it up to the gospel of Jesus Christ. Calvin's theology of the Spirit helps to develop missional theology in dealing with people outside the walls of the Christian church. The gospel is to be preached indiscriminately to all people, and the decision about who will believe is to be left to God.

MISSION AND THE KINGDOM OF JESUS CHRIST

Calvin was indebted to Augustine (354–430) in his understanding of two kingdoms: the city of God and the city of the world. Calvin continued to develop Augustine's theory of two cities in his view of the two kingdoms: the spiritual kingdom and the political kingdom (*Inst.* III.19.15). These two kingdoms under a providential view of history is moving toward its ultimate consummation in the kingdom of God or kingdom of Christ. Jesus Christ is the Lord of history. The Father has set Christ "over us to exercise his dominion through the Son" (*Inst.* II.15.5).

Given Calvin's notion of the reign of Christ, David Bosch maintains that for Calvin the Christ who was exalted to God's right hand is the active Christ par excellence. Calvin used the reign of Christ in an eschatological framework while seeing the church as intermediary between the exalted Christ and the secular order. Such an aspect remains an undercurrent in extending the idea of mission toward the reign of Christ by inward spiritual renewal as well as in the transformation of the face of the earth through the knowledge of the Lord.[23]

Furthermore, Calvin's political ethics concerning resistance has been sharpened in the midst of persecution in France. Calvin's advice to the members of the Reformed Church in France was related to life and death matters. Calvin moved very carefully into active resistance, even indicating the possibility of breaking the law. In his letter (to the Brethren of Poitou, September 1554), Calvin mentioned "a quiet and deliberate civil disobedience,"[24] while rejecting the use of violence. Calvin's reflection on

23. Bosch, *Transforming Mission*, 256.
24. Wallace, *Calvin*, 162.

the duty to resist is still alluding to his *Institutes* (IV.xx.30–31). However, he leaves a space for open resistance in emergency situations. In fact, Calvin's political ethics of resistance gained more of a democratic shape alongside the resistance movement of French Calvinists. Calvin's plea for religious autonomy carried the seeds of revolt into social and political matters, revolutionizing the whole of contemporary life.[25] This influence is obvious in Scotland and America in their subsequent historical development. Calvin's political ethics comes out of our confession and obedience to the gospel of Christ's kingdom which is in resistance to the worldly powers. Calvin proclaimed not two kingdoms, but one kingdom of God in Christ because the world should be obedient to the lordship of Christ. Praying and acting, faith and deed are brought together into realization in this direction.

The kingdom of Christ over both secular and spiritual matters implies that all of life belongs to God in Christ. All are valid fields of mission and evangelization, because human life in relation to religion, politics, science, art and the future is not exempt from the reign of Christ. All life should be consecrated to God's service, serving God in the world engaged in every position in life. Christ as the Lord of God's kingdom and Lord of history reigns, thus all fields are undertaken on behalf of the gospel. Richard Niebuhr classified Calvin as one seeing "Christ as the transformer of culture."[26] Nonetheless, Calvin does not ignore recognition of the Other framed within the universal horizon of the Holy Spirit.

MAX WEBER: CALVINISM AND CAPITALIST SPIRIT

Max Weber (1864–1920) contends that there is a selective affinity between Protestantism and the spirit of capitalism in *The Protestant Ethic and the Spirit of Capitalism*. In his sociological analysis, Calvin's theology of predestination is revealed as the ideological seed bed for creating a religious-ethical worldview leading to the rise of capitalism. For Weber, capitalism is a restraint, or rational tempering of the irrational impulse or unlimited greed for gain. In his definition, capitalism is "the pursuit of profit, and forever renewed profit, by means of continuous, rational, capitalistic enterprise."[27] For Weber, Luther's concept of vocation, or calling, is

---

25. Stankiecwicz, *Politics and Religion in Seventeenth-Century France*, 17.
26. Niebuhr, *Christ and Culture*, 206–18.
27. Weber, *Protestant Ethic*, 17.

not consistent with the spirit of capitalism. Luther translated vocation as *Beruf* (profession or occupation) in the German Bible. Thus Luther's view is very new because the fulfillment of duty in worldly affairs is valued as the highest form which the moral activity of the individual could assume. This inevitably gives every-day worldly activity a religious significance, first of all creating the concept of a calling in this sense.[28] Luther's conception of calling or vocation (*klēsis*) as *Beruf* means that each must keep to the divinely allotted sphere of work.

Unlike Luther, however, Weber argues that Calvin marked a new chapter in the ethical consideration of labor. Calvin saw work as the key task of a Christian who gives glory to God alone. Calvin's theology of election in its subsequent development of Calvinism and the Puritan sects has underlined the spirit of capitalism. In short, every person had the divine obligation to work—regardless of the kind of work and the kind of economy.

According to the Westminster Confession of 1647, by the decree of God, and for the manifestation of God's glory, some people and angels are predestinated into everlasting life, and others are foreordained to everlasting death (chapter III of "God's Eternal Decree"). For Calvin this *decretum horribile* is derived from the logical necessity of his theology. Even Christ died only for the elect. This eliminates salvation through Word and sacraments.[29]

Paradoxically, Weber arguably maintains that the doctrine of predestination became foundational for the idea of proving one's faith through worldly activity, that is, practical syllogism. As a matter of fact, "God helps those who help themselves."[30] The Calvinist doctrine of double predestination and work ethic led to the ascetic action of Puritan morality in the sense of methodically rationalized economic–ethical conduct. In this development, Puritanism is called the staunchest champion of the capitalistic ascetic movement.[31]

For instance, Richard Baxter, a Presbyterian and an apologist of the Westminster Synod, was the embodiment of Puritan ethics. For Baxter the providential purpose of the division of labor was structured more

---

28. Ibid., 80.
29. Ibid., 102, 104.
30. Ibid., 115.
31. Ibid., 96, 105.

than in Adam Smith's emphasis on the division of labor.[32] Although the pursuit of riches for their own sake was condemned as covetousness or the search for mammon, the religious valuation of restless, continuous, systematic work in a worldly calling was valued as the highest and the surest means to asceticism. It is also the most evident proof of rebirth and genuine faith. From this perspective, accumulation of capital occurs as the inevitable consequence, and it is accelerated through ascetic compulsion to save, enabling the productive investment of capital.[33]

JOHN CALVIN: THE MISSION OF THE GOSPEL AND ECONOMIC JUSTICE

It is argued that the capitalism of Geneva was incorporated into the later development of a Calvinist ethic. Calvin's cooperation with the economic administration of the State demonstrated an inner connection between economic progress and moral elevation.[34] The Protestant ethic of the calling was stamped with the Calvinistic adaptation of the capitalist system. However, in contrast to Weber's analysis, we must not ignore Calvin's anti-mammon stance in his political economic ethic.

Calvin had the situation of refugees who had come to Geneva needing financial assistance before they could make a profit in business themselves in mind. Calvin allowed only productive credit for business purposes, not usury credit. The usury credit should not be used for living on interest. The rate of interest must be fixed legally according to the needs of the situation. In Geneva, economic life was regulated in accordance with these principles. We find the protocols of the council and of the Consistory full of the fight against usury and the exploitation of the poor. Calvin's economic ethic, in the face of the modern development of capitalism, showed a tendency toward merging into a form of Christian social humanism.[35]

In his commentary on Ezekiel 18:7-8, Calvin states that God wishes the good offices of life to be reciprocal, because God commands the individual not to oppress anyone.[36] The restoration of the pledge to the debtor

---

32. Ibid., 161.
33. Ibid., 172.
34. Troeltsch, *Social Teaching*, 2:643–44.
35. Ibid., 649.
36. Calvin, *Commentaries on Ezekiel*, 224.

(Ezek 18:7) is not bound with the poor and the needy since God forbids taking a pledge of a widow or a poor individual. The destruction of the poor person's house, which is forbidden by God, would be a species of robbery or violence. The prophet condemns increase by making a profit at the expense of others. Because usury is odious, no usurer is tolerated even in the profane state. To take usury is almost the same as murder.[37]

Calvin's concern about social economic life was an expression of biblically grounded Christian faith. The purpose of human occupations was useful and in service of the common good by the sharing of the common benefits and seeking solidarity with humanity. Calvin also was very critical of idlers and good-for-nothing individuals. Human work in a secular calling became creative and liberating, by stopping an occasion of pain and oppression.[38]

In his exposition of 2 Cor 8:13–15, Calvin states that according to God's will there should be proportions and equality among human beings.[39] Each individual is to provide for the needy according to the extent of the individual's means. Consequently, no one has too much or too little. In the story of manna, Calvin holds that it is prohibited to hoard it, either from excessive greed or from distrust. No one is to be allowed to starve while no one is to hoard their abundance at the cost of defrauding others.[40] What is unique in Calvin's economic ethic is his consideration of the ancient Jewish law (Jubilee year) in which a periodic redistribution of lands and liberation from debts should be kept well. Thus property never became a source of social oppression through individual hoarding and general involvement in debt. The sumptuary laws inspired by Calvin's economic ethic were introduced in Geneva by Calvin's successors.[41]

To restore the genuine function of the economic relation, Calvin spoke in favor of the intervention of the state in terms of regulating commercial and traffic operations, for the commonwealth (*Inst.* IV.xx.130). In Geneva the state was openly involved in economic enterprise as it regulated buying and selling and making contracts for the protection of or search for the common good of society.

37. Ibid., 227–28.
38. Biéler, *Humanism of Calvin*, 45–46.
39. Calvin, *Commentary on Corinthians*, 294.
40. Ibid., 297.
41. Graham, *Constructive Revolutionary*, 110–15.

Calvin's model of the redistribution of the manna among the Israelites maintains that the rich are the ministers to the poor, and the poor are the receivers of God, the vicars of Christ, or the proxies or solicitors of God.[42] Insisting on the mutual communication of wealth within society, Calvin runs toward mutual emancipation and solidarity—the rich from selfishness and the poor from slavery. Calvin's economic concern is expressed in the principle: from each according to ability, to each according to need.[43] As St. Paul states, "the one who had much did not have too much, and the one who had little did not have too little" (2 Cor 8:15).

CALVIN AS OUR CONTEMPORARY

Given our study of mission and evangelism in Calvin's theology, Calvin proved himself to be genuinely concerned for the spread of the gospel. In light of the situation of the world around him, his writings show that the gospel should be preached to all. Thus, a generalizing argument, according to which Calvinism is incompatible with evangelism and obstructs all missionary enterprise, becomes ill-discoursed. Calvin's theology cannot be adequately comprehended without paying attention to his practical church planting and missional organization at his time. Wherever the Reformation went on, "poor relief and the concern for philanthropy was to be an important stress . . . running through its story like a gold thread among all too much venality."[44]

The unity of the whole church in Christ remains fundamental in Calvin's ecumenical concern, because believers are united with Christ, within His one body. Calvin made an attempt to establish concord with the Lutherans through his friendship with Melanchthon. He was deeply saddened and frustrated by the death of Melanchthon in April 1560. Calvin sought to develop ecumenical fellowship with Archbishop Cranmer's proposal for a consensus (1552) and also continued his concern in a letter to Archbishop Parker (1560). Calvin proposed "a free and universal council" to cease the divisions and reunite all Christianity.[45]

---

42. Biéler, *La Pensée Économique et Sociale de Calvin*, 327.
43. Ibid., 336.
44. Wallace, *Calvin*, 175.
45. McNeil, *History and Character of Calvinism*, 200.

In dealing with Calvin's ethics in relation to political government, Barth characterizes Calvin as "a man of the world" rather than a monk coming from the cloister. Calvin investigated the questions of public life and participated all his life in high politics. He might have been a most industrious reader of newspapers and writer for public issues. Thus modern politicians of all parties and countries would learn something from Calvin. Calvin may be called "a father of the political and economic ideal of Western European liberal democracy."[46]

Calvin's theology is also of public, missional, and prophetic character concerning political responsibility as church discipleship and economic justice in solidarity with those vulnerable and economically weaker. The state is invoked to offer a counter weight to the autonomy of the money-accumulation mechanism. The church is called to corporately reject and offer resistance to what is not compatible with biblical rules and social justice in the public sphere.

Calvin's legacy in matters of economic justice and ecological stewardship remains an enduring inspiration for the church's endeavor in the ecumenical context of the World Communion of Reformed Churches (formerly the World Alliance of Reformed Churches). Concerning the issues of economic justice, preservation of creation, and empire, we read from the Accra Confession: Covenanting for Justice in the Economy and the Earth (in the 24th General Council of the WARC, meeting in Accra, Ghana). "The earth is the Lord's and the fullness thereof" (Ps 24.1). This biblical statement challenges the current economic order imposed by global neoliberal capitalism and any other economic system, which dares to nullify God's covenant by excluding the poor, the vulnerable, and the whole of creation. Any claim of economic, political and military empire is rejected, because it attempts to subvert God's sovereignty over life, acting in contradiction to God's just rule.

A hermeneutical retrieval of Calvin's teaching of the Holy Spirit, which is an undercurrent in his mission and evangelism, finds its consonance and actuality in today's context of God's mission and World Christianity. Calvin should be spoken of much in the field of mission and evangelism. This is because the church is in need of ongoing renewal concerning the gospel in light of the lordship of Jesus Christ.

---

46. Barth, *Theology of John Calvin*, 202, 204.

3

Hermeneutics of the Word-Event in the Jewish-Christian Context

IN STUDIES OF MISSION, it is of special significance to develop mission as prophetic dialogue. When mission is comprehended as prophetic dialogue, it deals with interreligious dialogue, inculturation, and reconciliation. In this framework, we develop mission as public theology on behalf of justice, peace among faith communities, and the integrity of creation. Public missional theology undergirds the church's faithfulness to the word of justice, liberation, and the acknowledgement of creation in light of a biblical vision of a new heaven and a new earth (Isa 66:22; Rev 21:1).[1] Mission without dialogue and recognition becomes a monologue discarding the contexts in which people live. If Jesus Christ as eternal Word of God came to us through Israel, Jewish-Christian dialogue becomes an indispensable part of shaping and characterizing mission as prophetic dialogue between Christianity and Judaism.

David Bosch presents a substantial exegetical study in the field of Jewish-Christian relationship for the renewal of missional theology. Bosch's argument is that the mission of Paul can only be understood against the background of prophecy in the Hebrew Bible and contemporary Jewish apocalyptic literature. Bosch applies this observation to his reading of Romans 9–11, notably concerning 11:25–27. The gospel in this context does not mean the displacement of Israel by the church as the "new Israel," but is rather "an enlarged Israel."[2] The relation of Christians

---

1. Bevans and Schroeder, *Constants in Context*, 369–73.
2. Bosch, *Transforming Mission*, 164–65.

to Jews throughout Christian history has been misused and distorted in terms of perversion, hatred, and persecution.³ Thus Bosch insists that a serious dialogue between the church and Israel is of utmost importance for the paradigm shifts in a theology of mission.

Driven by Jewish-Christian renewal in the studies of mission as word-event for the sake of public missional theology, I take an interest in engaging the legacy of Bonhoeffer in connection with Martin Luther. Recent debates and conflict over the legacy of Martin Luther and Dietrich Bonhoeffer in the Jewish-Christian context impel us to carefully examine their orientation toward the Hebrew Bible against the unilateral charge of anti-Judaism in their works.

BONHOEFFER AND THE JEWS

Barth reviewed "The Barmen Theological Declaration" retrospectively in 1968, and he confessed that he had not challenged the Barmen Synod to accept the confession regarding the Jews. Barth appreciated Bonhoeffer as the one who had earlier discerned and keenly spoken of the issue of the Jews. Bonhoeffer was the first in the years after 1933 who energetically concentrated on and dealt with the theological issue of the Jews.⁴

Pincas Lapide, a Jewish theologian, maintains that Bonhoeffer's theological reflection during the time of his imprisonment demonstrates an extraordinary affinity for Torah. Lapide values Bonhoeffer's statement in 1941: "An expulsion of the Jews from the West must necessarily bring with it the expulsion of Christ. For Christ was a Jew."⁵ Lapide also draws attention to Bonhoeffer's sentence of 1936 about King David: "The people Israel will remain God's people eternally, the only people that will not disappear, because God has become its Lord, God has settled in it and built God's house."⁶ Lapide acknowledges Bonhoeffer as a forerunner who paved a way toward re-Hebraizing the church in our day.⁷

---

3. Ibid., 173.
4. Barth, *Fragments*, 119; Bethge, "Bonhoeffer und Juden," 211–48.
5. Bonhoeffer, *Ethics*, 90–91.
6. Bonhoeffer, *Illegale Theologenausbildung*, 894.
7. Bethge, "Bonhoeffer und Juden," 215.

In his theological writings, Bonhoeffer was bound to his teachers in Berlin such as Karl Holl and Adolf von Harnack. However, Bonhoeffer was critical of Harnack's statement concerning Marcion:

> Despising the Old Testament in the second century was an error that the great church has rejected rightly. Retaining it in the sixteenth century was a destiny that the Reformation could not avoid. However, conserving it as canonical document in the Protestantism of nineteenth century is the consequence of religious and churchly paralysis.[8]

In *Sanctorum Communio,* Bonhoeffer states that Jesus Christ places his life under the law (Gal 4:4) and takes his place within Israel's community of God. Israel's community is constituted by God's law. The law of God for Israel is the calling properly heard. Law and calling belong together. Both God's call and God's law point toward God's community. By placing himself within the community of Israel in vicarious representative action for all, Christ fulfills the law through love.[9]

In "The Church and the Jewish Question" (15 April 1933), Bonhoeffer showed himself as one who stood for the conversion of Israel to Christ: "The church of Christ has never lost sight of the thought that the 'chosen people', who nailed the redeemer of the world to the cross, must bear the curse for its action through a long history of suffering."[10] Given this, Stephen Haynes unfortunately categorizes Bonhoeffer as part of the anti-Jewish tradition of Christian "witness-people myth."[11] Witness-people myth refers to a theory which uses Israel as a negative example in witnessing to God's righteousness and judgment, because the Jews rejected Jesus Christ as Messiah.

However, even in this 1933 writing Bonhoeffer proposes the church's direct resistance on behalf of the Jews.[12] In Bonhoeffer's response of solidarity with the suffering people of God, he offers a vision of the political activation of the church. The church's undertaking is not just to bandage the victims under the wheel, but to jam the very spokes of the wheel.[13]

---

8. Harnack, *Marcion*, 248.
9. Bonhoeffer, *Sanctorum Communio*, 148.
10. Bonhoeffer, *No Rusty Swords*, 226.
11. Haynes, *Bonhoeffer*, 118.
12. Bonhoeffer, "Church and Jewish Question," 139.
13. Ibid.

Accordingly, Pangritz provides a convincing explanation of Bonhoeffer's position in "The Church and the Jewish Question" in agreement with Heinz E. Tödt:

> [Bonhoeffer] was the only one who considered solidarity with the Jews, especially with non-Christian Jews, to be a matter of such importance as to obligate the Christian churches to risk a massive conflict with that state—a risk which could threaten their very existence.[14]

Bonhoeffer speaks out against the Aryan paragraph, which refers to Paragraph 7 of a "Law for the Restoration of the Civil Service" (passed by the German Reichstag on 7 April 1933). This paragraph claims that Jews and anyone of Jewish descent must be resigned and banned from any appointment in any public office. "German Christians" (*Deutsche Christen*) refers to those who supported Adolf Hitler and Nazi ideology through the assimilation of the church into the ideology of the Nazi state. Their first national convention took place in Berlin from April 3–5, 1933. They applied this paragraph to the German Protestant Church, calling for the establishment of a united *Reichskirche* and for the single leadership principle within it.

The Barmen Synod challenged the Nazification of the German Reich Church and adopted "The Barmen Theological Declaration" which is the rejection of Nazi ideology in the Reich Church. However, "The Barmen Theological Declaration" unfortunately did not articulate the theological issue of Jews.[15]

THE CHURCH IN SERIOUS ENCOUNTERS WITH ISRAEL

In *The Cost of Discipleship* (1937), Bonhoeffer described a disciple as one who is conformed to the image of Christ. The concept of conformation to Christ, which comes by being drawn into the form of Jesus Christ, is decisive for Bonhoeffer's ethical formation. "The image of Jesus Christ impresses itself in daily communion on the image of the disciple."[16] In his chapter, "The Righteousness of Christ," Bonhoeffer connected dis-

---

14. Pangritz, "Sharing the Destiny," in Gruchy, ed., *Bonhoeffer*, 259.
15. Chung, *Christian Mission a Diakonia of Reconciliation*, 155.
16. Bonhoeffer, *Cost of Discipleship*, 299.

cipleship as a binding to Christ with the binding of the disciples to the law of the Old Testament. In commenting on Matt 5:17–20, Bonhoeffer challenges the traditional position of accusation toward the Jews since Marcion: "Think ye that I am come to fulfill the law and the prophets? I am not come to fulfill, but to destroy." Many others since Marcion have read and expounded this saying of Jesus as if that were what he said. But Jesus says: "You must not imagine that I have come to destroy the law or the prophets." In so saying he vindicates the authority of the law of the old covenant."[17]

Bonhoeffer's concept of discipleship cannot be aptly understood without reference to his statement, "The disciples are bound to the Old Testament law," that is, "the law of the old covenant."[18] Jesus came to fulfill the law of the old covenant, manifesting his perfect union with God's will, which is revealed in the Old Testament law and prophets. For Bonhoeffer, Jesus' fulfillment of the law is the fundamental presupposition of the whole Sermon on the Mount. "Only the doer of the law can remain in communion with Jesus." Thus, "with the disciple also righteousness could only take the form of obedience to the law."[19] The law of the old covenant belongs to Christ, as conversely Christ belongs to it. According to Bonhoeffer, there is an evangelical rejoicing in Torah, to which Christian discipleship is deeply bound. The gospel of Jesus Christ stands in deep conversation and relationship with the world of the Torah. Bonhoeffer comprehends the relationship between Jesus Christ and discipleship in terms of Jesus's faithfulness to the Torah while affecting it. Bonhoeffer characterizes Jesus as the affirmer of the law of the Mosaic covenant which transcends a charge of prejudice of witness people myth.[20]

Crystal Night, known as "the Night of Broken Glass," took place when the Nazi Party instigated the destruction of Jewish property and the synagogues. Some 7,500 shops were vandalized and 171 Jewish synagogues were burnt to the ground. After Crystal Night (November 9, 1938),[21] Bonhoeffer changed his attitude toward the Jews dramatically

---

17. Ibid., 121.
18. Ibid.
19. Ibid., 124.
20. Bonhoeffer, *Cost of Discipleship*, 126. See Haynes, *Bonhoeffer Legacy*, 79.
21. Additionally, we must mention Helmut Gollwitzer's sermon against anti-Semitism after the Crystal Night. Since the imprisonment of Martin Niemöller, he worked as his unofficial successor in the Dahlem church. Pangritz, "Umkehr und Erneuerung" in

and radically. Bonhoeffer advocated for God's grace to Judaism in historical time, while announcing God's punishment to the Nazi government and German Christians.

Psalm 74 is underlined in Bonhoeffer's Bible ("They burned all the meeting places of God in the land"), and "9.11.38!" (November 9, 1938) is written in the margin in his small handwriting.[22] A student of Bonhoeffer, Gottried Maltusch, reported in *"Beim Brand der Synagogen,"* how Bonhoeffer reacted with his illegal seminary, located at Pommern, over the destruction of the synagogues.

> Among us ... several students spoke about the curse, which would fall down on the Jewish people.... Bonhoeffer rejected the interpretation most sharply, that in the destruction of the synagogue by the Nazis, the curse is fulfilled upon the Jews ... Against this, and with this violence, the godless face of National Socialism has showed itself anew.[23]

In response to this violent act of destruction Bonhoeffer made reference to Matt 27:25 and Luke 23:28 in regard to Rom 9–11. He provocatively argues that "if today the synagogues are in flames, then the church tomorrow will be inflamed."[24]

In the culmination of Hitler's power in 1941, Bonhoeffer stated that

> Jesus Christ was the promised Messiah of the Israelite-Jewish people, and for that reason the line of our forefathers goes back beyond the appearance of Jesus Christ to the people of Israel. Western history is, by God's will, indissolubly linked with the people of Israel, not only genetically but also in a genuine uninterrupted encounter. The Jew keeps open the question of Christ ... An expulsion of the Jews from the West must necessarily bring with it the expulsion of Christ. For Jesus Christ was a Jew.[25]

Jesus was in solidarity with his people who became God's enemy for the sake of the Christian. The people of the world and Western history are bound to the Israelite-Jewish people for whom Jesus came as the promised Messiah. Therefore, Bonhoeffer understands the indispensable task

Berliner Zeitschrift, 269–84.

22. Bethge, "Bonhoeffer und Juden," 237.
23. Zimmermann, *Begegnung mit Bonhoeffer*, 118.
24. Ibid.
25. Bonhoeffer, *Ethics*, 90–91.

of the church to have genuine uninterrupted encounters and dialogue with contemporary Judaism, dialogue that keeps open the question of Christ. Just eleven days after the flaming of the synagogues, Bonhoeffer wrote to his brothers: "In the last days I have meditated so much on Rom 9:4 and 11:11–15. This leads me so much into prayer."[26] Therefore, he develops a Christology in continuity with the Old Testament and also in regard to contemporary Judaism.

During his imprisonment, Bonhoeffer presented his concept of the world's coming of age in which God should not be relegated to the gaps. Doing theology "without recourse to the working hypothesis called God"[27] gains importance. Bonhoeffer learned a great deal about the relationship between God and scientific knowledge from Weizäcker's book about *The World-View of Physics*. It is a mistake to use God as a stop-gap for the incompleteness of human knowledge.[28] God in Jesus Christ is not a stop-gap.

Bonhoeffer appreciates that the Enlightenment runs counter to the fascist "deification of the irrational, of blood and instinct, of the beast of prey in man."[29] However, Bonhoeffer does not ignore the limitation of the Enlightenment, because it indicates that history has begun at the hands of unshackled human beings along with the cult of reason, the deification of nature, faith in progress, the revolt of the bourgeoisie and the revolt of masses, nationalism, and anti-clericalism.

Bonhoeffer's theology of world orientation, which is relevant to his view of the Enlightenment, cannot be properly understood without reference to his orientation to the Hebrew Bible. Here, he takes seriously that the Israelites never utter the name of God.[30] Bonhoeffer wrote to Bethge, a close friend and confidant, that he was reading the Hebrew Bible much more than the Greek Bible. He noted that one might speak of God's grace only when one submits to God's law. "It is not Christian to want to take our thoughts and feelings too quickly and too directly from the New Testament."[31]

---

26. Klappert, *Miterben der Verheißung*, 93.
27. Bonhoeffer, *Letters & Papers*, 325 (= LPP).
28. LPP 311.
29. Bonheoffer, *Ethics*, 55.
30. LPP 135.
31. LPP 157.

BONHOEFFER CONCERNING KARL BARTH AND RUDOLF BULTMANN

Bonhoeffer's main concern is how to conceptualize the relationship between Christ and the world that has come of age on the basis of the gospel in reference to the suffering life of contemporary Jews. Bonhoeffer presupposes that God cannot be reduced to some secret place. But it is of special significance to recognize that the world and its people have come of age by way of confrontation with God. His theological project is to take into consideration "this revolt from below."[32]

In his orientation toward the Hebrew Bible, Bonhoeffer reveals, in his critique of the positivism of revelation in Barth's theology, that the religious *a priori* of humanity is "a historically conditioned and transitional form of human self-expression."[33] According to Bonhoeffer, Barth is the first theologian who seriously undertook a critique of religion. Although Barth started from a critique of religion, he arrived at its restoration rather than carrying his critique to completion in its ultimate deconstruction. He undergirds a positivist doctrine of revelation replacing religion.

Barth grounds the sum of the gospel in God's gracious election in the inner trinitarian framework of predestination (dialectical predestination), which undergirds the triumph of grace and revelation from above. In contrast to Barth's theological rationalization of predestination, Bonhoeffer, based on the incarnation of Christ, sought to restore a secret discipline which keeps the mysteries of the Christian faith from profanity. As Bonhoeffer argues,

> "God revealed in the flesh," the God-man Jesus Christ, is the holy mystery which theology is appointed to guard. What a mistake to think that it is the task of theology to unravel God's mystery, to bring it down to the flat, ordinary human wisdom of experience and reason! It is the task of theology solely to preserve God's wonder as wonder, to understand, to defend, to glorify God's mystery as mystery.[34]

According to Bonhoeffer, Barth does not take seriously the reality of the world, because "the world is in some degree made to depend on itself

---

32. LPP 346.
33. LPP 280.
34. *Testament to Freedom*, 472.

and left to its own devices."³⁵ Leaving the reality of the world to its own devices, Barth replaced religion with a positivist doctrine of revelation. This Barthian view says, in effect, take it or leave it: virgin birth, Trinity, or anything else. This theological metaphysics must simply be swallowed as a whole or not at all.³⁶

Bonhoeffer understands that the church based on *theologia crucis* is in service for the world as being for others, while Barth understands the existence of the church for others in light of the triumph of God's grace. Bonhoeffer's Christology for others is deeply connected with God's embodiment in Jesus Christ, emphasizing Jesus' solidarity with the working class. This aspect entails a hermeneutical learning from the standpoint of those who suffer, those who bear the status of outcast: the suspects, the maltreated, the powerless, the oppressed, and the reviled in the world.³⁷ Such a perspective radicalizes his hermeneutical theology of the gospel, putting it in deep dialogue with the world come of age, yet under the reality of brokenness and suffering.

According to Bonhoeffer, Bultmann remains fundamentally liberal and still religious based on his program of demythologization that separates God from miracles. Interpretation in a religious sense has a metaphysical character as well as having an individualistic character. Although Bultmann is aware of Barth's limitations, his liberal process of reduction dropped the mythological element of Christianity, reducing it to its essence. The primary task of exegesis and translation in Bultmann's demythologization is to interpret myth as an expression of a distinctive human self-understanding. As we compare Paul and John with the Synoptic gospels, we are convinced that a process of interpretation in the New Testament occurs, tending toward demythologizing. In the language of the New Testament, the worldviews of late Judaism and Hellenistic Gnosticism are distinctively reflected—directly or indirectly.³⁸

Against Bultmann, however, Barth attempts to seek understanding from the Word of God regarding what causes faith. The revelation of God in the life, death, resurrection, ascension, and *parousia* of Jesus Christ is the cardinal truth of the kerygma. This content must not be

---

35. LPP 286.
36. LPP 286.
37. Bonhoeffer, *Christ the Center*, 35; LPP 17.
38. Barth, *Modern Theology*, 86.

demythologized. Barth charges that Bultmann was not capable of making anything of the Old Testament because of Bultmann's tendency to run into docetism.[39]

Bonhoeffer also insists that mythology such as the resurrection remains the thing itself. The Greek Bible should not be interpreted as a mythological clothing of a universal truth.[40] In the Hebrew Bible, righteousness and God's kingdom on earth are the focus rather than the salvation of one's soul. Paul's teaching in Rom 3:24 articulates the view that God alone is righteous, rather than endorsing an individualistic doctrine of salvation. What is in the gospel "[is] intended to exist for this world . . . in the biblical sense of the creation and of incarnation, crucifixion, and resurrection of Jesus Christ."[41]

Given this, Bonhoeffer maintains a worldly interpretation influenced by the Hebrew Bible and John 1:14.[42] Underlying the interconnection between Jesus Christ and the Hebrew Bible, Bonhoeffer does not want to subsume the Hebrew Bible into the Greek Bible. Rather, the Greek Bible must be interpreted in terms of the Hebrew Bible from below and in the worldly, political, and material dimension. At issue is how to interpret important concepts such as repentance, faith, justification, rebirth, and sanctification in the Greek Bible from the worldly and non-religious perspective. According to Bonhoeffer, Bultmann's hermeneutics does not take seriously the worldly dimension of the Hebrew Bible, while in Barth the positivistic demand of revelation and church fails to grapple with the seriousness of the world. The world's coming of age is better understood on the basis of the gospel and in the light of Christ.[43]

THEOLOGIA CRUCIS AND THE SUFFERING OF ISRAEL

As he states,

> [T]he faith of the Old Testament isn't a religion of redemption. . . . But isn't this a cardinal error, which separates Christ from the Old Testament and interprets him on the lines of the myths

39. Ibid., 92.
40. LPP 329.
41. LPP 286.
42. LPP 286.
43. LPP 329.

about redemption? To the objection that a crucial importance is given in the Old Testament to redemption (from Egypt, and later from Babylon—cf. Deutero-Isaiah) it may be answered that the redemptions referred to here are historical, i.e., on this side of death . . . Israel is delivered out of Egypt so that it may live before God as God's people on earth . . . This world must not be prematurely written off; in this the Old and New Testaments are at one. . . . Christ takes hold of a man at the center of his life.[44]

Bonhoeffer made an audacious attempt to see world events from the perspective of those who suffer, which is grounded in his reflection on Isaiah 53. Here we see a correlation between *theologia crucis* and the suffering of the Jews. "Misery, suffering, poverty, loneliness, helplessness, and guilt mean something quite different in the eyes of God," because Christ was born in a stable.[45] *Metanoia* in this sense refers to participation in the suffering of God. It allows people to be caught up into the way of Jesus Christ and thereby fulfilling Isaiah 53.[46] Bonhoffer seems to identify the prophetic song of the suffering servant in Isaiah 53 with Israel in the Jewish tradition. The prophecy is fulfilled through our participation in the powerlessness of God in the world and our solidarity with the suffering of Israel.

Bonhoeffer's sentence, "God lets himself be pushed out of the world onto the cross,"[47] reflects the concrete event of the Jews being pushed out of the European world to a place of deportation and destruction.[48] "Behold, the Lamb of God, who takes away the sin of the world" (John 1:29) is embedded within Jesus' table-fellowship with public sinners and tax collectors. The suffering of the Jews is seen in their bearing the burden of the sins of the Christian church in the present context.[49] Following the messianic way of Jesus, Bonhoeffer argues that

> The church is the church only when it exists for others. To make a start, it should give away all its property to those in need . . . The church must share in the secular problems of ordinary human life, not dominating, but helping and serving.[50]

44. LPP 336–37.
45. LPP 166.
46. Chung, *Christian Mission a Diakonia of Reconciliation*, 160.
47. LPP 360.
48. Klappert, *Miterben der Verheißung*, 97.
49. LPP 362.
50. LPP 382–83.

Bonhoeffer places the relationship between the church and the world in mutual dialectical tension, by imploring the church to run in the direction of doing something courageous for God's sake "in a bold venture of faith."[51]

As Christians, we must share in the liberating and redeeming love of Christ for all who suffer. Since Jesus, being for others, was a Jew responsible for the innocent victims, the Jews may represent Jesus' existence through their weakness and suffering, as projected in Isaiah 53. Bonhoeffer was aware of Isaiah 53 being fulfilled in his time, seeing the connection of suffering between the messiah of Israel and his people. This fulfillment of the prophecy of Israel is relevant to his statement of confession in *Ethics*:

> "She [the church] was silent when she should have cried out because the blood of the innocent was crying aloud to heaven... And indeed she has left uncontradicted... even open mockery of the most holy name," with respect to "the physical and spiritual suffering of countless innocent people," "the deaths of the weakest and most defenseless brothers of Jesus Christ."[52]

BONHOEFFER'S REFLECTION ON "LUTHER AGAINST LUTHER"

God's promise in Jesus Christ is meaning for life, which is turned from being curved into oneself toward upright walking filled with hope, justice, and peace.[53] From here, life has *meaning* for us. The term *meaning* translates a biblical notion of *promise*. Furthermore, Bonhoeffer proposed Martin Luther as the one who lived a this-worldly life in such a direction anew.[54] Bonhoeffer consciously protected Luther from the nationalistic, anti-Jewish misuse of his theology. The "pro-Hebrew" Luther was accepted by Bonhoeffer as the one who would critically question the juridical and social separation of the Jews. This connection interpreted and portrayed Luther as an enemy of the anti-Semitic policy of 1933.[55]

---

51. LPP 6.
52. Bonhoeffer, *Ethics*, 114.
53. LPP 374.
54. LPP 369.
55. Bethge, "Bonhoeffer und Juden," in Kremers, ed., *Die Juden und Martin Luther*, 225.

The nationalistic misuse of Luther comes from Julius Streicher, the infamous "Jew devourer" of the Third Reich. He justified his actions on the basis of Luther's later anti-Jewish writings on the occasion of his indictment for a Jewish massacre in the year of 1946.

Albert Friedlander, a Jewish theologian, accuses that Luther's understanding of the Jews eradicates a space for Judaism. Luther's early friendly attitude toward the Jews does not hide his desire for the conversion of the Jews to the church. Although Luther expressed a hope for the Jews, he did not actually hold such hope for his contemporary Judaism.[56]

In contrast, Pincas Lapide appreciates Luther's early reflections on the Jews in a different manner. In the Reformation breakthrough, Luther emphasizes the importance of the Old Testament, advocating for coming back to the original Hebrew text. Insofar as Luther understands that word and deed are one in God, it refers to the Hebrew word *dabar*, that Luther expresses as *"verbum facere"* (to do the Word). Luther comprehends Torah in the Latin term *"instructio"* and *"doctrina"* (command and promise) as divine instruction in the Jewish sense.[57]

LUTHER'S ATTITUDE TOWARD THE OLD TESTAMENT

Unfortunately, there has been little attention paid to the influence of the Old Testament and Jewish faith on Luther's theology. Clarifying the importance of the Decalogue (in *The Small Catechism*), Luther holds that we should fear, love, and trust God above all things.[58] This is a clear translation of the Christian faith. God's grace and all good things are promised to the doer of the commands.

In his *Preface to the Old Testament* (1523, revised 1545),[59] Luther values the Old Testament as "the very words, works, judgments, and deeds of the majesty, power, and wisdom of the most high God." That is, "the swaddling cloths and the manger in which Christ lies."[60] The law,

---

56. Friedlander, "Luther und Wir Juden," in Kremers, ed., *Die Juden und Martin Luther*, 292, 295. Chung, *Public Theology in an Age of World Christianity*, 81.

57. Lapide, "Stimmen jüdischer Zeitgenossen," in *Juden und Luther*, 172.

58. Luther, "Small Catechism," in Kolb and Wengert, eds. ,BC 351.

59. The translation of the 1545 text can be found in LW 35:235–51.

60. "Preface to the Old Testament," in Lull and Russel, eds., *Luther's Basic Writings*, 114.

more than having an accusatory function, contains the sense of gratitude and delight of the justified who is willing to do the law for the grace of Christ and the neighbor. As Luther states,

> Now in the New Testament there are also given, along with the teaching about grace, many other teachings that are laws and commandments for the control of the flesh . . . Similarly in the Old Testament too there are, beside the laws, certain promises and words of grace, by which the holy fathers and prophets under the law were kept, like us, in the faith of Christ.[61]

In discovering the Old Testament and the Jewish roots of Christianity, Luther was accused by his enemies of being a Judaizer. In 1524, Rome branded Luther as a *"semi-Judaeus."* According to Luther's lecture on Deuteronomy, the synagogue emerged first. Christ, the apostles, and the Word had come from the Jews. The Jews became the first Christians. A hatred of the Jews has nothing to do with a Christian teaching and life.

In his *Table Talk,* Luther expressed an interest in learning the Hebrew language, if he were younger. Although the Greek Bible is written in Greek, it speaks in a Hebrew manner. "The Hebrew drinks from the spring source; but the Greek from water that flows from the source. The Latin drinks from the puddles."[62]

LUTHER AND MOSES

As Luther says,

> It is Christian freedom. If the law does not change itself, but if the humans change themselves, then this law . . . become joyous and loving. So we become *legis amatores*, who love the law in heart.[63]

According to Luther, Christians become *legis amatores* (lovers of the sacred law of the scripture) through God's grace. The emperor could take an example from Moses for establishing a good government.[64] Without claim for salvation, people may follow Moses' law without coercion.

---

61. Ibid.

62. WATr 525; see also Chung, *Public Theology in an Age of World Christianity*, 86.

63. WA 2:498, 528, 560.

64. "How Christians Should Regard Moses," in Lull and Russel, eds., *Luther's Basic Theological Writings*, 128.

Moses is the *Sachsenspiegel* (Saxon code of law) for the Jews, so that the Gentiles are not under obligation to follow Moses. However, the natural law is written in the hearts of the Gentiles (Rom 2:14–15, 3:22), and it comes from the commandments of Moses.

Luther wrote to Justus Jonas (June 30, 1530) that the Decalogue is the dialectics of the gospel, while the gospel is the rhetoric of the Decalogue. Therefore we have, in Christ, all of Moses, but in Moses, not all of Christ. Luther confessed that he became a new student of the Decalogue.[65] The Decalogue becomes the reason-reflecting ground of the gospel. Likewise, the gospel becomes the assertion, the art of language, the rhetoric of the Decalogue. Luther takes Moses out of Jewish external law and incorporates him into natural reason. Moses entails a christological dimension, because the Decalogue gives divine voice to all.[66]

In *How Christians Should Regard Moses* (1525) Luther is interested in learning from Moses as a moral teacher rather than a lawgiver. The best thing in Moses is "the promises and pledges of God about Christ."[67] He reads Moses for the sake of the promise about Christ: "what urges Christ." Thus the law is evangelically conceptualized.[68] The Ten Commandments are a mirror, reflecting our life. Luther relates Moses to beautiful examples of faith, love, and the cross. In fact, in Moses there is a fine order, a joy about the gospel of Christ.[69]

According to Luther, the laws retain three dimensions in terms of underlying laws for protection against the wicked, upholding laws for instruction, and finally acknowledging laws about faith and love. All laws are directed toward faith and love, and every law of God is good and righteous (Rom 7:7–16). God is reconciled through Christ for all and the human heart begins to feel kindly toward doing the law and enjoys it. As Luther states, "For Moses is, indeed, a well of all wisdom and understanding, out of which has sprung all that the prophets knew and said. Moreover, even the New Testament flows out of it and is grounded in it."[70]

---

65. Iwand, *Luthers Theologie*, 84.

66. Chung, *Public Theology in an Age of World Christianity*, 82.

67. Luther, "How Christians Should Regard Moses," in Lull and Russel, eds., *Luther's Basic Theological Writings*, 129.

68. Iwand, *Luthers Theologie*, 203–4.

69. Luther, "How Christians Should Regard Moses," in Lull and Russel, eds., *Luther's Basic Theological Writings*, 132.

70. Ibid., 121.

Furthermore, Luther sought to provide a third kingdom for the Jews, in regard to his two kingdoms.

> Between these two kingdoms still another has been placed in the middle, half spiritual and half temporal. It is constituted by the Jews, with commandments and outward ceremonies which prescribe their conduct toward God and men.[71]

Deliberating the Christian hermeneutical engagement with Moses, Luther demonstrates his notion of another kingdom, which is half spiritual and half worldly. Luther grants a space for Judaism as a moral religion while rejecting assimilation of them into the Christian sphere. The Jewish kingdom becomes meaningful for Luther as a kingdom of Jewish service before and toward the world. It is neither in the temporal nor in the spiritual realm of God, but rather it is set up in the middle between the spiritual and the secular.

As an intermediary, Moses exists only for the Jewish people, not a representative of the Gentiles. However, Luther appreciates the core value of the Torah for Christian faith: the Decalogue.

CHRIST AND THE OLD TESTAMENT

Luther's hermeneutic of "what promotes Christ" can be heard in his preface to the book of James.

> All righteousness-creating holy books are in agreement that they preach and promote Christ. This is also the right criterion to criticize all books, if one sees whether they drive Christ or not.[72]

Subsequently, the criterion to test every scripture is undertaken in light of this hermeneutical principle—whether or not it conveys Christ. The true touchstone for testing all scriptures lies in discovering whether they emphasize the prominence of Christ or not. This perspective maintains that Scripture is the prophetic word in the Old Testament, not contrary to Christ. The New Testament is the living and oral proclamation that opens up the prophetic word.

---

71. Ibid., 126.

72. Luther, "Preface to the Epistles of St. James and St. Jude," in Dillenberger, ed., *Luther: Selections*, 36.

In Luther's theology, the Scripture is originally only the Old Testament, which, as the law, entails the promise. Scripture wants to become a living and spoken word, which is the task of exegesis and interpretation. Luther's slogan, *sola Scriptura*, retains profound meaning for making a distinction between the text and interpretation. This conveys a movement of bringing Scripture to spoken word.[73]

In his exegetical work, "what promotes Christ" lies on a spectrum and entails new horizons. In other words, "what promotes Christ" is a wide breadth of interpretation and is open to innovative interpretation, so that the Old Testament is not simply Christianized, but the faith of the holy fathers in the Old Testament can be interpreted as Christian faith per se. Certain promises and grace in the Old Testament reveal that the holy fathers and prophets remained in the faith of Christ.[74] Luther appreciates the Old Testament as the First Testament, preaching the five books of Moses in the fashion of *lectio continua* for the Christian faith and the church in the city church of Wittenberg.[75]

The Word of God makes alive, and right faith arises there. The word of covenant, this promise of salvation, is the same Word that is revealed in Jesus Christ. Luther's mission to the Jews is based on his recommendation that the Jews return to their fathers in the Old Testament. In the *Preface to the Old Testament*, Luther asks:

> What is the New Testament but a public preaching and proclamation of Christ, set forth through the sayings of the Old Testament and fulfilled through Christ?[76]

The Torah is more comprehensive than the accusing law, because in the Old Testament there are certain promises and words of grace, which kept the holy fathers and prophets in the faith of Christ.[77]

For Luther, the gospel is essentially a joyous cry about Christ driven by the human mouth. It is no accident that Christ did not *write* the gospel message to apostles, but rather he spoke it. In the New Testament,

---

73. Ebeling, *Lutherstudien*, 1:288–89.

74. "Preface to the Old Testament," in Lull and Russel, eds., *Luther's Basic Theological Writings*, 114.

75. Chung, *Public Theology in an Age of World Christianity*, 84.

76. "Preface to the Old Testament," in Lull and Russel, eds., *Luther's Basic Writings*, 114.

77. Ibid.

preaching happens verbally and publicly with the living voice. Insofar as the "Bible" for Luther essentially refers to the Old Testament, the New Testament refers to the living voice of God.

CONCLUSION

Luther's writing, "That Jesus Christ was a born Jew," highlights his friendly attitude toward the Jews:

> I hope that if one deals in a kindly way with the Jews and instructs them carefully from Holy Scripture, many of them will become genuine Christians and turn again to the faith of their fathers, the prophets and patriarchs.... we are but Gentiles, while the Jews are of the lineage of Christ . . . The Jews are actually nearer to Christ than we are.[78]

The preaching of Christ as law and gospel is God's blessing for all people. The gospel as *viva vox evangelii* goes out over everyone as a pure blessing in which all are blessed, although not all have become Christian.[79] Luther's missional activity for the Jews is characterized by friendly dialogue and encouragement for the Jews "to turn again to the faith of their fathers, the prophets and patriarchs" while recognizing their Judaism.[80] Luther's mission of dialogue with the Jews implies an encouragement for them to return back to the faith of Abraham. In Luther's writings, Jesus has been sent to transform the whole of creation, the whole world. Christ has come to fulfill God-given and graced-filled Torah.[81]

In this regard, Luther's understanding of the gospel in terms of mutual conversation needs to be actualized and contextualized through Lutheran dialogue with the Jewish people, as brothers and sisters in the Bible. This aspect may also result in the physical and lively communication of interfaith relationship with Jewish brothers and sisters. For Luther, Abraham is the consummate example of evangelical life.[82] Abraham's faithfulness to the promise of God is recognized and accepted in the sight of God, like the Christian faith in Jesus Christ. Abraham was effective as a

---

78. LW 45:200.
79. Stolle, *Luther Texts on Mission*, 29.
80. Ibid., 53.
81. Ibid., 23.
82. WA 57:3.236.4–5.

missionary in Egypt, preaching God's mercy to the people.[83] God's promise with Abraham means that all the nations of the earth will be blessed (Gen 22:18) Christ as the descendent of Abraham has blessed the entire world through the gospel (Gal 3:16).

Bonhoeffer took Luther's Old Testament thinking a step further, arguing that the Jews keep open the question of Christ. Bonhoeffer's Christology retains a positive contour in dealing with the disobedience of Israel (Rom 10–11). Following in his footsteps, F. W. Marquardt deepens Bonhoeffer's Christology by arguing that, in the Jewish self-understanding, the "No!" is an act of loyalty to the God of the Torah, who is the free and transcendent God. If the Jewish "No!" to Jesus Christ means faithfulness to the God of the first commandment, Christians may pay attention to Jewish obedience to the First Commandment in which the Jewish "No!" expresses its protest to the final ecclesial passion of Christianity.[84]

According to Paul, the gifts and the calling of God are irrevocable. God has imprisoned all in disobedience so that God may be merciful to all (Rom 11:28–32). Thus, Paul proclaims the eschatological subjection of Jesus Christ to God the Father. "When all things are subjected to him, then the Son himself will also be subjected to the one who put all things in subjection under him, so that God may be all in all" (1 Cor 15:28).

God's faithfulness to God's people is irrevocable, despite their disobedience, because Jesus was obedient until his death on the cross (Phil 2:8): To sanctify God's name until death. The Christian confession of Jesus Christ is related to the particular Son of God who stands as the border between Israel and all nations, identifying himself with the lowest of the low of his brothers and sisters (Matt 25:31). The prophetic mandate of biblical Israel also urges the state of Israel to take seriously God's shalom with the fragile and vulnerable in Palestine. According to Bonhoeffer, the church is always guilty and responsible for innocent victims and also for today's Lazarus in Abraham's bosom. This prophetic voice is contextualized where a reality of injustice and violence prevails on behalf of those who suffer under the dominion of powers and principalities.

---

83. Stole, *Luther Texts on Mission*, 16.
84. Pangritz and Chung, eds., *Theological Audacities*, 24.

4

Georg F. Vicedom and God's Mission in a Larger Framework

THE GERMAN MISSIOLOGIST GEORG F. Vicedom (1903–1974) was trained in the seminary of Neuendettelsaus, which is well known for the legacy of the confessional mission and *diakonia* of Wilhelm Loehe (1808–1872).[1] Vicedom was a propagator of the theology of God's mission in an ecumenical and global context, providing a larger framework of God's mission by paving the way to public missional theology and World Christianity.

Vicedom received ethnological preparation and learning at Hamburg University. In 1929, he undertook mission service in the highlands of central New Guinea. The outbreak of war in 1939 forced him to return to Germany. There, he was assigned to a teaching position at the church faculty of Neuendettelsau, and later at Erlangen University. His massive ethnological survey of the Mbowamb tribe in New Guinea established his reputation as a missiologist and as a cultural anthropologist.[2]

Vicedom's theological and confessional acumen fully incorporates ethnographical research and its scientific method into the biblical and systematic framework of missiology. He contributed to the shaping of a larger framework in the field of mission studies, emphasizing the study of cultural ethnography and world religions. Although the term *missio Dei* was coined by Karl Hartenstein under the influence of Karl Barth,

---

1. Chung, *Mission and Diakonia*, 100–116.
2. Vicedom, *Myths and Legends*; Anderson, ed., *Biographical Dictionary*, 701–2.

Vicedom can truly be regarded as a father of *missio Dei* theology through his two influential books: *The Mission of God* and *Actio Dei*.[3]

In the ecumenical discussion of the theology of God's mission, Georg Vicedom played a normative role, undertaking the first major study of *missio Dei* theology in a biblical, systematic, and ecumenical manner. His book *The Mission of God* includes his reflection on the Willingen Conference, elaborating missional themes in a biblical, hermeneutical, and systematic manner. Scripture as *norma normans* (the norming norm) must speak first about the purpose of church work and mission. His book entails a practical guideline and guidance for missionaries and pastors, with an introduction to the theology of God's mission to the present-day theology of missionary work. Vicedom appreciates the contribution of dialectical theology, notably Karl Barth, in initiating a shift from an anthropocentric approach to a theocentric-Trinitarian one. However, he maintains that this paradigm shift comes through the rediscovery of reformation theology, notably refurbishing a model of the two kingdoms underlying God's mission. Vicedom's basic conviction is that mission is "an essential trait and expression of the life of the church . . . thus every justification for the mission must touch the basic faults of the church."[4]

TRINITARIAN DRAMA AS SALVATION HISTORY

The church is only the outcome of the activity of God. This is an affirmation of the concept of *missio Dei* as described in the Conference at Willingen: "[T]he mission is participation in the sending of the Son, in the *missio Dei*. The missionary movement . . . has its source in the Triune God Himself."[5] The concept of God's mission undergirds a concept of God's lordship and the church's obedience to God. According to Vicedom, God becomes the Sender as well as the One sent. Divine sending is best understood as an expression of divine love and mercy in the presence of the Son and the Spirit. The immanent Trinity in the process of the intra-divine sending is of eminent significance, becoming foundational for the mission and the work of the church. Theologically, there is a connection between God's mission as lordship in communion and God's activity of grace *extra nos*. God's

---

3. Vicedom, *Mission of God*; *Actio Dei*.
4. Vicedom, *Mission of God*, 3.
5. Ibid., 5.

creativity and activity in the history of *missio Dei* is exhibited in the entire *Heilsgeschichte*.[6] God's sending in the present takes place in the relationship between grace and judgment. In the discussion of a missionary motif, Vicedom integrates humanity into the kingdom of God. In this integration the grace of justification remains central in his theological-missional-integrative framework. Justification means reception into the kingdom of God (in the sense of the kingdom of grace).[7]

The grace of justification, built on Christology and the kingdom of God, remains central in Vicedom's Trinitarian mission in a salvation-historical framework. In Jesus Christ, the reign of God is different from the kingdom of the world. His death and resurrection are presuppositions for the announcement of the gospel for all, beginning with his exaltation (John 12:23).[8]

The church's mission came into existence when God's eschatology in the death and resurrection of Jesus, with the gift of the Holy Spirit, created a space for the church's mission to the world. God's eschatology in Jesus Christ is the mother of theology and mission. The eschatological place of the mission to the world is accentuated in Vicedom's theological refining of *missio Dei*. Thereby, the church becomes an eschatological entity and the church's mission becomes a continuation of God's mission in the sense of the history of salvation.[9]

Jesus Christ is the bearer of God's kingdom and provides its content and directive. The kingdom of God that Jesus bestows is a new life through *metanoia* and justification. The reign of God in relationship to human beings comes as a gift, presupposing a receptive, petitioning, expectant attitude in the human being (Matt 10:15; Luke 18:17; Mark 15:43). It has little to do with dominance, coercion, or usurpation.[10]

Israel was the bearer of the promise and the mediator of the blessing by God's act of election. The election of Israel is a service of God toward the nations. The other nations are included in God's promise through this election (Gen 12:1). Vicedom's contribution to the theology of God's mission lies in his appreciation of the Old Testament, notably Israel's place in

---

6. Ibid., 8–9.
7. Ibid., 14.
8. Ibid., 37.
9. Ibid., 41, 39.
10. Ibid., 26–27.

God's mission. God's promise to Israel comes to us as the gospel of Jesus Christ. Thus, *pro-missio Dei* is the foundation for *missio Dei*.

As he states, "the particularity of the salvation of Israel became the presupposition for the fact that salvation became meaningful for others also."[11] The understanding of mission in the Old Testament must remain crucial for the church and its missional practices.

According to Vicedom, the special *missio Dei* begins with Jesus Christ who fulfills and confirms Israel's mission. The incarnation and enthronement of God makes the very content of the sending. Jesus fulfills the work of the Father (John 4:34) and this is the proof that God has sent him and is at work (John 9:3). The cross accomplishes salvation, giving content to every sending. The resurrection gives the assurance of everlasting life. Reconciliation makes the fellowship with God perfect and the proclamation of the gospel receives its urgency in its eschatological emphasis.[12] The mission to the world becomes possible because God continued God's sending and makes a continuing mission through the gift of the Holy Spirit. Vicedom emphasizes that the Holy Spirit is the impulse to the Apostle's missions. The triune God is present in God's Spirit.

Vicedom emphasizes Luther as a missional thinker. Luther understands the gospel as the living Word, which is to be spread and communicated. The Word of God should be proclaimed to people in their own unique language and culture. It is certain that the Reformation was the movement of mission in its own way.[13] Thus mission can find its expression in fellowship with the gospel. Furthermore, Vicedom's notion of special mission cannot be properly understood apart from his reinterpretation of Luther's model of two kingdoms for public, missional implication. Vicedom not only outlines a classical approach to the *missio Dei*, visible in his book *The Mission of God*, but also paves the way for a larger framework for God's mission and the kingdom of God in the context of younger churches and world religions (notably in his book *Actio Dei*).

---

11. Ibid., 50.
12. Ibid., 53.
13. Vicedom, *Mission*, 22.

MISSIONAL CHURCH AND DUTCH THEOLOGY OF THE APOSTOLATE

Vicedom takes issue with Hoekendijk's theology of the apostolate in which the latter sees the apostolate indicated in the sending of the Holy Spirit. For Hoekendijk the area of the apostolate, whose content is the lifting up of the banners of shalom (salvation), is the world: "The apostolate becomes a reality in the kerygma, the public proclamation of the shalom, in the *koinonia*, the corporative participation in the shalom, and in the *diakonia*, the ministering demonstration of shalom."[14] According to Hoekendijk, the church stands nowhere except in the act of the apostles under the power of the Holy Spirit. A notion of the visible church is discarded for the sake of the Holy Spirit.[15] Vicedom is aware in this context that the doctrine of predestination is prioritized, undermining the place of the church in service to God's mission. The doctrine of predestination implies that God's immediate relationship to the world and God's effect upon the world comes into focus. God's mission in the context of the Dutch theology of the apostolate sees more than Christology, arguing that the gospel of God's kingdom is not completely identical with the Gospel of Jesus Christ.[16]

Dutch theology of the apostolate learns from Barth's definition of "the apostolic": the church "exists through the continuing work and word of the apostles." Moreover, the church also exists in doing "what the apostles did and by virtue of the nature of what their words and deeds continue to do."[17] Dutch theology understands the apostolate as an ongoing activity of the Holy Spirit. However, Vicedom argues that this apostolic teaching must be grounded in Luther's teaching of the universal priesthood of all believers. "Apostolic" in the Nicene Creed, in which the church rests upon the foundation of the apostles and prophets, has a different meaning than how the Dutch theologians used the same term.

Vicedom understands the apostolic nature of the church through Word and sacrament (*Augsburg Confession*, art. VII), in which a congregation must emerge and an office must be present. The church, as a visible congregation, lives not only in the proclamation, but above all in the hearing of the gospel as the prerequisite for witnessing. Through hearing,

14. Vicedom, *Mission of God*, 68.
15. Ibid., 85.
16. Ibid., 69.
17. Ibid., 70.

the church lives in the love that becomes effective through Christ. The church lives in adoration and doxology, living in the sacrament and in fellowship with Jesus Christ. In fellowship with Christ, the church lives in proclamation, service, and worship. The missional church should be directed to the praise of God, to worship, thereby also to mission.[18] The basic statement for Vicedom's notion of the missional church is seen in that the church is the strongest proof that the gospel also belongs to the people in the world.[19] There is a deep connection between the gospel narrative and the world, which is acknowledged as God's created realm and reconciliation.

Christ gave the church an office, which should lead to missionary service: the ministry of the divine Word in its fullness. Everything in the church concerning the pastoral office can be applied primarily to the missionary service of the church (2 Cor 3–5), leading the congregation to influence the world and making it fit for missionary service.[20]

In appreciation of Bonhoeffer's theology of discipleship,[21] Vicedom regards discipleship as important to God's mission because the preaching of God's kingdom is always a call to discipleship. Jesus Christ selected his apostles from among the disciples and sent them out into the world for service. Discipleship was the prerequisite for the call to be an apostle. Although not every disciple was called as an apostle, every apostle was a disciple.[22] The disciples who are brought to faith through the work of the apostles do not regard themselves as pupils of the apostles, but as followers of the Lord. All disciples are called to the extension of God's kingdom. Discipleship is the presupposition for the apostolic ministry of the church. As the disciples fulfill apostolic functions, the apostolate belongs to the distinguishing marks of genuine discipleship.[23]

Vicedom articulates that the reason for the church's mission is that the gospel is intended for the world. If the church makes itself lord of the gospel, it abuses the ministry of reconciliation. Even without a missionary command there would be a mission. As church is called from

18. Ibid., 87.
19. Ibid., 82.
20. Ibid., 90.
21. Ibid., 85.
22. Ibid., 77.
23. Ibid., 79.

among the heathen, the church becomes an instrument of God's activity, which is leading the world to its ultimate end.[24] The basic statement of the Willingen Conference is important for Vicedom: the church as God's people among the nations is defined as the pilgrim people of God.[25]

GOD'S MISSION AND THE KINGDOM OF GOD

Evangelical mission in the German context has been influenced by Pietism. Because of this, the message of God's kingdom within the churches is reduced to soul saving in terms of the church, although Pietism contributed to social reform, service, pedagogy, and institutions. Through the influence of Gustav Warneck (1834–1910), who saw the realization of God's kingdom only in the service of the church, mission began to be understood as the Christianization of a nation. God's kingdom exists only in the church, although no one taught that the church is identical with the kingdom of God. In the history of mission stamped by the pietistic orientation and Warneck, a notion of the kingdom of God has been narrowed to the spiritual and ecclesial sphere. Warneck dominated missional theology until the beginning of the Second World War.[26]

Critically reviewing the relationship between the church and the kingdom of God, Vicedom examines the notion of God's kingdom in the American context. According to Richard Niebuhr, the concept of God's kingdom plays the normative role in shaping the congregational life in American society. Based on the principle of separation between the government and church, the Puritans developed the message of God's kingdom in the direction of God's providence and manifest destiny, a different direction than the Protestant church in Europe took. American mission and its motive has become propaganda for the American way of life and culture, because the purpose of democracy and the ideal of Christianity have become unified in the program of social redemption.[27]

On the other hand, the Social Gospel movement made the message of God's kingdom into a central pivot, but tended to conflate God's kingdom with immanent, historical progress. It is certain that in Rauschenbusch's

---

24. Ibid., 83.
25. Ibid., 94–95.
26. Vicedom, *Actio Dei*, 18–19.
27. Ibid., 37.

line of thought the kingdom of God is always coming. God's kingdom is realized as a renewal of society in the brotherhood and sisterhood among people. Nevertheless, the church sidestepped from the reign of God's kingdom in the world. At any rate, the term mission remains an undercurrent in the context of the Social Gospel.[28]

In contrast to this immanent and inner-worldly side of God's kingdom, Hartenstein presented a missional theology with an eschatological outlook. According to Hartenstein, the kingdom of God is greater than the church, and mission is only the organ or instrument of service between the times of the ascension and the second coming of Jesus Christ. The church always lives out of the power of the coming world that is the ultimate gift of the Holy Spirit. Belonging to the kingdom of God, the church representatively demonstrates the witness of the kingdom of God for the world. However, the empirical church must not be identical with God's kingdom. Hartenstein blocks the possibility of conflating the kingdom of God with an inner-worldly programmatic understanding of God's kingdom.[29]

The experience of World War II destroyed all optimism in mission. In Willingen 1952, a theological basis for mission was undertaken in a new and fresh way. Evanston 1954 presented the theme: Christ the Hope of the World in connection with the concept of God's kingdom. In the 1968 WCC assembly in Uppsala the eschatological relevance was emphasized in the understanding of God's kingdom. Mission is not merely defined as sending, but participation in God's on-going work in history and the world. The new life is defined as the purpose of mission, like every activity of the church. The sending of God in which we participate is described as a gift of the new creation.[30] The social and political responsibility of the church is emphasized in missional service, witness, and evangelization.

However, Vicedom takes issue with an extreme case of the "comprehensive approach" represented by the Dutch theological circle. According to the comprehensive approach, the kingdom of God exists only in the form of the kingly rule of Christ. Humanity exists only in the form of becoming Christian and true culture becomes possible through Christianization. The kingdom of God is fulfilled to the degree that the church realizes the work of humanization among people in society. The

28. Ibid., 21, 23.
29. Ibid., 33–34.
30. Ibid., 54.

comprehensive approach has fallen into the gray zone of reducing the message of God's kingdom into the optimism for the progress of faith.[31]

Against the comprehensive approach, Vicedom introduces a counter proposal which is raised in the German Protestant context: There is no mission without *diakonia* and no *diakonia* without missional implication. Faith community occurs among the people and it becomes the bringer of God's love through the announcement of the gospel. *Diakonia* to the world is an echo of the Word of God in the public realm. Where the church takes place through the gospel, *diakonia* begins to break through.[32] A public missional theology of evangelization and *diakonia* remains complementary to the Dutch missional notion of the comprehensive approach, which aims at Christianization of the world through humanization.

Taking a further step, Vicedom accentuates that the new life brought by the gospel is greater than an idea of progress, implying a revolutionary character without violence. The new life grounded in God's eschatology is oriented toward the completion and coming of God's kingdom. The message about God's kingdom retains its great importance in the history of mission. The task of mission says that God works in human history, inviting people to the area of God's love. The world is renewed and changed through the message of God's kingdom and missional service. Thus, mission and the kingdom of God belong together.[33]

MISSION AND CHRISTIAN POLITICAL RESPONSIBILITY: VICEDOM AND GOLLWITZER

For his public missional theology, Vicedom takes into account Helmut Gollwitzer's concept of the kingdom of God: "The kingdom of God is the life of the new humanity, which can believe and love, liberated from sin and death . . . Because the kingdom of God in its present and coming form is fulfilled only through the power of God, not through the power of human being, it is the absolute utopia."[34] The kingdom of God, which is not to be fulfilled by us, is the content of the promise that revolutionizes

31. Ibid., 59–60.
32. Ibid., 67, 83.
33. Ibid., 142.
34. Ibid., 98.

the present status quo. The promise of God's kingdom enters against the lordless powers of the idols.

According to Gollwitzer, the heart of the gospel, the justification of the godless, is the core message of the kingdom of God, which is understood in a verbal sense: God's reign (in Hebrew, *malkuth YHWH*).[35] Forgiveness of sin and justification of the godless is conceived of as the liberating act of God in the context of the history of the kingdom of God. God's reign in the full sense refers to the eschatological kingdom of glory (*regnum gloriae*) in the consummation of seeing face to face (1 Cor 13:12), where even the last enemy, death, is overcome (1 Cor 15:26; Rev 21:4). God's reign is always to be spoken of as belonging to the eschatological future and to the present in grace (*regnum gratiae*). God comes through Jesus in Israel to the world. The story of Jesus Christ is the coming of God into the world, characterizing the present reality of God's kingdom. The *paranesis* (the apostolic exhortations, or line and trajectory of the gospel) characterizes the life of the primitive Christian church, filling this community with participation in God's kingdom in Jesus Christ and in anticipation of God's future kingdom, although it lived under the condition of the old age.[36] The church lives in the grace of communion and the new social life of *koinonia* under the reign of God.

God is defined biblically in terms of the content of the promise of the kingdom of God, because God is a word of promise, hope, and indwelling with people (Rev. 21:3). Creation is grace and is not yet complete, on the way to still greater glory. The act of creation entails an emancipatory dimension in a fight against all obstacles to salvation, preservation, and consummation of the creature in God's reign (*regnum naturae*) in the sense of *creatio continua*. The *paranesis* coming from the message of God's kingdom in the gospel is assigned to the church, emphasizing its public responsibility and missional discipleship for the world in collaboration with those in the world that has come of age for the sake of God's shalom and life-enhancing emancipation.

Thus, according to Gollwitzer, the ecumenical argument that the church is missional by its very nature means that it is permanently oriented toward those without. Mission is solidarity with non-Christians together with a dimension of self-renewal in the sense of *metanoia* that is focused

---

35. Gollwitzer, *Introduction to Protestant Theology*, 141–42.
36. Ibid., 150–51.

upon the in-breaking of God's kingdom in Jesus Christ. Mission has a political consequence concerning reality in the aftermath of colonialism. The Lord's Supper means God's promise, pointing to the solidarity of the fellowship of the Body of Christ (1 Cor 10:16–17). The Lord's Supper says, "Those who are starving out there are also members of your fellowship."[37]

Political independence did not bring economic emancipation to the formerly colonized countries. The colonial economy is one of the most important economic sources for the mother countries, which is characteristic of colonist hypocrisy, thus the previously colonized countries retain a right to speak out against the reality of neocolonialism. The church's mission finds its validity in the struggle for peace, social justice, and political freedom, characterizing a political responsibility and discipleship of Christian fellowship in terms of endless approximation of the second petition of the Lord's Prayer: "Thy will be done on earth as it is in heaven."[38]

This perspective shapes the direction of Gollwitzer's prophetic, political theology to which Vicedom relates a socio-critical dimension of God's mission and prophetic *diakonia*.[39] If God's *promissio* comes to us as the gospel of Jesus Christ and our life through the power of the Holy Spirit, a biblical language of God's *promissio* remains foundational for God's mission in a special and revealed manner (in light of God's two strategies), which stands in deep dialogue with the life horizon of the first function of the law. Given this, *missio*, which comes from God's *pro-missio*, is the underlying dynamism of the gospel in the sense of *viva vox evangelii* accompanied by God's work in the world. This public, ethical, missional aspect becomes the motive and impulse for the imperative of accompaniment with the Other in light of God's reconciliation with the world in Christ. This promotes the mutuality, interdependence, and solidarity that breaks through a colonialist, merchant, crusading mentality. A public ethical theology and discipleship of God's mission retains Christian political responsibility in Vicedom's notion of God's mission and missional church.

---

37. Gollwitzer, *Rich Christians and Poor Lazarus*, 5.
38. Gollwitzer, *Introduction to Protestant Theology*, 153.
39. Ibid., 120.

GOD'S MISSION AND GOD'S UNIVERSAL REIGN

What Vicedom contributes to the theological deliberation concerning God's kingdom and world is his creative reinterpretation of Luther's model of two kingdoms. According to Vicedom, Luther's model is of a hermeneutical character in understanding God's work in history. God is revealed and hidden in the unity of divinity, so God, who loves people, remains in both grace and judgment. Thus Luther saw two areas of God's reign: God's preservation of the world and God's salvific work. The two areas are distinguished, but not separated from each other. Luther acknowledges that God's act of salvation in faith is connected with the rule of Christ in the distinction between the church and the world. However, God also works among the non-believers in ways that are different from God's salvific work in the church. God's work in the creation is not necessarily the same as God's work of redemption in the church. The distinction between the church and the world becomes a basis for the church's mission because God wants to redeem the people of the world. However, Vicedom is cautious about an attempt to reduce all other humanity into the ruling area of Jesus Christ. This is because Luther had struggled against the Catholic Church's absolute claim. In fact, we cannot establish a theocracy in society in the name of Christ. The world and the society have their own distinct orders.[40]

In the framework of the two kingdoms, God rules the world in a twofold manner. The first way, belonging to God's left hand, is for preservation of the world while the other, belonging to God's right hand, is for eternal life, that is, for the redemption of the world. It is certain that God remains the same Lord in these two different strategies. There remains a creative tension between the area of redemption and that of creation in an eschatological dynamism. God may speak in the area of creation through the dialectical logic of distinction without separation. However, the salvific order of redemption cannot be brought and established in the world through human revolution. In the genuine care for the kingdom of God there is concern about all human society. When we do not distinguish between the kingdom of God in the area of redemption and God's on-going work in the creation, a notion of God's mission is diminished and even distorted by conflating redemption with creation. When we overemphasize Christ's lordship over the world as a general, visible reality, the church

---

40. Ibid., 110.

becomes no longer the servant to the world, but lord of the world. It is vulnerable to ecclesial triumphalism.

Having considered this, Vicedom argues that God's mission in light of God's universal reign entails great meaning for the development of God's mission in terms of eschatological dynamism concerning the grace of justification and the kingdom of God.[41] Here, Vicedom provides a new model of God's mission by dialectically integrating Christ's rule in redemption within God's universal reign in the creation. The present and eternal salvation that God offers in Christ through the grace of justification and that is received by faith has a public, missional mandate to be expressed and practiced in the world of creation in light of God's act of reconciliation. God's mission in the special grace of Christ and God's universal reign in terms of *creatio continua* corrects any attempt to reduce the message of God's kingdom merely to a worldly agenda or to conflate the realm of salvation with that of creation as seen in the Dutch's comprehensive and universalizing approach.

Vicedom further develops his missional theology as a publicly and ethically accountable theology in terms of God's mission and God's universal reign. His stance concerning church, the peace movement, and the nuclear disarmament movement demonstrates his missional theology as a public ethical theology. Vicedom argues against the traditional idea of just war, because he clearly sees that totalitarian ideology always leads to total war. Thus, no theory of just war is justified. The church must seek to hinder every war and establish peace through the witness to the Word of God.[42] The government is assigned to exercise the divine mandate. The Christian collaborates with the government insofar as it promotes a divine mandate seeking justice and peace.

However, this does not justify the totality of the government. The government is a servant of God, but the gospel requires preservation of the government as far as it carries out the ordinances of God and exercises love in these ordinances. When the magistrates and laws command sin, Christians owe greater obedience to God than to them (Acts 5:29).[43] The church is not a flight from the world, but it, the kingdom of God's right hand, has to

---

41. Ibid., 113.
42. Vicedom et al., *Lutherische Stimmen*, 32.
43. "Augsburg Confession," in Kolb and Wengert, eds., BC 16.

live responsibly for and in the world.⁴⁴ In leading people from the nuclear question to peace, the church announces *metanoia* and judgment.⁴⁵

MISSIONAL CHURCH: LOCAL CULTURE AND WORLD RELIGIONS

In the discussion of the missionary goal, Vicedom takes into account Hoekendijk's critique of German missiological thought in light of ethnic fervor. According to Warneck, the missionary command directs the church to all nations. The conversion and Christianization of the nation is the purpose of the mission in opposition to Pietism's notion of individual conversion. Hoekendijk rejects the Christianization of the nations as the goal of missionary work, calling such a mentality German ethnic fervor.⁴⁶ Here Christianity is synthesized with nationhood. There is a danger of placing nationality above the gospel. Vicedom appreciates Hoekendijk's critique.

Together with Hartenstein and Freytag, Vicedom sharply distinguishes the congregation from its national and natural environment. Critiquing Warneck' notion of Christianization, Vicedom upholds the disciple's recognition of local cultures and belief systems.⁴⁷ According to the Scripture, the Greek term *ethne* includes people and nations outside of God's congregation. The 'all' in the missionary command is underlined by Matt 24:14. The message is to be proclaimed in the entire *oikumene* (the living space of the nations), because the gospel is intended for all. However, the Scripture is realistic, saying that a portion of humankind will accept the message.⁴⁸ According to St Paul, social relations are permitted to be adapted to the people in the congregation. However, he did not see the hallmark of Christianization in the transmission of new social patterns. The new life created by the gospel transcends them. Religion formed by revelation determines nationality, not vice versa.

Vicedom is aware that the questions about nation, nationality, and the indigenous character of the church are of special significance for the younger churches. Their striving for independence is not only a reaction against

44. Vicedom et al., *Lutherische Stimmen*, 35.
45. Ibid., 37.
46. Vicedom, *Mission of God*, 99.
47. Ibid., 113.
48. Ibid., 103.

colonization but also a struggle for their own development in their environment. Hoekendijk argues in his comprehensive approach that all areas of human life are to be permeated with Christian thought. However, Vicedom is critical of this approach, because it entails the inability of the missionary to recognize the value and uniqueness of the indigenous factors.[49] He further critiques such a missionary inability to acknowledge the indigenous factors as the confrontation between "civilization vis-à-vis nationalism."[50]

Based on his enriched experience of church and people in New Guinea, Vicedom finds it necessary that the younger churches discover their own characteristic forms of expression. The mission must not impose foreign forms on the younger church. At issue is the translation of the Word of God. For instance, the phrase "Son of Man," if literally translated into the Guinean language, means "young man." Instead, the word "chief-pillar-man" is chosen, because Jesus, like the principal pillar of a house, carries the whole weight of the building on his shoulders. This term conveys the significance of Jesus as the Son of Man. Furthermore, the kingdom of God became "the *miti* of heaven." *Miti*, which has no English equivalent, stands for peace, measure, and custom. This term can include everything that is good and beautiful. Vicedom's basic conviction is that the indigenous Christians gradually Christianized their language and worked out theological phrases and concepts in the course of time.[51]

In reference to the relationship between Christianity and non-Christian religions, Vicedom bases his thinking on Rom 1:18—12:24. He is aware that people in the world of non-Christian religions are recognized as God's people, because God is the creator and the Lord of all. People of other faiths retain a possibility of experiencing and acknowledging the existence of God. Jewish-Christian relations shape an example for further relationships between Christianity and other religions.[52]

Vicedom understands the religions as *praeparatio evangelica* or everyone has a Christian soul by nature. According to Augustine the human heart is restless until it finds rest and peace in God. Religion awakens the human soul to have desire for the infinite ocean: God.[53] In dealing with

---

49. Ibid., 111.
50. Ibid.
51. Vicedom, *Church and People*, 68–69.
52 Vicedom, *Mission*, 33.
53. Ibid., 35.

the position of the Second Vatican Council, Vicedom is convinced that world religions have a definite meaning. The gospel is a critique of the religions (including Christian religions, too), but is also fulfillment of them. Vicedom carefully distinguishes the content of the gospel from Christian culture or civilization or confessional-denominational splits. The Christian religion lives always out from the gospel, which always implies a critique of Christianity as a religion. In light of God's reconciliation with the world, we announce this Good News for all to serve and renew the world.[54]

His position may be characterized in terms of evangelical inclusivism. Vicedom argues that the universal claim of the gospel has little to do with establishing Christianity as the absolute religion. God makes salvation possible, letting the forgiveness of sin be proclaimed through the death and resurrection of Jesus Christ. The grace of God always remains the salvation, and faith in the death and resurrection of Jesus Christ affects a new life in which the missional power of attraction undergirds the faith community. The gospel sharply distinguishes mission from Western propaganda.[55]

Vicedom takes seriously the disillusioning voice about Christianity in a missional context. Christians bring and sow division. The Christian mission is associated with the Western urge toward the expansion of its civilization. This understanding of mission came as a result of colonial power and the colonial power used mission to extend its domination.[56] The whole colonization process rested on the profit motive. "Their [the Western people's] desire for world domination transformed the simple faith of Jesus into a fiercely proselytizing creed."[57]

Vicedom is convinced that Christianity always lives from the gospel, thus the gospel is always the critique of Christianity when its mission is deviated from the subject matter of the gospel.[58] The missional church is grounded in God's reconciliation through Christ's suffering. It does not escape the suffering. In suffering, it receives the mandate to suffer vicariously for the world. The church participates in the rule of Christ and thus becomes an eschatological reality. The missional church is characterized

---

54. Vicedom, *Mission der Weltreligionenen*, 165–66.
55. Vicedom, *Actio Dei*, 141–42.
56. Vicedom, *Challenge of World Religions*, 62.
57. Ibid.
58. Ibid., 143.

as the one engaged in the ministry of reconciliation that assigns the ministry to prepare the church for the times of suffering (Acts 14:22).[59]

GOSPEL AND CONTEXTUAL THEOLOGIES

Vicedom expects that the gospel can be understood in all its profundity in dialogue with other religions, which the Western church and theology have sidestepped. The Indian Theologian Devanandan brings up primarily the cosmic salvation of Christ on the basis of the cross through which the human being, according to Asian understanding, is then liberated to the personal salvation. A Japanese theologian Kazoh Kitamori demonstrates that God's wrath is expressed in the pain and suffering of God for the sinners. In God's pain, God's wrath is overcome, because it took place in the suffering life of the Son. Every human suffering is a symbolic witness to the pain of God.[60] For the relation between gospel and contextual theologies, Vicedom cites the theological basis for modernization by the Asian Conference for Church and Society held in October 1967 in South Korea: "Although we believe in the impact that divine providence makes on the progress of history we doubt whether we can recognize God's activity in modernization or in any other event of history."[61] This statement reflects on the beginning of Asian *minjung* theology, which culminated in the church's solidarity with people suffering and victimized by the process of modernization in the 1970s and 80s.

Vicedom's contribution to public missional theology can be furthered in current studies of mission in regard to congregational mission, the church's socio-political responsibility as public theology, interreligious dialogue, cultural and contextual studies of World Christianity. His legacy remains an inspiration for embodying missional church with public responsibility for the world and taking up the challenges of younger churches in the context of World Christianity. Thus Vicedom is a public missional theologian who provides a larger framework for God's mission and missional church in postcolonial World Christianity.

---

59. Vicedom, *Mission of God*, 138–9.
60. Vicedom, *Mission*, 140–41.
61. Vicedom, ed., *Christ and Younger Churches*, 15.

II

God's Mission, Public Ethics, and Israel
Karl Barth Revisited

Barth's theology of divine sending became foundational for the 1952 meeting of the IMC in Willingen, Germany. The *missio Dei* theology in Willingen is popular and influential in the recent study of God's mission and the missional church conversation. In the Willingen conference we read that the kingdom of God means the lordship of Christ over the world and the entire cosmos. The statement of the conference emphasizes the sending of the Son, the *missio Dei*, with the comprehensive goal of establishing the lordship of Christ over the whole creation.[62]

Scholars in the project of the *missio Dei* and missional church conversation have made an important contribution to missional ecclesiology rooted in the Trinitarian perspective, extending its horizon to public engagement and World Christianity. In the biblical definition of the church's mission the church is essentially multicultural. God's people are formed in distinctive and unique ways in each time and place, interacting with every culture through which the church is shaped and constituted as a community of witness.[63]

---

62. Freytag, ed., *Mission zwischen gestern und morgen*, 54.
63. Guder, ed., *Missional Church*, 233.

In recent studies there is an argument that Barth never used the term "*missio Dei*" nor phrased the term "God as a missionary God." Furthermore, it is argued that Barth did not take a Trinitarian approach, as was central at Willingen.[64] However, Barth's theology of election is structured in the inter-Trinitarian framework in which God's mission is comprehended as God's gracious election through Trinitarian activity. In Barth's theological development from election to reconciliation his systematic-constructive theology entails our participation in Christ's reconciliation as that which underlies God's mission, with a strong public and ethical component. A hermeneutics of God's mission in the study of Barth's theology contributes to public ethical theology and discipleship of God's mission which confesses Jesus Christ in postcolonial World Christianity. In the studies of God's mission, public ethics, and Israel, it is important to clarify the prophetic legacy of Karl Barth, by stimulating and theologically advancing the study of God's mission and missional church conversation.

---

64. Flett, *Witness of God*, 12.

5

Theology of Reconciliation

God's Mission and Missional Church

GOD'S ELECTION AS THE GROUNDS FOR MISSION

IN HIS SEMINAL PAPER "Die Theologie und die Mission in der Gegenwart" (delivered at the Brandenburg Missionary Conference, April 11, 1932),[1] Barth grounds mission in the divine sending of God's Son in the presence of the Holy Spirit. The church can be missional only in so far as it is obedient to God. Thus Barth argues that mission and theology should be founded upon the solid rock of God's election. Underlying the connection between mission and theology is God's free and non-prejudiced grace.

Barth insists that the term *missio* is an expression of the doctrine of the Trinity, which refers to mission as God's initiative. Grounding the church's mission in God's initiative, Barth argues that the mission becomes the subject matter for itself. We must beg the action, will, and power of mission always and only from God.[2]

According to Barth, theology is not conflated with mission, because theology entails the exegesis of the Holy Scripture as its unique and central task. The motive of mission must be grounded in God's free grace.[3] The actual point of contact for mission does not lie in the realm and power of human language, but in God's grace—where and how the language wants to connect itself—proclaimed as God's miracle of grace.[4] As the task of

1. Barth, "Theologie und Mission," 100–126.
2. Ibid., 110–11.
3. Ibid., 115.
4. Ibid., 125.

mission, announcement of the message of the kingdom of God is more than conversion of individuals.[5]

GOD'S MISSION AND TRINITY

Barth undertakes an exposition of the Trinity at the very beginning of his discussion of the nature of revelation.[6] The root of the Trinity is expressed in the statement: God revealed God's self as the Lord.[7] According to this perspective, God only revealed God's self as Lord in Jesus Christ. Eberhard Jüngel expounds Barth's Trinity by claiming that "God's being is in becoming,"[8] with an emphasis on Barth's theory of the analogy of relation (*analogia relationis*). In Jüngel's study of Barth's Trinity in the christocentric sense, Jüngel does not relate the Christian Trinity to an interpretation of the God of Israel. This is so especially in deliberation of the God of Israel in God's coming: God's being shares itself in the history of God's coming in the life of Israel and culminates itself in Jesus Christ for all. Jüngel's expression, "God's being is in becoming," is rather ontologically structured and is comprehended in terms of God's self-correspondence (God corresponds to God's self).

Barth further comprehends God as the One who loves in freedom. There is a tension between the love of Christ and the freedom of God in this formulation because Barth reduces God's freedom into the sphere of revelation rather than grounding the revelation of Christ on the freedom and love of the God of Israel. More sharply, Barth sees the love of the triune God in freedom in light of the one who changes, renews, and transforms all in all.[9] This perspective entails a political and socio-critical dimension in an analogical manner in which the socialist movement is accepted as one analogical witness to God's being wholly other in revolution.[10]

It is a substantial task to investigate the three aspects—lordship, God's freedom in love, and God as the Wholly Changing (Revolutionary Transforming)—in a Trinitarian, analogical, social-critical framework.

5. Ibid., 120.
6. Barth, *Church Dogmatics* (=CD) 1/1:295–489.
7. CD 1/1:307.
8. Jüngel, *God's Being is in Becoming*.
9. CD 2/1:258.
10. Chung, *Reclaiming Mission as Constructive Theology*, 109.

Barth argues that in the mystery of God's loving, God communicates God's self to the beloved. To be a person means to be what God is, that is the One who loves in God's way.[11] In this way, God is the personifying person. Barth's concept of God's modes of being is connected with God-in-person as the personifying God. A personal aspect of Barth's Trinitarian theology contradicts a charge of Sabellian modalism.

THE TRIUNE GOD-IN-BECOMING

In Jüngel's interpretation of Barth's Trinity, revelation in the Barthian sense is *Dei loquentis persona* (God speaking in person).[12] This aspect implies that language is commandeered by revelation, or that God comes to speech as God. Where revelation commandeers language, the word of God takes place.[13] The triune God is a speaker, as God is present in the communicative act of human language. God's being-as-object is God's being-revealed. God's objectivity is to be thought of only as event, because God makes God's self objective. Barth makes the distinction between primary and secondary objectivity. The primary objectivity of God is God's innertrinitarian being, which is differentiated from God's secondary objectivity in historical revelation. God's primary objectivity in God's true lordship demonstrates God's self for us in the secondary objectivity of revelation in the historical and economic context. God speaks of God's self in a human way, thereby, in the humanity of Jesus Christ.[14] God's being-as-object consists of the fact that God as God has become speakable. Faith occurs in the event of God's speakability, which comes to speech in human words. The knowledge of God in the certainty of faith is mediated knowledge.[15]

When revelation is comprehended as God's self-interpretation, which is the root of the doctrine of the Trinity, language is an interpretation of revelation, which grasps the language. Thus, Jüngel contends that God's being (the immanent Trinity) is not identified with God's becoming (the economic Trinity), rather God's being is ontologically and relationally lo-

---

11. CD 2/1:284.
12. Jüngel, *God's Being is in Becoming*, 27.
13. Ibid., 23, 26.
14. Ibid., 64–66.
15. Ibid., 59.

cated. God's being can be understood as the ontological place of the being of God.[16] Thus, God corresponds to God's self. God's being *ad extra* corresponds to God's being *ad intra*. God's self-interpretation is interpretation as correspondence. The triune God in the economic and historical reality of revelation corresponds to God's immanent Trinity only in the sense of an *analogia relationis* (analogy of relation).[17] Explicating "God's being is in becoming," Jüngel grounds the hermeneutical circle (of the doctrine of appropriation) in an ontological circle (of the doctrine of *perichoresis*).

The doctrine of *perichoresis* refers to the modes of the being of God as encountering one another in mutual condition, permeation, and unrestricted participation. The unity of *perichoresis* demonstrates itself as a concrete unity by the doctrine of appropriation, because God expresses God's self in the sense of Creator, Redeemer, and Sanctifier. Jüngel characterizes the doctrine of appropriation as a hermeneutical process, because such a doctrine brings God to speech.

A CRITICAL VIEW ON JÜNGEL'S INTERPRETATION OF BARTH'S TRINITY

Jüngel's limitation can be seen in his incapacity to deal with God's objectivity, whether primary or secondary, in terms of God in the transforming act. Barth's fundamental thesis in his doctrine of God is that God's Being is revolutionary and transformative (*Alles in allem real verändernde Tatsache, dass Gott ist*).[18] The objectivity of God is the transforming and revolutionary fact underlying God's existence as the Lord loving in freedom. For Barth, God's being is in becoming not merely in the sense of ontological correspondence, but in the coming of God's kingdom in a transforming and eschatological sense.

In Jüngel's interpretation, the God of Israel, who exists in freedom and mystery, is reduced to the secondary objectivity of revelation. However, For Barth, the God of Israel, who is the primary objectivity, is revealed as the Lord loving in freedom underlying God's act of reconciliation, revolution, and transformation in the sense of God's act of speech.

---

16. Ibid., xxv.
17. Ibid., 36, 38.
18. Barth, *Kirchliche Dogmatik*, 2/1:289; CD 2/1:258.

With excessive emphasis on the primal action of God's gracious election in analogy of relation, Jüngel tends to undermine God's sustaining activity in creation, reconciliation, and revolution in light of God's act of speech in the Trinitarian sense concerning the coming of kingdom of God.

In taking issue with Jüngel's Trinitarian theology, I maintain that the Word in John's prologue was in the beginning with God. All things came into being through the Word. What has come into being in the Word was life, the light of all people (John 1:1–4). The sending of the Son and the mystery of the incarnation are described in terms of the Word. In the Word as a power of communication, God speaks in, with, and to the Son and the Spirit for the world. The self-manifestation of the divine life in the Trinitarian salvific drama is mediated and communicated by God's Word as event, or God's Word-in-action (*dabar*) which creates the world. The creation of the world by the Word breaks through a Greek metaphysical idea of logos because the living Word of God in the presence of the Holy Spirit is self-revealing and manifest in the life of Israel and the life, death, and resurrection of Jesus Christ, who is the Lord of the church and the world.

In the Trinitarian history of salvific drama, people's experience of divine life and blessing in the context of God's ongoing creation is taken up in unity with the reconciliation of God in Christ through the power of the Holy Spirit and in light of God's act of speech in love and freedom. Creation and reconciliation are not juxtaposed in an antithetical manner, but dynamically interconnected with the universal reign of the triune God, which embraces the church and the world.

God's word-in-action is more than analogical expression, because it points to the fecundity and rich resources of the divine life, related to the creation that is embedded within the reality of reconciliation. Jesus Christ comes to us through the world of God's creation, in which God's covenant with Abraham interacts with God's covenant with Noah. Thus, *verbum relationis* breaks through Jüngel's notion *analogia relationis* which is dissociated with God's transforming act. The Word of incarnation is not a copy, nor a mere duplicate of the original, resembling the original, because God's being-in-becoming is fulfilled and culminated in Jesus Christ who is not the principle of *analogia relationis*, but the embodiment of the eternal *verbum Dei*. Indeed, the Word is the original.

AESTHETIC DIMENSION OF TRINITY

In contrast to Moltmann's social model of the Trinity (running into tritheistic panentheism), Barth sharply rejects a mythology of partially equating the identity of God with the world under the rubric of panentheism.[19] Barth's notion of Trinitarian theism contradicts a social model of the doctrine of the Trinity which underpins panentheism and human participation ontologically in divine *perichoresis*. In the Trinitarian sending the three modes of being are always together in a *perichoresis*. God's triunity (*Dreieinigkeit*) insists that the one whole divine being, as the Father, the Son, and the Holy Spirit, must be always at the same time identical with itself, a unity both in movement and at peace.[20] The triune being of God is beautiful to the extent that the triunity of God is the secret of God's beauty. God is beautiful because God loves us as the One worthy of God as love.[21] The work of the Son reveals the beauty of God, helping us to recognize the beauty of God in Jesus Christ.[22] Barth's theology of triunity expresses the secret of the beauty of God who is incarnated in Jesus Christ, the ground of the church's mission. An aesthetic dimension of God's mission is conceptualized by Barth who argues that theology is the most beautiful of all the sciences. Mission is related to the beauty of God in sending the Son and the Holy Spirit.[23] If Barth maintains that God's glory is God's overflowing self-communicating joy,[24] an aesthetic dimension of missional theology must be sought in our ecological stewardship and sustainability. Stewardship of creation is one indispensable part in public ethical theology and discipleship of God's mission.

For Barth, God lives eternally in a *perichoresis*, that is, a mutual indwelling and interworking of the three forms of eternity.[25] The eternity is the living God as such. The time of mission is grounded in the *perichoresis* of the Father and the Son in the fellowship of the Holy Spirit. God's mission is actualized historically in God's historical time in Jesus Christ in connection to God's future (post-temporality, God's Sabbath rest). Then

---

19. CD 2/1:312.
20. CD 2/1:660.
21. CD 2/1:651.
22. CD 2/1:664.
23. CD 2/1:656.
24. CD 2/1:653.
25. CD 2/1:640.

God will be all in all. The kingdom of God consists in the fact that God is all in all.[26] Our past is overcome and dissolved by God's future, because God is the God of hope. If time itself is with and in eternity, if God is in the midst with us, mission follows God's historical activity in Jesus Christ through the Holy Spirit in eschatological dynamism. This is Barth's attempt to conceptualize the theological concept of eternity by setting it free from "the Babylonian captivity of an abstract opposite to the concept of time."[27] This is Barth's contribution to overcoming an Augustinian dualistic understanding of time and eternity. Such a perspective entails a strong political implication. The triune God in historical-eschatological dynamism always stands unconditionally and passionately on the side of the threatened innocent, the oppressed poor, widows, orphans and aliens against the lofty. On behalf of the lowly, God is against those who already enjoy right and privilege.[28]

For Barth, God is God in a special way as Father, as Son, and as Spirit in terms of the doctrine of the relations of origin. According to the doctrine of *perichoresis*, the Father, Son and Spirit as the three distinctive modes of being of the one God subsist in their relationship one with another.[29] *Perichoresis* (*circumincessio*, John Damascus) is grounded in the relationship between the unity of the Trinity and the Trinity in unity. However, this view does not eradicate the classic notion of relations of origin and appropriation, which entails a hermeneutical dimension of designating God the creator, God the redeemer, and God the sanctifier. Without hermeneutical designation we cannot affirm God's triune identity. For Barth, God's works, like the *missio Dei*, are assigned to God's acts, not conflated with God's essence or *perichoresis* as such. The *mysterium trinitatis* remains a mystery to us. Barth's missional theology upholds the church's participation in God's reconciling work in Christ with the world and in openness to freedom of God's act of speech in the world.

---

26. CD 2/1:630. Chung, *Reclaiming Mission as Constructive Theology*, 111.
27. CD 2/1:611.
28. CD 2/1:386.
29. CD 1/1:366.

THEOLOGIA CRUCIS IN THE TRINITARIAN LIFE

Barth emphasizes that God dared to be "God against God" without falling into a contradiction within God of God with God's self, upholding the importance of *theologia crucis*.[30] The mystery of the divine passion is found in the person and mission of the crucified One. His mission is grounded in the Judge who, in this passion, takes the place of those who must be judged. The reconciliation of the world with God takes place in this divine mission.[31]

In the suffering of God and the man Jesus, Barth argues for the passibility of God even in theopaschite fashion. He recognizes that there is a particular truth in the teaching of the early patripassians. God the Father co-suffers in the offering and sending of God's Son, and co-involved in the abasement. God assumes the alien suffering of the creature in a profound manner and without reservation. The fatherly fellow-suffering of God refers to the mystery of the humiliation of the Son, transpiring on the cross of Jesus Christ.[32]

Given this, Moltmann reproaches Barth for his use of a simple concept of God without Trinitarian differentiation. However, Barth's concept of God's fatherly fellow-suffering must be seen primarily in terms of the innertrinitarian life of God (*perichoresis*).[33] God's suffering in the Trinitarian framework corresponds to God's being-in-action. God's being is in the act of suffering. In this regard, Jüngel insists that the existence of Jesus Christ in the Trinitarian communion with God includes the proper concern of the *communicatio idiomatum*.[34]

GOD'S MISSION AND THE CHURCH IN THE HORIZON OF RECONCILIATION

Barth fully develops and elaborates a theological understanding of mission in his doctrine of reconciliation (CD 4/3.2, §72, "The Holy Spirit and the Sending of the Christian Community"). Jesus Christ is the liv-

---

30. CD 4/1:185.
31. CD 4/1:247.
32. CD 4/2:357.
33. Moltmann, *Crucified God*, 203.
34. Jüngel, *God's Being is in Becoming*, 97n91.

ing Word of God, and becomes the eternal subject of the gospel. This challenges a missionary attempt to propagate and defend "any supposed Christian worldview of its own."[35] The gospel is distorted and ossified when it is domesticated and controlled by the dominant philosophy or scientific method or general hermeneutical principle.

According to Barth, God's reconciliation in Christ upholds the missional nature of the church. In becoming incarnate and in reconciling sinful humanity to God, Jesus Christ has constituted an ontological connection with all humanity. In virtue of the Holy Spirit, humanity comes to share in the work of Christ and thus a church is created and born.[36]

Jesus Christ is the incarnate Word, who is the baby born in Bethlehem. He is the one Word of the *Deus pro nobis*, the gracious address of God and the gracious claim of God.[37] The old things have passed away and all things have become new. This is what God has done in Christ through reconciliation. This aspect is grounded in St. Paul's ministry of reconciliation.[38] In the context of reconciliation Barth corrects the previous formula, "God everything and man nothing,"[39] by saying that it is complete nonsense as a description of grace, not merely a shocking simplification. In the divine act of reconciliation a new human subject is introduced as the faithful covenant partner of God, namely the covenantal partner of God's initiative of salvific drama.

In the upbuiliding of the Christian community, sanctification is a special form of God's reconciliation. Jesus Christ builds up church as his body, his earthly-historical form with the quickening power of the Holy Spirit. Jesus Christ "to give [the church] a provisional representation of the sanctification of all humanity and human life as it has taken place in Him."[40] Thus, the risen Lord and the Holy Spirit are fundamental to the doctrine of sanctification and the upbuilding of the faith community. Here, Barth appreciates Calvin's definition of the church as the mother of all believers.[41]

---

35. CD 4/3.2:837.
36. Chung, *Public Theology in An Age of World Christianity*, 98.
37. CD 4/1:53.
38. CD 4/1:74.
39. CD 4/1:89.
40. CD 4/2:614.
41. CD 4/2:614–15; Calvin, *Institutes*, 4.1.4 (2:1016).

The classical description of the church as *una, sancta, catholica,* and *apostolica* in the Nicene Creed can be applied to the divine operation that takes place in the church.[42] Barth gives credence to the Lutheran understanding of the church in the *Augsburg Confession* (art. V), according to which faith is mediated and attained through preaching and the sacraments. The Holy Spirit awakens faith by preaching and the sacraments, that is *tamquam per instrumenta—ubi et quando visum est Deo* (through instruments the Holy Spirit is given, who effects faith where and when it pleases God).[43]

The true church has its goal in the revelation of the sanctification of all humanity and human life, as it has already taken place *de jure* in Jesus Christ, rather than becoming an end itself. The church is provisional, fragmentary, incomplete, insecure, and questionable because it is only on the way to the return of Jesus Christ for all.[44] Jesus Christ in the quickening power of the Holy Spirit acts where this provisional representation takes place, namely, where the true church is an event—with a view to *diakonia*. The church is empowered to serve in the edification of the body of Christ.

In speaking of God's reconciliation, Barth has always in mind: first, the act of God in Christ, which is inclusive of all; second, the inevitable thrust to embrace the cosmic sphere of the earth. This inclusive-universal thrust reveals the ontological connection between Christ, the church, and the world. The *totus Christus* to whom the church looks and moves (Eph 1:10) includes "all those elected and justified and sanctified and called in Him."[45] With the *totus Christus* in mind, the church looks to the future of Christ, as Christ is absolutely future to the church. This church in the future is transcended since the New Jerusalem (Rev 21:2) comes down from God. The holy city is future and transcendent to the church. Christian eschatology is to be understood in christological-ecclesiological terms rather than merely from the standpoint of God's advent or prolepsis.

In this christological-eschatological perspective, the church is edified and edifies itself in worship, so public worship continually takes place. Christian worship is the action of God, Jesus Christ, and the com-

---

42. CD 4/1:668.
43. CD 4/2:618.
44. CD 4/2:621.
45. CD 4/2:624.

munity for the upbuilding of the community, "spread out into the wider circle of everyday life of Christians and their individual relationships."[46] Worship and the everyday life of Christians are two concentric circles in which worship as the inner circle gives to the outer sphere of the Christian daily life its content and character. "Assembling for divine worship is self-evidently the centre and presupposition of the whole Christian life."[47] The lordship of Jesus Christ taking place in divine service summons the community to be the confessing community (in the confessing of law, baptism, the Lord's Supper, and prayer as the fellowship of believers).[48]

CREDO ECCLESIAM: ONE HOLY CATHOLIC AND APOSTOLIC CHURCH

The Holy Spirit is the awakening power in which Jesus Christ has established and continues to renew his body, the one holy catholic and apostolic church. This refers to Christ's own earthly-historical form of existence.[49] In light of the earthly-historical body, Barth expounds the essence of the church in terms of *una, sancta, catholica, apostolica*, in keeping in line with the Nicene Creed. *Una* refers to its singularity while *sancta* implies the particularity in this singularity. The community of the saints is the body of Jesus Christ, that is holy. This is because Christ, the Head of the body, is holy. *Catholica* implies the essence in the self-manifestation of the particularity and singularity. *Apostolica* refers to the concrete spiritual criterion known only in faith. That is the one and only *nota ecclesiae*.[50] The unity of the community in diversity should be mutually attested and affirmed while acknowledging differences. The complete unanimity of the churches can only be brought to completion by Jesus Christ, who is Lord of all the churches.

The earthly-historical form of Jesus Christ is in the unity of the visible and the invisible. Believing in the *ecclesia invisibilis*, we will enter into its earthly and historical existence of *ecclesia visibilis*. Without serious participation in the historical life of community—its upbuilding

46. CD 4/2:639.
47. CD 4/2:640.
48. CD 4/2:707–8.
49. CD 4/1:643.
50. CD 4/1:712.

and its mission—no one understands the critical and serious meaning of the *credo ecclesiam*.[51] Gathering in the faith community, the invisible triune God controls the church so that the visible attests to the invisible. Jerusalem, which is above, is the mother of us all (Gal 4:26).

Each community has its own locality, its own environment, tradition, language, etc. In this locality the community is established and appointed by Jesus Christ so that it may be the one complete community. The adjective "catholic" means general, comprehensive. It speaks of an identity and a universality, in spite of all the differences. For Barth, "catholic" denotes, first of all, ecumenical in the narrower sense. In a broader sense, it is identical in the whole inhabited world, where it can exist as the church in all parts of the globe.[52] The very existence of the church is based on reformation in the sense of *ecclesia semper reformanda*. The church is catholic and ecumenical, insofar as it participates in this ongoing renewal (*semper reformari*).[53]

"Apostolic" means participation in discipleship under the instruction and direction of the apostles. Apostolic refers to the being of the community as an event. The apostolicity of the church and its mission may be imparted and emphasized by the witness of a bishop. God moves where God wills and pleases.[54] This perspective corrects a notion of apostolic succession on historical and juridical grounds. Jesus Christ has chosen, ordained, and sent the apostles for witnesses about the gospel of the kingdom of God. In the life and work of the church, the teaching and instruction of the apostles must always be maintained and confirmed, because their teachings are the apostolic witness to Jesus Christ in affirmation of their authority, power, and mission.[55]

Along this line, there is a legitimate apostolic succession of the church in the following of the apostles. It becomes possible only when "the apostolic witness finds in a church discipleship, hearing, obedience, respect and observance."[56] The authority, mission, and power of the apostles must be seen as a matter of service to Jesus Christ, the service to incarnated Word (*ministerium Verbi incarnati*).

---

51. CD 4/1:654.
52. CD 4/1:703.
53. CD 4/1:705.
54. CD 4/1:717.
55. CD 4/1:718–19.
56. CD 4/1:719.

CREDO ECCLESIAM AND HOPE OF THE ESCHATON

We exist in the *communio sanctorum*, otherwise a private monadic faith has nothing to do with the Christian faith.[57] Jesus Christ lives and exists in the heavenly-historical form of existence. Coexisting as the Head with his body, he exists already in the light of Easter Day, the dawning of the Last Day, which is within the as yet unbroken continuity of earthly history. It is important to consider an eschatological dimension of the church, which corresponds to the *already* of Easter Day, that is, the dawning of the Last Day within the earthly history. Ecclesiology and mission exist in the time between in the eschatological expectation .God wills (1 Tim 2:4) through the church that all people should be saved and come to knowledge of the truth.[58]

On Easter Day, Barth conceptualizes the first *parousia* which has only the provisional, transitory, and particular form, a penultimate character. It was the end in this penultimate character.[59] A new time commenced, that is, the beginning of the eternal Sabbath. We have a promise, an admonition, and a warning in the temporal Sabbath of the resurrection of Jesus Christ, which is the penultimate end. God has received praise from the heart of the human creation before the dawning of God's eternal Sabbath. The postponement of the second *parousia* of Jesus Christ is time given for the work of the Holy Spirit. This is because it is time for faith and repentance, time for preaching the gospel throughout the world, time for the church, service, and mission.[60]

Faith includes hope by generating it in the fulfillment of the promise of God. Because hope springs from faith, Barth maintains that faith is the basis and presupposition of hope. Thus Barth is critical of a theological trend of the pan-eschatological dream, which is unilaterally anchored in the future of God.[61] For Barth, the justification of believers has taken place in Jesus Christ. The Spirit who raised up Jesus from the dead dwells within them (Rom 8:11). Christian eschatology begins with the life,

---

57. CD 4/1:678.

58. According to Barth, *extra Christum nulla salus* implies that in the hidden ways, God may put into effect the power of atonement made in Jesus Christ (John 10:16) even *extra ecclesiam*. CD 4/1:688.

59. CD 4/1:734.

60. CD 4/1:739.

61. CD 4/3.2:912.

death, and resurrection of Jesus Christ, which becomes an eschatological reality in the churchly life in expectation of the one who is finally to come.

Looking back to Easter Day and forward to the Last Day, the church's life can only follow the movement and mission of Christ's life.[62] In the faith community the term "body" is used to refer to humanity as a whole: the totality of Jews and Greeks, slaves and free people, males and females. In a dispensing and eating of the bread that is broken in common, the visible fellowship of this body perceives and attests a real presence of Christ's body. Thus, the union of a concrete human fellowship with Christ is recognized in the faith community (1 Cor 10:16).

In the fullness of time God made known God's mystery of salvation to all through Christ–both in heaven and on earth (Eph 1:9). This aspect emphasizes the *Magna Carta* of the church in Jesus Christ.[63] The future outpouring of God's Spirit on all flesh (Acts 2:17) is promised, thus the life of the church is located between Christ's reconciliation and the final consummation of God's kingdom.

THE VOCATION OF THE COMMUNITY

According to Barth, the Word of the living Jesus Christ is the creative call by awakening person to be witness into the service of Jesus's prophetic work. A theology of vocation is conceptualized in the service of the prophecy of Jesus Christ, in the *ministerium Verbi divini* of the Word of reconciliation. By the calling Word of God Barth understands the one revelation and prophecy of Jesus Christ attested by the Holy Spirit and in the Scripture.[64]

Barth agrees that Luther's teaching of vocation is addressed to every person in his or her status, vocation, and sphere of operation in contrast to the medieval doctrine. Luther translates *klēsis* in 1 Cor 7:20 as vocation, insisting that each must keep to the divinely allotted sphere of work. God's presence is in every moment of life and is renewed in terms of a realization of the true call of God within the world and its work.

However, Karl Barth sees the concept of vocation or calling (*klēsis*) in a way that it is the divine calling, namely the act of the call of God

62. CD 4/1:661–62.
63. CD 4/1:665–66.
64. CD 4/3.2:482–83.

issued in Jesus Christ. By this calling, a human being is transplanted into the new state as a Christian. He or she is made a participant in the promise (Eph 1:18, 4:4) bound up with this new state. It assumes the duty (Eph 4:1; 2 Pet 1:10) corresponding to this state.[65]

However, Barth takes issue with Luther's co-ordination between the word of God and the word of the superior or parent, by emphasizing the superiority of the divine calling over all the prescribed stipulations of the human sphere. Acknowledging Luther's strength, Barth seeks to widen the range of vocation.[66] At this juncture, Bonhoeffer's statement—vocation is the place of responsibility—finds its consonance with Barth's theology of vocation.[67] This is the *terminus a quo* of all recognition and fulfillment of the command. The person is called to freedom by the command of God. For Barth, the calling of God is revolutionary, shaking what is worldly. Every person has his or her calling in correspondence with *charism* and *diakonia*.[68] Every person retains the special responsibility in vocation. The vocation of each person is the *terminus a quo* of his or her obedience and also the place of responsibility. Every person in their calling is wholly responsible to God alone.[69]

Furthermore, Barth holds that the *homo incurvatus in se* (humans curved in on ourselves) is the one who does not hear the command of God, because the command of God genuinely demands the active life in accordance with *diakonia* and freedom. Human participation in the service to the kingdom of God takes the form of correspondence to divine activity, that is, the covenant-partner of God rather than becoming a co-creator or co-agent in God's activity.[70] A human being concerned in encounter with the divine calling is wholly responsible to God alone, because the vocation is the source of human obedience.[71] The church must engage in mission, casting the net to catch people, hence the church is as such a missionary community in its commission to announce the gospel to the world. Otherwise, it is not the Christian community.[72]

65. CD 3/4:600.
66. CD 3/4:644–45.
67. CD 3/4:598.
68. CD 3/4:603.
69. CD 3/4:607.
70. CD 3/4:473, 476, 482–83.
71. CD 3/4:606–7.
72. CD 3/4:504–5.

Barth insists that the church as the living community of Jesus Christ exists in and for the world. The very nature of the church is a missional one, based on the triune God, on Christ's reconciliation and on the power of the Holy Spirit. Here, Barth defines the church as the community of vocation.[73] As the earthly-historical form of Christ's post-ascension existence, it pertains to the church's mandate. The church is entrusted to undertake the ministry and mission of Christ's prophetic Word.[74]

The church's solidarity with the world is not its accommodation to the world, because the church is different from the world. The church is salt and light for the world, becoming the light of life: Jesus Christ. The church's solidarity with the world lies in its acknowledgement that Jesus Christ can exist as the Savior of the world, in a worldly and non-religious fashion.[75] The world is led by the enlightening power of the Holy Spirit. Now that no one can evade what God has done in Christ for humanity, the church is under obligation to the world (John 4:35), in solidarity with it, and in pledge and commitment to it without reservation.[76]

The church, visible in its participation in God's mission and Christ's prophetic work, finds itself as a subsequent and provisional representation of the kingdom of God. The kingdom of God, which begins and is already revealed in the resurrection of Jesus Christ, establishes the exclusive, all-penetrating, all-determining lordship of God, in the Word and the Spirit, throughout the whole sphere of creation.[77] As the body of Christ, the current earthly-historical form of Christ's existence, the church is his likeness, analogously corresponding to the glory of Christ's own image.[78]

Mission is not an optional work, but the whole task of the church. Christian mission receives its prophetic profile and character from the reconciling action of God in Christ. This worldly reality of mission is now concealed and will be revealed only in the absolute future of the redeeming and consummating action of God. The reality of the eschaton is vis-

---

73. CD 4/3.2:682.
74. CD 4/3.2:681.
75. CD 4/3:2:773–74.
76. CD 4/3.2:784.
77. CD 4/3.2:792.
78. CD 4/3.2:793.

ible and partially and provisionally realized here and now through the reconciling action of God.[79]

MISSION, EVANGELIZATION, AND *DIAKONIA*

In the German Protestant context the sole purpose of mission is the proclamation of the gospel (evangelization) and social *diakonia* (with respect to the succession from J. H. Wichern through C. Blumhardt). Barth is strongly influenced by the Blumhardts and knew that a German missionary, Richard Wilhelm, son-in-law of Christoph Blumhardt, undertook anti-colonial mission in terms of prophetic *diakonia* in Tsingtau, China.[80]

The main direction of *diakonia* was the helping of God, the brethren, and the state. Although Barth in his early stage of Safenwil withstood *diakonia* work of A. Stoeker and F. Naumann because of their nationalistic support of the war, he later appreciates and values the social work of *diakonia* in his ministry of the community. The churchly *diakonia* was in competition with Marxist socialism through evangelization and *diakonia*. They were combined in the name of Home Missions represented by John Wichern. For Barth, the Christian *diakonia* should be extended to reach out in the political and social context.[81]

In this light Barth argues: "The goal of missions is not to convert the heathen in the sense of bringing them to a personal enjoyment of their salvation. Neither at home nor abroad can it be the work of the community to convert men. This is the work of God alone."[82]

The Christian is called to do service to the Word of God (*ministerium Verbi Divini*) as a witness to the free grace of God. Sharing itself in solidarity with the suffering of Christ, Christian mission is a reflection of and analogy to the suffering of Christ, upholding the church's solidarity with the world embedded within affliction and suffering.[83]

---

79. CD 4/3.2:489.

80. For the relation between Barth's theology of *diakonia* to the tradition of Wichern and Blumhardt in reference to Richard Wilhelm, Chung, *Mission and Diakonia*, 83–100, 116–33.

81. CD 4/3.2:892.

82. CD 4/3.2:876.

83. CD 4/3.2:637.

Evangelization attests to the goodness of God in the humanity of Jesus Christ, since Jesus Christ is the goodness of God. Humanity is the object of God's goodness. The gospel is the good, glad tidings of Jesus Christ, who reveals the great and unconditional "Yes" of the eternal goodness of God to the world.[84] Proclamation of the living Word of the living Lord challenges any attempt at appropriation, control, and domestication of the gospel by dominant philosophical, scientific, and hermeneutical principles. Evangelization takes issue with the inevitable domestication and deformation of the gospel.[85]

Given this, Barth presents his strategy of interpretation by focusing on the living Word of the living Jesus Christ. This provides a new insight into the hermeneutics of God's act of speech for God's mission and evangelization. With emphasis on the living Word of the living Prophet Jesus Christ, Barth prevents possible deformation, distortion, and falsification of the gospel in light of freedom of God's act of speech. Thus, the next chapter will further examine a hermeneutical dimension of God's mission and prophetic *diakonia* imbued with socio-critical and political orientation.

---

84. CD 4/3.2:798–800, 805.
85. CD 4/3.2:821.

6

Hermeneutics of God's Mission and Prophetic *Diakonia*

BASED ON THE STUDY of Barth's theology of God's mission in terms of reconciliation and missional ecclesiology, I further develop a hermeneutical horizon of God's mission through God's act of speech by taking note of Barth's Reformation-oriented hermeneutic, which is central to his concept of evangelization and prophetic *diakonia*. Underlying his missional direction and endeavor is Barth's theological hermeneutic and biblical exegesis. For the theological hermeneutic, a discussion can be made about the relationship between Luther and Barth. Then I shall deal with Barth's theological analogy in a dialectic of *extra nos* and inclusivism with a strong political implication as compared to Quenstedt. An account must be taken of an analogical political hermeneutic, by speaking in terms of a horizon of evangelization and the socio-critical aspect of Christian mission and prophetic *diakonia*. Integrating Barth's social ethics and reconciliation into his public hermeneutic of evangelization, Barth's notion of God's mission paves the way to holistic mission.

REVELATION AND SCRIPTURE

For Barth, Scripture constitutes itself as the Canon insofar as it imposes itself upon the church. The self-imposing of the Scripture is made possible by virtue of its content, that is, God's revelation. Scripture is God's Word in the form of attestation, if it bears witness to God's revelation in Jesus Christ.[1] This does not uphold a direct identification between revelation and Scripture in the literalist sense. This identification becomes possible only in terms of internal testimony of the Holy Spirit. For this reason Barth maintains that historical criticism or critical –scientific study of the Scripture is accepted on theological grounds, that is, on the basis of God's revelation. Given this, Ebeling appreciates Barth's hermeneutical contribution.[2]

According to Barth, the demand for a historical understanding of the Bible means that the Bible was written "in the human speech uttered by specific men at specific times in a specific situation, in a specific language and with a specific intention."[3] Understanding is a return to and an inquiry into the Word itself, fraught with all its linguistic and factual propositions.

As Barth states in agreement with Martin Noth, "The human and historical limitations of the Old Testament text are real and boundless."[4] Reading the Scripture would be impossible without realizing the uncertain ground offered by the Scripture, which is evident in all the limitations of the Hebrew and Hellenistic tongues. In this regard, Scripture exposes its human character and limitation to full view. The biblical writers speak as particular human beings embedded within the social, historical and cultural situation of the time. They communicate in the languages and patterns of human thought.[5]

Concerning the relation of the biblical words to revelation, Barth argues that theological hermeneutics is valid by virtue of the Bible as the witness of revelation, which is the real substance of the Bible.[6] Deriving the hermeneutical principle from Scripture as such, Barth maintains that the Scripture is the special form of the universally valid hermeneutical principle. The writers of the Bible speak as fallible, erring people. We can evaluate their words as human words, by bringing them to immanent critique. We are free to critically distance ourselves from their philosophical, social, cultural and religious assumptions and limitations. In the world of the Scriptures the human imperfection is obvious in the face of divine

---

1. CD 1/1:111.
2. CD 1/2:464; Ebeling, *Word and Faith*, 318.
3. CD 1/2:464.
4. Barth, *Against the Stream*, 221.
5. Ibid., 224.
6. CD 1/2:466.

perfection, while divine perfection is confirmed in spite of human imperfection.[7] The writers of the Bible are set and conditioned historically, socially, and culturally. Obvious overlapping and contradictions are found between the Torah and the prophets, between John and the Synoptics, and between Paul and James.[8] Already in the second edition of *Romans* (1922), Barth articulates a unity between exegesis and socio-historical criticism: "The historical critics, it seems to me, need to be more critical!"[9]

In the face of the subject matter of theological hermeneutics Barth maintains that the sovereign freedom of the subject matter speaks of itself. The reader is really gripped, mastered, and subdued by the subject-matter of the Scripture: God's revelation in Christ by the power of the Holy Spirit. The theological hermeneutics prescribed by the content of revelation is guarded against the totalitarian claim of a general hermeneutics based on a general anthropology.[10]

Given this, Barth does not accept the doctrine of so-called verbal inspiration, which affirms literal inspiration of the writings of the Old and the New Testaments. Herein, the Bible becomes the actual words of God. Barth maintains that verbal inspiration does not mean the infallibility of the biblical words as human words in their linguistic, historical, and theological character. Here we see Barth's choice of verbal inspiration grounded in the internal, living testimony of the Spirit and a free Word of God, as opposed to verbal inspiredness in a mantic-mechanical sense. For Barth, the texts of the Bible are documents of the story and the person of Jesus Christ, so that the center of the Scripture is the revelation of Jesus Christ incarnated.[11]

The entire scripture, despite its differences, is a testimony to the one revelation of Christ. The Word of God awaits us in the words of the prophets and apostles. On the basis of the revelation of God, the Scripture is the source and the guiding principle of Christian doctrines and exposition

---

7. CD 1/2:508.
8. CD 1/2:509.
9. CD 1/2:533; Barth, *Epistle to Romans*, x.
10. CD 1/2:470, 472.
11. Barth, "Christian Understanding of Revelation," in Barth, *Against the Stream*, 218.

for preaching the Word of God. Insofar as the scripture is of kerygmatic character, the church must also be kerygmatic.[12]

Furthermore, the Barthian notion of special biblical hermeneutics must not abandon the validity of the principle of general hermeneutics, but rather it must engage with the general hermeneutics in light of freedom of God's act of speech through the world. There is no confident approach to mastering and subduing the subject matter of Scripture. Insofar as the subject matter of the biblical word is grounded in the mystery and freedom of God, human interpretation of the Word of God, in approximation of God's truth, takes place in an open-ended and eschatological direction. God's revelation is heard in the human word of the Scripture.[13]

However, Barth warns that the purpose of critical method must not be in mediating a historical truth that lies behind the texts. Rather, the historical truth that biblical scholarship has to mediate is the true meaning and context of the biblical texts as such. Barth identifies this biblical-exegetical position in terms of Luther's principle: *veritas scripturae ipsius*[14](the verity of the Scripture itself) in reference to the internal testimony of the Spirit within the Bible.[15]

Although Barth's theological hermeneutics guards against the totalitarian and universal claim of a general and ontological hermeneutics,[16] he does not necessarily undermine linguistically oriented hermeneutics. According to Gadamer, Barth's way for a special hermeneutics is informed and prescribed by, and concerned with, the subject matter of Scripture.[17]

KARL BARTH AND REFORMATION-ORIENTED HERMENEUTICS

Given Barth's theological hermeneutics, I sense that there is an affinity between Barth and Luther. Certainly, Barth appreciates Luther's notion of a canon within the canon. Luther tests every Scripture by whether it sets forth Christ or not. What does not teach Christ is not apostolic, even

12. Ibid., 221.
13. CD 1/2:471.
14. CD 1/2:494.
15. CD 1/2:536.
16. CD 1/2:472.
17. Gadamer, *Truth and Method*, 521.

though Peter or Paul may teach it. What preaches Christ is apostolic, even though Judas, Annas, Pilate, and Herod may teach it. Christ is the criterion or yardstick that the church has applied to the canon in its own way in every age.[18] According to Luther, "the Scripture is the garment which our Lord Christ has put on and in which He lets Himself be seen and found."[19]

Appreciating Luther's insights into the Bible, Barth agrees that "to have the Gospel without understanding is to have no Gospel. And to have the Scripture without knowledge of Christ is to have no Scripture."[20] In this light, Barth affirms his understanding of the Word of God by recognizing "its human imperfection in face of its divine perfection, and its divine perfection in spite of its human imperfection."[21]

Luther grounds his biblical hermeneutic in the conviction that the whole of Scripture is to be understood in connection with Christ. The New Testament should really be only the living Word (*viva vox evangelii*) corporeally. It is not the Scripture as the written whole.[22] We are incorporated into the new world of the Scriptures. The words, "when we first believed," should be related to faith in the promise to Abraham: "In thy name shall all the nations in the earth be blessed."[23]

The New Testament comprehended as an opening and revealing of the Old Testament, the books of Moses and the prophets are also gospel for Luther. This is because they preached and described the same thing about Christ beforehand like the apostles in the New Testament. As Barth comments on Luther, the gospel should be proclaimed and put in a living voice. It must sound forth and be proclaimed and heard everywhere in the world.[24] Having the unity of the Word of God in mind, Luther comprehends the truth of the Word of God in terms of Scripture by books, word by proclamation, and thought by the heart. Barth concurs with Luther concerning three forms of the Word of God. Luther's statement—all scripture has its light from the resurrection—restores the doctrine of the inspiration of Scripture as the doctrine of a divine mystery, true and

18. CD 1/2:478.
19. CD 1/2:484.
20. CD 1/2:508.
21. CD 1/2:508.
22. CD 1/2:76–77.
23. CD 1/2:76.
24. CD 1/1:122–23.

redemptive (*Deus incomprehensibilis*).[25] For Barth, the proleptic dimension (Mark 3:14) acquires its proper sense only through the message of the resurrection.[26] God cannot be mastered or conceived. Rather, God inspires and controls human interpretation of the Word of God.

Furthermore, Barth appreciates Calvin who views that the Word of God becomes the word of Scripture as the sign of the Word of God. The thing itself (the Word of God) is present and active in the word of Scripture.[27] The reformers' teaching of the verbal inspiration of the Bible is valued in terms of the revelation as the theme of the biblical witness. The biblical concept of *theopneustia* as an act of revelation points to the present, in order words, to the present event occurring for us.[28] Calvin's notion of revelation as *Dei loquentis persona* (God speaking in person) teaches that the literally inspired Bible is a witness to revelation.[29] As Barth states, "the Reformers' doctrine of inspiration is an honoring of God, and of the free grace of God. The statement that the Bible is the Word of God is on this view no limitation, but an unfolding of the perception of the sovereignty in which the Word of God condescended to become flesh for us in Jesus Christ, and a human word in the witness of the prophets and apostles as witness to His incarnation."[30]

THEOLOGICAL ANALOGY IN THE DIALECTIC OF *EXTRA NOS* AND INCLUSIVISM

According to Barth, the idea that "God is knowable" means that "God can be known" only by God in the grace and mercy of divine revelation in Jesus Christ. Human readiness to know of God is encompassed and determined by the readiness of God, as God's grace is mediated in revelation.[31] The human being can be a recipient of God's grace in God's Word and sacrament. Barth's epistemology, "God is known by God," does not abrogate, abolish, or alter human cognition, rather it is fulfilled in views,

25. CD 1/2:521.
26. CD 1/2:487.
27. CD 1/2:501.
28. CD 1/2:506.
29. CD 1/2:520–21.
30. CD 1/2:522.
31. CD 2/1:128–29.

concepts, and imagery. In the act of the knowledge of God, we are active as the receivers of images and creators of counter-images, becoming capable of receiving images of the divine.[32]

In faith we know God in utter dependence, discipleship, and gratitude. The hiddenness of God is the content of a statement of faith, thus it concerns human knowledge and intention as God's revelation concerns us.[33] Knowing God in revelation, we know the hiddenness or incomprehensibility of God. God is not One whom we can dialectically encompass and control.[34] Nevertheless, God is visible only to faith and attested only by it. Our capacity of viewing, conceiving, and speaking, which is awakened and actualized by revelation and faith, are placed in service because God imparts the truth to our capacity. Having known God's hiddenness, we have known God by the grace of revelation because God is apprehensible in the revelation. However, our knowledge of God is self-critical, because it consists only in approximation, always remaining incomplete and open-ended. It is in need of correction at every point.[35]

In deliberating the veracity of human knowledge of God, Barth avoids the terms parity or disparity. The word parity implies that God had ceased to be God and become merely a creature. The term disparity implies that *de facto*, we do not know God at all. There is no veracity of human knowledge of God under the rubric of a simple disparity, not to mention the fellowship between God and human being. Here, God's revelation as a simple veiling is not to be understood as revelation. Barth's dialectic of God's veiling and unveiling leads him to a theology of analogy. A theological dialectic from above remains connected with a theological analogy of faith.

Barth's theology of analogy, set within the dialectical framework of veiling and unveiling, attempts to radicalize Luther's doctrine of justification *extra nos* and faith. Barth engages in a critical conversation with Quenstedt, a Lutheran Orthodox theologian. Quenstedt expounds the Lutheran teaching of analogy in terms of *analogia attributionis*. A similarity of two objects consists in the fact that what is common between the two exists primarily and properly in the first. Thus, the second is de-

32. CD 2/1:182.
33. CD 2/1:183.
34. CD 2/1:188.
35. CD 2/1:202.

pendent upon the first. The *analogia* is *analogans* (one who makes the analogy) in the first while it is *analogata* (that which is analogized) in the second. This teaching refers to the similarity between God and the creature. Furthermore, according to Quenstedt, there is an *analogia attributionis extrinsecae* but also an *analogia attributionis intrinsecae*. The first form of analogy implies that the analogy of the *analogatum* (the creature) is proper to the creature only externally in the existence and form of its relationship to the *analogans* (God). The second form of analogy internally is proper only to the *analogans* as such. However, according to Quenstedt, this analogy belongs both to the *analogans* and to the *analogatum*, inwardly both to God and to the creature.

Barth concurs with Quenstedt's notion of *analogia attributionis*, arguing against the notion of *analogia inaequalitatis* (similarity existing between the different species of one genus) or *proportionalitatis* (the similarity existing in the agreement when some determinations of two objects agree, while others disagree) concerning the relationship between God and the creature. The idea of a calculability of the correspondence and agreement must be rejected.

For Barth, the analogy in an attribution is sought in the relationship of an *analogans* with an *analogatum*. This analogy is undertaken as *analogia relationis* in which the Creator-creature relationship is established by the Creator. The humanity of Jesus, his fellow-humanity, his being for human beings indicates, attests, and reveals the correspondence and similarity between the Creator and the creature.[36]

Barth's disagreement with Quenstedt lies in the notion of analogy of *attributio intrinsecae*, which belongs both to God and to the creature, inwardly and properly.[37] For the sake of the doctrine of justification by grace alone, Barth adopts the analogy of *attributio extrinsecae* against *attributio intrinsecae*. If Barth develops his teaching of *analogia fidei*, strictly grounded in the teaching of justification *extra nos*, Quenstedt applies his teaching of analogy to the distinction between special revelation and general revelation.

Nonetheless, Barth's theology of analogy entails a horizon of natural-material and socio-political life, notably in a political correspondence between God's kingdom as *analogans* and the democratic-socialist op-

---

36. CD 3/2:220.
37. CD 2/1:238.

tion as *analogatum*. Barth's notion of analogy is not merely of scholastic character, but is also shaped in the context of political activity during his pastoral time in Safenwil. Barth comprehends the Reformation doctrine of grace in terms of a radical image of revolution and transformation in the social-political realm rather than in an individualist manner. In his 1919 Tambach lecture ("Christian's Place in Society"), Barth articulates a social, political horizon of analogy concerning the relationship between God's kingdom and worldly affairs, especially the socialist movement.

Furthermore, in his 1946 article "The Christian Community and The Civil Community," Barth justifies the civil community as the parable, thus as correspondence and analogy, in relation to the kingdom of God for the sake of more democracy and more social justice.[38] Given the dialectical relation between the grace of justification *extra nos* (*analogia fidei*) and inclusivism of reconciliation, it would be safe to say that Barth's theology of analogy is of particular character (*extra nos*) in matters of the grace of justification. All the while, it is of inclusive and socio-critical horizon in matters of God's kingdom in analogical relationship with the world, notably with an emphasis on a democratic-socialist direction.

THEOLOGICAL EPISTEMOLOGY AND ANALOGICAL HERMENEUTICS

Analogy means a partial correspondence and agreement, which is helpful in investigating God's truth in revelation, which is the basis of the veracity of human knowledge of God. In the revelation of God coming to us, we, with the word of similarity, participate in the incomprehensible similarity which is posited in God's revelation. On the basis of the similarity, Barth contends that the relationship between God in self and God in our work is only a relationship of similarity. Despite the limitation of human language, our concepts and words that are rooted in God's revelation can be legitimately applied to God. This is because our thought and our language are also God's creation.[39] For Barth analogy is understood as the work and proposition of revelation as such, because an analogy of human views, concepts and words should not be established apart from God's revelation.[40]

38. Chung, *Karl Barth*, 188.
39. CD 2/1:227.
40. CD 2/1:232.

Barth considers a circle in the undertaking of faith: human participation, God's adaptation to analogy, and analogy in relation to revelation. This hermeneutical circle in the undertaking of faith acknowledges God's movement and experience in the sphere of Jesus Christ. Barth's thesis, "God is known by God," develops an analogical hermeneutic in light of the *circulus vertitatis Dei* (circle of verity of God). A dialectic of God's veiling in unveiling avails ourselves of the concept of analogy.

Human participation in the truth of God takes place in the analogy of God's truth itself, or the truth of the similarity with God. Our participation in the veracity of God's truth depends on our appropriating God's promise with the permission and command of God's revelation. Given this, our words possess the entire veracity in which God places human language at our disposal, by which to describe God. The human word becomes God's own word, receiving the momentum of *parrhesia*, which distinguishes genuine preaching from a mere speaking about God.[41]

Human language and word receive concrete content and form from God, spoken on the basis of the strength of God's permission and command, so that language has definite similarity with the truth of God promised and bestowed by God's revelation. For Barth a linguistic concept of similarity, analogy, and partial correspondence and agreement becomes foundational for his theological hermeneutic in contrast to parity or disparity. An ordered dialectic between veiling and unveiling in light of the *circulus vertitatis Dei* designates a way of speaking God's coming with us; God is gracious in unveiling and veiling.

Given this, Barth still remains indebted to Aristotle who distinguishes three different possibilities and predications: univocal, equivocal, and analogous. Analogous speech is in the middle between equivocity and univocity. According to analogy, the concept of proportion is expressed in the mathematical sense (a:b::c:d). A relates to B as C relates to D. In the sense of God by analogy, God's relation to God's self and to other creaturely beings must be known in correspondence. However, in the analogy of attribution, B, C, and D all relate in varying ways to A. In contrast to the analogy of proportionality, the analogy of attribution implies that the many things are all related to that one common thing in a relationship of dependence.

---

41. CD 2/1:231–32.

In my view, Barth uses the theory of correspondence regarding the relationship of the Father and the Son in the Trinitarian sense, and furthermore he also uses the theory of attribution concerning the relationship between God's kingdom and the world. The analogy of attribution, according to Jüngel, is hermeneutically constituted by an *analogans* on which the *analogatum* depends. The relation of dependence in the fashion of Scholasticism is translated into the ontological context.[42]

A CRITICAL VIEW OF NARRATIVE THEOLOGY

Following in the footsteps of Karl Barth's analogical theology, Jüngel contends that there can be no responsible talk about God without analogy. *Analogia fidei* is the precondition for proper talk about God. Gospel as correspondence refers to event in discourse. What is spoken of is described as a language event. In this event the analogy of faith is performed. Analogy works according to the gospel. If God is the One who is "above everything which can be thought," analogy as a pendulum never arrives at a conclusion. An analogy of advent that expresses God's arrival among people makes this world-relationship anew in an eschatological light. To be concise, according to Jüngel, the gospel is comprehended as the event of correspondence, thus the man Jesus is the parable of God. The analogy itself is a language event in an eminent sense whereby God's relationship to the world is expressed in language.

Furthermore, Jüngel refers to the parable as an extended metaphor while the metaphor is called an abbreviated parable. The narrative structure is imminent in the metaphor, which is understood as "the epiphora [transference] according to analogy."[43] What is expressed in both metaphor and parable is addressing speech. Analogy grips us, causing the character of address, which is found in metaphor and parable. Language is originally metaphorical and parabolic. Analogy characterizes the sociality of metaphor and parables, which thus express more in language.

According to Jüngel, discovering the language of metaphors and parables supports a language event of creative freedom that undergirds their concreteness as social discourse. The subject of discourse becomes concrete in language itself, defining anew the people addressed in their own

42. Jüngel, *God as The Mystery of the World*, 272.
43. Ibid., 290.

existence.⁴⁴ Parables in Biblical talk about God serve as the language of faith in which Jesus's parables of the kingdom of God are notably instructive. A parable as an event makes something else happen. Great dissimilarity is emphasized in a still greater similarity in the parables of the kingdom of God. The kingdom of God expresses itself in the language form of the parable understood as analogy. God comes into language to the extent that God also can be brought to language. The language in correspondence to the humanity of God is narrative in structure, telling a story. God's humanity is introduced to the world as a story that is to be told.⁴⁵

Human consciousness is constituted not only by the egocentricity of "I think," but rather by history or narrative. Consciousness is entangled in history or story-telling. The church can correspond in language to the humanity of God only by constantly telling the story anew. This is characteristic of the church as a missional community. In the presence of the Holy Spirit God's humanity constantly encounters human life as a story to be told anew. The gospel of the humanity of God has been introduced to the world in the form of narrative in the word of the cross. A narrative construction of history can be undertaken with an emancipatory intention. Metz's narrative theology, based on the dangerous memory and dangerous tradition, tells us of dangerous stories.⁴⁶ Jüngel proposes a dialectical discursive theology in the narrative framework because discursive theology needs a discursive theory of narrative.⁴⁷

Jüngel's hermeneutical theology, which develops Barth's theology of *analogia fidei*, emphasizes a discursive theory of narrative that incorporates Metz's political theology in light of the gospel of the humanity of God. However, Jüngel's theology of language event tends to sidestep a living discourse of the gospel in the sense of *viva vox evangelii*. This sense remains an integral part in shaping Barth's theology of God's act of speech through the world and in the otherness of the Other in Christ's reconciliation. Jüngel's naiveté lies in his understanding of language-event as narrative theology which undermines an irregular, socio-critical, even transforming dimension in Barth's political-analogical theology in light of God's act of speech. Barth's theology of God's Word-in-action later

---

44. Ibid., 292.
45. Ibid., 302.
46. Ibid., 311.
47. Ibid., 312.

radicalizes his early understanding of revelation as God the Subject of God's Word (*Dei loquentis persona*) in an unexpected and extraordinary broader spectrum within the universal horizon of the reconciliation and the eschatology. However, Jüngel's narrative theology remains narrow minded and even reduces Barth's theology of God's speech-deed and its irregular and extrabiblical orientation to the intratextual narrative.

Barth's theology of God's act of speech, which is the event of God's work and activity, breaks through a narrative theology because it actually speaks in all directions. Like the periphery of a circle, something is said in all directions to be heard and repeated. Barth expresses this provocative, irregular, and audacious side of God's act of speech in the following manner: "God may speak to us through Russian Communism, a flute concerto, a blossoming shrub, or a dead dog. . . . God may speak to us through a pagan or an atheist, and thus give us to understand that the boundary between the Church and the secular world can still take at any time a different course from that which we think we discern."[48]

Barth's dialectical theology in an analogical fashion is in service of God's act of speech, its freedom in love, its revolutionary irregularity and transformation, and God's mysterious challenge for theology and church to begin anew at the beginning. This aspect entails a possibility to interpret Barth as the theologian of God's Word-action who could overcome a limitation of his analogical-narrative theology in hierarchical manner under influence of Aristotle. God may speak to us through the underside of history which shapes our dangerous memory of Jesus as "the partisan of the poor" in a Barthian sense. Furthermore, Barth's dialectical theology becomes socially concrete and engaged in emphatic listening to marginalized stories and discourse for the sake of the dangerous memory of the gospel of Jesus Christ concerning the kingdom of God.

THEOLOGICAL HERMENEUTICS AND HUMAN EXPERIENCE

Concerning the relationship between the Word of God and human experience,[49] Barth states that God is involved in the human experience of the Word of God. The human being as a historical being experiences

---

48. CD 1/1:55.
49. CD 1/1 § 6.3.

the Word of God in a particular social and historical context.[50] In God's coming to us as revelation, human social existence is embedded in the contingent contemporaneity, while encountered in the hermeneutical circle of the veiling and unveiling of the Word of God. In this hermeneutical circle of encounter, the Word of God as subject matter guides and shapes human experience of the Word of God in terms of movement from the experience or thought to the opposite experience and thought. In this encounter and movement we acknowledge the mystery of the Word of God and Christian experience is located only within the confinement of faith. *Illic et tunc* (there and then) becomes *hic et nunc* (here and now) in this hermeneutical encounter and mediation.[51]

Thus Barth does not protest against the introduction of feeling or conscience or especially the intellect into experience of the Word of God.[52] However, this perspective does not imply a specific form of indirect Christian Cartesianism, making the Word of God become a predicate or self-certainty of human existence in general.[53] For Barth, human self-understanding becomes significant, to the degree that we understand ourselves as confronted with the living Word of God in terms of revelation, Scripture, and proclamation.[54] In the hermeneutical circle of promise and faith, we are driven anew and freshly to the actualization of God's grace as experienced in faith, by clinging freshly to the promise of God. And we look anew for such an event and encounter.[55] This hermeneutical perspective in eschatological openness enables Barth to promote human experience and analogy to be socially engaged in regard to relationships between the secular sphere and the kingdom of God.[56]

Insofar as revelation is *Dei loquentis persona*, God comes to us as speech event which is remarkably of hermeneutical character and significance. Later on, Barth managed to open a universal dimension of God's act of speech in the sphere of creation. Creation is the external basis of the

50. CD 1/1:200.
51. CD 1/1:206.
52. CD 1/1:208–9.
53. CD 1/1:214, 218.
54. CD 1/1:218.
55. CD 1/1:225.
56. For the connection between political analogy and the Kingdom of God, see Gollwitzer, "Kingdom of God and Socialism in Theology of Barth," in Hunsinger, ed. and trans., *Barth and Radical Politics*, 91–100.

covenant, which is the internal basis of creation. In Barth's thought, there is a hermeneutical conversation between creation and covenant in light of God's reconciliation in Christ.

In correspondence to God's faithfulness to the creation, the language of the self-witness of the creaturely world is discovered, integrated, and instituted in terms of God's self-interpretation in Christ. God's self-interpretation and communication in Christ makes the self-witness of the world into a parable of the kingdom of heaven, that is, the *ministerium Verbi Divini* (service to the Word of God).[57] This is because the whole creation is the theatre of God's glory and the recipient and bearer of God's Word. The secular sphere is allowed to become a parable of God's Word, it speaks of God in an analogical witness to God's kingdom, which is qualified as the free communications of Jesus Christ.[58]

EVANGELIZATION AND PUBLIC HERMENEUTIC IN LIFE CONNECTION

According to Barth, all exegesis and hermeneutics demonstrates "the life lived at this period, here or there, by the fraction of humanity concerned, and the awareness of life experienced by them." That is to say, "their particular culture, civilization and technique, their historical past and present . . . their national qualities, aspirations and disillusionments, their moral standards and customs, their political order and disorder, their retrogressive or progressive commercial relations and . . . their particular degree of religion or irreligion."[59] These historically conditioned documentations and social connections remain the arbiter in shaping the interpretation of Scripture in a decisively political and social-critical manner. Barth incorporates understanding, seen as a social category, into interpretation of the Scripture in terms of life connection and condition.

Likewise, Barth contends that the mission of the Word of God is proclaimed in the sense of *viva vox evangelii* by engaging in the public sphere. Its ministry is to be discharged *voce humana* in human words, in terms of declaration, explanation, and evangelical address to the world. Evangelization also awakens the sleeping, lifeless, and dead church, as it

57. CD 4/3.1:164.
58. CD 4/3.1:157.
59. CD 4/3.2:821.

is in need of renewal by way of evangelization.[60] We encounter here a hermeneutical dimension of the explanation or explication of the gospel, as the human skill and power given to the church is explored in light of the living word of Jesus Christ.[61] Evangelical address (proclamation and explication in the form of application) cannot be achieved in a vacuum.[62]

If grace, the covenant, reconciliation, the life of Jesus Christ and the kingdom of God are not being demonstrated to the world, then the church is not the Christian community.[63] Insofar as the gospel gives itself to be understood, and wills to be understood—so that human historical fact corresponds to the content of the Word of God—hermeneutical explanation will follow the elucidation of that which issues as the self-declaration of Jesus Christ.

The Word of God concerning reconciliation, the covenant, the kingdom of God, and the new reality of the world is the promise and assurance given to the church, sustaining its witness to the risen and living Jesus Christ who is the origin, theme, and content of the church's witness. Promise and assurance are given and received in the power of the Holy Spirit.[64] The church lives by the promise of its ministry, fulfilled in Jesus Christ.

GOD'S ACTIVITY OF RECONCILIATION AND PROPHETIC *DIAKONIA*

For Barth, the cosmic character of the reconciliation that is accomplished in Jesus Christ makes *diakonia* indispensable by being involved in human physical and material existence. This is a sign of the kingdom of God. *Diakonia*, like other missionary works, is an affair of the church which engages in helping the needy in the totality of their human existence. *Diakonia* to the needy is not blind to the prevailing social, economic, and political conditions.[65]

---

60. CD 4/3.2:874.
61. CD 4/3.2:849.
62. CD 4/3.2:850.
63. CD 4/3.2:845.
64. CD 4/3.2:840.
65. CD 4/3.2:892.

The Christian church would become a dumb dog and serve the ruling powers if it withdraws tackling social evils at their roots.[66] In this regard, Barth requests the Church to keep itself over and against the political, economic disorder of society. The church is fundamentally on the side of the victims of this disorder, and espouses their cause regarding various forms of social progress or even of socialism in the specific time, place, and situation. In the proclamation of God's revolution as it has already come and comes, evangelization means denouncing all the ungodliness and wickedness of men (Rom 1:18).[67] The direction and orientation coming from the gospel recognizes in social movement or democratic socialism an affinity to the gospel. Evangelization means participation in the relative counter movements in immanent opposition to the social system so that the relation between the Word of God and espousing social progress is likened to "the relation between center and circumference, origin and consequence, grace and living from grace."[68]

Barth elaborates the theological-prophetic meaning of *diakonia* by emphasizing the this-worldly aspect of the active life in obedience to the Word of God. This perspective emphasizes the biblical concept of service, which Barth would call implicitly, "the objective character of obedient human action."[69] The word "God" denotes the Lord of covenant, also the concept of serving God. To serve God is to choose God. The service demanded of human beings is the free self-expression of the recognition that humanity belongs to God on the basis of God's gracious resolve and act.[70]

St. Paul understands his work in the service of the gospel as a free continuation of work in the Old Testament sense, undertaken in the tabernacle and temple. According to Daniel 7, the king of the last time comes to serve. God in the New Testament appears as God's self, the servant. Jesus fulfills the picture of serving God as spoken through the prophet Isaiah (Matt 12:18–21). In the gospel of John the story of the Last Supper is replaced by the foot-washing. God has placed God's self in the service of humanity. This is revealed and affected in the sacrifice of Jesus. The word *diakonia* is established more strongly and concretely in the foreground

66. CD 4/3.2:893.

67. CD 3/4:544.

68. Gollwitzer, "Kingdom of God and Socialism," in Hunsinger, ed. and trans., *Barth and Radical Politics*, 84.

69. CD 3/4:475.

70. CD 3/4:476.

by including service among and for people (because of the self-evident presupposition of the service of God).[71]

God acts and is revealed as a servant, in this way as the Lord, in the person of Jesus Christ who took upon himself the form of a servant (Phil 2:7). To follow Jesus means to follow his way of service. In this way one becomes an imitator of God (Eph 5:1) and co-worker for the kingdom of God (Col 4:11). Our active participation in discipleship and service of the kingdom of God takes the form of a correspondence to the divine activity, in the undertaking of faith as the covenant-partner of God.[72]

With that in mind, Barth elaborates the church's mission in service of the coming of God's kingdom. The faith community as the living people awakened and assembled by Jesus Christ discharges its service to the kingdom of God. All its members are summoned to this service in the sense of universal priesthood.[73] Thus, faith rests on the recognition of the kingdom of God in a witness to the *causa Dei*. We are called to the active life for the cause of God. All members of the congregation are bound together only by the Lord and the Holy Spirit and by their mutual perception of the kingdom of God.[74] The espousal of God's cause finds expression in activity on behalf of the world, not in a crusade against it.[75] The church is, as such, a missional community otherwise it is not the church. Every Christian is to be a missionary, a recruiting officer for new witnesses. The congregation must recognize it and act as the missional congregation. Otherwise, it cannot be truly Christian.[76]

The community as missional community is commissioned to preach the gospel to the world. It lives by its commission to the gospel of the coming Kingdom of God not by its numerical growth.[77] Barth articulates the interconnection between evangelization and the prophetic *diakonia* of the church by interpreting the signs of the times. A Christian ethic as public ethical theology is integrated with the prophetic service of mission or the ministry of the gospel. Under God's effective rule, a Christian ethic

---

71. CD 3/4:477.
72. CD 3/4:483.
73. CD 3/4:490.
74. CD 3/4:499.
75. CD 3/4:502.
76. CD 3/4:505.
77. CD 3/4:508.

should not depreciate the work of the non-Christian. Rather it must give it respect and esteem for the sake of discipleship of God's mission.[78]

When the command of God is heard, there is always a summons to counter movement to the perverted world stamped by competition, thoughtlessness, serious conflict and the struggle of existence. Barth argues that the so-called progress of Western civilization and culture is based on these assumptions. It is hardly denied that in Western society the modern industrial process rests *de facto* on the principle of the exploitation of some by others.[79] Human labor under the sign of competition always implies labor in the form of conflict. In it one encounters another with force and cunning, ending up with innumerable prisoners, wounded and dead.[80] The proclamation of the kingdom of God as the end of all strife, inhuman activity, competition and conflict is central to the work of a humanity resisting decisive repentance.

GOD'S MISSION AND EVANGELIZATION IN HOLISTIC FRAMEWORK

Evangelization remains central in Barth's concept of God's mission in the context of reconciliation and prophetic *diakonia*. Barth's theology of the God in the gospel in terms of transformation of the human situation penetrates his theological consideration of the christological and Trinitarian foundation in light of the kingdom of God, which is transcendently and immanently a prototype of the grace to be emulated in public, missional praxis here and now. The grace of God is actualized and revealed in the concrete divine claim, the law as the necessary form of grace.[81] Jesus Christ as the gospel is always as the doer of the law, clothed in the law. The unity of dogmatics and ethics[82] that implies human conformity with divine grace emphasizes that the human being lives by the grace of God and, therefore, for the grace of God. Human action is committed to correspondence with God's gracious action.[83]

78. CD 3/4:524–25.
79. CD 3/4:540, 542.
80. CD 3/4:541.
81. CD 2/2:566.
82. CD 1/2: §22 (782).
83. CD 2/2:576–77.

Being the provisional representation of the humanity justified in Jesus Christ, the church is elected from the world so that it should perform the service the world most needs. In the discussion of the order of the community, Barth insists that true church law has to declare and maintain the radical openness of the whole life of the community in its determination to service. Church administration is a question of service, having nothing to do with bureaucratization or commercialization. Theology is also a question of service. The same is true of the discipline of the church. In the church's affairs we are in the sphere of service, so Barth proposes a rule of the church on a christocratic basis, which must be firmly interpreted as "outstanding service."[84]

Barth's public missional theology contradicts an attempt at undergirding confessional positions, imposing Western culture and civilization upon non-Western people who receive the gospel. Barth's theology of *missio Dei* challenges the Western missionary desire for colonial or general political interests and aspirations. Other religions and cultures are allowed to contribute to the understanding of the gospel in their own manner: psychologically, sociologically, aesthetically, and ethically.[85] Cultural constructions and contributions are appreciated as a way of eliminating the crass arrogance of Western people, who dampen and domesticate the gospel "in all its radical uniqueness and novelty."[86]

The mission concerning the establishment of the whole ministry of the church must be carried out in the form of preaching and evangelization as well as instruction and diaconate. Here Barth contends that conversion is the work of God alone; neither at home nor abroad does conversion belong to the work of the Christian community.[87] In the ministry of its witness, *Ecclesia semper reformanda* (church is in need of continual renewal) is imbued with its prophetic awareness of the "signs of the times."[88] The church's mission takes issue with the racial question. Racially different people must be taken seriously in recognition of their cultural particularity and orientation. The church's witness to the world nullifies an attempt at dividing the church into special white, black or

---

84. CD 4/2:693.
85. CD 4/3.2:875.
86. CD 4/3.2:875. See Chung, *Public Theology in an Age of World Christianity*, 104
87. CD 4/3.2:876.
88. CD 4/3.2:895–96.

brown congregations.[89] In no way should the church justify and uphold class distinctions, racial segregation, and political, economic ideology. The church's mission must not be misused by supporting and strengthening a class, its concerns, and its interests, its faith and its ideology; or its ethos with its morality.[90]

Driven in the light of the gospel of the kingdom of God, church mission struggles with unsolved social problems by seeking a new and third way which transcends capitalist ideas and attitudes as well as the proletariat. This perspective is Barth's contribution to public ethical theology and discipleship of God's mission, confessing Jesus Christ in our reconciled world for the sake of solidarity, recognition and emancipation.

As we already examined, Barth's concept of God's mission of reconciliation opposes the general notion that mission is an instrument of an ecclesial, religious, or civilizing program and propaganda, or is associated with an economic-political power strategy in the non-western country and culture. The church is missional by nature because it is grounded in the Trinitarian sending for and Christ's reconciliation with the world. The Trinitarian sending based on the lordship of God is connected with Barth's understanding of God who loves in freedom, reconciliation, and transformation. The transformative character of the church's mission comes from Barth's definition of God as *ganz ändernde* (the Wholly Changer) who "materially changes, all things and everything in all things."[91]

The faith community has to confess that it is fundamentally on the side of the victims of the social order and to espouse their cause, whether the social order appears in its capitalistic or its socialistic guise. That God "is" is the revolution of God, in which evangelization means prophetic denouncement of all the injustice and unrighteousness of humanity.[92] Mission should be carried out with the greatest respect for the value of other religions. Mission involves the whole person and so cares for humans in their totality. Education, healing, help, and the needs of all are rightly associated with mission. This aspect is Barth's contribution for theology of God's mission to become prophetic, emancipatory, and postcolonial in the context of World Christianity.

89. CD 4/3.2:899.
90. CD 4/3.2:900.
91. CD 2/1:258.
92. CD 3/4:545.

7

Theological-Political Ethics and the Discipleship of God's Mission

IN THE NORTH AMERICAN context, public theology deciphers the role of the institutional church in the public realm or characterizes the public orientation of the ecclesial community.[1] In his public theology and political economy, Stackhouse critiques Barth as a representative of existential theology (in the fashion of Kierkegaard) and the sort of dogmatic confessional theology that is incapable of offering guidance on public issues of political economy.[2]

In contrast to Stackhouse, Ronald Thiemann appreciates Karl Barth in the task of constructing a public theology.[3] Here, public theology is defined and conceptualized in Anselm's fashion ("I believe in order that I may understand"), utilizing Clifford Geertz's concept of "thick description." This cultural-anthropological concept "begins with 'exceedingly extended acquaintances with extremely small matters' and moves slowly and cautiously to 'broader interpretations and abstract analyses.'"[4] In order to gain a detailed and thick understanding of the social, cultural, and moral context, this type of public theology begins from the standpoint of faith, which is based on the revelation of Jesus Christ. This public theology is of a non-foundational and descriptive character, seeking to provide a justification of Christian belief that is specific and unique to

1. Marty, *Public Church*; Thiemann, *Constructing Public Theology*.
2. Stackhouse, *Public Theology and Political Economy*, 82.
3. Thiemann, *Constructing Public Theology*, 75–95.
4. Geertz, *Interpretation of Cultures*, 10.

the Christian faith, ecclesial community, and church tradition. Here, a "non-foundational" model redescribes the internal logic and narrative of the Christian faith.[5] In this light, Karl Barth is explored as part of the task of constructing a public theology.

Furthermore, Stanley Hauerwas appreciates Barth's contribution to ethics based on the concreteness of God's command as found in Jesus Christ. Barth provides extensive discussions of issues such as suicide, euthanasia, marriage and singleness, the ethics of war, and the Christian calling to serve the neighbor. Barth rejects the notion that casuistry can predetermine God's concrete specific command here and now. There can be no ethics apart from theology because theology is understood as the primary activity of the church.[6]

A public theology evaluates the church in a pluralistic culture, seeking to describe Christian thought and practice with attention to the broader social and cultural realms within which Christians seek to live in accordance with the narrative of the Christian gospel. In short, public theology is faith seeking to understand the public relevance of Christian theology in a social-cultural location. A public theology in a Barthian fashion, which is grounded in a non-foundational model and Anselm's epistemology, calls for an exploration of prophetic-ethical insights within Barth's ethical framework in the public sphere.

As we have already examined Barth's notion of God's mission in terms of reconciliation and prophetic *diakonia*, Barth's theological ethics assumes a public and prophetic character, one that is socially and politically engaged. His deliberation of the discipleship of God's mission entails a demand for public theologizing in witness to the coming reign of God for social engagement and public action. However, a non-foundational model in a neo-orthodox fashion undermines Barth's hermeneutical-analogical model in which theology and issues of the public sphere come together in light of the Word of God. For Barth the Word of God inspires human understanding and engagement with itself in the public context, rather than remaining non-foundationalistic in a transcendental, non-participatory manner. This chapter is a study of Barth's public-political ethics, which assumes the character of special ethics embedded within contextuality, emphasizing Jesus's solidarity with the poor. It furthers

---

5. Thiemann, *Revelation and Theology*, 74–75.

6. Hauerwas, "How 'Christian Ethics' Came to Be (1997)," in Berkman and Cartwright, eds., *Hauerwas Reader*, 49.

critical analysis of lordless powers in the socioeconomic, cultural, and political realms. God's mission is thus integrated with public ethical deliberation concerning discipleship, solidarity, and emancipation.

THE COMMAND OF GOD AND THEOLOGICAL ETHICS

Theological ethics represented by Barth is called "rule ethics" because the task of ethics is defined as the teaching of Christian obedience to God's commands, beginning with the ethical consideration of the commandments. Barth subsumes ethics under the task of the doctrine of God in which the command of God is scrutinized as the ethical problem in a threefold sense: the command as the claim of God, the decision of God, and the judgment of God.[7] Ethics interprets the law as a form of the gospel, namely, sanctification. The law is completely enclosed in the gospel. The law is valid because God is the doer of the law. The divine claim is always a concealed repetition of the totality and promise of grace. The law is the form of the grace of God that is actualized and expressed in the divine claim. The grace of God has teleological power in the person of Jesus Christ.[8] This is the most crucial point in Barth's public and political ethics. God's claim on human existence is grounded in God's self-giving to humanity in Jesus Christ, God's being-in-act is gracious in Jesus Christ. The event of grace is grounded in divine election as the sum of the gospel. The moral life, which is dependent on God in Christ, is preserved in its integrity as the answer to the command of God. Responsibility and answer are interwoven. A theological-confessional understanding of God in God's own salvific, missional drama cannot be separated from the ethical deliberation of the faith community concerning the issues of the public sphere.

Barth's construction of ethics in the doctrine of God counters Schleiermacher's attempt to maintain the general religious self-consciousness with its moral content or orientation as a necessary element in a general philosophical and ethical enquiry.[9] The way of theological ethics, according to Barth, lies in the knowledge of the electing grace of God in Jesus Christ. This aspect decides the nature and aim of theological

---

7. CD 2/2 §37, §38, §39.
8. CD 2/2:563, 566–67.
9. CD 2/2:520.

ethics.[10] Barth's endeavor of establishing unity between dogmatics and ethics should not be regarded as applied theology or rule ethics. This is because Barth's unity between dogmatics and ethics entails a contextual character in a critical analysis of the sociohistorical reality.

In the doctrine of creation, Barth develops the task of special ethics. Human good action can be viewed only from the standpoint of the true and active God and God's goodness. Thus, ethics should not be isolated from dogmatics.[11] If human sanctification by the command of God in human real action is a problem of ethics, ethics becomes concrete, particular, or special ethics. Special ethics takes the understanding of the command of God as a prescribed text, which is encountered in the biblical texts, in which reside universally binding divine ordinances and directions. Certain propositions are presumed to be universally valid and the natural moral law is generally perceptive to human reason. Particular norms have been handed down historically in the tradition of Western Christianity claiming universal validity.[12]

SPECIAL ETHICS AND CONTEXTUALITY

Special ethics argues against the moralist's wishes (casuistic ethics) to set him or herself on God's throne. The commands of God are not general, moral doctrines and instructions. Rather, they are specific directions concerning the behavior, deeds, and omissions of definite human beings in a social, historical context. The Word of God cannot be properly understood when detached from the context. Casuistry violates the divine mystery and freedom in the ethical event, and destroys Christian freedom.[13]

The contextual character of Barth's special ethics allows a space for *Grenzfall* (limiting case or extreme case) because the *Grenzfall* of necessary participation in war can be undertaken only with strict reserve and caution. The *Grenzfall* as a sign and safeguard of the liberty of God is also seen as a sign and safeguard of human responsibility. It finally points to the finitude of all human values. Despite his harsh critique of the traditional notion of just war and his appreciation of pacifism, even Yoder claims

10. CD 2/2:543.
11. CD 3/4:3.
12. CD 3/4:6.
13. CD 3/4:11, 13.

that Barth's ethics of *Grenzfall* causes him to be cautious in regard to the principle of pacifism as well as in the case for justifiable tyrannicide.[14]

Barth deals with the issue of tyrannicide in reference to Dietrich Bonhoeffer. This question was faced by many seriously minded and even Christian Germans in regard to Adolf Hitler between the years 1938 and 1944. Belonging to these circles, as Barth argues, Bonhoeffer was really a pacifist grounded in his understanding of the gospel, even while Bonhoeffer did not give a negative answer to the question of tyrannicide. Theologically, encouragement to tyrannicide can be traced to the dictum of Thomas Aquinas. On the Protestant side, Calvin, Theodore Beza, and John Knox did not conceptualize tyrannicide as a general possibility, but they pointed to extreme public emergences in which God would raise up an avenger and deliver. The latter's work would be done in obedience to God's command rather than as an act of murder. According to Barth, a strange form of capital punishment is a matter of the pure heart, clean hands, and untroubled conscience since it is the command of God.[15] In the Zurich reformer Zwingli's *Schlussreden* (1523) we read that "a faithless government, which has abandoned the rule of Christ, must be *dismissed with the help of God*." In the Calvinistic *Confessio Scotica* (1560) the Christian task is "to support the life of the good people, *to oppress the tyrant*, and to defend the weak against the violence of the malicious."[16]

To support his political resistance, Barth quotes even Luther himself at the time of his earliest anger against Rome. This is, for Luther, a possible way to meet emergencies even within the *communio sanctorum*: "Thieves, robbers and heretics must be destroyed."[17]

Barth's activist and contextual ethics, rooted in the living Word of God, argues against considerable casuistic teaching, which means application of general rules to specific cases. Barth accepts Bonhoeffer's ethical view that God's commandment is the speech of God in concrete form to human beings. It can only be heard in a local and temporal context. The Word of God comes to us as word-event in a concrete time and place.[18] This perspective paves the way to a hermeneutical-ethical dimension of

14. Yoder, *Barth and Problem of War*, 41.

15. CD 3/4:450.

16. Pangritz, "Sharing the Destiny of His People," in De Gruchy, ed., *Bonhoeffer for a New Day*, 262.

17. CD 3/4:449.

18. CD 3/4:14.

the Word of God, overcoming limitations of casuistic conclusions from generalities. Special ethics can become a formed reference to the ethical event and performs its service as instructional preparation. The ethical event is known to us through the Word of God as the event of God's claim, decision, and judgment concerning our conduct.[19]

Interpreting the ethical event in light of the Word of God, Barth rejects Brunner's ethics of order according to which the doctrine of justice in family, industry, and state is to be grounded upon a natural law as interpreted in an Aristotelian fashion.[20]

In venturing toward a true special ethics, a radical and comprehensive consideration of the Word of God becomes foundational for the unity of ethics and dogmatics. The radical character of the Word of God as God's act of speech can only be approximately described in all human words, retaining a certain breadth and openness.[21] Barth's hermeneutics is articulated in the statement: "Even the understanding of man from the Word of God will always be affected in practice in the language, categories and framework of the possibilities of human self-understanding."[22] The Word of God as theological subject matter shapes and guides the ethical event of human conduct in a specific and particular context, affecting human self-understanding and linguistic expression.

Barth's hermeneutical perspective strengthens his ethics in a contextual and socio-critical manner. Barth's hermeneutic of theological subject matter challenges the limitations of historical criticism by integrating a socio-critical dimension into a theological, political hermeneutic.[23]

ANALOGY AND POLITICAL-HERMENEUTICAL LANGUAGE

At the Tambach Conference in Germany in the year of revolution, 1919, Karl Barth delivered his lecture concerning Christian political responsibility in the public sphere. This conference was held from September 22nd to 25th at Tannenberg, a sanatorium in Tambach. The participants were pastors and theologians who, amid post-revolutionary confusion in

19. CD 3/4:18.
20. CD 3/4:20.
21. CD 3/4:31.
22. CD 3/4:44.
23. Marquardt, "Exegese und Dogmatik," in Marquardt, *Verwegenheiten*, 381–406.

Germany, "were deeply concerned about the revolution which had taken place in recent years and now as Christians were on the look-out for new ways in political and church life."[24] According to F. W. Marquardt, the years of 1917–1919 characterize the third phase of revolution and the Third International in relation to Barth's political theology, which finds itself in the direction of Eisner, that is, pointed toward the goals of the Munich Soviet Republic.[25]

In his lecture entitled "Christian's Place in Society,"[26] Barth's language of analogy offers an insight into human life in a particular social location in pursuit of a new, different society. He advocates establishing a new church with democratic manners and socialist motives.[27] The solution lies, for Barth, in our hope in God, and Christians are called to priestly agitation of this hope in God.[28] A public ethic is thus conceptualized in light of the living God. The Word of God breaks through and appears in the secular and public spheres through the bodily resurrection of Christ from the dead.[29]

Barth's idea of analogy is grounded in the eschatological critique of all that exists. The realm of creation or the public sphere must be seen critically in the interest of eschatological renewal *per analogiam*. The affirmation of the kingdom of creation can be found in Jesus's parable. Social and political realms stand in need of and are capable of becoming an analogy for the kingdom of God, indirectly reflecting the kingdom of God in a mirror image.

During the revolutionary period after World War I, Barth sees Christianity as the place of "hope-sharing and guilt-sharing comrades"[30] in solidarity with social democracy. He discovers the likeness of the kingdom of God in this social democracy that is regarded as the best option for Germany in the postwar revolutionary period.

Barth considers an element of analogy in demanding continuity, arguing that this continuity is taken as eternity in the human heart. In

24. Busch, *Karl Barth*, 110.

25. Chung and Pangritz, eds., *Theological Audacities: F. W. Marquardt*, 116, 119.

26. Barth, "Christian's Place in Society," in Barth, *Word of God and Word of Man*, 272–327.

27. Ibid., 280. Chung, *Karl Barth*, 173.

28. Ibid., 282.

29. Ibid., 287.

30. Ibid., 319.

search of this eternity, "the children of this world are wise; judged by their own standards they do their work well—better than the children of light judged by theirs—and the Lord praises them for it."[31] This remains a fundamental biblical statement for Barth, which he continues in his theology of social analogy in his Amsterdam lecture "Church and Culture" (1926) and later in the so-called "doctrine of lights of reconciliation."[32]

In his seminar study of Anselm, Barth does not undermine Anselm's dictum that faith seeks understanding in connection with the world. *Credo ut intelligam* does not mean a fanatic appeal to heaven, which is *sacrificum intellectus* (sacrifice of the intellectual). The revelation of God as *ratio vertitatis* (reason of truth) is not merely reduced to the fulcrum of the dogmatics of dialectical theology. Rather, Barth pays attention to the significance of Anselm for the outsider of Christian faith. In light of God as that which nothing greater can be conceived (*id quo maius nihil cogitari nequit*), all theological statements are under eschatological reservation because they are incomplete, broken, and inadequate expressions of the *ratio veritatis*. Barth's analogical theology in an eschatological fashion finds Anselm to be a theologian in solidarity with the world. "There is a solidarity between the theologian and the worldling . . . because the theologian is determined to address the worldling as one with whom he has at least this in common—theology."[33] According to Barth, Anselm "did not really remain standing on this side of the gulf between the believer and non-believer, but crossed it."[34]

Barth's theology of *analogia fidei* undergirds his concern about secular humanism and the solidarity between the church and the world in light of the humanity of God. As Barth maintains, "the unbelievers' quest is not simply taken up in any causal fashion and incorporated into the theological task but . . . it is in fact treated as identical with the quest of the believer himself."[35]

Furthermore in "The Christian Community and the Civil Community" (1946), Barth's language of analogy has a connection with his later political–analogical theology. For Barth, the line and direction of Christian

---

31. Ibid., 307.
32. CD 4/3.1, § 69.
33. Barth, *Anselm*, 68.
34. Ibid., 71. Chung, *Karl Barth*, 284.
35. Ibid., 67.

judgments, purposes, and ideals in socio-political affairs is undertaken concerning the parabolic capacities and needs of political organizations in view of the coming kingdom of God.[36] From a Christian perspective, the civil community is justified to be capable of becoming the parable and desirable of the parable, as correspondence and analogy in relation to the coming of kingdom of God. The public, political sphere, which stands in support of democracy and "the greatest measure of social justice," can serve as an analogy or a parable in the service of the kingdom of God.[37]

Given Barth's analogical politics in relation to the coming of the kingdom of God, it is important to examine H. Richard Niebuhr's comparison of Barth's theology with the Social Gospel in terms of the kingdom of God and eschatology.[38] According to Walter Rauschenbusch, "if theology is to offer an adequate doctrinal basis for the Social Gospel, it must not only make room for the doctrine of the kingdom of God, but give it a central place and revise all other doctrines so that they will articulate organically with it."[39] The Social Gospel seeks the symbol kingdom of God in terms of teleology and a specific standard of value rather than assuming a theocenric horizon. It is of a teleological, this-worldly direction by means of a goal of society. The telos is a humanity that is organized according to the will of God in a kingdom of ends, based on an association in love of intrinsically valuable persons. The meaning of Jesus is found in his human endeavor toward the realization of the kingdom of ends. Underlying the Social Gospel is a religio-empirical theology as well as teleological ethics. It is precisely "social" because the Social Gospel apprehends the eschatological ideas of judgment in history.

In this light, H. R. Niebuhr benchmarks Barth's theology against the Social Gospel. Barth's theology is not a reaction against Social Gospel, but a critique of teleological theology. What matters in Barth's thought is that theology starts from God's way toward humanity through the revelation of Jesus Christ. Then, humanity begins on this path as responsible agent. H. R. Niebuhr introduces Barth's theology of the relationship between eternity and time (God is pre-temporal, super-temporal, and

---

36. Green, *Karl Barth*, 280.

37. Ibid., 284.

38. H. R. Niebuhr, "The Kingdom of God and Eschatology in the Social Gospel and in Barthianism," in Johnson, ed., *H. Richard Niebuhr, Theology, History, and Culture*, 117–22.

39. Rauschenbusch, *A Theology for the Social Gospel*, 131.

post-temporal), stating that time is bounded by eternity on every side while eternity enters into and conditions time. Niebuhr's interpretation contradicts a popular, specious interpretation of Barthianism, according to which an emphasis on divine action excludes the human initiative as well as all significance of human action.

Niebuhr underscores that Barth's theology calls for the response of the temporal concerning the kingdom of God. Christian life is understood as the response to divine action in preceding, accompanying, and awaiting human responsible action in society and history. Such Christian life in response to divine action is precisely life under the kingdom of God.[40] Nonetheless, H. R. Niebuhr sidesteps an important dimension of analogical theology connecting Barth's theology with political ethics.

Given the political and social-critical dimension of analogical theology, Moltmann takes issue with Barth's model of correspondence, because he argues that Barth bridges the gap between God and the world only by analogies from the side of God, the church, and faith. In the relationship between the Christian community and civil community, the church is idealized as the model of society. Against the model of political analogy, Moltmann presents a model of anticipations and promises in the process of realization. To arrive at a political hermeneutics of the crucified Christ and a theology of real liberations, Moltmann proposes a liberating presence of God in the extremities of inhuman misery and emphasizes the incarnations and anticipations of the presence of God in a history of the transformation of God. It goes beyond analogical reflection of difference and parable toward a perception of God's identification in history, whose criterion is the identification of God with the crucified Christ. History is the sacrament of Christian ethics.[41]

It is certain that Barth understands the correspondence and likenesses in the historical movement of the life of God. The church is not idealized, but critically viewed in light of the coming kingdom of God, unlike Moltmann's critique. Correspondence and likenesses are not only reflections and images of the completed reconciliation but also signs and anticipations of the future of God in the world. Furthermore, there is a theological-ethical task to establish distinctive marks of the kingdom of God on earth in a direction toward social democracy and justice,

40. "The Kindgdom of God and Eschatology in the Social Gospel and in Barthianism," in Johnson, ed., *H. Richard Niebuhr, Theology, History, and Culture*, 121–22.

41. Moltmann, *Crucified God*, 321.

which becomes crucial for Barth's political theology. Nonetheless, Barth would reject Moltmann's understanding of history as the sacrament of Christian ethics, because God's revolution in Christ is the sacramental basis for Christian ethics.

THE PLACE OF THE POOR IN BARTH'S ETHICS

In reflection on poverty, Barth insists that in many places in Scripture the rights of the poor are proclaimed. God declares God's self to be the upholder and avenger of these rights. Thereby, the rich are commanded not to forget the rights of the poor, but rather to be rich for the sake and benefit of the poor. In many places in scripture, the gospel is proclaimed to the poor, the poor are extolled as blessed, called the chosen of God. Thereby the words, "the poor," are synonymous with "the righteous."[42]

In Jesus' proclamation that rich men will enter the kingdom of God as "easily" as a camel enters through the eye of a needle, the distinction is made as sharp as a knife. The blessing of wealth is not seen to be on an equal footing with the blessings of poverty. The God of Scripture is on the side of the poor, the impecunious and the destitute, and God's coming kingdom will put an end to poverty. This kingdom has come already.

The Son of God eternally rich becomes the source of the fullness of life for everyone. The kingdom has come in poverty, because Christ was born in poverty in the stable at Bethlehem. He died in extreme poverty, nailed naked to the Cross. He is the companion of the poor of this world. For that reason Jesus Christ called the poor blessed, thereby he is here and now to be found in the company of the hungry, the homeless, the naked, the sick, and the prisoners. Poverty, rather than wealth is the mark of the kingdom of God, the mirror of eternal salvation. The Christ of poverty is for all who are poor, all who are truly destitute and suffer any privation. In great humility the most High God becomes the Lord of all humanity.[43] The church must follow the example of the humanity in Christ's life in companionship with those who are destitute and needy. The church grows rich in Christ by confessing his poverty.

---

42. Barth, "Poverty," in Barth, *Against the Stream*, 244.
43. Ibid., 246.

THE WORD OF EMANCIPATION AND ECONOMIC JUSTICE

In the discussion of active life within the special ethic,[44] Barth sharpens his economic analysis of capital. He cites the verdict of August Bebel as an instructive example: "Strictly speaking, the worker who drains sewers to protect humanity from unhealthy miasmas is a very useful member of society, whereas the professor who teaches falsified history in the interests of the ruling class, or the theologian who seeks to befog the brain with supernatural, transcendental doctrines, is an extremely harmful individual."[45]

The amassing and multiplying of possessions is expressed in financial calculation or miscalculation. In view of the organization of the process of labor, Barth argues that the work of the employee is performed and executed "in the service of a sinister and heartless and perpetually ambiguous idol."[46] Led to the disadvantage of the other, the means has become an end. However, the command of God aims at the corruption of the root, remaining in force in spite of all the human perversity for the sake of possession and profit-seeking. Where the command of God is heard, there will always be a summons to counter-movements against capitalist revolutions of empty and inordinate desires.[47]

The prophetic witness of the Christian community has many opportunities to influence both the social and political sides to promote the criterion of humanity. This aspect has led to open struggle for existence in terms of ignoring and even thwarting and suppressing the existence of others. Barth critiques this situation as "inhuman humanity in isolation from and opposition" to the neighbor.[48] Without the neighbors, without fellowship with them, a human being becomes only a shade of a human being.[49] Human labor is a social act involving association and comradeship, measured by the criterion of humanity. The "revolution of empty and inordinate desires" happens where the transgressions of impelling and eliminating the community of industry take place.[50]

---

44. CD 3/4.
45. CD 3/4:534.
46. CD 3/4:532.
47. CD 3/4:538–39.
48. CD 3/4:536.
49. CD 3/4:537.
50. CD 3/4:538.

This is the revolution of lust for a superabundance that is the overflow of nothingness, not the natural and beautiful abundance of life. This is the revolution of the lust for possessions that are desired only as a security and pledge against future use, or only for the sake of the idea of possession. Here, the acquisition of the power of even the mightiest instrument is regarded as an increase of one's own real power over life. Against this revolution of capitalist lust, Barth argues that the genuine and vital claims of humanity are not empty and inordinate desires. Work in the service of their genuine and vital claims must not lose the character of peaceful co-operation.[51]

The reign of empty and inordinate desires gives the process of human labor its profound sinister character because of the deeply discordant aspect and the character of the struggle for existence. One's work would cause both oneself and others more trouble and sorrow, becoming the victim of incurable discontent, and occasioning a good deal of suffering.[52] The Capitalist process of production is based on the principle of the aiming and obtaining of a profit, which accrues to the economically stronger (the owners of the means of production). They turn to their advantage the contract of labor with the economically weaker and dependent. This reality is social injustice grounded in co-ordination of the free contract of labor. However, it is even more oppressive and provoking in the ostensible show of justice, making industrial peace more radically impossible to attain.[53]

In state socialism, Barth argues, this injustice perpetuates itself in a different form and basis directed by a ruling and benefit deriving group. State socialism finally amounts to a new and even crasser form of the oppression and exploitation of some by others as useful objects. The command of God calls for a counter-movement for the sake of humanity by championing the cause of the weak against every kind of encroachment on the part of the strong or the powerful elite. The command of God remains in force above and in spite of all human perversity, challenging the root of corruption. The root of the trouble lies deeper in human aberration, generating the exploitation that attempts at counter-movement can modify but not entirely remove.[54]

---

51. CD 3/4:538. In this light see Gollwitzer, *Kapitalistische Revolution*.
52. CD 3/4:539.
53. CD 3/4:542.
54. CD 3/4:545. Chung, *Karl Barth*, 442.

In the hope of the kingdom of God, the church stands in immanent resistance and opposition to the system of exploitation, whether in the capitalist or socialist form. It does so by constantly advocating freedom and emancipation in face of the exploitation, injustice, and violence of the system and mitigating the prevailing injustice and its consequences.[55] Barth implores the Christian church to keep to the left in opposition to every kind of encroachment on the part of the strong. The church must confess that "it is fundamentally on the side of the victims of this disorder and to espouse their cause," announcing "the revolution of God against all ungodliness and unrighteousness of man (Rom 1:18)."[56]

God's mission in this regard may be furthered in terms of God's *oikonomia* in critical analysis of possessive individualism and neoliberal principles embedded within the process of economic globalization. The Christian community cooperates with God's work and is pledged and committed to the world. It is ascribed, allotted, and promised the grace of liberation to enable solidarity with the world and responsibility for it.

JESUS CHRIST IN SOLIDARITY WITH *MASSA PERDITIONIS*

The Word of God that "swims against the stream"[57] becomes visible in Jesus' table fellowship with publicans and sinners.[58] Barth provocatively argues that Jesus Christ as "partisan of the poor" is in solidarity with *massa perditionis* (the mass and multitude lost, the public sinners and tax collectors), who belong to the party of the godless and are thusly assailed by the Pharisees. Barth asks whether Jesus "does not call men out of the *massa perditionis* to set them at God's side within the world."[59] Jesus' solidarity with *ochlos-minjung* "can consist only in the attestation and proclamation" of God's free grace, which means Jesus Christ as "the saving coup d'état of God."[60] The Pharisees were not prepared to recognize this *am ha'aretz* and take responsibility for their actions and impulses.

---

55. CD 3/4:545.
56. CD 3/4:544–45.
57. CD 4/3.2:581.
58. CD 4/3.2:586.
59. CD 4/3.2:587.
60. CD 4/3.2:620.

They refused to participate in the hope that dawned for this *am ha'aretz*, this *profanum vulgus* (wretched people profaned and vulgar).[61]

In this political orientation, Barth's reflection on *parrhesia* is of special significance to evangelization and mission. Through our participation in the veracity of God's truth our words become God's own word, receiving the momentum of *parrhesia*, which distinguishes genuine preaching from a mere speaking about God.[62] In *parrhesia* we live as Christians or as witnesses to the world. Our life is undercut by the threat of inhumanity and exploitation of the neighbor. The Christian discourse of *parrhesia* resists ideologically distorted forms of inhumanity and exploitation.[63] Evangelization is undertaken in the spirit of speaking the truth of the gospel with boldness and audacity, following in the footsteps of Jesus of Nazareth and his disciples. Jesus Christ, who comes in Jewish flesh, announces God as "the One whose will is that [God's people] should be totally changed and renewed."[64] Jesus Christ stands in God's "corresponding partisanship of those who are lowly in this world."[65]

SPECIAL ETHICS: CRITICAL ANALYSIS OF LORDLESS POWERS

The uniqueness of Barth's theology lies in his prophetic and ethical contour. In his deliberation of the ethic of the active life,[66] Barth develops a prophetic ethic of *diakonia* for the responsibility of the church's mission. Integrating the church's responsibility with the coming kingdom of God, Barth insists that when the command of God is heard there is always a summons to a counter-movement in protest of the perverted, unredeemed reality of the world, which is stamped by competition, thoughtlessness, serious conflict, and the struggle for existence. In light of God's kingdom, Barth challenges both the capitalist society, labeling it a revolution of empty and inordinate desire,[67] and also the injustice and

---

61. CD 4/3.2:774.
62. CD 2/1:231–32.
63. CD 4/2:442.
64. CD 4/2:180.
65. CD 4/2:248–49.
66. CD 3/4.
67. CD 3/4:538.

oppression of state socialism,[68] thereby undergirding the socio-critical dimension of the church's mission. The kingdom of God has come in the poverty of Jesus Christ, the companion of the world's poor. He is now to be found in the company of the hungry, the homeless, the naked, the sick, and the prisoners.[69]

Barth's hermeneutic of the poor becomes one of the main thrusts in shaping the socio-critical and political horizon of *Church Dogmatics*. Barth develops his special ethics as a task of the doctrine of reconciliation in connection with the grace of election and creation in his posthumously published ethics of reconciliation.[70]

Special ethics in the doctrine of reconciliation considers human life and conduct in their particular time and place. God alone is good and God decides what human action may be good or not good. Special ethics does not adopt any supposed natural or rational truths or any timeless truths supposedly taken from the Scripture or the Christian tradition, because God's command is not the timeless truth of a general principle, but the specific content of a special event between God and human beings in the context of a particular historical reality. The task of special ethics is to explicate the *kairos*—the event between God and human beings. Where the Word of God speaks of God's act of sanctifying God's name and God's future manifestation, there will necessarily be acts that repudiate the status quo, and the Christian's wrestling with the law of the recurrence of all things that partially determine human life.[71]

In the acts of repudiation, we are aware that the non-Christian world knows the one, true, and living God who is reconciled to the world.[72] Knowing that the world is not dark and without light leads the Christian church to take seriously its solidarity with those outside and to take their place alongside them.[73]

Bonhoeffer's theology from below in solidarity with those who suffer finds its impulse in Barth's ethical consideration of the struggle for human righteousness. Here, Barth contextualizes his political ethics in

---

68. CD 3/4:544.
69. Barth, "Poverty" in Barth, *Against Stream*, 244–46.
70. Barth, *Christian Life*, 205–60.
71. Ibid., 180.
72. Ibid., 196.
73. Ibid., 200.

revolt against the disorder and critical analysis of the lordless powers in light of the kingdom of God. There can be no reconciliation or peace in worldly occurrences. The Christian is called to rebel against the human plight in the world in all circumstances, rising up against it.

Human beings try to live a lordless life in isolation from God. "Lordless indwelling forces" (Goethe) unleashed the rebellion, exalting human abilities as lordless forces, pretending to be absolute, against human beings themselves. They have won a certain autonomy, independence, and superiority in relation to humanity.[74] They are also the real factors and agents of human progress, regress, and stagnation in politics, economics, scholarship, technology and art; they are also factors and agents of the evolution and retardation of the whole personal life of the individual.[75] Barth's view of the lordless powers has a parallel to Weber's notion of the mechanism of the iron cage, or mechanism of the colonization of the lifeworld (Habermas), or apparatus of reification built on the capitalist mode of production (Marx), or the hegemony nexus of knowledge and power in the society (Foucault). Barth clarifies the state as political absolutism for the sake of the establishment of sovereignty and dominion and the exercise of power and force by human being over human being. Here the demonism of politics arises. The establishment and strengthening of power is seized and exercised by some in the subjugation of others.

The demonism of politics consists of the notion of empire, which both the ruled and the ruling have to serve, in any forms whether monarchical, aristocratic, democratic, nationalistic or socialistic. Hobbes' political idea of the state as Leviathan is grounded in fear of the war of all against all. This is because people have handed over and entrusted to the state all their political, social, economic, intellectual, and even ethical and religious freedoms, possibilities, and rights. Leviathan in the hellish vision of the coming iron cage may be seen in the so-called totalitarian states of Fascism, National Socialism, and Stalinism.[76]

Mammon is another of the lordless powers, referring to the material possessions, property, and resources that have become the idol of human beings. Mammon, the very mobile demon of human beings, is the close relative of Leviathan. The spirit of this world is also the spirit of Mammon

---

74. Ibid., 215–16.
75. Ibid., 216.
76. Ibid., 220–21. Chung, *Karl Barth*, 438–40.

attempting self-absolutization. Mammon in the form of money is the lordless power of material resources holding absolute sway over person and humanity. Money is "a capital epitome and standard not merely of economic values but of all human values."[77]

Human beings make their ideas into a system, an ideology, in independence of the living Spirit of God. Within this framework and under its direction, the ideology exerts on human life such a fascination, becoming the object of human reflection, its backbone and norm, the guiding star of human action. People are made the functionaries of the ideology, measuring and evaluating others only from the standpoint of one's ideology. The ideology of the "-ism" rises up like monstrous bubbles, with all their changing colors and their fascinating effect on individual and social life; it stands in concurrence with Leviathan and Mammon, and in competition with them, creating slogans or catchwords, and propaganda. Words of propaganda color the world in black and white, as do acts of propaganda. This is the particular art and masterwork of ideologies.[78]

Barth further brings chthonic destructive forces, threatening the life of the earth under his critical analysis. This sphere is called "earth" in the Scripture, in distinction from heaven. Human beings are to make the earth their own world, having dominion over it (Gen 1:28) and shaping it as a tool of human historical existence. Finally, the human beings put spirits of the earth in their service as their lord. Human beings, investigating, using, and exploiting the earth, are captive to the chthonic powers of which technology is an example. The industrialization and commercializing of sport has been made remunerative. Barth observes the example of chthonic powers and forces in the field of transportation. The daily rate of traffic accidents and their victims (the total numbers in 1960 were 65,000 in Europe) have already reached and even surpassed the numbers of those who are lost in war. Unfettered and palpably lordless chthonic power is aroused in all its rational irrationality. Lordless powers have one thing in common: they do not work for human beings but against them. Breaking away from God, they are inhuman. They oppress people, moving them according to the laws of their own dynamics and mechanics.[79]

---

77. Ibid., 224.
78. Ibid., 225–26.
79. Ibid., 233.

Insofar as a society legitimatizes the death of the poor, the myths that justify this treatment of victims are strictly rejected. If a scientific rationality justifies victimization, it is wrong-headed under any circumstances. A scientific theory is valid if it does not demand a victim through history, but unearths the mechanism generating the victims. The political responsibility of the Christian community is directed toward a better communal life, that is, an ever-changing self-renewal in deconstruction of the rule of privilege, dominion, and violence. A movement toward life, which comes from God's reign, finds its active fulfillment in the second petition of the Lord's Prayer: "Thy will be done on earth as it is in heaven." Against the lordless powers, "the coming world" of God, in which many from east and west sit at table with Abraham, Isaac, and Jacob (Matt 8:11–12), breaks into our midst here and now, moving into the future.

David Tracy views Barth's analogical theology in his study of Anselm, in which Barth develops ever-new reformations of theological languages in connection with his *Church Dogmatics*. Barth's language of analogy of faith (or grace) in *Church Dogmatics* always includes a constitutive dialectical component within its general analogical form. However, Tracy argues that Barth's theological language of all the negations in the *Church Dogmatics* is to be seen in light of the "yes" of the gracious and merciful God, especially because of Barth's emphasis on the triumph of grace. Tracy's evaluation of Barth's language of analogy remains defective because it neglects the liberative dimension of Barth's analogical politics in its negative-critical force.

However, Barth's theology does not sidestep a socially engaged dimension of Jesus's parables in discursive connection with public sinners and tax collectors. Barth's political ethic remains an important arbiter for the development of public ethical theology and discipleship of God's mission in the aftermath of colonialism and World Christianity. Barthian analogical theology from above supports public ethical theology and discipleship of God's mission from below concerning discursive analysis of religious institutionalized knowledge and socio-political hegemonic power.

8

God's Mission and Israel in the Jewish-Christian Context

DABRU EMET, A JEWISH Statement on Christians and Christianity, signals a dramatic and groundbreaking shift in the longstanding and often hostile relationship between Jews and Christians. In this statement, we read of the Jewish understanding of God, the Torah, land-promise, peace, and social justice in a theocentric-eschatological framework. Moreover, the *Dabru Emet* remarkably states that "Jews can respect Christians' faithfulness to their revelation" through Jesus Christ.[1] If Jews respect a Christian understanding of the God of Israel through Jesus Christ, it is essential for Christian theology to conceptualize a Christology that does not deny the place of Israel, while still maintaining the Christian faith in Jesus Christ. Thereby, Christian faith in Jesus Christ would be a form of accompaniment and solidarity with the Jews rather than a source of division.

For this task of the church's accompaniment and solidarity with Israel, Barth's theology of God's mission is worth considering. Some argue that bringing Karl Barth into dialogue with Judaism is out of the question because of his Trinitarian theology and Christology that are based on the Hellenistic Council of the ancient Church. Furthermore, it is noted that Barth's doctrine of election tends to subsume Israel into the ecclesial sphere. Thereby, Barth's theology of Israel in his dogmatic theology is blamed for dislodging the place of Judaism. In taking issue with critique of Barth's theology of election and Israel, it is essential to explore Barth's

---

1. Frymer-Kensky, et al., *Christianity in Jewish Terms*, xv-xviii.

theology of election and Israel in *Church Dogmatics,* considering his several writings, letters, and interviews on this topic.

BARTH AND THE SECRET OF ISRAEL

In the hands of Nazi ideologists a general doctrine of election was violently manipulated to gratify the nationalistic extermination. The German Volk was idealized and idolized as God's new chosen race. Consequently, Israel was stripped of the status of election. The Jews were condemned to the penalty that is worthy of the rejected. Vilified as life unworthy of living, the Jews were elected to death—a death executed in the hells of Auschwitz, Belzec, Chelmno, and Sobibor. In his letter to Rabbi Emil Bernhard-Cohen in 1934, Barth expressed his worry and shame over what was happening to the Jewish people in Germany. For Barth, the election of the people of Israel retains an on-going theological significance for the Christian church. In Israel there was the last secret of divine covenant and grace in the midst of the political and historical enigma of the year 1934.

In his doctrine of election Barth understands Jesus Christ in a Jewish environment and in connection to the Hebrew Bible which is of special significance for God's mission. His understanding of the triune God bears witness to the God of Israel and the Father of Jesus Christ. Barth's perspective on mission in his Trinitarian election model provides an insight into the renewal of relationship between the church and Israel. His theology of Israel occupies a central place in his doctrine of election.

THE CHURCH'S MISSION AND THE ELECTION OF ISRAEL

As we already examined, Barth's concept of mission opposes the general notion that mission is an instrument of religious or civilizing propaganda on the part of western Christianity. Barth interprets the decree of election to be identical with that of salvation. This Barthian perspective on election accentuates that Christ's election is all-inclusive and universally reaching out in a meaningful and efficacious way. Barth takes the road of the Trinitarian election of Christ to avoid the Scylla of the Calvinist concept of *decretum absolutum* and the Charybdis of Pelagianism.

God's Mission and Israel in the Jewish-Christian Context 135

According to Barth, the dynamic of election is grounded in divine condescension.[2] God in God's movement toward humanity is personalized in the Jewish man of Nazareth. Barth states that Israel and the church are the people represented in the election of the man Jesus of Nazareth. Barth underscores the doctrine of election as the dialectical relationship between Jesus Christ and his people Israel. Jesus Christ is the electing God and the elected man.[3]

Discussing the community of those who are elected in Christ, Barth understands the reality of this elected community as embracing both Israel and the church. Jesus Christ, as the Messiah of Israel, is the Lord of the church.[4] This understanding of Jesus Christ is the grounding principle that Barth uses to underline the relation of Israel to the church. Both, together in unity, stand under the one covenantal grace of God grounded in Christ's election. Fundamental to Barth is the affirmation, clarification, and development of "the bow of the one covenant [that] arches over the whole"[5] in speaking of Israel and the church.[6]

However, in his typical dialectical fashion, Barth treats Israel as a witness to God's judgment, while the church witnesses to God's mercy. This dialectical model provokes a criticism from the circle of theologians who promote Jewish-Christian renewal. Additionally, Barth's material on the doctrine of election in *Church Dogmatics* was developed before the start of the Holocaust. The Nazis' "Final Solution" for the "Jewish question" was planned at the Wannsee Conference (20 January 1942). In this background, Barth's reflection of Israel in the form of passing humanity becomes questionable, thus remaining a source of controversy.

According to Katherine Sonderegger, Barth conceptualizes Israel's election only for rejection. Barth allows full expression of a form of nationalistic and dogmatic anti-Judaism. Similarly, Soulen also critiques Barth's concept of christocentric theology as carrying the logic of economic supersessionism for the sake of integrating Israel into the ecclesial sphere.[7]

2. CD 2/1:311.
3. CD 2/2:103.
4. CD 2/2:197–98.
5. CD 2/2:200.
6. Busch, *Unter Bogen des einen Bundes*.
7. Sonderegger, *Jesus Christ Was Born a Jew*, 123, 129, 146. Soulen, *God of Israel and Christian Theology*, 89–93.

Unlike these charges, however, Barth recognizes that the gospel pre-exists even in the realm of the law. The law becomes a necessary form of the gospel. The law is a call to freedom, responding to God's grace with praise and thanksgiving instead of servitude or accusation. The historical event of the revelation of Jesus Christ is pre-actualized within the history of Israel. Therefore, Israel is not merely dissolved into the church. Rather, Israel is involved in the universal mission of God together with the church.[8] As Barth states, "By the church of the coming man pre-existing in Israel, Israel's election is also confirmed positively. It does not alter Israel's special determination, but illumines and interprets it."[9]

Israel's participation in Jesus Christ–even for unbelieving Jews–does not necessarily mean that Israel is superseded or converted into the sphere of the church. Thereby, Barth articulates the concept of a christological embrace of unbelieving Jews, whom Barth describes as the natural environment of Jesus Christ. Insofar as the church lives on in Israel, Israel also lives on in the church: they co-exist. In his doctrine of election Barth does not compartmentalize his theology of election in terms of ascribing Israel for rejection and the church for election.

REVELATION IN THE ENTIRE SCRIPTURE

For Barth, the Christ of the New Testament is the Christ of the Old Testament, that is, the Christ of Israel. The Hebrew Bible is the witness of recollection alongside the original Canon, which is the witness of expectation. This perspective implies the decisive issue between the church and the synagogue. Seen in light of the resurrection of Jesus, Moses and the prophets are the prophetic heralds of Jesus Christ together with the Evangelists and apostles.[10] Scripture is produced by the Jewish spirit and humanity. The whole of the Bible as a Jewish book cannot be understood without engaging in the language, thought, and history of the Jews. The continuing existence of the Jews is the natural proof of God in world history. Christians must not hesitate to be primed to become Jews with the Jews.[11] If the church demonstrates hostility toward the Jewish people,

---

8. CD 2/2:266.
9. Ibid.
10. CD 1/2:490, 494.
11. CD 1/2:511.

it becomes blind, dangerous, and ungodly. For Barth, rejecting the Jew leads us to reject God.[12]

KARL BARTH AND CHRISTIAN ANTI-SEMITISM

Barth maintains that the church stands or falls by way of fellowship and solidarity with Israel. The hearing of Scripture in church does not replace the hearing of the Jewish witness in the past or the present.[13] Christian anti-Judaism is essentially grounded in the notion of the church's replacement of Israel. However, the person who believes in Jesus must accept the Jews as the ancestors and relatives of Jesus. Otherwise, one rejects Jesus himself along with the Jews. Against Christian anti-Semitism, Barth challenges the church *not* to say that the Jews crucified Jesus. In such an attitude, Israel has ceased to be the chosen–the holy people of God. Into its place the church enters as the historical successor of Israel. Then Israel is outsider, so that they are forsaken by God.[14]

Sharply criticizing Christian anti-Semitism, Barth interprets the resurrection of Jesus as eradicating the Jewish rejection and disobedience. "The finis arbitrarily written by the unbelieving will of Israel in the betrayal and crucifixion of Jesus has been finally cancelled by a higher hand in His resurrection from the dead."[15]

The exchange between God and humanity took place on Golgotha when God chose as God's throne the malefactor's cross. It took place once and for all in fulfillment of God's eternal will. "There is no condemnation–literally none–for those that are in Christ Jesus."[16]

Two-edged predestination in Christ implies that God's judgment did not take place on the cross for the rejection of Israel. In the vicarious death of Jesus Christ, Jacob and Esau, church and synagogue, pagans and Jews are bound together in solidarity. Jesus Christ is the substance of both the elected and the rejected communities. Therefore, Barth accentuates that the doctrine of election is "the sum of the Gospel."[17] When it comes to

12. CD 1/2:511.
13. Barth, *Briefe 1961–1968*, 420.
14. CD 2/2:290.
15. CD 2/2:291.
16. CD 2/2:167.
17. CD 2/2:3.

Barth's doctrine of election, we need to distinguish *praedestinatio gemina* from *praedestinatio dialectica*. The former is the election of one and the rejection of the other, which is exemplified in the Calvinistic teaching of double predestination. But the latter places the judgment of election and rejection upon the one person of Jesus Christ. When we take seriously Barth's doctrine of election from the perspective of dialectical predestination, it is unfair or even unqualified to one-sidedly force Barth's theology of election into a dualistic model of Israel-rejection and church-election.

Barth advances his reflection by considering that Israel is the natural environment of Christ and the church is Christ's historical environment. The arch of God's eternal will embraces Israel and the church together within the environments of Jesus Christ. God's mercy is the final ground and justification for establishing a relationship between Israel and the church. Even in the face of a Christ-rejecting Judaism, God's mercy remains as the first and final word for the election of Israel. "Beloved! This is the last word which in every present and in respect of every member of this people has to be taken into account in relation to Israel's history from its beginnings into every conceivable or inconceivable future."[18]

KARL BARTH UNDER CHARGE OF ANTI-JUDAISM

However, Barth's view of the synagogue can arouse suspicion of an anti-Jewish residue, remaining a stumbling block to Barth's contribution to Jewish-Christian relations. In the section entitled, "The Determination of the Rejected,"[19] Barth tends to fall into a gray area, seeming to dispute Israel's right to exist: "Israel's right to existence is extinguished, and therefore its existence can only be extinguished."[20] Although Barth does not intend to reject the right of the Jewish people for physical existence, he is careless in disqualifying it as unreal life.

In the determination of the rejected, it is important to scrutinize Barth's concept of the rejection of Judas. For Barth, the elector-elected Jesus of Nazareth is rooted in his Jewishness and offers a ground for co-existence between Israel and the church. Barth depicts Judas as the archetypal figure of rejection and as representative of Israel. Judas himself

18. CD 2/2:303.
19. CD 2/2 § 35. 4.
20. CD 2/2:505.

stands paradoxically in the closest proximity to the church. Like Jesus, "Judas . . . belongs to the tribe of Judah, the seed of David."[21] He was genuinely elected, although rejected. It is certain that Barth distances himself from identifying Judas exclusively with Israel because "Jesus was handed over by one of His own . . . from within the Church. The Church stands and acts in identity with the Israel which rejected its Messiah."[22]

The work of Judas is done within the life of the apostles. Likewise, "the apostles have to share the guilt of Israel and the Gentile world towards Jesus."[23] In this regard, Barth is far from viewing the church idealistically. He doesn't ascribe guilt for Jesus' death exclusively to Judas or Israel. Although the Jews were not innocent of the death of Jesus, the church is also indicted with the same charge. Barth insists that Judas' basic flaw can be seen in the apostolate as a whole because "Judas and the other apostles belong together."[24]

Highlighting the Jewish character of Jesus Christ as confirmation and fulfillment of the Torah, Barth argues that the church, in harmony and continuity with the Old Testament, runs counter to the synagogue—as a place of "the nationalistic-legalistic Messiah-dream" or "the Synagogue of death."[25] Barth's hostile language goes very far, arguing that the synagogue is the terrible, shadowy side of the history of Israel, both disobedient and idol worshipping. Such a description of the synagogue as perpetually non-believing causes the charge of anti-Judaism or anti-Semitism to be brought against Barth. The synagogue as the non-believing community is characterized by an arrogant lie, which is caught up in nationalistic-legalistic messianic dreams. Israel stands as the enemy of God and practices obstinacy, melancholy, crankiness, and fantasy. It is "the personification of a half-venerable, half-gruesome relic, of a miraculously preserved antique, of human whimsicality."[26]

The synagogue must live the pattern of a historical life without absolutely having a future. Despite the anti-Jewish overtones, Barth, in point of fact, does not use these aggressive remarks to speak out against the syna-

---

21. CD 2/2:459.
22. CD 2/2:460.
23. CD 2/2:461.
24. CD 2/2:471, 475.
25. CD 2/2:264.
26. CD 2/2:263.

gogue without reservation. Barth illustrates this reality of the synagogue in accordance with the life of St. Paul. Barth's critique of the synagogue must be seen in his exegesis of St. Paul's life in terms of a dialectical affirmation of the synagogue through Jesus Christ. In the same place as his controversial description of the synagogue and the Jews, we observe that Barth does not forget to speak positively of God's eternal election of Israel.

When the church confesses that salvation is for the Jews, the church's confession asserts, teaches, and defends the eternal election of Israel in defiance of all Gentile arrogance. This is because, in his argument against the synagogue, Barth is at the same time concerned to highlight both Israel and the church standing "beneath the bow of the covenant that arches over both."[27] Barth's interpretive mode illustrates this complicated fact, viewing the life of St. Paul and drawing upon the prophets' critique of Israel in the Old Testament context.[28] Barth's interpretive strategy can be outlined: the synagogue has aroused the hatred and envy of every kind of Gentile and "has been the subject of its own dilettante dreaming." But the church must not embrace anti-Judaism to dispute it, but rather assert and teach God's eternal election of Israel in response to the synagogue. Barth's fundamental conviction is expressed in the following statement: "Confessing Jesus Christ, it confesses the fulfillment of everything that is pledged to Israel as promise, the substance of all the hope of the fathers, of all the exhortations and threats of Moses and the prophets, of all the sacrifice in the tabernacles and the temple, of every letter in the sacred books of Israel."[29]

Barth does not explicate Israel-synagogue only for rejection; nonetheless he is not prepared to affirm the Jewish rejection of Jesus Christ as an act of Israel's "faithfulness to the Torah."[30] Bertold Klappert argues that if Barth remained faithful to his actual dialectical christological approach to the doctrine of Israel, Barth would have to say that the crucified and risen Christ, who as such is the future of Israel, is also the reconciler and Lord of the world and the church. Israel should have received a positive qualification from the resurrection of Jesus Christ, becoming the witness to the promise received and heard from God's covenant.[31] More sharply

27. CD 2/2:204.
28. Marquardt, *Entdeckung des Judentums*, 335, 337.
29. CD 2/2:204.
30. Marquardt, "Feinde um unsretwillen," in Marquardt, *Verwegenheiten*, 315.
31. Klappert, *Israel und Kirche,*, 64.

against Barth's negative description of Israel-synagogue, F. W. Marquardt argues that Israel is even in its bruised form a witness to God's condescending goodness. Israel as a witness to the death of Jesus Christ is also a witness to his resurrection.[32]

BARTH AND GOD'S FAITHFULNESS TO ISRAEL

We have viewed Barth's dialectical language of Christ's election regarding the relationship between Israel and the church. It is no wonder there are limitations in his theology of Israel that remain a stumbling block to a Jewish-Christian relationship. This negative side belongs to Barth's face looking backwards. It is important to critically distance ourselves from this backwardness. In his later stage, however, Barth demonstrates a transition, that is, a face looking forward, considering the future of Israel—including the present state of the unbelieving Jews—and the future of the church. This perspective is already implied in Barth's early reflection on God's gracious love for Israel and the church.[33]

Grounded in God's faithfulness, Barth is willing to affirm a hopeful future for Israel. The fundamental blessing and election are still confirmed, because the final word is the divine "Yes" to Israel.[34] In Barth's interpretation of Romans 9–11, Barth legitimizes St. Paul and his apostolic office as the evidence that God has not thrown away God's people.[35] If God makes a new creation, the new covenant is proof of God's active will in terms of the eternal covenant with all of Israel. Although the whole of Israel is not sanctified, the rest represents the whole. What is represented in the rest is the root, that is, Jesus Christ, the last-born, but, in fact, the first-born brother.[36]

Barth already perceived in the doctrine of election that Israel is a witness to humanity passing away. Referring to the Jewish cemetery in Prague, together with Jewish obduracy and melancholy—even Jewish caprice and fantasy—Barth states that all these contain "objectively and effectively more genuine Gospel" than all of the unbelieving (and much

32. Marquardt, *Entdeckung des Judentums*, 352.
33. CD 2/2:303.
34. CD 2/2:15.
35. CD 2/2:275.
36. CD 2/2:300.

of the Christian) Goyim-wisdom.[37] Israel remains elect, a symbol of the innocent victim, testifying to a humanity that is perishing and passing away in the midst of a Gentile world, which first of all pushes Israel out of the way. A Gentile Christian falls into sheer paganism or anti-Semitism when he or she does not hear Israel's witness. Israel, as the people of the risen Christ, has a hopeful, new, and gracious beginning that dawns in the resurrection of Christ. God's faithfulness in Jesus Christ for God's people—whether they are faithful or unfaithful—becomes the hermeneutical principle in Barth's approach to the Jewish people. The Jews constitute the universal horizon for the goyim as well as solidarity with the reality of the innocent victim.

Given this, we observe that Barth's pro-Jewish activity in Switzerland was remarkable between 1935 and 1945. In his lecture to the Swiss Evangelical Relief Organization (after the Night of Broken Glass in 1938), his motto was John 4:22—"Salvation is from the Jews." The God of the Jews is the God of the Christian church. His claim spoke out against resentment toward the God of the Jews in Germany—replete with a plague of anti-Semitism, the destruction of Jewish synagogues and Torah scrolls, and the physical extermination of the Jews. Anyone who was in principle an enemy of the Jews was to be recognized as, in principle, an enemy of Jesus Christ.[38] "Anti-Semitism is a sin against the Holy Spirit."[39]

For Barth, the promise of Jeremiah 31 is applied to the suffering Jews in Germany. However, the offspring of Israel will never cease to be a nation before God. Such a nation as Pharaoh's Egypt, which murdered Jews, had necessarily met a horrific end.[40] At the height of the Holocaust in July of 1944, Barth stated, "What kind of picture is it that it is raised to our eyes in the middle of today's contemporary occurrences just in the groundless and defenseless slaughtering of the Jewish people? Is it not that punished and tormented servant of God for the sake of others from the book of Isaiah? Is it not our crucified Lord Jesus Christ himself who becomes visible in the destiny of those countless Jews who are shot or finally murdered through poison gas?"[41]

37. CD 2/2:236.
38. Barth, *Schweizer Stimme*, 69–107.
39. Ibid., 90.
40. Ibid., 307–33.
41. Ibid., 18–19.

At this juncture, Rabbi Geis responds, "Who, other than Karl Barth, could have demonstrated more clearly the struggle and courageous resistance that develops from grace?"[42]

According to Barth, Jewish existence becomes the natural environment of Jesus Christ, constituting a formal Christology in accordance with the factual Christology of the Christian church. Not a rejection, an expropriation, and a paganization of Israel, but an appreciation of Israel must be done in terms of the natural environment of Jesus Christ.

BARTH AND POST-BIBLICAL JUDAISM

In the doctrine of providence, Barth began to speak positively of post-biblical, Christ-rejecting Judaism, as the single natural proof of God.[43] The existence of Judaism is the sign of the divine reign, and it functions as the natural environment of Jesus Christ. Barth's understanding of the enigmatic existence of the Jews in world history indicates his interest in viewing the history of Israel in light of God's providential care. What shapes Barth's position in approach to the history of the Jews is God's faithfulness in Jesus Christ for Israel.[44]

Barth, in his doctrine of providence, sees traces of divine world-governance in the special history of the Jews. They are not "antique-dealers," but rather God's partners in the covenant upon whose fulfillment the church is founded. God appoints and constitutes Israel as the bearer of light and salvation to all nations. Jesus Christ is the remnant of the Jewish remnant of Israel. He definitely died and rose again on behalf of this remnant, indeed of Israel as a whole.[45]

The Christian community must condemn anti-Semitism as a barbaric insult to Western culture and civilization, as a breakdown of Christian values. Such a condemnation will do the utmost for the victims of anti-Semitism, welcoming the Jewish establishment in Palestine. It hopes to see a wider interchange of ideas and a new brotherly and sisterly cooperation between Christians and Jews.[46] The Jews as the reluctant wit-

---

42. Geis, *Leiden an Unerlöstheit der Welt*, 240.
43. Barth, *Dogmatics in Outline*, 75.
44. CD 3/3:216–17.
45. CD 3/3:217.
46. Barth, "Jewish Problem and Christian Answer," in Barth, *Against Stream*, 195.

ness of Jesus Christ are sustained and preserved by the free grace of God. Christians from among the Gentiles are guests in their house like new wood is grafted into the old tree. The defiance of the Jews against the one Jew on the cross of Golgotha is so closely associated with Christian anti-Semitism. However, Jesus Christ has already overcome all human defiance and healed division among us, especially the division between the Jews and other nations.[47]

The Word became Jewish flesh,[48] becoming a man of Israel. The self-designation, the *I*, of Jesus originates from Israel. Jesus as a Jew is the fulfillment of the meaning of the history of Israel. The covenant of God should be confirmed and fulfilled by God's faithfulness in the coming of the Son from the tribe of Abraham. The natural and biological dimension of Jewish hope must not be mystified in an anti-Semitic direction nor should the tribe of Abraham be spiritualized in a Christian way.[49] The proof for God's existence is the Jews. This notion is reminiscent of remarks of Fredrick the Great's assistant: The Jews are a people ordained as bearers of light and salvation to all nations.[50]

ISRAEL-COVENANT AND CHRIST-RECONCILIATION

Barth regards the prophecies from the messianic history of Israel as an adequate pre-figuration of the messianic prophecy of Jesus Christ. In other words, Israel is "an exact representation and adequate pre-figuration of the prophecy of [Christ's] history."[51] A new model of correlation occurs between the entire messianic history of Israel and the messianic prophecy of Jesus Christ. This model of correlation presents and systematizes Israel's relevance to Barth's Christology, comparing Jesus with the entire history of Israel without reservation.[52]

God's reconciliation in Jesus Christ is the confirmation and the fulfillment of Israel's election and covenant. *Missio Dei* in Barth's sense becomes God's mission of reconciliation that embraces the place of Israel.

47. Ibid., 201.
48. CD 4/1:171.
49. Barth, *Dogmatics in Outline*, 217.
50. CD 3/3:219.
51. CD 4/3.1:66.
52. CD 4/3.1:48–49.

The covenant is the presupposition of reconciliation, while God's reconciliation is the fulfillment of the broken covenant.[53] In Jesus Christ a new humanity is introduced so that humanity may be God's people, newly created and grounded in the free act of God's grace in Jesus Christ.

God's unchangeable faithfulness to Israel is spoken in contrast to the unfaithfulness of Israel. There is the emphasis on the imperishable nature of God's covenant with Israel in Jer. 31:31–37. Jer. 31 is the final word in matters pertaining to "the covenant of the free but effective grace of God."[54] This is the universal purpose of Israel's mission.[55]

Seen in the framework of God's mission of reconciliation, Barth bases his articulation of the final mission of Israel to the nations on Isaiah. In the eschatological perspective God's covenant with Israel is not an end itself, but it has "a provisional and a provisionally representative significance."[56] Jesus Christ is the eschatological realization of God's covenant with Israel, and for the whole of humanity. The general covenant with creation and the special covenant with Israel are integrated into God's free grace in Jesus Christ, the first born of all creation (Col 1:15).

Church as the earthly-historical form of the existence of Jesus Christ is also provisional, fragmentary, incomplete, insecure, and questionable. With this provisional representation in mind, we consider the way and the movement of the true church.[57] In this eschatological understanding of the church, Barth opens a space for the future of Israel. The bow of the one covenant stretches over the whole.[58] The "Jewish question," according to Barth, is really a "Christian question."[59]

The temporary pruning of its natural branches and the grafting of wild shoots onto it in the parable of the olive tree does not say that the church supplants Israel. Instead, the originally non-elected Gentiles would come into the place of Israel through God's mercy. The church, therefore, must stand in alliance with Israel and witness to the gospel among the pagans rather than pursuing missions to the unbelieving Jews. The

---

53. CD 4/1:67.
54. CD 4/1:34.
55. CD 4/1:31.
56. CD 4/1:28.
57. CD 4/2:621.
58. CD 4/1:670.
59. CD 4/1:671.

connection between people and land belongs to the essence of Judaism. Because this connection is biblically grounded, Christian theology has to take it into account. The occupation of land must be understood as an indispensable and concrete implication for the covenant that is fulfilled in Jesus Christ as the Messiah of Israel. In light of the founding of the state of Israel in 1948, Barth's statement is fundamental for his theology of Israel-Land: "They are again there, they are there still. They are remarkably representing the remnant of Israel."[60] There they are not antique-dealers, but God's partner in the covenant upon whose fulfillment the Church is founded.[61] This perspective implies that Barth's witness renders all anti-Jewish Christian theology null overnight.[62]

A NOTE ON BARTH AND A MODEL OF ENGRAFTING

In a collection entitled *Gespräche: 1964–1968*,[63] Barth writes several sporadic passages and assertions about a relationship between Israel and the church. His contention is that "we all stem from the Jews. Christ was a Jew and so were all the people who wrote the New Testament."[64] If the church turns its back on the Jews, it is turning against God. The experience of the Jewish people with God in world history is of special significance to Christianity. They cannot be eliminated, just as the Bible cannot be eliminated. In the Jews we have before us a living Bible down to the present day.[65] Jesus came from the Jewish people and as a result they are the people of Jesus, whether they acknowledge him or not.

In light of this corporeal and eternal relationship, the church is not entitled to replace Israel. Rather, the church is invited to be grafted into Israel, sharing and forming a covenantal solidarity with the Jews. According to Barth, we Christians are a so-called expanded people of Israel.[66] God's constant and unfailing faithfulness to Israel brings hope to all of us. That God keeps God's promises and sustains God's people is

60. CD 3/3:212.
61. CD 3/3:212–13.
62. Marquardt, "Israel, Judentum, Zionismus," in Marquardt, *Verwegenheiten*, 293.
63. Barth, *Gespräche: 1964–1968*.
64. Ibid., 207.
65. Ibid., 208.
66. Ibid., 422.

something wonderful and marvelous to behold. This is a consolation, and also a witness.[67]

Thus, Barth calls for the abandonment of Christian mission to the Jews in a post-Shoah era. The concept of Christian mission to the Jews is theologically impossible. "In relation to the Synagogue, there can be no real question of 'mission' . . . Mission is not the witness which [the church] owes to Israel."[68] Barth states that "the Jew, even the unbelieving Jew, so miraculously preserved . . . through the many calamities of his history . . . is the natural historical monument of the love and faithfulness of God." The Jew "as a living commentary on the Old Testament is the only convincing proof of God outside the Bible."[69]

According to Barth, what should become of the conversation in the long run for the Jews, who have already rejected Jesus Christ as their Messiah? A conversation for the purpose of converting the Jews to Christianity is meaningless. Barth's recommendation in this context is for the church to make Israel and the synagogue jealous (Rom 11:14). The church must live together with the synagogue since both possess the Old Testament as their root, from which the church has emerged. The ecumenical movement today suffers much more from the absence of Israel than from the absence of Rome and Moscow.[70]

As a result, his previous negative description of the synagogue and Israel is transformed into his reclaiming of Christians as guests grafted into God's original covenant with the Jews. Barth argues that Christology does not need to be muffled and decreased in order to amplify and expand eschatology, despite the christological disagreement on both sides. On this christological basis, the Christian looks forward into the future in expectation of and hope for the coming Messiah. However, Moltmann's critiques sounds unfortunate and enigmatic in this regard, because Moltmann argues that Barth's christological eschatology has annulled the Old Testament's surplus of promise beyond the coming of Christ, so that Israel in Barth's Christology "has no future other than conversion to the Christ who has come."[71]

---

67. Ibid.
68. CD 4/3. 2:877.
69. CD 4/3. 2:877.
70. CD 4/3. 2:878.
71. Moltmann, *Ethics of Hope*, 23.

FURTHER DEVELOPMENT: KARL BARTH AND F. W. MARQUARDT IN EXCHANGE

As we have examined, Barth's doctrine of Israel is revealed to have two different faces: a face looking backwards and a face looking forwards. Barth failed to take seriously the Jewish "No" to Jesus as the Messiah in light of the Jews' faithful act in obedience to the first Commandment. His typical dialectical description of Israel and synagogue remains controversial and even under considerable critique. This aspect continues to be a limitation of and impediment to Barth's theology of Israel, and is part of the face that looks backwards.[72]

Challenging Barth's paralyzing element in the doctrine of Israel, Marquardt attempts to introduce and integrate Judaism's own understanding of God and the Torah as a further categorical dimension in the theological discussion about Jewish-Christian renewal. Therefore, Marquardt critiques Barth's theology of Israel for oftentimes dismissing Israel's self-understanding as a *quantité négligeable*.[73] In Marquardt's view, "God has not thrown away his people. Israel is not degraded to a puppet figure. It has self-consciousness as well as existence, and both are not to be separated from each other. Physical description is deliberate, not involuntary description."[74]

In a letter to Marquardt, however, Barth writes: "Biblical Israel as such gave me so much to think about and to cope with that I simply did not have the time or intellectual strength to look more closely at Baeck, Buber, Rosenzweig, etc."[75] Additionally, Barth does not identify himself unreservedly as a Philo-Semite. To some degree, Barth made the sigh of "Pfui!" to his allergic reaction against the Jews.[76]

Furthermore, Barth maintains that Marquardt has discerned "the beginnings of improvement" in him, "or at least a serious attempt at it," which is alluded to by Marquardt. Barth refers to his continuing development in several places, namely in his 1954 seminar, which was a supplement to the declaration of "Christ—The Hope of the World" in the World Council of Churches. Additionally, Barth referred Marquardt

---

72. Marquardt, foreword to *Entdeckung des Judentums*.
73. Ibid., 296.
74. Ibid., 320.
75. Letter to F.-W. Marquardt, September 5, 1967, in *Letters 1916–1968*, 262.
76. Chung, *Karl Barth*, 415.

to his summons in 1938, drawn up by W. Vischer, in which Barth's debate with Emil Brunner became central regarding whether salvation is or was of the Jews (John 4:22).

As Barth states in *The Hope of Israel*, "We have to say first of the people which bases its hope on the same object, which is also the ground of our hope, namely in the coming Messiah . . . [this hope] is based namely in the promises of God, which he has given his chosen people . . . Israel is the people of hope."[77]

In considering Marquardt's critique, it is also essential to take into account Barth's response to Vatican II's declaration on Non-Christian religions in his book *Ad Limina Apostolorum* and his contribution to a panel discussion held in Chicago in 1962.[78] In his book *Ad Limina Apostolorum* (1967), Barth undertook a serious study of the sixteen Latin texts in Vatican II. According to Barth, it would be dubious if the Declaration speaks of the past and present history of Israel in the same manner as Hinduism, Buddhism, and Islam, all non–Christian religions. It should be important for the church to make an official and public confession of guilt in regard to the anti-Semitism in the ancient, the medieval, and the modern church.[79] In the light of "the primal form of the one God's revelation,"[80] it is essential for Barth to advocate the entire messianic history of Israel and Judaism as the configuration of Jesus Christ.

In Rome in 1966, Barth emphasized anew the significance of the Jewish-Christian relationship for the unity of Christians. "There are today many good relations between the Roman Catholic Church and many Protestant churches . . . But we should not forget that there is finally only one actual great ecumenical question—our relation to Judaism."[81] If the church and the Jews stand "beneath the bow of the covenant that arches over both,"[82] the church consists only of transplanted aliens,[83] which are grafted into the Old Testament as the primal form of Christian revelation; then the church must read and learn from the Jewish understanding of

---

77. Busch, *Karl Barth*, 402.
78. Letter to F.-W. Marquardt, September 5, 1967, in *Letters 1916–1968*, 262–63.
79. Barth, *Ad Limina Apostolorum*, 36–37.
80. Ibid., 39–40.
81. Klappert, *Israel und Kirche*, 76.
82. CD 2/2:204.
83. CD 2/2:288.

God and the Torah. This thought-form enables Barth to take a step further in affirming an engrafting model in which the Christian church is in an on-going process of dialogue and learning as it encounters God's living voice in the life of Israel.

TOWARD GOD'S MISSION OF RECONCILIATION IN THE POST-SHOAH ERA

In Jewish-Christian dialogue, the particular-universal significance of Jesus Christ encourages the church to enrich and deepen the subject matter of the Gospel as it encounters and learns God's Torah in both written and oral form from a Jewish understanding of God. The *Logos* speaks the word of the faith of Israel, *Dabar*, together with Israel.[84] Therefore, Christian faith hears both words: *Logos* in the Greek Bible and the *dabar* of Israel in the Hebrew Bible. David Bosch, in his model of transforming mission, finds the Jewish-Christian relationship to be of utmost important for the paradigm shifts in the theology of mission.

However, his approach is driven by the missionary mentality of transforming the Jews to Christian church. Bosch is suspicious of Romans 9–11 (particularly 11:25–32), because this passage appears to be anachronistic in appeal to today's question. He also argues that there should be a distinction made between the place of Israel in the covenant of God and the empirical modern state of Israel. It is a dangerous theological misconception to establish a direct connection between the biblical Israel and the survival of the Jews in a nation state.[85] Thus, the issue of a continuing evangelistic mission to Jews remains an unfinished issue in the agenda of the church. Since Romans 9–11 is characterized by an almost unbearable and yet creative tension, the text remains significantly ambiguous in deciding Jewish-Christian relations.[86]

However, it is important to unfold a mission as dialogue with and recognition of the Jews in terms of appreciation, critical-constructive mutual renewal, and critical solidarity concerning the issues of justice in Palestine. From the beginning, Jesus Christ is *dia-logical*, embodying God's Torah. The Hebrew Bible belongs to the Gentile Christians through Jesus Christ,

---

84. Marquardt, *Entdeckung des Judentums*, 110.
85. Bosch, *Transforming Mission*, 173.
86. Ibid., 174.

who was born a Jew and sent in the service of the God of Israel. The theology of mission is grounded in God's reconciliation, and in the reconciled world God may speak in Israel in terms of the one general covenant with all through Noah, which finally reached its climax in Jesus Christ.

Moreover, it is especially important to be involved in exegetical work on the passages in the New Testament that have been associated with anti-Judaism. Some verses have been misused to legitimize the church's position in support of anti-Judaism. Insofar as God at Golgotha is no less than the God of Abraham, Isaac, Jacob, and the father of Jesus Christ, Jewish-Christian relations should be pursued, renewed, and transformed in light of the mystery of God in *Dabar* as well as in *Logos*.

Barth's theology of Israel, despite its shortcomings, may serve as a point of departure for us to move toward renewal of Jewish-Christian relations, solidarity with those victimized in Palestine, and also in view of its implication for religious pluralism. It enables a new discussion and improvements in a postcolonial study of God's mission and the missional church conversation, encouraging the Christian church to break ground through self-renewal in the post-Shoah period.[87]

---

87. Chung, *Karl Barth*, 408–18.

III

Public Ethical Theology and a Transformative Construal of the World

IN PREVIOUS STUDIES OF God's mission and public ethics I sought to investigate Luther, Calvin, Bonhoeffer, and Vicedom in a broader horizon. Furthermore, I examined the theology of Karl Barth when it comes to God's mission, theological hermeneutics, public political ethics, and Jewish-Christian renewal.

Part III seeks to undertake public ethical theology in terms of a transformative construal of the world by attending to diverse horizons of theological ethics. Broadly speaking, ethics is defined as the theory of the conduct of human life, in which ethical questions become life questions and thereby construct meaning. Thus ethics considers concrete life situations that generate moral reflection upon particular issues, which are intertwined with the institutional life of families, schools, churches, social and public institutions, and the state. Given this, public ethical theology relates a discipleship of God's mission to life situations and develops theological, moral reflection in a broader horizon of diversity, plurality, and difference.

Chapter 9 investigates a theological reflection and characterization concerning the method, framework, and epistemology underlying public ethical theology in relation to the discipleship of God's mission. This chapter deals with the relationship between God's mission in the economic realm, while exploring the relevance of Christian ethics in the life of God's creatures.

Chapter 10 evaluates Troeltsch's Christian social ethics and his historical-critical method in terms of public ethical theology and the discipleship of God's mission.

Chapter 11 explores the ethical-hermeneutical correlation in dealing with Gadamer's philosophical hermeneutics, which incorporates Aristotle's notion of *phronēsis*. Evaluating Gadamer's contribution and limitation, I shall introduce Habermas' discourse ethics and communicative theory. Critically appreciating Gadamer's hermeneutics and Habermas' critical theory, I shall develop public ethical theology in relation to diversity, plurality, and difference.

Chapter 12 is a study of moral deliberation and the ethical approach to race, gender, and inequality as I relate public ethical theology to social cultural life-conditions and deal with an aspect of ethical emancipation. A black theology can be taken as an example that demonstrates the connection between the issue of race and its historical consciousness. A black theology shapes and reinforces theological ethics for equality, justice, and emancipation. Furthermore, a feminist approach to sexuality, patriarchy, and inequality shall be included in the liberation perspective.

9

Public Theology and the Discipleship of God's Mission

PUBLIC ETHICAL THEOLOGY AND ITS CHARACTERIZATION

A notion of social ethics became a public discourse in the circle of the "Social Gospel movement" in the early 1880s in the United States. The social ethical mission was to transform the structures of society in the direction of social justice and solidarity. Theologians and ethicists have construed the social meaning of Christianity in this perspective. Reinhold Niebuhr's influential blend of realist politics and neo-Augustinian theology, together with H. Richard Niebuhr's ethics of the responsible self, remains a catalyst and watershed in propelling the further development of social ethics. Along the path of this Christian realism and responsible ethics, liberation ethics has also arisen out of an eruption of the voices of those repressed and excluded.

Without losing its basis in the Christian narrative and its prophetic manner, public theology entails a horizon and dimension of social ethics in relation to social-critical and scientific method and moral theory. The Christian character of social ethics is undertaken analyzing human life and its connection in social, political, economic, and cultural realms. Thus, social ethics becomes, at its best, a public discourse of the academy and church in dealing with ethical responsibility and the discipleship of God's mission in relation to public issues and social problems.[1]

---

1. Dorrien, *Social Ethics in the Making*, 2–4.

Insofar as Christian ethics considers and analyzes human moral conduct and practice in light of a biblical faith, it should not preclude the other theological reflection, that is, the systematic–dogmatic-hermeneutical reflection on ethical theology in the deliberation of human behavior, attitude, and public responsibility.

According to Trutz Rendtorff, "ethics is thus an intensified form of theology."[2] Theology and ethics are integrally related, with distinct disciplines, methods, and themes. Ethics, also termed moral theology, explores human relationships, predicament and obligation involved in human action and accountability concerning God, humanity, and the world. Public and contemporary ethical questions force theologians and ethicists to meet their challenges in a theologically intensified manner.

Unity exists between systematic theology and the ethical realities of life, while ethical theology comprehends the basic theological-ethical problem in the interpersonal, social context and the publicly communicative realm. Given Rendtorf's ethical theology, I seek to advance ethical theology in connection with public theology in terms of public ethical theology. Public ethical theology brings theological reflection to contemporary problems and situations in terms of interdisciplinary dialogue, critical renewal, and mutual learning in a dynamic, creative, and continuous manner.

Faith in the tradition of the Reformation finds its full expression in ethics of discipleship and social *diakonia* which upholds and characterizes public ethical theology. Faith active in love seeks God's shalom, justice, and reconciliation in society and the world, protesting the unredeemed reality of lordless powers (Eph 6:12).

A social aspect of *diakonia* insists that God's salvific economy takes place in Christ's *diakonia* of reconciliation to the world. This train of thought may further seek to create a space for the subaltern to speak for themselves and for the church's emphatic listening to them, because such a train of thought suggests that God continues to work and speaks through the voice of the subaltern in today's world. This aspect underlying theological ethics of discourse sharpens a language of God from above and from below in light of God from the Other concerning race, gender, culture, and religion.

For further characterization of public ethical theology within the tradition of the Reformation, I include Calvin's theological deliberation

---

2. Rendtorff, *Ethics*, 1:7.

of ethics and Christian life. Calvin understands the divine law through the lens of Jesus Christ as the fulfillment and the end of the law. The Holy Spirit provides inward obedience to the meaning of the law, while strengthening ethical responsibility and renewing the human heart within. In Christian discipleship, the Holy Spirit mediates the death and resurrection of Christ to the life of believers in ethical terms of self-denial and cross-bearing. Advancing regeneration and justification, Calvin presents his ethical theology in relation to the Christian life.[3]

For Calvin, Christian freedom willingly observes the divine ethical commandments in obedience to God's will.[4] Christian freedom entails a freedom from indifference to any religious obligations, while preventing us from indifferently using outward things or arbitrarily avoiding their use.[5]

Furthermore, Calvin presents a theology of hope, in his meditation on the future life. A right estimate of the present life in light of Christ's resurrection leads us to meditate on the life to come, in right longing for eternal life, and in aspiration for it.[6] According to Calvin, hope invigorates faith again and again with perseverance and in terms of unremitting renewing and restoring.[7]

Given this, Moltmann places Calvin as the one allied with a theology of hope. Faith in Christ gives to hope its assurance, while hope gives to faith its breadth by leading it into life.[8] Calvin's ethical theology, imbued with eschatological hope, facilitates our understanding of his theology of predestination in a more qualified sense. This is because the reprobate are sometimes affected by almost the same feeling, guided under the power and efficacy of the Holy Spirit, as those predestined to salvation.[9] This aspect runs counter to an argument, according to which Calvin retained the distinction between the hidden and the revealed God, transforming the whole idea of God through his doctrine of predestination.[10]

---

3. Calvin, *Institutes of the Christian Religion*, 3.6–10 (1:684–725). Chung, *Christian Spirituality and Ethical Life*, 81–103.

4. Calvin, *Institutes of the Christian Religion*, 3.19.4 (1:836–37).

5. Ibid., 3.19.7 (1:838–39).

6. Ibid., 3.9.1–6 (1:712–19).

7. Ibid., 3.2.42 (1:590).

8. Moltmann, *Theology of Hope*, 20.

9. Calvin, *Institutes of the Christian Religion*, 3.1.11 (1:555).

10. Troeltsch, *Social Teaching of the Christian Churches*, 2:583.

Insofar as we desire the good, we must also desire a world in which that good reigns. Public ethical theology engaged in a practical and transformative construal of the world implies the construction of a better world in a moral and social context. In a theological context, the true meaning of "good" works becomes a social reality when they are performed on behalf of others, that is, for the good of the neighbors in the sense of *diakonia*. Good can be defined as a prophetic *diakonia* to the needy, having little to do with the hedonism of the religious individual. The teaching of justification by faith in the grace of Christ, sanctification, and reconciliation becomes a distinctive feature characterizing public ethical theology in relation to the discipleship of God's mission.

Furthermore, an ethical reflection of work as vocation within the Reformation tradition refers to a paradigm shift from the privilege of a special and spiritual calling to the activity of a secular calling. However, the division of labor in modern industrial production has transferred the meaning of work from individual vocation to the greater satisfaction of needs through a social relationship between the owner and the worker underlying an exchange value of the commodity. The work has been regarded as a form of alienation and exploitation, because money is central in the concrete expression of the self-determination of the employee. Nonetheless, work as vocation is the most indispensable factor in the social economic structuring of human life.[11]

In the ethical context, Luther's theology of the priesthood of all believers rejected the special vocation to the monastic life and affirmed the special value of lay life. Any special form of life as a privileged locus of the sacred is denied and a distinction between sacred and profane is eliminated. This aspect entails the affirmation of ordinary life as more than profane. Reaffirmation of daily life is a central locus for the fulfillment of God's purpose. The fullness of Christian existence was to be found within the activities of this life: in one's calling, marriage, family, politics, and the economic realm. In this light, Charles Taylor maintains that the entire modern development of the affirmation of ordinary life was foreshadowed and initiated in Reformation ethics.[12]

---

11. Rendtorff, *Ethics,* 2:46.
12. Taylor, *Sources of Self,* 218.

DISCIPLESHIP OF GOD'S MISSION AND GOD'S ECONOMY

If God's mission is conceptualized in a Trinitarian-economic sense, it must further take the form of God's salvific economy for the world. The real concern of theology—gospel—can be expressed in relation to the ethical commandment, in a critical, affirmative, and liberating manner. Theology makes itself understood and heard as it seeks and encounters humans in concrete ethical reality. This aspect strengthens a public ethics of vocation in the socioeconomic context concerning God and economic justice.

Considering public theology and discipleship of God's mission, I draw attention to developing a prophetic correlation between God's mission and God's *oikonomia* in light of God's act of speech through the church, the world, and in the otherness of the Other. The economic Trinity integrates the life of the household and economic realms into God's missional, redeeming history, emphasizing the public ethical dimension of God's mission. Economy (*oikonomia*) as the law or the management of the household is a compound of *oikos* (household) and *nomos* (law or management). *Oikos* as access to livelihood and its relationship to the living household include family, institution, market, state, and nature.[13]

According to Karl Polanyi, the market became the dominant force in the economy, thereby generating a market economy. Then it gave rise to another extreme development, a market society that denotes that a whole society was embedded in its own mechanism.[14] In a market society, exchange relationships replace all other social relationships. Thus the logic of accumulation and exchange invades and rules every dimension of life. Like an "invisible hand" the market works without a system of justice based on natural law. This refers to the self-regulating character of the economy implying the natural economic equilibrium. Market society based on the supply-demand-price mechanism has made God's *oikos* superfluous.

If economic realities influence our relationship to God, it suggests that unjust economic conditions would destroy the true worship of the triune God. If our concept of God influences our economic life, it suggests that worshipping God in distorted ways would contribute to the dehumanization of economic life. God's economy of the public household, which is foundational for the understanding of the church, is meant for

---

13. Meeks, *God the Economist*, 33.
14. Polanyi, *Livelihood of Man*, 9. Also see Meeks, *God the Economist*, 50.

people and the world. Public ethical theology has the task to serve the church's mission to contribute to the renewal of the economic system and structure in its current dehumanizing form and to promote the integrity of a life-enhancing direction in the ecological context.[15]

The Greek word *oikonomia* (economy), which combines *oikos* (household) with *nomos* (law or management), denotes the management of the public household. An ethics of vocation and discipleship, which requires a metaphor of God's mission as God's economy, finds it important to think of economic issues and participation in economic activity in light of the criterion of God's righteousness in Torah and Jesus Christ.[16] The issue of economy is an indispensable component in shaping and characterizing public ethical theology in relation to God and political economy, because economic existence is lived in the horizon of God's economy (Col 1:25; 1 Cor 9:17; Eph 3:2; 1 Tim 1:4).

This perspective challenges the notion of possessive individualism that is attached to the modern market society, which grounds the principle of modern economics on the abstract concept of the "individual" in the tradition of Thomas Hobbes, John Locke, and Adam Smith. God's mission concerning Christian eschatology and God's righteousness in Jesus Christ finds its sharp contour in ethical deliberation on God and economic justice.[17]

Ethical theology "must speak of a reformulation of the purpose of the ethics."[18] In this reformulation, Rendtorff contends that the christological mediation of love is determinative. Christian freedom enters into the service of the public sphere that God establishes with humanity.[19] Nonetheless, Rendtorff does not manage to refine a biblical theme of reconciliation as an ethical theme in terms of a practical and transformative construal and construction of social reality, which is in accordance with the ethics of discipleship, solidarity, and emancipation. His ethical theology remains in increasing our sensitivity to the world's problems.[20]

---

15. Meeks, *God the Economist*, 20, 27.
16. Ibid., 3.
17. Ibid, 11. Further see Duchrow and Hinkelammert, *Property*, 29–42.
18. Rendtorff, *Ethics*, 1:70.
19. Ibid., 70–71.
20. Ibid., 71.

However, if love as life in freedom and service can be understood as the realization of the highest good, this realization must uphold a practical engagement of Christian ethics for the reconstruction of social reality in light of God's reconciliation and eschatology. The ethical value of the eschaton in striving for God as the ultimate good in our present reality locates the *summum bonum*, the highest good underlying the imperative of public ethical theology confessing Jesus Christ in postcolonial World Christianity.

Given the eschatological foundation of theological ethics, I utilize a notion of public ethical theology by reconfiguring a hermeneutical theology of speech-event and God's economy in light of Christ's reconciliation in solidarity with those who are fragile, vulnerable, and poor. All the while, I incorporate history and social location as effecting human moral consciousness and reasoning for the sake of the fusion of horizons between the biblical narrative and social discourse of the Other in the world. Public ethical theology remains an undercurrent in refurbishing discipleship of God's mission through God's economy in light of God's speech-event in the reconciled world, while standing in expectation of the coming of the kingdom of God.

THE PLACE OF NATURE IN GOD'S CREATION

Globalized civilization is expanding and penetrating the whole of the global lifeworld through political power, the export of capital, and the global network of information through mass media. Human dominance of nature in the form of economic use and exploitation and its continuing use as a source of economic value to human life should be under ethical scrutiny regarding God's economy and ecology.

Nature as the environment for human life has been intensively appropriated and exploited by the development of scientific and technological culture. Ethical deliberation on technological control and exploitation of nature is a major component in characterizing public ethical discourse in terms of God's economy and our ecological stewardship. Nature and other living creatures find their place and dignity in God's Shalom as partners in companionship with humans.

The Bible sees humanity as rooted in nature, sharing finitude, creaturliness, and death with all other living creatures. It finally returns "to the ground, for out of it you were taken; you are dust, and to dust you shall return" (Gen 3:19). The breath of God's life was given "to every beast of the earth, and to every bird of the air, and to everything that creeps on the earth." (Gen 1:30). God gives "drink to every animal," and "the young lions roar for their prey, seeking their food from God" (Ps 104:11, 21). God's image is fulfilled in and transformed into the second Adam, Jesus Christ, the image of God. Noah's covenant includes God's universal covenant relationship with all living creatures and the earth.

The world of nature is driven by natural law and rhythms, and is open to God's promise and ongoing creativity. A theory of evolution and the earth's own system (its ecology) can be instituted, installed, and ordained for the service of the promise and freedom of God's act of speech in accordance to God's creation, covenant, and reconciliation in Christ. Insofar as ecology denotes the system itself in sustaining and enhancing life on earth, it may come from God's promise: "As long as the earth endures, seedtime and harvest, cold and heat, summer and winter, day and night, shall not cease" (Gen 8:22). God as alpha and omega includes God's final rest within creation (God may be all in all, 1 Cor 15:28), which is already projected in the protological sense of God's Sabbath. God's Sabbath as God's ecology articulates God's covenantal "yes" to all creatures through divine ongoing action (*creatio continua*), which is discovered in the dynamic rhythm and life-circle of the world. We are God's collaborators in God's ongoing creative activity.[21]

An ecological conscience integrates humanity as a part of nature, though God's special delight is in humanity (Prov 8:27–31). It is imperative to advance the ethical duty of sustaining and respecting the order and dignity of nature in light of God's ecology for the integrity of life and its life-enhancing culture.

A critical evaluation of technological activities is necessary in the ethical discussion of environmental problems regarding the economic application of scientific outcome and technological progress. Ethical significance is the precondition and guidance for moral evaluation of a scientific and technological culture and its related economic system and orientation. These must not be driven toward the domination or demise of nature. Rather, scientific progress and economic activity must

---

21. Peters, *God—The World's Future*, 141.

be understood as part of a living world for the sake of the integrity of life on earth.[22]

We recognize the God-givenness of all that is good. The Holy Spirit is invoked at the heart of the eucharistic prayer (epiclesis). We acknowledge that the Spirit animates and indwells both the bread and wine, underlying the heart of the Christian approach to the nonhuman creation.[23]

---

22. Rendtroff, *Ethics*, 2:154.
23. Gorriange, *Capital and the Kingdom*, 15.

10

Christian Social Ethics and Public Theology

CHRISTIAN SOCIAL ETHICS AND ITS CHARACTERIZATION

Given the relation between discipleship of God's mission and social ethics, it is important to examine Ernst Troeltsch's division of the social teaching of Christianity into church, sect, and mystic types. Ernst Troeltsch (1865–1923) can be regarded as a public theologian, who was involved in his social and political context in seeking to make the religious ethical contribution to the future course of history. His task was to bring the sociological significance of Christianity to its contemporary relevancy, while refusing to relegate its meaning only to the private, personal sphere.[1] In Troeltsch's investigation concerning the relation of the Christian ethos to the social environment, ethics regarded as the apex of theology entails a comprehensive horizon to shape the future afresh.[2] His approach is compared with Max Weber's sociological response to the problem of modernity.

Troeltsch's project is undertaken in the context of the whole religious, cultural situation of the time as well as through the standpoint of the historical consciousness. Religion should find concrete expression in the real world, because it is not separated from history. What matters is to examine the reciprocal relationship between Christianity and its social historical context. He is concerned with further development

---

1. Chapman, *Ernst Troeltsch and Liberal Theology*, 4–8. See further Gayhart, *The Ethics of Ernst Troeltsch*, 232.

2. Gayhart, *Ethics of Ernst Troeltsch*, 182.

of Christian thought and life in frank interaction with the forces of the modern world.³

Social and political context or the facts of modern world determined theological and ethical action, while theology could provide a realistic unified vision for the modern world by engaging in it. The modern world has created new foundations and presuppositions which are differentiated from the ecclesiastically unified period of European culture.⁴ This changed situation challenges Troeltsch to prepare for a new Christian ethic in terms of an all-embracing compromise in relation to the Enlightenment ideal of humanity.

Social ethical teaching of Christianity has been radically conditioned throughout its history in the different historical situations and environments in which Christianity has lived. Troeltsch focuses on analyzing the social ethics of the churches, because Christian social ethical teaching depends on the sociological conditions and concepts. This perspective undergirds essentially sociological-realistic-ethical outlook through compromise,⁵ which is also crucial in his study of social teaching of the Christian churches. Troeltsch develops such sociological method as a fundamental tool of interpretation in his historical study of social ethical teaching of churches.

For Troeltsch, the Enlightenment breaks through European culture dominated by the church and theology, undergirding "a complete reorientation of culture in all spheres of life."⁶ However, it is in part a religiously inspired process of liberation, which discovers the autonomous self-legislating individual as the most important feature of the modern world.⁷

According to Max Weber, a sociological method, based on the ideal-typical meaning, seeks to investigate the meaning of an individual's social action. For the method of the ideal type Weber maintains that there is selective affinity underlying connection between religious ideas, ethical conduct, and socio-economic stratification and development. This historical-sociological perspective does not explain all social religious development through consequences of idealist elements. It also takes issue with a unilateral materialist interpretation of cultural and historical causes.⁸

---

3. Troeltsch, *Social Teaching of the Christian Churches*, 1:19.
4. Ibid., 140.
5. Welch, *Protestant Thought in the Nineteenth Century*, 2:293.
6. Chapman, *Ernst Troeltsch and Liberal Theology*, 152.
7. Ibid., 153, 155–56.
8. M. Weber, "Protestant Asceticism and the Spirit of Capitalism," in *Selections in*

IDEAL TYPES AND THE CHURCH'S SOCIAL TEACHINGS

A methodological function of ideal types remains influential in Troetsch's study of social teaching of Christian churches along with the church-sect-mystic type distinction, which is central in his analysis of the historical process of compromise. The basic distinction of the three types of Christian church implies that the church type and its principle is universal, open, and in accommodation to the world through the communication of grace and salvation. Ascetic monasticism is incorporated into the system of the church type which includes it as a special element of religious achievement.

The church type is best represented in medieval Catholicism, while also characteristic of the main-line Reformation. The sect type seeks personal inward perfection and direct personal fellowship. It gives up the idea of dominating or incorporating the world and its social institution to itself in opposition to the state and society. Asceticism in the sect type is expressed in the detachment from the world. Mysticism is an instance of direct inward and personal experience rather than a type of social organization. Forming groups on a purely personal basis, mysticism tends to weaken the significance of forms of worship, doctrine and the historical element.[9]

The church-sect-mysticism distinction shapes Troeltsch's social teaching to present the whole of Christian history for the understanding of the social teachings of the gospel, the early church, the Middle Ages, and the post-Reformation confessions in relation to the formation of the new situation in the modern world.[10] Church, sect, and mysticism have appeared alongside one another and interwoven through the whole history of Christianity.

Similar to Weber's evaluation of Puritan Calvinism, Troeltsch insists that Calvinism in its form of ascetic Protestantism had attained comprehensive historical significance, and created a completely comprehensive social ethic. It became more systematic, uniform, and rigorous than all previous theories.[11] A Calvinist type of comprehensive historical significance and influence which Troeltch envisions as a normative Christian

---

Translation, 172.

9. Troeltsch, *Social Teaching of the Christian Churches*, 2:993.

10. Ibid., 1:25.

11. Ibid., 2:603.

ethic is grounded in the fusion between the church and sect ideal types through the practicality of compromise.[12]

In the modern world Christian social teaching has faced an extremely difficult situation, because Christianity must seek free spirituality and adaptability of the church without the compelling guarantees of ecclesiasticism.[13] As the old Christian ethic was a compromise, so any ethical compromise has to take place in the conditions of the modern world. Indeed, we have to make a new synthesis valid for the present.

Nowhere does there exist an absolute Christian ethic, which only awaits to be discovered, nor an absolute ethical transformation of material life or human nature. What matters is a constant wrestling and struggling with the problems. A Christian ethic of the present day and the future will also only be an adjustment to the world-situation, desiring to achieve what is practically possible.[14]

In the interaction between the Christian ethos and sociological forms, Troeltsch strives to engender the constructive task of public ethical renewal, in which the critical study of history provides vital information about how to achieve a constructive synthesis as a creative act in the present. A longing for universally valid laws can be found only in religion.[15]

HISTORICAL RELATIVISM AND ETHICAL INVOLVEMENT

The entire domain of the ethical standard is relative, since it is embedded within the historicism based on the triadic principle of critique, analogy, and correlation. The principle of critique places all tradition and materials under critical examination and scrutiny through the historian's critical reason. The principle of analogy facilitates the historical critic to discern analogy between events in the past and events in the present. An analogical critique can be undertaken in the sense of similarity in the historical activities of human beings, despite its difference. The principle of correlation pays attention to interconnection between all happenings and events

---

12. Gayhart, *Ethics of Ernst Troeltsch*, 202.
13. Troeltsch, *Social Teaching of the Christian Churches*, 1:381
14. Ibid., 2:1013.
15. Chapman, *Ernst Troeltsch and Liberal Theology*, 158.

in historical life. Knit together in embracing correlation, all is made relative embedded within the correlation and interconnection.[16]

However, it does not necessarily mean a rampant and aimless relativism, that is, denial of the values appearing in the individual configurations. But it refers to relativity implying that all historical phenomena are unique and individual configurations acted on by influences from a universal context. This historical influence comes to bear on all historical phenomena and individual configurations in varying degree of immediacy.[17]

According to Troeltsch, "there is no absolute ethical transformation of material or human nature; so current and future Christian ethics will be adapted to the situation and will pursue only what is possible."[18] Thus the ethical work will never be completed. In the mutual interpenetration of the chief sociological categories, the central life of the church type is permeated with other categories of the sect and mysticism. Thus these categories are united and reconciled in the future task.[19]

A particular significance of historical relativism for Christian social ethics is expressed in terms of compromise which describes the historically inevitable relationship and accommodation of Christianity to its historical and social context in different epochs and situations. Compromise also refers to "the phenomenology of involvement,"[20] whose task is to think through and formulate independently the Christian world of ideas and life, in terms of unreserved and practical involvement in the modern world.[21] It seeks to interpret the development of medieval Catholicism out of the initial radical impulse of the gospel and the kingdom of God. Compromise as the phenomenology of involvement can be seen in the Reformers' protest against medieval Catholicism, while continuing to do the process of Christianity in their own ways. Even the sect in protest against compromise cannot escape such a historical process. A new comprehensive union of the church-sect-mysticism categories lies in an all-

---

16. Welch, *Protestant Thought*, 2:281–89.
17. Ibid., 298.
18. Troeltsch, *Social Teaching of the Christian Churches*, 2:1013.
19. Ibid., 2:1009.
20. Reist, *Toward a Theology of Involvement*, 161.
21. Ibid., 17.

embracing synthesis for the future. Religion should be placed at the heart of ethical life in Troeltsch's vision of public theology.

For Troeltsch, the ethos of the gospel as an ideal cannot be realized without the dialectic between compromise and involvement. Christian ethos is a constantly renewed search for the compromise in involvement with historical and social context, while providing a fresh opposition to the spirit of compromise and engagement.[22] Compromise shapes an ethical task for the present time in seeking a new Christian ethic, as seen in light of historical relativism.[23] The complexity and diversity of ethics in our world is essentially incapable of completion and is open-ended. But it is always searchable and practicable in each new case.[24]

This aspect paves a way to recognition of religious and ethical pluralism. There is a religious and ethical pluralism even within Christianity. Christian social ethics will be shaped and developed in the interpreter's engagement with the whole of Christian history, while its content will be presented at different times and from different standpoints. Christian social ethics is in the making, remaining a creative act through faith, which is expressed in ethical decisions in an act of responsible decision. Christian social ethics will be made anew as a creative act, because an ethical assertion of validity remains relative for us in the particular present.[25]

According to Troeltsch, there is something of permanent value which serves the present in the content of the Christian ethos. In the varied history of the Christian social doctrines, there are the conviction of personality and individuality; a socialism through the idea of the inclusive divine love; a way of resolving the problem of equality and inequality through the values of mutual recognition, confidence, and care for others; a charity that is indispensable in any social order; and a goal, in the idea of the kingdom of God, for social life and aspiration that lies far beyond all the relativities of this earthly life.[26]

---

22. Troeltsch, *Social Teaching of the Christian Churches*, 2:999–1000.
23. Ibid., 2:1001–2.
24. Welch, *Protestant Thought*, 2:299.
25. Ibid., 301.
26. Troeltsch, *Social Teaching of the Christian Churches*, 2:1004–5.

CRITICAL REFLECTION: PUBLIC ETHICAL THEOLOGY AND SOCIAL INVOLVEMENT

A social ethics in the fashion of Troeltsch is driven by correlation between religious idea and its social and historical context, because the whole Christian world of thought and dogma depends on the fundamental sociological conditions. The Christian ethos based on the idea of the future kingdom of God provides all social life and aspiration with a goal which goes far beyond all the relativities of this earthly life.

However, Troeltsch is excessively attached to religious individualism and historical relativism within the European ideal of Enlightenment and humanity. He relegates an idea of the kingdom of God to Christian asceticism in opposition to all social utopias. The kingdom of God is within us. Thus, the Christian ethic can be a form of adjustment and accommodation to the world situation,[27] rather than renewing and transforming its status quo in light of the gospel about the kingdom of God: a new heaven and earth. Driven by the Enlightenment principle of the autonomous individual, Troeltsch's search for the possibility of a single unifying principle implies that autonomy is related to freedom and responsibility. In other words, this refers to human participation in divine creativity, that is, "autonomy and theonomy become one in divine love."[28] However, I contend that divine love reconciling autonomy with theonomy must be sought in accordance with the righteousness and peace of the kingdom of God on earth underlying Christian ethics of discipleship.

Furthermore, Troeltsch's historical critical method needs to be rearticulated by including a critical question of the historian's standpoint concerning his or her own social location as well as proposing a prophetic and social critical dimension of the biblical message. The principles of critique, analogy, and correlation are to be comprehended in a qualified sense by incorporating social discourse of power-knowledge interplay as well as material economic formation, which, in turn, shape and condition religious institution and its ethos.

The kingdom of God must be neither confused with the establishment of a just society on earth without reservation, nor with relegating it to the inwardness of Christian individualism. Nonetheless, it is not indifferent to the society. The announcement of the gospel about the coming

---

27. Ibid., 1013.
28. Chapman, *Ernst Troeltsch and Liberal Theology*, 165.

kingdom of God inspires the church and the world for a just society in relation to the promise and hope of communion of all with God. YHWH is a God of life also a God of justice and righteousness (Amos 5:24; Isa 1:16; Jer 22:15–16).

A public ethical deliberation of social justice and reconciliation undergirds an ethics of discipleship and involvement through transformative construal of the world. It is connected with a critical analysis of social, political, cultural and economic formation and structure in the yet unredeemed reality of the world, which stands in expectation of the coming of the kingdom of God.

Furthermore, a public ethical theology emphasizes the living dynamism of the gospel and promotes the hermeneutical dialogue with the world and people in ways that God continues to work on and sustain lives of people and nature in the universal horizon of the Holy Spirit. A biblical notion of God's act of speech (*dabar*) integrates the natural and moral law of people in all different contexts in light of God's reconciliation. God's creation and its integrity are fulfilled in God's reconciliation with the world in Christ. It is certain that reconciliation does not overwrite the eschatology, because the world is still in an unredeemed reality under the reality of lordless powers, waiting for the final consummation. This view challenges a dialectic between compromise to and involvement with world-situation through adjustment and accommodation, rather it proposes a public ethical theology which is driven by God's social-economic concern for the world in terms of God's act of speech, particularly in solidarity, emancipation, and recognition of the Other.

Given this, it is important to support interdisciplinary interaction in studies of ethical theology, culture, religion, and socioeconomic realm for the sake of a thick description of gospel about God's mission. This endeavor facilitates Christian ethics of discipleship in faithfulness to mission of God's kingdom in terms of listening to those on the margins and their voices under the dominion of Empire.

Neoliberal globalization, whose outcome is the total market, has the sole goal of removing all social and ecological barriers for expanding and globalizing the accumulation of the capital and establishing world-market society. The neo-liberal ideology of the absolute market is presented as the only option and its empire appears as the invisible hand of the absolute possessive market.[29]

In fidelity to the invisible hand, ethics is reduced to the functional ethics of market action which undercuts the interventional and regulating actions of the government for the common good. Furthermore, Max Weber's view of capitalism in rational terms remains naïve in its ramification of cutting loose the irrationality of the market society. In a distinction between conviction ethics and responsibility ethics Weber bases the conviction ethics on the biblical brotherhood ethics, which remains in the individual decision, while the responsibility ethics paradoxically implies legitimization of institutionalized irresponsibility.

Weber's notion of responsibility ethics in relation to conviction ethics finds its place only in the personality of the solitary individual, who is a parliamentarian charismatic leader in the world of politics.[30] This preference for a few heroic individuals might support a nihilism of politics, which would allow for the charismatic leader in non-democratic, authoritative manner. Such an aspect has parallels with Troeltsch's social teaching based on religious individualism and ethical significance in relation to historical relativism, which undertakes ethical reconstruction on the basis of the European ideal of humanity in universally realizable manner. However, his ethics of compromise discourages an ethic of engagement and solidarity through a transformative construal and construction of the world as exploring ethics of discipleship in expectation of and participation in a society-renewing horizon of the kingdom of God in the sociopolitical and cultural realm. An ethic of social engagement and solidarity in this regard is needed by starting from the standpoint of the victims of the globalized system.[31]

Given this, a dimension of discourse ethics—telling the truth of the gospel in light of God's economy in the area of political economy and creating a space for and solidarity with those on the margins and innocent victims—occupies a central place in the public ethical project of God's economy and solidarity in postcolonial World Christianity.

Insofar as Christian ethics is concerned with fullness of life, economics is at the heart of public ethical concern for the control of the pro-

---

29. Duchrow and Hinkelammert, *Property*, 107.
30. Chung, *Hermeneutical Self and an Ethical Difference*, 152.
31. Duchrow and Hinkelammert, *Property*, 107, 160.

duction of wealth for choosing life against the death culture of Moloch. In the struggle for fullness of life the church is summoned to take a stance on the side of the God of life against the culture of mammon based on greed, power, violence, and dominion.[32]

---

32. Gorringe, *Capital and the Kingdom*, 170.

11

Ethical Hermeneutics, Discourse Ethics, Moral Plurality

E THICAL REFLECTION BEGINS WITH the givenness of life embedded within tradition, history, language, and social world. The life history of an individual becomes the context for ethical reflection to unfold in the public forms of social world. An ethical norm is responsibility for the concrete reality of human life history rather than remaining timeless norms and laws of conduct prior to social life. This chapter is a study of hermeneutical relevance to practical moral reasoning and discourse ethics based on communicative rationality in relation to social, cultural life setting embedded with plurality, diversity, and difference.

PHILOSOPHICAL HERMENEUTICS AND MORAL REASONING

Hans G. Gadamer makes an issue of understanding relevant to Aristotelian ethics. In the Kantian framework, the logical basis of judgment subsumes a particular under a universal and recognizes something as an example of a rule. Thus judgment requires a principle to guide its application of the rule to a particular context in a universal manner. However, the logical basis of judgment cannot be demonstrated and taught in the abstract, because it can only be practiced from case to case. What matters is not the application of the universal but internal coherence. Kant calls it reflective judgment or aesthetic judgment. This judgment is understood according to real and formal appropriateness.[1]

However, according to Gadamer, Aristotle shows a reflection to break through the limitation of Kant. It is certain that Aristotle is not concerned with the hermeneutical problem and its historical dimension. Rather, Aristotle tried to estimate the role that reason plays in moral action. Reason and knowledge according to Aristotle are not detached from a being that is becoming, but determined by it while they also are determinative of being in becoming. In contrast to Plato who sees the idea of the good as an empty generality, Aristotle considers this codetermination by questioning what is humanly good or what is good in terms of human action. The basis of moral knowledge in human is striving and its development into a fixed demeanor. Aristotle grounds the good on practice and ethos, so that his ethics indicates such an aspect. Encountering the good in the form of the particular practical situation, the task of moral knowledge is regarded as that which determines what the concrete situation asks of the acting person. When knowledge cannot be applied to the concrete situation, it remains meaningless and even obscures what the situation calls for. Such ethical perspective demonstrates a methodologically difficult problem because ethics is not capable of achieving the extreme exactitude of mathematics.[2]

Likewise, the hermeneutical problem is clearly distinct from pure knowledge which is detached from any particular kind of being. It is because the interpreter belongs to the tradition that he or she is interpreting and understanding itself is a historical event. Moral knowledge is not standing over a situation that a person merely observes, rather the knower is confronted with what he or she sees in the particular context. Hence Aristotle makes a distinction between moral knowledge (*phronēsis*) and theoretical knowledge (*epistēmē*). Knowledge of the particular situation is necessary to supplement moral knowledge. The moral task of application or correlate between understanding and context is also central to the problem of hermeneutics.[3]

For Aristotle, sympathetic understanding stands beside *phronēsis*, the virtue of thoughtful reflection. Understanding is seen as a modifi-

---

1. Gadamer, *Truth and Method*, 31.
2. Ibid., 312–13.
3. Ibid., 315.

cation of the virtue of moral knowledge. Given this, Gadamer incorporates Aristotle's analysis of virtue of moral knowledge to the problem of hermeneutics. In reading a traditional text, for Gadamer, the text is not given as something universal, so that the reader understands it per se, while afterward using it for particular application. Against this mechanical application, Gadamer argues that the interpreter seeks to understand the text and what it says, and what constitutes the text's meaning and significance. In so doing, the interpreter relates his or her particular hermeneutical situation to the text. The interpreter's own thought plays a role in re-awakening the text's meaning for the sake of fusion of horizons between the text and the reader.[4]

We understand the text in a different way, because in all understanding the efficacy of history is at work. For Gadamer, language is the universal medium in which understanding takes place, in other words, understanding transpires in interpreting. The linguistic dimension of understanding is the concretion of historically effected consciousness.[5] Projecting a historical horizon is overtaken by our own present horizon of understanding (incorporating our proleptic expectation or hope). In this process a real fusing of horizons occurs. As the historical horizon is projected, it is also superseded. A concept of historically effected consciousness is to bring about this fusion in a regulated manner.[6]

Furthermore, in dialogue with the text or the Other we expand our own horizon and particular vantage point, opening up new horizons in an open-ended manner. This is because knowledge of oneself in hermeneutical and historical sense can never be complete, thus it is driven in an open-ended manner. Hermeneutical situation acquires the right horizon of inquiry for the questions which is raised and evoked by the encounter with tradition and in a conversation with the Other in the social location. Gadamer's hermeneutics paves a way of acknowledging the otherness of the Other involving the fundamental understanding of the truth. This is hermeneutical conversation,[7] which provides an insight to break through the limitation of historical-critical method and its ethical orientation in Troeltsch's sense.

4. Ibid., 324. 388.
5. Ibid., 301, 388–89.
6. Ibid., 307.
7. Ibid., 304.

Gadamer's contribution lies in bridging the hermeneutical self with moral reasoning. A theory of interpretation in a linguistic and ontological manner correlates with a philosophy of morality. Appreciating this correlation, I further argue that this integration needs to be sharpened in the project of interpretive reasoning as it engages with communicative rationality and anamnestic reason in remembrance upon the reality of the innocent victim and mass suffering in the past and the present. In hermeneutical conversation with the Other, a fusion of horizons should incorporate the otherness in regard to social, cultural, and political-economic location.

Thus *phronēsis* can be social-critically sought in archeological reasoning concerning the social history irregularized and buried. I perceive public ethical theology in terms of transformative construal of the world, by attending religious moral background and orientation embedded with sociohistorical setting and condition. This aspect finds it substantial to seek to develop a social biographical approach to ethics by attending to the ideological aspect of distorted dialogue or communication (Habermas) and the interplay of discourse between knowledge and power (Foucault) that Gadamer ignores.

DISCOURSE ETHICS AND COMMUNICATION RATIONALITY

The question "what is good" is to be sought under the giveness of life in a social historical context. Ethical reflection anticipates community, and involves communication in reality as ordinary conversation. An anticipation of community is achieved through the development of the capacity to communicate with others.

Circumscribing Gadamer's hermeneutics, Habermas's discourse ethics based on communicative rationality has contributed to a sociological understanding of morality in terms of a double framework of lifeworld and system. His discourse-communicative ethics provides a critique of ideology (communicatively distorted language and discourse). It also refines self-reflection of emancipation and undergirds a social critical deliberation of public ethics in taking a stance for lifeworld against system as steered by money, politics, and mass media. In the framework of system, language becomes a medium for domination and social power, hence ideological. The process of emancipation aims at revealing and overcoming the system of systematically distorted communication in critical reflection of dominion and power in a given society.[8] Habermas presents his ethic of discourse within the universalist framework of communicative rationality. He refers to morality as the foundational question of right and wrong in the Kantian sense while the term 'ethical' refers to the question of living a good life in a particular time and place to the common good. Habermas differentiates the issue of the moral from evaluative, ethical issue for a good life.[9]

He also provides an important insight for public theology, because civil society entails the plurality of institutions, associations, movements emerging out of the lifeworld. Religion, speech, and association are important realms for undergirding civil society. Religious community and ethical norms can be seen and in the social space of communication, in which religious community and ethical practice are advanced through the public process of interpretation and through network for communication, information, and consensus. Religious discourse is asked to be free of all forms of coercion, dominion, and authority in search for communicative reason and action. Habermas' perspective helps religious community concerning whether it is on the side of lifeworld or the system. The unfortunate alliance between the altar and the crown in the Christian tradition needs to be critically analyzed for the sake of the prophetic, ethical factor.[10]

Nonetheless, Habermas tends to confine plurality of lifeworlds and moral difference to the universal of communicative rationality still in Kantian framework. It remains a barrier to incorporating the different horizon of moral theory to communicative consensus. Habermas's assumption of the justification of the principle of universalization as a rule of argumentation shows a lack of taking seriously the discourse of those unfit, deviated, and underprivileged in the public sphere.

Ethical reflection derived from communication constitutes the public nature of one's personal life. We are born in our locality and our own language. Underlying one's consciousness and ethical orientation is primarily one's history, tradition, social world, and language as the site

---

8. Habermas, *Theory of Communicative Action*, 2:119.
9. Habermas, *Justification and Application*, 8, 117.
10. Chung, *Cave and the Butterfly*, 101.

of effect. This perspective seeks to redefine and renew moral theory, by contextualizing qualitatively universal–linguistic reason in terms of an archeological, hermeneutical reasoning and its sociobiographical practice: in terms of appropriation of one's local tradition, critical distance from its provincial and even parochial element and backwardness, and reconstruction of one's moral and ethical theory in emphatic listening to the life narrative of the Other.

Driven in this archeological-hermeneutical fashion, I frame public ethical theology in a practical and transformative construal of the world concerning change of its course, moral self, justice, and goodness. It also considers diversity, difference, and plurality. Thus, justice based on a categorical imperative should not overwrite "the moral" over "the ethical" or relegate the moral to a domain significantly narrower than the ethical.[11] If modern moral theory endeavors to define the moral domain by giving priority to the domain of justice over questions of the good life, the goods underlying modern moral theory (freedom, justice, and universalism) have become hypergoods. Hypergoods are goods from whose standpoint other goods must be evaluated, judged, and decided about.[12] Thus hypergoods are generally a source of conflict and tension.

Regarding the relationship between moral norms and life goods, I am interested in developing such a dialectical relationship between "the moral" and "the ethical" in relation to God's speech-event and the Other. The sense of the good has to be woven into one's understanding of one's life as an unfolding social story and discourse in hermeneutical dialogue with the Other.

DIVERSITY, PLURALITY, AND DIFFERENCE

Ethics implies a tradition. A way of life includes a specific world view and ethos which are influenced by the history, tradition, and culture. It is also mediated socially and culturally through the universal-particular medium of language. It is important to establish tradition as a necessary step in the process of forming ethical judgment. Nonetheless, we act for good moral reasons, not only according to traditional norm or convention, but also to social material life formation.

11. Taylor, *Sources of the Self*, 64.
12. Ibid., 63. Chung, *Hermeneutical Self and Ethical Difference*, 157.

A fusion of horizons can be performed in many more ways than Gadamer expects. First, it transpires in correlation or interplay between tradition and one's historical consciousness in reading and understanding the classic texts. In the process of understanding, one's historically effected consciousness is co-shaped by one's place in social location in which language as social discourse (power, knowledge, and dominion) influences and also distorts one's identity. It is also conditioned by socio-economic formation through labor, capital, and market. Religion is not merely subsumed under institution or material life formation. Diversity, difference, and plurality in religious cultural worldviews are important factors in shaping and characterizing our understanding of morality and religious ethics in a comparative manner.

A deliberation of God's speech-event imbued with *creatio continua* in the universal horizon of the Holy Spirit has a task to incorporate moral theory and religious ethical orientation in different places and times by appreciating their contribution, renewing their limitation, and installing their place on behalf of respect of integrity of life, responsibility, reconciliation, and solidarity. Here, responsibility, reconciliation, solidarity, and emancipation remain crucial to an approach to the public ethical theology through practical, transformative construal of the world in linguistic, creational, and emancipatory terms. God speaks and the human responds in diverse, different, and plural lifeworlds.

We live in a plurality of social words, driven by the midst of global complexity, confusion, and whirl. An ethics of peace, compassion, justice, and the integrity of life in a global-ecumenical context can be developed by learning from moral and ethical sources of great religious traditions which facilitates improving on the inadequacy and limitation of Westerncentric ethics based on ideal of Enlightenment and the autonomous individual.

According to Troeltsch, Christianity among the great religions is comprehended as "the strongest and most concentrated revelation of personalistic religious apprehension."[13] It is not only the culmination point but also the convergence point of all the developmental tendencies, synthesizing separate tendencies and suggestions into one common goal.[14] Although Christianity is "the focal synthesis of all religious tendencies

---

13. Troeltsch, *Absoluteness of Christianity*, 112.
14. Ibid., 114, 112.

and the disclosure of what is in principle a new way of life,"[15] we cannot prove that it will always remain the final culmination point. Absolute truth belongs to the future appearing in the judgment of God.[16] Thus, Troeltsch is reluctant to affirm the idea of Christianity as the culmination or convergence point, because the absolute lies beyond history.

Troeltsch's final position is expressed in the 1923 lecture on the place of Christianity among the world religions (delivered at the University of Oxford). He argues that Christianity is a thoroughly historical, individual, and relative phenomenon, which has arisen among the Latin and Germanic races. Other religions such as Buddhism and Brahmanism are also humane and spiritual religions. In their historical individuality they ensure the inner certitude and devotion to their followers, like Christianity appeals to its followers.[17] Christianity only entails validity for Christians, while other religious groups can also affirm their experience of the divine life just as valid as Christianity.

This perspective on religion in terms of religious individualism and historical relativism sidesteps that no historical situation could be understood except in its own terms grounded on the social situation of thought. Religion is an eminently social and cultural entity, implementing its spiritual and cognitive meaning. Spiritual experience of religion or its social ethical teaching is embedded within a sociohistorical framework. Religions exist because human beings exist only as social beings and in a humanly shaped world,[18] though it is expressed in diverse ways concerning social and ethical teaching.

Religion as a sociocultural reality entails an epistemic system of religious knowledge, institutionalization, and world-building. All the while, such an epistemic system is intertwined with church-sacramental, mystic-spiritual, moral-prophetic, eschatological, and apocalyptic motives. This view complements and overcomes a historical-critical study of religion merely based on religious individualism and historical relativism.

Religions have resources for ethics in the time of many worlds, underlying a construal of the world in different sociohistorical settings for moral aspirations. In the context of Christianity a correlation between

15. Ibid., 114.
16. Ibid., 115.
17. Welch, *Protestant Thought* 2:288.
18. Durkheim, *Elementary Forms of Religious Life*, xix.

creation, Torah, and the responsibility for the Other remains an undercurrent in Jesus's gospel on the coming kingdom of God in bringing good news to the poor, proclaiming release to the captives, healing the sick, and feeding the hungry. The Sermon on the Mount provocatively insists that God makes all the goods like rain and sunshine on the undeserving folks, even the evil doer and the unrighteous (Matt 5:45). Creation and God's reign provide a moral space as they link to God's reconciliation and ongoing activity in those outside the churchly sphere, especially in light of God's act of speech.

Given this, a comparative religious ethics has the task to respecting the integrity of life, enhancing the imperative of ethical responsibility, recognizing the moral value and dignity of the Other and their contribution to moral value, peace, justice, and integrity of creation.

The biblical notion of creation implies a pluralist reality, related to abundance and fecundity and the integrity of life.[19] A correlation between creation and God's reconciliation remains a fulcrum for a concept of moral goodness more amenable for an age of religious pluralism and the co-existence among religious communities. Moral diversity implies the ethical challenge of pluralism, offering an opportunity to reflect and deepen the multidimensional meaning of diversity in terms of moral theory and religious ethics. Responsibility and reconciliation make the interreligious dialogue an opportunity for creating moral space in a broader global spectrum.

In our experience of society we engage in differing worlds. Plurality and complexity become significant concepts for understanding our social nature and ethical reflection. The life story and social biography of an individual can be comprehended as the history of relations with the Other. In such a biographical approach we share the reality of the everyday world with others. The world is already constituted as a social entity, which shapes a background for any specific actions, intentions, or moral obligations.[20] The social structure of reality articulates that ethical subjectivity can be framed in interaction with the Other: Ethical self-in-the-world-with the Other. This offers a basis for construing Christian ethics as publically oriented and socially engaged ethics.

---

19. Schweiker, *Theological Ethics and Global Dynamics*, 31.
20. Berger and Luckmann, *Social Construction of Reality*, 28.

In openness to differing interpretations of moral theory, I seek to unearth the narratives and discourses of the Other as marginalized, foreclosed, and unproblematized in the construal and construction of social reality. Terms such as plurality, complexity, and irregularity characterize a postcolonial character of public ethics in the context of World Christianity.

Norm and situation do not appear as an alternative, but they can be refined and deepened in hermeneutical-ethical correlation in a practical, transformative construal of the world and in construction of social reality. A stalemate between normative ethics and situation ethics can be broken through a sociobiographical approach to publically framed ethics in a hermeneutical and archeological formation concerning plurality, complexity, and irregularity.

12

Moral Deliberation, Sociocultural Embeddeness, and Emancipation

IN PRESENTING PUBLICALLY FRAMED and socially engaged ethics, it is important to hermeneutically mediate moral norms and ethical life with social cultural reality. Here social discourse, narrative of innocent victims, dialogue, and emphatic listening play a central role in practically shaping and transformatively driving ethics in terms of God's act of speech underlying discipleship of God's mission through God's economy concerning the kingdom of God. Public debates shape the social character of theological ethics concerning the daily ethical discourse, goals of human actions, and responsibility in a given society or faith community. Faith in this regard begins with the question of its relationship to life.[1]

Given this, it is important to incorporate social cultural and ethnic factors such as ethnicity, culture, gender, and language into our undertaking of publically oriented and socially engaged ethics, because these elements are crucial in influencing one's moral deliberation and orientation. Gospel is embodied in our sociocultural and political economic life context, calling for new and creative interpretation of it in a different time and a particular context. An attempt to restructure ethnic ethics argues that morality is socially, historically, and culturally shaped and constructed.

---

1. Ebeling, *Dogmatik des christlichen Glaubens* 1:79.

ETHNICITY, RACE, AND BLACK THEOLOGY

A sociology of religion such as that of Emile Durkheim emphasizes a social embeddedness of ethical conduct, because human nature is basically social. Insofar as the morality can be found in the structure of society and in social relations, ethnic background, gender roles, religious orientation, cultural value system, and socioeconomic status need to be considered and articulated in the construction of ethnic ethics. A notion of ethnic ethic in the fashion of Durkheim's sociology of religion views morality as a social fact.[2]

However, I am more interested in analyzing social factors in terms of discourse in the power-knowledge-nexus imbued with archeological hermeneutics, which aims at rewriting the irregularized and foreclosed side of history and society. It promotes a public ethical project of recognition of the ethnicity of the Other, while advancing theological humanism based on the humanity of God in Jesus, and emancipation. Insofar as language is of analogical implication in terms of similarity-in-difference, I argue that our current history and society, as seen in light of *similarity*, must be also comprehended and challenged in an archeological rewriting of the *dissimilarity* of the marginalized history concerning ethnicity, race, and inequality. This archeological hermeneutic entails an emancipatory horizon of the hermeneutical circle through long route via social critical science, critique of dominating discourse, political hegemony, world-economy, while taking issue with hierarchically institutionalized religious discourse.

People in the United States are inclined to use the terms race and ethnicity in everyday conversations as functionally synonymous or interchangeable. Race emphasizes biological connection with a group while ethnicity articulates cultural connections within the same group.[3] Ethnic identity is more complex than racial categories, because it is rooted in a wider variety of characteristics. Language and religion may be considered indispensable components of the ethnic identity. Ethnicity changes with people's interests and context in which ethnic identities are shaped, expressed, and maintained in response to social cultural and political economic circumstances. Likewise, ethnicity is conditioned through linguistic, cultural, and social markers.

The marginalized ethnic individuals begin with less access to occupation, education, and power by virtue of who they are. An unequal distri-

---

2. Cortese, *Ethnic Ethics*, 2.
3. Meneses, "Science and the Myth of Biological Race," 33–46.

bution of social sources constitutes social stratification which means the organization of people into ranked groups, or hierarchies. In varying degrees in all societies, social stratification is related to social inequality, which implies more the differential access to economic resources, political powers or social prestige resulting from stratification. Given this, race is also a cultural category which divides the human race into subspecies in terms of biological differences. Racial category exists as a powerful social one which continues to be used to support social inequality and other phenomena. Race correlates with social problems such as unemployment, violence, and imprisonment. It is indicated in high percentages of Black and Hispanic people, the majority of whom are poor in comparison with white people in the United States. A concept of ethnic ethics challenges racial hierarchies and repudiates race as a valid scientific category. It also values and celebrates the cultural diversity which affects moral reasoning and orientation.

History as effect should not be left behind in the sociological and anthropological approach to ethnic ethics. Insofar as ethnic background affects moral reasoning and moral judgment, cultural-religious background plays a major role in underscoring social economic stratification of ethnic groups, social classes, and genders. Ethnic and cultural differences in moral reasoning and judgment come into an encounter with historical, religious background and diversities. A universal ethical system in the Kantian sense can be corrected and renewed in terms of social analysis of ethnicity and the hermeneutical notion of self, being-in-the-world of the other. Western colonial misrepresentation or universalization needs to be countered by the ethnic endeavor of re-presenting or re-writing its own moral tradition, history, and virtue.[4]

A Black theology of liberation or a theology of African-American Christian consciousness raises the important place of Black experience and the wounds of racial violence in the religious meaning of the African American struggle for justice and wholeness. The racial identity and experience constitute a correlation with the theological norm of the Word of God or revelation: "I was black before I was Christian."[5] A theology of African-American Christian consciousness seeks to "rethink African American theology in light of the common practices and experience of generations of black Christians."[6]

4. Chung, *Hermeneutical Self and an Ethical Difference*, 259–60.
5. Cone, *Cross and the Lynching Tree*, xvii
6. Noel and Johnson, eds., *Passion of the Lord*, vii.

African-American interaction with the biblical narrative, especially the story of Christ's passion and its theological expression are deeply rooted and embedded in real, concrete horror and terror which was suffered in Middle Passage, slavery, Jim Crow, lynchings, and other acts of oppression and racial violence. This theological form incorporates the rich religious heritage and spiritual and social experience of African-Americans to its hermeneutic of refusal of white dominant culture and appreciation of black identity by not only illuminating African-American culture but also contributing to the universal struggle with evil through God's redemptive action in Christ.[7] Here theological ethics becomes a form of struggle and liberation correlated with God's love and justice revealed in Christ's forsaken suffering.

Language is not merely historically mediated, but also socially, culturally, and racially discoursed when it is embedded within dominion, knowledge, and ethnicity. Language as social discourse, seen in the sociohistorical and diverse cultural settings, can become social episteme or cultural framework. Morality, understood within a particular cultural and sociohistorical context, is inseparably related to language as communication and social discourse. Language is crucial to the teaching of morality, thus language-morality-correlation upholds that no knowledge is value-free. In other words, truth is seen in reference to a particular sociohistorical standpoint. Moral theory, seen in this regard, affirms that each group retains its own moral and language system. Subcultural groups which are based on ethnicity, race, gender, or religion underpin different and even contradictory systems of morality and ethical thought as compared to the dominant group.

A concept of ethnic ethics and moral reason cannot be politically neutral, because it reflects on the concrete life connection and reality of social situation. Ethnic identity and ethnic diversity are part of God's creation. In Revelation 7:9, we read that every nation, tribe, people and language worship God before the throne.

---

7. Ibid, vii.

FEMINIST CRITIQUE, CULTURALLY CODED TEXT, PATRIARCHY

Christian interpretation of human nature or natural law sees human nature as created divinely and directed to certain goods recognizable by reason. This ethical aspect provides a realist approach to morality and seeks common ground with other religious and philosophical traditions. This natural-law ethics assumes that natural and intelligible goods orient virtuous activity in the practical realms of life and all culture shares such disposition.

However, a new emphasis on the historical production of knowledge takes issue with the biblical teaching of sexual life, patriarchy, and its morality as naturally given and fixed. It raises the question whether biblical writings on patriarchy, homosexuality, monogamy, gender, and divorce are no more than artifacts of cultural bias and byproduct. Sex and gender are fundamental questions and some of the most challenging issues facing contemporary Christian ethics.

Patriarchy is the term used by feminist theology to refer to an institutionalized system of sexual hierarchy and cultural mechanism for justifying men's dominion over women. This male sexism in analogy to racism affirms a privilege and the particular characteristics of the male sex dominant in culture, religion, politics, and economy.

A critique of patriarchy is a demand for equality of man and woman in seeking emancipation of women from social norms and traditional ways of life which subordinates the role of women to men. Paul's statement has been used to support a biblical patriarchy: "The women should keep silent in the churches." (1 Cor 14:34). Against this, Paul also affirms that "there is neither male nor female, for you are all one in Christ Jesus" (Gal 3:28). What matters in this regard refers to a hermeneutical strategy concerning how to interpret the text for the construal of the world.

The Biblical texts were written in the patriarchal world. Feminist critique of patriarchal culture and language in the biblical context takes issue with gender as a matter of men's power and dominion over women socially, religiously, politically, and economically. Such hierarchy is inscribed in biblical texts as if it were natural law rather than a historical and cultural construct. A critical feminist hermeneutic requires a revision of biblical code and narratives; for instance, the Levitical laws about the purity and impurity of women, the texts of terror about Hagar, Tamar, Jephthah's daughter, and the unknown woman violated in Judges 19 among others.

Women's own experiences such as suffering, joy, and emancipation were written over, altered, represented, and inscribed in subservience to what has been of special interest to men in the biblical texts. What matters in the biblical studies is to read behind what men have written, in seeking traces of invisible women, its irregularity, and hearing the silence of the voiceless. It debunks misogynist tendencies in the tradition of interpretation of the biblical texts. The Bible has prescribed our gender and our sexuality and defined our social roles to this day and this culture (Gen 2–3).

A gender-bias critical method of feminist theology reads biblical texts and their historical formulations within the socio-historical context. It argues that all texts are products of an androcentric patriarchal culture and history.[8] Feminist theology as a critical theology of liberation requires a feminist hermeneutic in seeking to overcome a symbolic androcentrism and patriarchal domination within biblical religion.[9]

A Jewish feminist critique of the profound injustice of Torah itself is undertaken to reconstruct the past in light of the feminist claim for recovering women's history within Judaism. The covenant community is the community of the circumcised (Gen 17:10). Moses addresses the community only as man.[10] Women did not participate in writing their experience and interpretation in *halakha*. A feminist hermeneutic of suspicion/remembrance informs and guides a feminist appropriation of religious texts which are pronounced patriarchal.[11] It emphasizes recollections of the histories of suffering and oppression of women in the patriarchal biblical culture, religion, and society. "Thou shall not lessen the humanity of women" is missing from the Torah.[12]

Despite the androcentricity (man-centeredness) and patriarchy imbued with the biblical texts, a theological subject matter, God's act of speech in the otherness of the Other, brings a critical catalyst to overcoming the fixed authority of the written and spoken text concerning androcentricity and patriarchy, helping women escape from the sameness of man. "The transcendence of God can help in the discovery of the other as other . . . The fecundity of God would be witnessed in the uncalcu-

---

8. Schüssler-Fiorenza, *In Memory of Her*, xv.
9. Ibid., xxii.
10. Plaskow, *Standing Again at Sinai*, 31.
11. Ibid., 13.
12. Ibid., 5.

lating generosity with which I love, to the point of risking myself with the Other."[13] Such a perspective requires an ethic of sexual difference. Feminist ethics helps man-centered theology from the deformation and accommodation of God's subject matter to patriarchy which has produced the patriarchal God complex as the gender of God, always masculine and paternal in the West.

ETHICS OF RESISTANCE, GENDER, AND SEXUALITY

Sex is known as sexual dimorphism which refers to biological maleness or femaleness, usually given at birth. Gender denotes what it means to be male or female in a particular culture. Even the gender of a new born is already influenced by culture. Gender is socially constructed. The social and cultural meanings are assigned to the sexual differences. Gender status is connected to a gender role regarding proper behavior and appearance for a particular gender. Sex and gender should be conceptualized as a spectrum of human diversity in relation to gender blenders, intersex or gender variations beyond biological dimorphism (for instance *bakla* in the Philippine, a man is dressed as a woman in the workplace, on public transportation, or even in church).

Cross-cultural understanding about sexual identity and sexual diversities provides an opportunity to see how one's own sexual culture is shaped and arranged by one's own culture. Gender ideologies are frequently hierarchically organized and deployed. Sexual inequality is embedded in thought, language, and social institutions. Gender issues are of great importance in contemporary society and culture, becoming arbiter for the critical analysis of unexamined androcentric presuppositions.[14]

In the Christian context there are arguments whether the sexual dimorphism and a binary system of gender statutes correlate with God's creation. In various cultures, gender traits are held by women, by men or by both genders. Gender traits such as affection for parenting, capacity for nurture or styles of childhood play are not taken commonly as natural, but culturally shaped and produced.[15]

---

13. Irigaray, *Ethics of Sexual Difference*, 204–5.
14. King, ed., *Religion and Gender*, 2.
15. Mead, *Male and Female*.

Feminist anthropologists have contributed to undertaking gender-focused studies in terms of analysis of entire sub-disciplines in light of gender and sex.[16] Sexually coded culture is the system of cultural meanings about sexuality and the social practices of sexuality. Sexual identity is an element of some sexual cultures. Homosexual, heterosexual, gay, lesbian, or LGBTQ (Lesbian-Gay-Bisexual-Transgender-Queer) are sexual identity categories which are crucial to the society's sexual culture, by challenging a unified understanding of human sexual nature.

A postmodern deconstruction of sexual identity can be seen in its rejection of Western bourgeois norms of sexual behavior and life conduct. Foucault's deconstruction of sexual identity and value is utilized to develop Christian ethics of sexuality and gender.[17] Foucault explores the exclusionary and silencing functions of power in regard to a knowledge system as seen in prison and sexuality. A modern medicalized discourse of sex is the entry point for the surveillance and regulation of individual bodies. Sexuality itself is a social construction and its ultimate effect is in control of sexual identity and body. Body is a site of power, that is, the locus of domination causing body docility and constituting subjectivity.

In Foucault's fashion, sexuality and sex come into being as a social power mechanism. A notion of sexuality is a historical construct as deployed in the service of bourgeois power. In Foucault's view, a nineteenth-century hermaphrodite was forced by legal and medical authorities to choose a sexual identity as male or female. Science, law, and bureaucracy formalized sexual essentialism. A powerful critique of essentialism pertains to discourse's relation to power/knowledge and practices of self as it challenges the operation of normalizing power and a demand for a unitary morality.

However, the body and sexual passion in the ancient Greek culture were differentiated from the modern understanding, thus the nature of sexual desire is variable with culture. Underlying knowledge-power discourse is an iconoclastic refusal of hegemonic dominion of sexuality. In his explication of power/knowledge, Foucault argues that there is a regime of truth for producing truth on the form of scientific discourse and the institutions. It is subject to constant economic and political incitement. It circulates through apparatuses of education and information relatively broad in the social body. It is produced and transmitted under

16. Di Leonardo, ed., *Gender at the Crossroads of Knowledge*.
17. Cahill, *Sex, Gender and Christian Ethics*, 3–4.

the control of a few great political and economic apparatuses such as university, army, writings, and media. It is the matter of ideological struggles in political debate and social confrontation.[18]

As a matter of fact, power operates in the modern era through the complex network of disciplinary systems and prescriptive technologies. Sexuality emerged in this historical period which refers to a mechanism of new ways of organizing knowledge and discourse. A reverse discourse about homosexuality has begun to speak in its own behalf, demanding that its legitimacy or "naturality" be acknowledged.

Western humanism is a privileged form of culture in the experience of the Western masculine elite underlying universals about truth, knowledge, and human nature. A strategy of debunking unrecognized or foreclosed modes of domination leads to ethics of resistance which is also influential in feminist gender/sexuality ethics.[19]

This ethics of resistance urges a search for styles of existence in terms of care of self and practice of freedom as different from each other as possible in resistance to normalizing power and a unitary morality. It also fosters ethical and political solidarity with the Other and embraces otherness toward non-fascist community of moral action. A search for a form of morality that everyone should accept is out of this consideration. Rather it is important to present a method in analyzing, dismantling, and debunking the totalizing proclivities of conventional ethical visions as rationalizing discourses, suppressing marginalized groups.[20]

Feminist critical hermeneutics entails 1) a descriptive dimension in retrieving women's status, role, images, and experiences so long neglected in the study of culture and religion, 2) the negative-critical dimension of the analysis and deconstruction of the androcentric framework, perspectives, and assumptions. This gynocritical analysis leads to understanding women as independent, autonomous writers. 3) a positive-critical dimension in women's undertaking of reconstruction of experiences, insights, and different elements of tradition for making them meaningful for us today. 4) the methodological dimension in woman's critical approach as A gendered self in relation to others. It requires different research methodologies from the traditionally established methodological paradigm.[21]

18. Foucault, *Power/Knowledge*, 131–32.
19. Diamond and Quinby, eds., *Feminism and Foucault*, x.
20. Ibid., xvi.
21. King, ed., *Religion and Gender*, 28.

PUBLIC ETHICAL THEOLOGY
AND THE LIVING WORD OF GOD

Since there is no human subject grounded outside or beyond historical condition, there is no moral sense which transcends power relations, sociohistorical background, and religious-cultural matrix. A cultural, ethnic, and racial version of being a woman celebrates plurality in resistance to assimilation and totalization of one's unique particular narrative to universalized metastory of essentialism. A strategy of plurality and difference becomes a catalyst for undergirding an ethic of sexuality and gender while resisting the dominant culture and becoming a resource for solidarity with the poor and the oppressed. Any essentialist search for sexual identity and the origin of gender is kept at bay and a warning is given to an attempt to assimilate to a white, middle-class paradigm of women's experience and liberation.

Given this, a cautious but essentially realist ethics is proposed to avoid the social ineffectiveness of moral relativism.[22] It seeks to develop a discourse of sex and gender justice by learning from multiple moral traditions in one's own culture and in other cultures. It attempts to reconstruct recognizable foundations for sex and gender ethics by incorporating postmodern critique of rationality and moral value to Christian ethical reasoning. Nonetheless, a suspicion is raised whether Christian ethics of sexuality and gender serves effectively gender equality for women embedded within more marginal condition by race, class, ethnicity, or nationality.

In view of gender ethics, whether in Foucauldian framework, or in natural-law ethical framework, however, I am more interested in emphasizing biblical correlation between God's creation and reconciliation in Jesus Christ for the public ethical theology in linguistic-creational-emancipatory framework. Comprehending God's act of speech through the face of the Other, I contend that that language of faith is that of communication with the world in announcing the gospel to the world which is reconciled in Christ.

In the Israelite belief in God, the masculine tradition and language stands in parallel with feminine traditions (Wisdom, Ruach, Shekinah). In the New Testament Jesus's disciples form a community of free and equal women and men which is in parallel with the family ethics in the pastoral Epistles. The Scripture was written in the world of patriarchy and

---

22. Cahill, *Sex, Gender and Christian Ethics*, 12.

slavery, but encountering God's act of speech in the universal horizon of the Holy Spirit, the biblical writers have brought their limited horizon to an understanding of the living word of God in a broader spectrum.

The living word of God revealed in Torah in a patriarchal culture and in Gospel in slavery society continues to transcend its cultural condition and confinement in speaking to our contemporary culture. It requires a new and fresh interpretation of the Word of God in terms of God's ongoing activity in the world and the otherness of the Other.

The language of faith, as seen in light of justification, justice, and reconciliation, has public ethical significance in de-patriarchalizing and de-essentializing the biblical histories, cultures, and laws of God, which contradict biblical subject matter of the gospel in embracing the difference and plurality concerning the kingdom of God.

Furthermore, a public ethical theology incorporates life connection and moral orientation embedded within sociohistorical setting in which the meaning of the gospel in the sense of *viva vox evangelii* needs to be translatable and reinterpreted in open-ended manner in fresh relation to ethnicity, plurality, race, and gender in different times and places. Reducing the social inequality and discrimination harming people based on their sex, gender, or sexuality, it is important to undertake public ethical theology and discipleship of God's mission concerning the coming of the kingdom of God, which does not nullify cultural diversity, plurality, difference, but transforms their meaning to God's new creation under a new heaven and earth.

Christian responsibility for the Other in the reconciled world embraces diversity, difference, and plurality. The role of gender and sexual nature are not essentially fixed, but eschatologically transformed. "For I am about to create new heavens and a new earth; the former things shall not be remembered or come to mind." (Isa 65:17). Likewise, there is no oppression or inequality in how Christians treat one another (Gal 3:28; Col. 3:11). "Nor height, nor depth, nor anything else in all creation, will be able to separate us from the love of God in Christ Jesus our Lord." (Rom 8:39).

IV

Theological Ethics and Missional Implication

PREVIOUSLY, WE REVIEWED PUBLIC ethical theology and its characterization in which God's mission is comprehended as God's economy in light of God's act of speech. This perspective remains foundational, given hermeneutical deliberation of virtue ethics, communicative discourse ethics, and moral deliberation in socio-historical and cultural context in relation to ethnicity, gender, and sexuality. Public ethical theology incorporates a hermeneutical reorientation for the ethical self. This model can primarily be seen in Gadamer's hermeneutical mediation with Aristotle's practical reasoning (*phronēsis*).

Part IV will explore the relation between theology and ethics in diverse perspectives and different models in order to present a correlation between theology and ethics in dealing with virtue, a theocentric approach, a biblical narrative position, realist ethics, and global public theology. In dealing with theology and ethics in diverse models, I shall seek to examine their implications for public missional theology.

To begin with, I pay attention to Schleiermacher's contribution to the integration of duty and virtue. Prior to Gadamer, Schleiermacher maintained that ethics is expressed and determined by history. For him "history is the picture book of ethical teaching, and ethical teaching is the book of formulas for history."[23] This perspective provides an insight into breaking through individual ethics, by articulating actual public life in connection with a given social structure.

23. Cited in Rendtorff, *Ethics*, 1:102.

13

Ethics in Integrative Framework

Duty and Virtue

SCHLEIERMACHER'S CONTRIBUTION CAN BE seen in his integration of moral duty and ethical virtue. According to Schleiermacher, Christian life precedes Christian moral teaching. Christian faith is also prior to Christian doctrine. Nonetheless, emphasis on life experience does not necessarily entail the separation of human experience and moral reasoning or theological reflection. Schleiermacher's position finds its validity in a theological discourse of public ethics as a practical construal of the world, which entails a missional character of the church. In order to appreciate Schleiermacher's contribution, it is important to start our argument with Kant's moral philosophy.

KANT'S MORAL DUTY AND ITS INFLUENCE ON THEOLOGICAL ETHICS

Kant differentiates between *noumena* (things in themselves) and *phenomena* (things as they appear to an active human mind). It is the *noumena* that give rise to our knowing, although we cannot gain knowledge of things in themselves. Transcendental realities such as God, the immortal soul, and human freedom are discussed in terms of practical and moral reason. The *noumena* are conceived of as free, the world of freedom, while *phenomena* is the world of necessity. The human mind imposes relationships between phenomena through reason. Human conduct is based on rationality, placing a primacy on the value of the individual in reaction to the dogmatic authority of the church and the state. The concept of freedom is key in Kant's explanation of the autonomy of the will. Morality is confined to the idea of freedom.[1] Practical reason as an effect of freedom and the particular relationship between practical reason and freedom are called "moral law."

Practical reason is coextensive with morality, thus reason and the will can attain unity only in autonomy. Practical reason enables the human being to grasp the moral law within. The basis of obligation must be sought *a priori* in the concept of pure reason rather than in the circumstances of the world in which we live. Moral philosophy gives laws *a priori* to a human as a rational being.

Moral law is deontological because right or wrong action is defined only on the basis of the character of the action itself; it has little to do with the consequences. Two kinds of imperatives play an important role: hypothetical and categorical. The former assumes teleological and consequentialist form, deriving from one's inclinations which are determined, shaped, and conditioned by the natural world. "If you want it, just do this!" If you want to maintain health, you ought to sleep enough. If the action is good only as a means to something else, the imperative is hypothetical. However, the categorical imperative is grounded solely in the notion of duty, telling us what we ought to do. An act is truly moral only if one acts out of duty, without regard to consequence. It is unconditional and non-hypothetical. If the action is conceived as good in itself, and consequently is necessarily the principle of a will in conformity to reason, it is categorical.[2] The categorical imperative belongs to real freedom, since freedom enables the agent to choose duty over inclination.

Kant's ethics focuses on this supreme principle of morality called the categorical imperative, according to which one will "act always on such a maxim as thou canst at the same time will to be a universal law; this is the sole condition under which a will can never contradict itself; and such an imperative is categorical."[3]

The moral agent must act purely from obedience to the imperative, without reference to consequences or ends. Freedom is the necessary condition for morality and an idea for the noumenal reality of human beings.

---

1. Kant, *Fundamental Principles of the Metaphysics of Morals*, in *Basic Writings of Kant*, ed. Wood, 203–5.
2. Ibid., 172.
3. Kant, *Fundamental Principles of the Metaphysics of Morals*, trans. Abbot, 54.

It postulates pure practical reason that specifies the conditions for the possibility of becoming moral agents. The supreme principle of morality and the postulate of freedom are intertwined. A person apprehends his or her existence as an end in itself, because persons are never to be used as means to other ends. It implies that all persons are members in the kingdom of ends.[4] Insofar as the categorical imperative is the first principle of ethics, Kant's ethics is a strong, agential theory of responsibility.[5]

What is interesting is Kant's understanding of Jesus Christ, the Word through which all other things are made. Jesus Christ is the archetype of moral disposition in all its purity, who has come down to us from heaven and has assumed our humanity. Our common duty is to elevate ourselves to this ideal of moral perfection, finding the archetype in ourselves, though we are natural persons.[6] For Kant, an ethical commonwealth under divine moral legislation is the church invisible, which refers to "a mere idea of the union of all the righteous under direct and moral divine world-government."[7] The true visible church exhibits the moral kingdom of God on earth.

Such an aspect finds its validity in a theological ethics, notably in the Ritschlian School, which was dominantly influenced by Kant's moral philosophy. This school accepted the Kantian critique of theoretical reason and the adoption of the moral as its theological basis. According to Albrecht Ritschl (1822–1889), Kant is the first one who perceives the supreme importance for ethics of the kingdom of God as an association of persons bound together by virtue.[8]

For Ritschl, Christianity is the perfected spiritual and ethical monotheistic religion, which consists of the freedom of divine adoption. The motive of love is directed to the ethical organization of humanity, establishing blessedness both in divine adoption and in the kingdom of God. Ritschl never identified the church with the kingdom of God. The church remains a means to an end by representing the idea of the ethical unification of the human race through activity inspired by the motive of love.[9]

---

4. Ibid., 46.

5. Schweiker, *Responsibility and Christian Ethics*, 81.

6. Kant, *Religion within the Limits of Reason Alone*, in *Basic Writings of Kant*, ed. Wood, 399, 402.

7. Ibid., 411.

8. Chapman, *Ernst Troeltsch and Liberal Theology*, 84.

9. Ibid., 16–17.

It is certain that Ritschl sees the ethical as historically grounded in Jesus and in the consciousness of the original Christian community. Religious dependence on God's grace and ethical orientation toward the kingdom of God remain the apostolic norm. *Lebensführung*, a religious ethical style of life, is a fundamental tool for interpreting the whole of Christianity in its development. Christianity is a moral religion of redemption through Christ. The moral focus can be maintained through a proper appreciation of the idea of the kingdom of God. Thus, the kingdom of God is both a religious and an ethical concept because the idea of the kingdom of God is the universal ground of moral conduct, making Christianity the specifically moral religion.[10]

The kingdom of God is divinely ordained as the highest good of the community founded by Christ. It forms the ethical ideal for whose attainment the members of the church bind themselves to each other, in the imperative for moral actualization in the world. Kant's kingdom of ends is echoed strongly in Ritschl's characterization. Ritschl as a theologian of culture incorporates a modern (and Kantian) understanding of the human ethical problem into his understanding of human vocation for the kingdom of God. Thereby, the demands of Christ remain in harmony with that of cultural values, undermining potential conflicts between the universal end of the kingdom and the regular claims of activity in the form of an ethical vocation for the common good.[11]

Our conduct is subordinated to the universal end of the kingdom, thus God's kingdom is conflated with the cultural achievement of the German nation. All the work of culture has its goal in the moral achievement of the kingdom of ends in the Kantian fashion, which is identified with the kingdom of God in the New Testament. The Christian community is also the true form of ethical society. The grace of justification as forgiveness of sin stands in no tension with ethical striving (reconciliation, that is, justification as effective) for the attainment of the perfect moral society.

By means of the idea of the kingdom of God, Albrecht Ritschl, a middle-class nationalist and also a supporter of Bismarck's policies, achieved complete reconciliation between Christianity and German culture. Troeltsch argues that Ritschl represented the middle-class voca-

---

10. Welch, *Protestant Thought in the Nineteenth Century*, 2:19.
11. Ibid., 23.

tional ethic of trusting in God and the best old Prussian morality, that is an admixture suited neither to Christianity nor to secular society.[12] Furthermore, Richard Niebuhr sees in Ritschl's theology the movement toward the identification of Christ with culture. Niebuhr portrays its contrast by pointing to Ritschl as the best illustration of the Christ of culture type.[13] This typology is also convinced that Ritschl's theology represents a cultural Protestantism.

RELIGION, LANGUAGE, AND ETHICS

For Kant, the predisposition to personality is the capacity to respect the moral law within us. This predisposition alone is rooted in practical reason in itself. Practical reason dictates moral laws unconditionally.[14] Practical reason is a dictating, transcendental from above, without consideration of history, society, and language, all of which are also important factors in conditioning and shaping human practical rationality in cultural and historical difference.

However, Friedrich D. E. Schleiermacher (1768–1834) provides a counterproposal to Kant, securing the place of religion in rejection of Kant's location of God and immortality in moral experience. Togetherness between God and faith and the experiential dimension of theology is elaborated in terms of religious self-consciousness. The religious subject and one's hermeneutical experience are systematically and ethically recognized in theological reflection. Revelation as a theological subject matter must be reinterpreted in the human linguistic and experiential context. Dogmatic theology is historically conditioned and shaped, and thus every doctrinal form has no absolute claim for its permanent validity. Dogmatics is intended only to give guidance in determining whether the expressions of religious consciousness are Christian or not. Schleiermacher presupposes that every Christian has already inward certainty in connection with the redeeming power of Christ.[15]

God the infinite horizon of human life is active and reveals God's self to us, affecting our religious feeling at every moment. The nature of reli-

---

12. Gayhart, *Ethics of Ernst Troeltsch*, 189.
13. Niebuhr, *Christ and Culture*, 94.
14. Kant, *Religion within the Limits of Reason Alone*, in *Basic Writings of Kant*, 378.
15. Clements, ed., *Friedrich Schleiermacher*, 115.

gion as a sense and taste for the Infinite does not necessarily mean its own individualistic and spiritualistic existence apart from social morality. The individual ability depends upon the prior activity of God the infinite. Our place in the universe implies that our "being-in-the world" is connected with God the infinite horizon of ontological dependence by transcending both our cognitive and practical activity.[16] God the infinite horizon as cause prior to human self-consciousness is the ground of all beings in guiding and shaping religious self-consciousness.

Schleiermacher takes his hermeneutical path, which is the art of understanding the discourse of another person correctly. The hermeneutical field marks his most significant contribution to theology and philosophy in the nineteenth century.[17] Hermeneutics plays an important role in his view of theology and ethics: "Christian doctrines are accounts of the Christian religious affections set forth in speech."[18] The task of theology is critical reflection in expression of the implication of the living religious consciousness in a new and fresh way in reference to the whole history of the faith community and the living Christ.

Schleiermacher's linguistically oriented hermeneutics in his early phase complements his theological way of locating religion in the realm of feeling or immediate self-consciousness for the redemptive work of Christ. As religious experience is expressed in a linguistic manner, theological or doctrinal expression acquires a new horizon of meaning. Schleiermacher's understanding of religious feeling or experience is so relational that it is incapable of surviving apart from a faith community. His view of religion is of a social and communal character. The individual learns the language only by participating in communal life. Relatedness, community, and language are interconnected, featuring human existence in a historical and social sense.[19] In his aphorisms on hermeneutics between 1805 and 1810, Schleiermacher proposed a fundamentally language-centered hermeneutics. Language is the key behind Schleiermacher's hermeneutics, which is the art of understanding.[20]

---

16. Schleiermacher, *Hermeneutics and Criticism*, xvi.
17. Clements, ed.,*Friedrich Schleiermacher*, 25.
18. Schleiermacher, *Christian Faith*, §15; Welch, *Protestant Thought*, 1:62.
19. Clements, ed., *Friedrich Schleiermacher*, 39.
20. Schleiermacher, *Hermeneutics: Manuscripts*.

Dealing with three main aspects of theology, Schleiermacher contends that philosophical theology demonstrates the distinctive nature of Christianity in its historical givenness in regard to that of other religious communities. Historical theology presents a knowledge of the whole in the present situation by understanding it as a product of the past (including church history, hermeneutics, and dogmatic theology). Practical theology develops rules for the leadership in service of a congregation and in the governance of the whole church. Thus, practical theology is the crown and goal of the entire theological task.[21] This aspect provides an insight into developing Christian ethics as a missional and practical construal of the world in light of the universal notion of the ontological dependence of all beings upon God.

Christian theology in a Schleiermachian fashion becomes public and missional because theological statements need to be intelligible to those who are outside the confines of the faith community. Other non-theological claims to truth enter correlatively into dialogue with theological truth claims. Schleiermacher's "theology of culture" is not based on a mere repetition of past formulations, but is undertaken in a hermeneutical circle in dynamic interaction with a contemporary world. His hermeneutical theology aims to create a covenant between the living Christian faith and independent and free science in which science is not obscured and faith is not excluded.[22]

The individual finds her/his validity only in belonging to a community. Human actions are always situated within the world, history, and community. Schleiermacher opens up space for recasting a moral action imbued with the faith community and also grounding its conduct of life and manifestation in a different history. One's ethic, influenced by tradition, is grounded in history, as expressed in one's own community and language. This mediation corrects the Kantian notion of the moral subject as an autonomous individual.

Schleiermacher's hermeneutical theology has implications for public missional theology because he retains a view of the proclamation of the gospel and it is historical in connection with a communal and relational view of humanity. As he states, "the whole work of the Redeemer himself was conditioned by the communicability of his self-consciousness by means of speech, and similarly Christianity has always and everywhere

21. Welch, *Protestant Thought* 1:70.
22. Ibid., 63.

spread itself solely by preaching. Every proposition which can be an element of the Christian preaching (*kerygma*) is also a doctrine, because it bears witness to the determination of the religious self-consciousness as inward certainty."[23]

The public, missional character of Schleiermacher's theology is best witnessed in the fact that the identity of knowledge is articulated in language and confirmed in real processes of communication. We know the individual not through intuitive or empathetic means, but through dialogue or communication. The locus of the ethical is in the relationship between language and the individual, in a way that the ethical is inscribed in language. Theological language should not be private or esoteric, because religion is grounded in the structure of human existence and feeling for the Infinite in the most comprehensive manner: personal, social, and cultural. Thus, Schleiermacher undergirds Christian participation in the public sphere, philosophy, politics, and the social life of his time.

ETHICS OF DUTY AND VIRTUE

Schleiermacher challenged Kant's dichotomy between the noumenal and the phenomenal worlds, seeking to develop a more dialectical model of the self; in this model reason and nature always exist together and condition each other. Inclinations play a major role in our moral choices and moral responsibility includes the development of a pattern of life shaping the inclinations. The moral life is conceived as a process, bringing inclinations more and more under the control of reason or bringing the flesh into harmony with the Sprit in a theological manner.

Thus, Schleiermacher seeks to develop a dialectical model of duty and feeling. His first philosophical work was a translation and commentary on Aristotle's *Nichomachean Ethics*. For Aristotle, the norm of the moral life is happiness or flourishing (*eudaimonia*), which is exercised in accordance with virtue or excellence.

Schleiermacher's question was how we could reconcile duty and feeling.[24] His early comment on Aristotle and his translation project of Plato indicates that ancient Greek philosophy is an important source of Schleiermacher's hermeneutics and ethical theory. At issue in

---

23. Clements, ed., *Friedrich Schleiermacher*, 45.
24. Schleiermacher, *Lectures on Philosophical Ethics*, ix.

Schleiermacher was bringing together of the teleological doctrines of good and virtue with a deontological doctrine of duty, in reference to one's linguistic competence. The word "religious" refers to all real feeling and to the synthesis present in the physical domain as spirit and in the ethical domain as heart. Feeling and linguistic depiction are essentially bound up together. The notion of a hermeneutical circle implies a continual reciprocity and interaction between ethical consciousness, human experience, and linguistic expression.

Schleiermacher distinguishes philosophical ethics from Christian ethics. The former is the foundation for the historical sciences, defined as "the science of the principles of history."[25] It stands in affinity to the philosophy of culture, the philosophy of history, or even sociology. Philosophical ethics provides the basic categories of understanding, to be employed in the construction of Christian ethics. Human life consists in the dialectical unity of nature and reason. The religious self-consciousness in absolute dependence on God coincides entirely with a notion in which all such things are conditioned and determined by the interdependence of Nature. Thus, religious dependence on God does not exclude its being, which is conditioned by the system of Nature.[26]

Schleiermacher's moral subject is not as radically free as Kant's noumenal self, which is unaffected by the phenomenal self. The dialectic of religion, reason, and nature is crossed by a second dialectic between the individual and the community. The self is not constituted in radical individuality but unfolded in its social relationships. Human inclinations are shaped by one's associations with other human beings, especially in communities like the church. Christian ethics is always only in and for the Christian church, because it contains the description of the same form of behavior developed from the Christian principle.[27]

CHRISTIAN ETHICS AND FAITH COMMUNITY

Schleiermacher's contribution expands moral theory as the hermeneutical way of construing human life in the relationship with community and world. The essence of religion is the feeling of absolute dependence,

25. Schleiermacher, *Brief Outline on Study of Theology*, §29.
26. Clements, ed., *Friedrich Schleiermacher*, 172, 180.
27. Schleiermacher, *Introduction to Christian Ethics*, 38.

which then becomes an impulse to thought and action. Ethics is not applied theology while theology is not reflection on praxis. Rather, Christian ethics is expression of the content of feeling, the primordial consciousness in Christian specific individuality engaging in construing the human self within the community or the world. Schleiermacher's concern about the role of Christian community in shaping its character and significance for moral decision is similar to themes in the ethical thought of Stanley Hauerwas.[28]

Christian ethics and philosophical ethics of duty presuppose an identity of subject and method, but with a difference. Insofar as Christian ethics contains expressions about the Christian moral feeling, its principle of behavior should be nothing else but the consciousness of God.[29] The principle of Christian ethics is the Holy Spirit. The task of Christian ethics assembling those propositions is actually followed and advanced as a result of the operation of the Spirit.

For Schleiermacher, the true essence of Christian ethics lies in communion with Christ. Christian experience, as participation in the perfect God-consciousness of Jesus himself, is that of an historical community. The God-consciousness of Christians is filled out in terms of the historical Jesus. Jesus Christ as the Redeemer is distinguished from all humanity by his God-consciousness, which is the veritable existence of God in Jesus. Christ as an absolutely powerful God-consciousness means attributing to him an existence of God in him.[30]

Through personal communion with Jesus, the inner life of the believer is recreated. Redemption and reconciliation are founded upon the union between Christ and the believer. Redemption and reconciliation should manifest the union of the life of the believer with Christ.[31] In his second *Synodic Letter to Lücke*, Schleiermacher regarded John 1:14 as the basic text of the whole of dogmatic theology and for the whole ministry of a clergyman.[32]

With the statement of John 1:14 in mind, Schleiermacher insists that Christianity is a faith, relating everything to the redemption that is

---

28. Hauerwas, *Character and Christian Life*.
29. Schleiermacher, *Introduction to Christian Ethics*, 45.
30. Clements, ed., *Friedrich Schleiermacher*, 56.
31. Schleiermacher, *Introduction to Christian Ethics*, 65, 91.
32. Ebeling, *Introduction to Language*, 49.

accomplished by Jesus of Nazareth. Christianity as a faith is wholly and completely oriented toward life in which the natural in human conditions is subordinate to the moral. Schleiermacher's historical Jesus grounded in his God-consciousness does, however, have a psychologizing tendency, which undermines a theology of the cross in which God appears as a participant in the death of Jesus rather than remaining "pure act." Schleiermacher's crux of soteriology in Jesus' God-consciousness downplays the aspects of suffering and anguish in Jesus' life and death.[33]

Nevertheless, Schleiermacher's notion of the moral is to be seen in his idea of an all-inclusive kingdom of God. In Christianity, all pain and all joy are religious as they relate to activity in the kingdom of God. However, Schleiermacher did not interpret the idea of the kingdom of God as the reduction of religion to morality in a Kantian sense.

According to Kant, the Word (the *Fiat!*) in John's prologue, through which all other things are, is the brightness of God's glory. Only in Jesus Christ, proceeding from God's very being, can we hope to become sons of God. Given this, Kant maintains that our common duty is to elevate ourselves to the ideal of the moral perfection of Jesus, who is the archetype of moral disposition in all its purity. Practical reason presents this moral idea itself to us for our zealous emulation of the archetype. Kant interprets this archetype in terms of a state of humiliation of the Son of God. We hope to become acceptable to and saved by God through a practical faith in the Son of God who serves as the archetype and moral exemplar of humanity.[34] Kant further defines God and the moral ruler of the world, thus an ethical commonwealth is conceived of only as a people under divine commands, under laws of virtue.[35] A people of God under laws of virtue are zealous for good works.[36] An ethical commonwealth under divine moral legislation is called a church invisible. The visible church, as the actual union of people into a whole, harmonizes with this ideal of the invisible church. The true visible church exhibits the moral kingdom of God on earth in terms of universality, which has no sectarian divisions. Its nature or quality is purity, and the union under moral motivation and its relation is under the principle of freedom. The administration of

33. Clements, ed., *Friedrich Schleiermacher*, 57.

34 Kant, *Religion within the Limits of Reason Alone*, in *Basic Writings of Kant*, ed. Wood, 400.

35. Ibid., 410.

36. Ibid.

the church may be changed according to time and circumstance, yet it remains under primordial laws for guidance. An ethical commonwealth in the form of a church is a mere representative of a city of God in the republican sense.[37]

In contrast to Kant's reduction of the Christian gospel to practical and moral reason, Schleiermacher acknowledged that the autonomy of the religious self-consciousness is embedded with other expressions of life, determining the whole of human existence. Religious self-consciousness must not be subsumed under practical morality. Rather, it can be properly understood in Schleiermacher's conception of Jesus of Nazareth as the ultimate source and point of reference regarding all theological statements.[38] Thus, practical action includes the whole scope of the process of life. Schleiermacher's famous statement—practical theology is the crown of theology—is comprehended in his christological framework. This aspect underlines church as missional community with an ethical character.

In this light, Schleiermacher makes John 1:14 the watchword for an understanding of a theology for practical action. The incarnation of the logos is the basis of the relation of theology to practical action because life itself has become the place of divine presence and the experience of divine glory. John 1:14 gives guidance to the whole practice of the church, becoming the basic text of dogmatic theology as well as the whole ministry of the clergyman.[39] A biblical notion of the incarnation remains foundational for Christian ethics and the missional church.

JESUS CHRIST AND GOD'S UNIVERSAL REIGN

Schleiermacher proposes Christ's lordship or the kingly power of Christ in terms of the inner vital relationship, distinguishing it from the power of God the Father. The sole lordship of Christ means that Jesus Christ is the climax and end of all spiritual kingships. Schleiermacher insists that Christianity is not a political religion, nor a religious state, nor a theocracy.[40]

Schleiermacher defines Christianity as a monotheistic faith, essentially differentiated from other faiths, grounded in the redemption

---

37. Ibid., 412.
38. Ebeling, *Introduction to Language*, 52.
39. Ibid., 51–52.
40. Clements, ed., *Friedrich Schleiermacher*, 252.

accomplished by Jesus of Nazareth. Christ is distinguished from all others as Redeemer.[41] Christ puts an end to the state of being in need of redemption and produces faith in Christ. The certainty of faith in Christ accompanies a state of the higher self-consciousness, which is different from faith in God, the certainty concerning the feeling of absolute dependence. Faith in Christ relates the state of redemption (as effect) to Christ (as cause). Faith springs from preaching, which must always take the form of testimony. Testimony arouses in others the desire to have the same experience of the believer. Language of faith in communion with Christ, on which Christian ethics is based, becomes language of dialogue and communication. The language of faith relates the proclamation of the gospel to the world by interpreting the world in terms of ontological dependence of all beings upon God.

All later believers received the impression from the influence of Christ, that is, from the common Spirit as communicated by him, and from the whole communion of Christians, which has been supported by the historical representation of his life and character. Likewise, contemporaries received the same impression from Christ directly. Those who remain unbelieving must not be blamed. Christ is the only One who can work conversion and redemption. The ground of unbelief is the same in all ages, as is the ground of belief or faith.[42] The church's mission consists of proclamation and testimony to Christ's priestly kingship, while conversion becomes effective through Christ's work as the cause. Unbelief is not strictly judged as a contradiction to Christ, but is dependent on the initiative of Christ's redemptive work underlying *universalismus verus* (true or real universalism.)[43]

The distinguished essence of Christianity exists in rest, a part of the communion with God that is characterized by divine rest. The highest human perfection is portrayed as rest in the contemplation of God and God's self. The situation of the Christian in perfection is called happiness. This is ethics of self-expression, or the ethics of virtue. Here we observe a parallel between Schleiermacher and Aristotle in regard to the priority of contemplation over moral activity. Nonetheless, what differentiates Schleiermacher from Aristotle is his christological understanding of

---

41. Ibid., 108, 113.
42. Ibid., 116.
43. Moltmann, *Coming of God*, 248.

faith in connection with God's universal reign, which stands behind the ontological dependence of human beings upon God. Schleiermacher's theocentric direction in monotheistic framework cannot be properly understood apart from Christian faith in communion with Christ.

MISSION AS THE SELF-EXPRESSION OF THE COMMUNITY UNDER THE HOLY SPRIT

Self-expressive behavior is a desire to express oneself in communication with another. Communion with God is an essentially universal Christian expression. Through the influence of Christ it is happiness or joy in Christ.[44] Through an active power of the divine Spirit, we remain in living community with the grace of God. Autonomous activity will grow in this community out of the self-actualizing Word.[45] This expresses the church triumphant, manifesting communion with God. Self-expressive behavior comes first and then comes efficacious behavior. The influence of the divine principle is efficacious, thus the self-expressive behavior turns into an efficacious behavior.[46]

On the other hand, efficacious behavior is motivated by pleasure or pain, moving toward perfection.[47] Efficacious behavior can spring from two different impulses: pleasure (disseminating behavior) and pain (corrective behavior).[48] According to the impulse of pain, Christian life in the real world is lived in the tension between sin and grace, between flesh and Spirit in the sense of *simul peccator et justus*. Pain is experienced when one's communion with God and the desire of absolute blessedness are suppressed and one's impulses are dominated by one's lower nature and selfish desires. Such an impulse also springs from corrective behavior because it seeks to correct or restore the proper relationship between one's higher and lower natures. This can occur by virtue of the consciousness of a power within us to remedy the deficiency.[49]

---

44. Schleiermacher, *Introduction to Christian Ethics*, 75.
45. Ibid., 89.
46. Ibid., 101.
47. Ibid., 72–73.
48. Ibid., 102.
49. Ibid., 74.

The religious impulse springing from disseminating behavior seeks to extend the rule of the Spirit over oneself, the church, and the world. "Christian piety must express itself in all connections as appropriate for its relationship."[50] Thus, Schleiermacher maintains that "there is no other way of obtaining participation in the Christian communion than through faith in Jesus as the Redeemer."[51] This expresses the church *militant*, which is set in opposition to the world, whose aspect emphasizes faith community as missional church, spreading the church's life in all life connection under the reign of the Holy Spirit. A spiritual dimension of communion between God and the believer leads to public behavior in terms of its self-expression in communion with the Other. Schleiermacher paves the way to a theology of the Holy Spirit, considering what is actually felt as the experience of God's activity in human consciousness.[52] This is Schleiermacher's important contribution to faith community as public, missional community.

FAITH COMMUNITY: SOCIAL JUSTICE AND RECOGNITION OF RELIGIOUS OTHERS

Schleiermacher considers two components: the essential aim of morality (the principle of ethics) and the essential ability to be moral (the freedom of the will). He defines Christian ethics "as the description of those ways of acting that have evolved in the Christian church from the effect of the Christian principle."[53] Schleiermacher's public ethics finds its appreciation in the circle of Social Gospel, especially in Walter Rauschenbusch.[54] Social justice occupies an important place in Schleiermacher's ethical framework.

Schleiermacher paves the way for the methodological construction of ethics in explication of the ontological structure of the formation of ethical tradition and its linguistic embodiment. An ethics always implies tradition and communication. Language places the individual life in the

---

50. Ibid., 82.
51. Clements, ed., *Friedrich Schleiermacher*, 115.
52. Ibid., 65. See Barth, *Theology of Schleiermacher*, 278.
53. Schleiermacher, *Introduction to Christian Ethics*, 87.
54. Rauschenbusch hailed Schleiermacher as one of the prophets of social Christianity. See Rauschenbusch, *Theology for Social Gospel*, 27. For Schleiermacher's prophetic-ethical critique, see Brandt, *All Things New*, 122–30.

wider context of the whole of life. The relationship of ethics and history is central in Schleiermacher's conception, according to which ethics is determined by history. Insofar as ethics is expressed in history, a perspective tied to language inheres in the discussion of morality and the conduct of life. If Schleiermacher comprehends Christian doctrine as "accounts of the Christian religious affections set forth in speech,"[55] dogmatic theology needs to serve Christian proclamation for Jesus Christ. Jesus Christ as the veritable existence of God on earth centers on the perfect God-consciousness of Jesus and the significance of Jesus Christ is expressed as the one in whom humanity is created anew. In dwelling in Jesus, God dwells in the whole world.[56] The gospel of Jesus Christ stands in connection with God's act of preservation of all things in the world underlying the ontological dependence of the world upon God. The false distinction between natural and supernatural knowledge of God can be overcome. Non-Christian religions are not to be categorized as utterly in error. Christianity, grounded in the centrality of the experience of redemption brought by Jesus, does not make itself discontinuous with the inwardness of other religions. There are other forms of piety that are related to Christianity in different forms but similar on the same level of historical development.

According to Schleiermacher, the monotheistic forms, in which all religious affections express the dependence upon one Supreme and Infinite Being, occupy the highest level, while all others are related to them as subordinate forms. In this light, Schleiermacher argues that there is at least a presentiment of one Supreme Being behind the plurality of higher beings, thus the way to monotheism is open. According to Schleiermacher, St. Paul also finds an obscure presentiment of the true God in the missional context. Each religion occurs in distinct, specific, historically conditioned forms of existence and each must be examined in its own particular case, which demands a scientific study of the historical religions. However, Christianity as the most perfect of the most highly developed forms of religion retains the exclusive superiority of Christianity as the purest form of monotheism.[57]

Despite the lack of a Trinitarian understanding of God, Schleiermacher becomes a pioneer in paving the comparative study of religions in mono-

---

55. Clements, ed., *Friedrich Schleiermacher*, 134.
56. Ibid., 209.
57. Ibid., 270–71.

theistic terms of the dependence of everything finite upon one Supreme and Infinite Being. God-consciousness and self-consciousness are not separated from each other, because God as the expression of the feeling of absolute dependence is given to us in feeling in an original way.[58] Religious self-consciousness, which is expressed by the feeling of absolute dependence, leads necessarily to fellowship or communion, that is, a church as a missional community characterized by proclamation, dialogue, justice, and the recognition of others.

---

58. Ibid., 104.

14

Theocentric Ethics, Theonomy, and Method of Correlation

SCHLEIERMACHER HAS INFLUENCED GUSTAFSON'S ethics from a theocentric perspective.[1] This chapter includes a critical and constructive study of Gustafson's ethics in connection with Schleiermacher, Niebuhr, reformed theological tradition, and David Tracy. In this study I also investigate Gustafson's position concerning Tillich by examining their ethical contributions and missional implications.

Gustafson proposes a theological ethic in its critical reference to an Other, an ultimate power. If the Deity is not bound to our judgment in service of our interests, theological ethics is radically altered. What is right for human beings has to be determined in relation to humanity's place in the universe, in relation to the will of God. Moral certainty is grounded in the will of God. The authorization is no longer human rationality, social customs, or civil law. The highest authorization is Divine. Man can no longer be the measure of the value of all things.[2]

In the development of Western Christianity, according to Gustafson's argument, theology and religion remain Ptolemaic in their basic outlook, since the salvation of humanity is claimed to be the ultimate intention of God. God acts exclusively for the benefit of humanity. The human being seems to be at the top of the hierarchy of beings, and the well being of human beings is the primary purpose of all other aspects of creation and of the Deity. Religion itself has become independent, anthropocentric,

---

1. Gustafson, *Ethics*, vol. 1.
2. Ibid., 99.

and Ptolemaic. Countering this Ptolemaic direction, Gustafson argues that the proper orientation is toward God; the chief end of humanity is to serve, glorify, and celebrate God. Human conduct has to be evaluated in this light of theocentricity rather than in consideration or reflection upon what is good for the human being.[3]

Gustafson argues that the first ethical question is "what is God doing?" rather than "what ought we do?" This question is especially inspired by H. R. Niebuhr who sought a larger framework for critical reflection about Christian action than Barth. Niebuhr's conviction is that ethics could not provide some prescriptive definition about some rules for responsible behavior or show how a responsible self should behave in one particular instance or another. Rather than analyze such regulative prescriptions, H. R. Niebuhr was interested in analyzing and laying bare ethos as the fundamental character of a community's moral life. He was reluctant to accept Christianity's claim of self-sufficiency or the superiority of Christian ethics over other patterns or non-Christian ethics.

For example, H. R. Niebuhr had reservations about attempts to derive all moral wisdom from Scripture or from Jesus Christ alone. His ethics, based on radical monotheism, are expressed as he argues: When Jesus is made the absolute center of confidence and loyalty, there occurs a form of the deformation of radical monotheism. Christian theology should not substitute the Lordship of Christ for the Lordship of God.[4] Niebuhr understands the task of ethics to be investigating the indirect effect of ethical analysis upon moral life and action, rather than constructing superior Christian plans for God's activity. Thus Niebuhr proposed "What is going on?" or "What is God doing?" as the prior question to "What should we do?"[5]

Insofar as the Christian community cannot claim superiority for its moral knowledge or its capacities to cultivate moral wisdom, ethics helps us to understand ourselves as responsible beings in this world in which the responsible existence of the human community is exercised. Affirming that only One is absolute and that all others are relative to the absolute One, H. R. Niebuhr argues that the Scripture is a mediate derived authority. This is because we cannot assign absolute authority to

---

3. Ibid., 110, 113.
4. H. R. Niebuhr, *Radical Monotheism*, 59.
5. Gustafson's introduction in H. R. Niebuhr, *Responsible Self*, 14.

Scripture.[6] H. R. Niebuhr develops his preference for the ethics of responsibility, which includes accountability and responsiveness, as being more adequate in a philosophical-theological manner. His ethics points to the Father of Jesus Christ who manifests the ultimate power through the resurrection of Jesus from death.[7]

Niebuhr's *Radical Monotheism* influenced Gustafson's argument on behalf of ethical theocentricity, which also turns toward a selective retrieval of a theocentric tradition within the reformed tradition (especially, John Calvin). If one's language about morality uses the terms good and evil (value terms), one is likely to fall under the teleological type. If one's language about morality uses the terms right and wrong, one is likely to fall under the deontological type. The two different types are distinguished by the primacy of the language of goodness and value on the one hand, and of oughtness and rightness on the other. In Gustafson's account, the normative material criterion for ethics in the West is "man." The West chooses Protagoras: "Man is the measure of all things." In most of the Christian tradition the purposes of God are finally for the benefit of human beings.

THEOCENTRIC ETHICS AND THEONOMOUS ETHICS

Gustafson takes issue with the method of correlation in which the question is determined by current moral and social interests. For Gustafson, theology and religion would not be instrumental to moral arguments or social interests (such as the case of abortion in the American context). Rather they play a greater role in shaping moral questions and describing the circumstances in which moral and social issues emerge.[8] The temptation is to simply put the Deity and religious piety in the service of the immediate needs and desires of individuals, communities, and societies. God is denied as God, becoming an instrument in the service of human beings.[9] For Gustafson, God is not an object that is subject to scientific

---

6. Ibid., 22.
7. See Gustafson's foreword in H. R. Niebuhr, *Radical Monotheism*, 7.
8. Gustafson, *Ethics* 1:24.
9. Ibid., 25.

investigation, but God poses an epistemological problem. The language of theology has to be analogical or metaphorical at best.[10]

For Tillich, symbols participate in the reality of that for which they stand. As a symbol for God the realm of reality is elevated into the realm of the holy. It is theonomous.[11] The moral act is a victory over disintegrating forces. Its aim is the actualization of the human being as a centered and free person.[12] The moral law is our essential nature expressed in terms of an imperative of conscience. The will of God is manifested in the good of our essential being, by which we accept the moral imperative as valid. This is the conscience, the silent voice of our own nature.[13] True freedom is thus theonomous because it is grounded in God. Morality is religious in its very essence.[14] Here we see Tillich's agential theory of responsibility. Nevertheless, our lives are marked by fragmentations. This reality makes it necessary that we encounter the moral law, the will of God, which is the testimony of the conscience against the self. The conflict between self-integration and disintegration is to be answered in love, agape, which is the ultimate principle of morality.[15]

Theonomous culture is Spirit-determined and Spirit-directed culture. Being itself is symbolized as Divine Spirit, or as Spiritual Presence. Spirit determines, directs, and fulfills the human spirit from within.[16] Human individuals and human cultures are grounded in being itself, the Spiritual Presence. What is antagonistic to the Spiritual Presence is judged to be heteronomous. It cannot communicate the experience of holiness as theonomous culture does.[17] Like culture, morality is to be theonomous when we are directed by the Divine Presence, the dynamism of being. Love makes this theonomous morality possible, because it is a matter of being. "Theonomous morals are morals of love as a creation of the Spirit."[18]

Assessing Tillich's method of correlation, Gustafson sharply separates himself from Tillich's "anthropocentric" direction that has made the Deity

10. Ibid., 33.
11. Tillich, *Systematic Theology*, 1:241.
12. Tillich, *Morality and Beyond*, 21.
13. Ibid., 24.
14. Ibid., 64.
15. Schweiker, *Responsibility and Christian Ethics*, 83.
16. Tillich, *Systematic Theology*, 3:250.
17. Ibid., 25
18. Ibid., 272.

a device of utility for the fulfillment of human interest and aims.[19] However, in contrast to Gustafson, Tillich himself described the overcoming of human alienation and conflict in a creative manner in his ontological analysis of love. For Tillich, love is the motive power of life, being in actuality, attracting all beings to other beings.[20] It is also the transcendent source of the content of the moral imperative, unifying our actual nature with our essential being. Tillich's position is not merely reduced to anthropocentric pitfall as Gustafson speculates. A theonomous ethics in light of the Spiritual Presence is always concrete and dependent on concrete traditions, thus, remaining in conflict with the autonomy of ethics.[21] Furthermore, Tillich's theonomous ethics under the presence of the prophetic Spirit revives expectation of the coming kingdom of God, which awakens the church to the task of witnessing to it in preparation for it.[22]

Furthermore, Tillich's method of correlation includes a theocentric-eschatological aspect. Tillich's dynamic-typological model, which is built on the religion of the concrete spirit, entails a sacramental, mystical, and ethical-prophetic element[23] in an eschatologically open-ended manner. The religion of the concrete spirit is actualized fragmentarily in history in moments of *kairoi*. Theonomy appears from *theos* (God) and *nomos* (law), which is the inner aim of the history of religions. If the autonomous forces of knowledge, aesthetics, law, and morals point to the ultimate meaning of life, we have theonomy. In their inner being they point beyond themselves to the Ultimate. Theonomy in the religion of the concrete spirit appears only in fragments, never fully, because its fulfillment is eschatological.[24] This theonomous structure keeps Tillich's ethical thought from merely becoming anthropocentric and autonomous.

---

19. Gustafson, *Ethics*, 1:41.
20. Tillich, *Love, Power, and Justice*, 25.
21. Tillich, *Systematic Theology*, 3:267.
22. Ibid., 375.
23. Tillich, *Christianity and Encounter of World Religions*, 71–72.
24. Ibid., 75.

TILLICH'S ONTOLOGICAL ETHICS AND MISSIONAL IMPLICATIONS

According to Tillich, all the ethical materials in the biblical resources are open to ethical criticism under the principle of Agape. Rather than producing commandments, the Spirit judges all commandments.[25] Love, power, and justice are central in ethics and jurisprudence, determining political theory and pedagogical method. Tillich asks for the root meaning of love, power, and justice from an ontological perspective.[26] Love is combined with the ethical imperative 'thou shalt,' justifying its ethical and its ontological interpretation. The ethical nature of love is dependent on its ontological nature, which gets its qualification from its ethical character.[27] Love is a matter of being rather than a commandment, a matter of ought-to-be. The human being is incapable of love because of his or her existential estrangement. "Theonomous morals are morals of love as a creation of the Spirit."[28] They transcend the estrangement between our fallen existence and the goodness of our created, essential being. This love also entails justice.

Power without justice and love is identified with compulsion. An ethical theism surfaces when the love of God is contrasted with God's power by neglecting the divine mystery and majesty.[29] In the ontological sense, there is interplay between love and power. Justice is just because of the love implicit in it. The relation of love to justice can be understood properly in the ontological analysis of the root meanings of both love and justice.[30]

Love in the sense of agape, which is the unambiguous criterion of all ethical judgments, enables us to think of the meaning of reconciliation, union, and reunion. The reunion of human existential being with human essential being must be expressed in love. This ontological aspect of love accepts and surpasses the Kantian formalism of the moral imperative, because love unites the unconditional character of the moral imperative with the conditional character of ethical content. It breaks through the

---

25. Ibid., 268.
26. Tillich, *Love, Power, and Justice*, 2.
27. Ibid., 5.
28. Tillich, *Systematic Theology*, 3:272.
29. Tillich, *Love, Power, and Justice*, 12.
30. Ibid., 15.

oscillation between the abstract and formalized and the concrete elements in a moral situation.[31]

As Schweiker asserts, ethical demand in Tillich, which is for the actualization of life against disintegrating forces, is conceptualized "in terms of the reunification in agape of actual life with essential being."[32] A Christian agential theory of responsibility is to be sought in the responsibility of the moral agent for self-actualization under the moral law of essential human nature. This aspect indicates a concern for an integrated ethics of responsibility, because it integrates the multidimensional reality of life and its various goods in terms of the essential and actual self. Tillich's understanding remains an undercurrent in the development of the integrity of diverse good in historical and social life.[33]

In speaking of the power of love, separation and contradictions among humans presuppose an original unity that encompasses both unity and separation through a reunion. Love makes unity a present reality. Life includes love as one of its constitutive elements. Emotions, their motifs and feelings can be explained in light of the ontological character of love. The feeling of love is the anticipation of a reunion and is contained in every human relationship. Thus, feelings or emotions must be interpreted as part of reality in ontological terms; in the interest of love as the meaning of action, feelings or emotions should not be denied. Agape as the depth of love is in relation to the ground of life. In agape ultimate reality manifests itself, transforming life and love. Agape is love cutting into love as the Word of God is the Word cutting into all words.[34]

Love, power, and justice are united in God and in the new creation of God in the world. Life is ambiguous in regard to love, power, and justice. In the new creation of the holy community, agape elevates qualities of human love beyond the ambiguities of humans' self-centeredness. The spiritual power elevates power beyond the ambiguities of its dynamic realization and compulsion. Justification by grace elevates justice beyond the ambiguities of its abstract and calculating nature. Love, power, and justice in the ontological structure of the new creation are affirmed and "their estranged and ambiguous reality is transformed into a manifesta-

---

31. Tillich, *Systematic Theology*, 3:273.
32. Schweiker, *Responsibility and Christian Ethics*, 84.
33. Ibid.
34. Tillich, *Love, Power, and Justice*, 33.

tion of their unity within the divine life."[35] In this light, ethical theology inspired by the ontological concept of love seeks to express the relationship between the receiving of life and the giving of life: "Love is a word that comes to us from everyday language and brings a rich variety of meaning to ethical theory."[36]

The message of the church's mission is God's love, which affirms that we are accepted in the sense of the grace of justification. According to Tillich, the core message of the church's mission is the grace of justification *extra nos* in a forensic sense, which means salvation as acceptance of the New Being.[37] Justification presupposes faith, which is the state of being grasped by the divine presence. Justifying faith is not a human act, but the work of the Spirit.

Tillich identifies the New Being with the being of Jesus, which means the New Being in Jesus as the Christ. Jesus Christ is the kingdom of God and in him the eschatological expectation is fulfilled in principle. Those who participate in Jesus participate in the New Being, even only fragmentarily and by expectation under their condition of the existential predicament. In the distinction between the first and the second coming of the Christ, the mission of the church proclaims the New being in Jesus Christ as the power of salvation.[38]

Tillich defines salvation in a threefold character. Salvation is (1) participation in the New Being (regeneration/conversion); it is the state that has been drawn into the new reality manifest in Jesus as the Christ. Faith accepts Jesus as the bearer of the New Being. Salvation is defined (2) as acceptance of the New Being (justification). Tillich emphasizes the priority of justification or regeneration in the process of salvation. In contrast to Melanchthon's notion of the third use of the law (emphasizing reception of the Spirit after the act of faith), Tillich puts regeneration as defined in the sense of participation in the New Being, before justification.[39] Tillich does not separate regeneration from justification, but both regeneration and justification are one as a divine act. Regeneration is the actual reunion while justification is the paradoxical character of this reunion

---

35. Ibid., 116.
36. Rendtorff, *Ethics* 1:63.
37. Tillich *Systematic Theology*, 2:177.
38. Ibid., 165.
39. Ibid., 178.

of that which is estranged. Furthermore, Tillich defines salvation (3) as transformation by the New Being (sanctification). Sanctification is the process in which Christ transforms personality and community, inside and outside the church. The sanctifying work of the Spirit as the actuality of the New Being aims at both the individual Christian and the church, both the religious and the secular sphere.[40] The church believes that the power of the New Being, active in itself, will conquer the demonic powers as well as the forces of profanization in society and history universally.[41] Tillich's understanding of salvation in the threefold sense is decisive for the church as the missional representative of the kingdom of God. In the context of justification by grace through faith, the cause is God alone, but faith is the channel through which grace is mediated to human beings. This is the *articulus stantis et cadentis ecclesiae*,[42] which shapes and guides the missional activity in service of the communication of the gospel of grace for all.

The church's message about the grace of justification brings the human state of estrangement and self-destruction to the justifying act of God. It is announced as salvation from despair, despite its in-spite-of character. Accepting that one is accepted, drawn into the power of the New Being in Christ, is the paradox of salvation. Without the grace of justification there would be no salvation but only despair.[43]

The church's mission also involves the inner-historical struggle of the kingdom of God against the forces of demonization and profanization. Under the presence of the prophetic Spirit, the church is awakened to the responsibility for and the witness to the kingdom of God in preparation and expectation of it. The mission of the church represents the kingdom of God in the universal sense, which embraces all realms under the standpoint of their ultimate aim.[44]

---

40. Ibid.,180.
41. Tillich, *Systematic Theology,* 3:376.
42. Ibid., 2:179.
43. Ibid.
44. Ibid., 3:375.

ETHICS AS WORLD CONSTRUAL, FAITH, AND HUMAN EXPERIENCE

Theology is a way of construing the world, to the extent that its concepts and principles function to interpret the world in light of the Deity that theology construes.[45] Gustafson's primary features of theology are of a hermeneutical character, because it is a way of "construing the world" (Julian N. Hartt).[46] "Construing" in a religious context intends to relate to all things in ways that are appropriate to their belonging to God. Gustafson starts his theological engine to describe the primary task of religious morality. The principle of construing as more than a linguistic-intellectual activity brings religion and morality together in a unity, allowing for the development of theology as a basically practical discipline. Gustafson's basic argument reads: "Theology primarily is an activity of the practical reason. This it shares with ethics."[47]

The impulse to reflect theologically arises from human experience, grounded in a religious intellectual enterprise more than in a linguistic-intellectual activity. Theology as a way of construing the world exists with practical impulses or practical consequences. There are diverse models of theological ethics visible in different theological ways of construing the world in relating all things appropriate to their relation to God. Different wellsprings of action are described and proposed. For instance, Luther's ethics is determined by the justification of the sinner through the grace shown in Jesus Christ and received through faith alone.[48]

The Lutheran teaching of justification presupposes an ethics of freedom (Gal 5:1), because Christ has set us free. The *kairos* of the gospel touches on the reality of human life in a particular situation and God's language brings human beings to participation in its powerful force. Luther's notion of passivity is contained in the conviction that "you are loved." It implies an inspiring, life-giving passivity, an experience of an *actus* of human being in the highest sense; it also determines human life and practical action.[49] This perspective makes the doctrine of justification relevant to ethical action,

---

45. Gustafson, *Ethics*, 1:140.
46. Ibid., 1:158.
47. Ibid.
48. Althaus, *Ethics of Luther*, 3.
49. Ebeling, *Introduction to Language*, 39–40.

making it foundational for ethical theology. The role of the human agent as an ethical subject is at the heart of the matter.[50]

However, aside from the Reformation teaching of justification and ethical agency, Gustafson expresses his preference for the Reformed tradition. Calvin's sayings—"Without knowledge of self there is no knowledge of God"; "Without knowledge of God there is no knowledge of self"; and "Piety is requisite for the knowledge of God"[51]—lead to a theocentric concept of the priority of human experience. For an ethical proposal of theocentricity Gustafson accentuates the priority of human experience, because human experience is prior to reflection. Religion and morality are aspects of human experience, theology and ethics are ideas about aspects of experience. Experience is of a deeply social character (although it does not sidestep private moments of experience) since it is a process of interaction between persons, between persons and natural events, and between persons and historical events. Experiences are articulated and explained in light of their meanings through cultures, which are the products of societies and social experience. Language is the most common evidence of this. The development of language is required for meaningful communication. Language and symbols are socially meaningful and are necessary for shared explanations of events in the world.[52]

In light of the priority of human experience, Gustafson argues that the dichotomy or polarization of reason and revelation is wrongly assumed and even unnecessary. Human experience is an indispensable aspect in religion and theology, since both revelation and reason are human reflections on human experience. Theology as reflections on religion and religion as a reflection on morality both seek to explain and justify religion and morality. Knowledge of what is right and good for human beings is gained from reflection on experience. Doctrine and dogma arose out of the experiences of persons and communities in the past; they are conditioned by the individual, natural, and historical circumstances in which those persons and communities lived. Here Schleiermacher's influence on Gustafson becomes evident, because human ontological dependence upon God (utter dependent feeling) remains a foundational undercurrent as we express such an experience in linguistic-doctrinal manner.

50. Rendtorff, *Ethics*, 1:65–66.
51. Calvin, *Institutes* 1.1.2; 1.2.1 (1:37; 39).
52. Gustafson, *Ethics*, 1:121.

For analytical purposes, Gustafson distinguishes between God as the object of human experience and human experience of God. Such a division tends to suppress God's priority through revelation, that is, God's self-communication in Christ by the power of the Holy Spirit underlying God's mission and the church's responsibility for the world. Therefore, Gustafson's ethics of theocentricity does not eschew a certain kind of anthropocentrism since knowledge of God is mediated only through human experience by undermining God's priority through revelation.[53]

Gustafson's basic thesis is that religion is a matter of the affections or the emotions which stand in relation to some cognitive and some more volitional aspects of life (Jonathan Edwards). In morality and in religion there are affective as well as cognitive and volitional aspects of experience. He contends that Kant's espousal of religion "within the limits of reason alone"[54] remains insufficient in regard to the religious aspects of experience. Religion is also a matter of the will, an attitude or volition that directs toward an object, which motivates worship and moral activity. A principle of theocentricity considers seriously the interconnections between the affective, volitional, and cognitive features in dealing with morality and religion as aspects of human experience.[55] Gustafson's basic argument—human experience is prior to reflection—shapes his ethical theocentricity in a hermeneutical configuration involved in construing the world, since the priority of human experience is the case in all ways of knowing and understanding in regard to science, ethics, and theology.[56]

PIETY AND ETHICS IN A REFORMED FRAMEWORK

Religion as part of human experience takes place within communities that have traditions. Religious affections and activities are evoked in human relationships. Aspects of experience evoke and sustain certain senses of responsibility called aspects of piety or aspects of religious affections. One of the most primal senses central to religion is the sense of dependence, which is a primal moment in religious life (Schleiermacher).[57] Human ex-

---

53. Ibid., 116.
54. Kant, *Religion within Limits of Reason Alone*, trans. Green and Hudson.
55. Gustafson, *Ethics*, 1:120.
56. Ibid., 129.
57. Ibid., 130.

perience, interpreted in terms of sense of direction, is incorporated into a religious and theological vision, *visio Dei*, which is the supernatural end of communion with God. The eschaton creates foretastes of that end in our present life.[58] Schleiermacher's notion of self-expressivity built on union with Christ finds its echo in Gustafson's theocentric ethics in this regard.

In the language of monotheistic piety, according to Gustafson, experiences of diverse others are seen as various manifestations of the divine Other. In human moral activity and in worship, life is seen as being directed toward the divine Other. Epistemological steps, phases, and aspects in monotheistic religious faith and life that Gustafson adopts move from experiences shared in common, to experience of others, to experience of the reality of a divine Other.[59] In his monotheistic theocentrism, Gustafson's preference for ways of theologically construing the world is rooted in the Reformed tradition in which he sees three components: (1) a sense of a powerful Other as the sovereignty of God; (2) the centrality of piety (a sense of devotion, duties and responsibilities) or religious affections in religious and moral life; and (3) an understanding of human life in relation to the powerful Other for the sake of the purpose of God.[60]

Piety is a response to the powers of God. The ethics deriving from Calvin are theonomous, since the divine law is present in the natural ordering of things. Action is to be in accordance with the natural law. The motive for obedience to God's law stems from piety both natural and Christian in which piety frames the moral and natural ordering of life in regard to human duties and obligations. Thus, piety and morality are unified in this view. Both are evoked and directed by God and toward God, There is no ethics of autonomy.[61] Affections are always part of distinctively Puritan piety related to the glory of God in which religion is experiential. Love is not emotive, but a settled disposition; it is the chief of the affections and fountain of all other affections in which there must be light in the understanding and an affected fervent heart as well. For Jonathan Edwards, piety and morality are oriented toward God while morality is corrected by piety.[62] Along the lines of Augustine, Calvin, and Edwards,

58. Ibid., 134.
59. Ibid., 136.
60. Ibid., 164.
61. Ibid., 126.
62. Ibid., 173, 176.

Richard Niebuhr developed his view of experiential religion in the study of Schleiermacher.[63]

Like Calvin, Schleiermacher contends that God has sown the seed of piety in the human heart. Religion is a fundamentally human affective response to God characterized by the feeling of absolute dependence. Christian doctrines are accounts of Christian religious affections and theology articulates this fundamental piety.[64] Piety or religious affections are prior to theological, rational formulations. In Gustafson's judgment, theology is a reflection on the religious self-consciousness because religion is prior to theology as a rational reflection on God. Schleiermacher entails a fundamentally organic vision of the relations: the powerful sense of the powerful One and the divine governance of all things remain central and congenial not only through historical events, but also in and through the nexus of relationships in and with nature.[65] Nonetheless, I observe that Gustafson sidesteps Schleiermacher's notion of John 1:14 which is defined as the basic text of the whole of dogmatic theology. Schleiermacher's statement of practical theology as the crown of theology is undermined in a theocentric ethical formation.

THEOCENTRIC ETHICS: CRITICAL, REVISIONIST, NOT PROPHETIC

In contrast to Gustafson's evaluation, David Tracy finds in Tillich a theological language that maintains fidelity to both the intensity of negative dialectics and the similarities-in-difference and order in all of reality. For the sake of the method of correlation Tillich does not sidestep a moment of negative dialectics ("Protestant principle and Catholic substance," in Tillich's parlance). In Tillich, the analogies are always intrinsically dialectical, thus negations are always present in the very expression of the equally real affirmations. A mutual dependence between question and answer is important, since "the method of correlation explains the contents of the Christian faith through existential questions and theological answers in mutual interdependence."[66] In this theological method, individual experi-

63. R. Niebuhr, *Experiential Religion*; idem, *Schleiermacher on Christ and Religion*.
64. Schleiermacher, *Christian Faith*, 76.
65. Gustafson, *Ethics*, 1:178.
66. Tillich, *Systematic Theology*, 1:25.

ence, traditional valuation, and personal commitment are central in the decision of the issue, and every understanding in this context is circular.

Taking a step further than Tillich, Tracy's correlation method in a revised and critical sense envisions theology as a mutually critical dialogue between interpretations of the Christian message and interpretations of contemporary cultural experiences and practices. His critical, revisionist model of correlation defines Christian theology "as philosophical reflection upon the meanings present in common human experience and language, and upon the meaning present in the Christian fact."[67] For the revisionist task of critical correlation, Tracy compares the meaning discovered as adequate to the common human experience to the meaning in the Christian tradition in order to discover similarity-in-difference between two meaning systems.

Tracy argues that we are all affected by the effects of history and the influence of tradition in our language. It is naïve to think that we can be faithful to the tradition to which we belong by merely repeating its *tradita* instead of critically engaging its tradition,[68] since all understanding assumes a radically finite and historical character. When dialectical language is embedded within a scientific method of critical analysis of society and culture, a systematic theology of analogical imagination may come along with a prophetic theology, which is mindful of the radical conflicts and massive human suffering present in all history and societies. Such a theology is anxious for a victimless society and history, trusting in God's promises of liberation.[69]

Tracy finds his revisionist model to be in agreement with the revisionist model of critical theory in the work of the Frankfurt School. A revisionist, practical theology assumes "the form of philosophical reflection upon the meanings of our common human experience and upon the meanings of the Christian tradition."[70] The critical-theoretical aspect (tied to critical social analyses and ethical analysis) and the hermeneutical aspect in the reinterpretation of Christian symbols undergird public ethical theology in the critical, revisionist model. This praxis of a revisionist theory that is implemented by a return to symbols and through symbolic

---

67. Tracy, *Blessed Rage for Order*, 43.
68. Tracy, *Analogical Imagination*, 100.
69. Ibid., 437.
70. Tracy, *Blessed Rage for Order*, 247.

meaning to praxis is achieved through the most critical reflection upon those symbols.

However, Tracy's hope of returning to symbolic meaning becomes questionable because the symbol of the cross is double and ambiguous: God's atonement in Christ's death and crucifixion in exclusion and genocide. It is unfortunate to see Tracy's Western-centric position in his argument: "A post-critical or second naiveté towards the Christian symbols present in Western culture might be a real possibility for the Christian and non-Christian alike."[71] This aspect leads Tracy to undertake the critical, revisionist model for the universal applicability to all experience and all symbol systems.[72] To what extent can a creative, revisionist model become self-critical and self-revisionist in encounter with the lifeworld of other history, tradition, and language?

Indeed, Gustafson finds in Tracy's revisionist model a useful method for contemporary fundamental Christian theology. Christian theology according to Tracy can best be described as philosophical reflection upon the meanings, which are present in common human experience and language, and Christian fact. What is given in Scripture as the concepts and symbols for the presence of God is itself reflection on the meanings of "common human experience" in light of an experience of the presence of God. The content of revelation in Gustafson's theocentric framework centers on the plurality of Christology in the New Testament and in the subsequent theological traditions. The various christological themes in the theological tradition can each be authorized from within the New Testament. Thus, Gustafson affirms that "revisionist" models of theology are present in Scripture. The Bible is understood not to provide one single Christian ethic.[73]

Thus, Gustafson's generalizing attitude of human experience does not acknowledge the particularity of biblical subject matter. For instance, a slogan "God's preferential option for the poor" becomes an example of drawing selectively from the Bible. He counters that prophets such as Micah, Amos, and a few others knew God's purpose in comparison with the priests in their temple sacrifices. We should not make an ideal a theo-

---

71. Ibid., 248.
72. Ibid., 246.
73. Gustafson, *Ethics*, 1:147, 150.

logical case and a normative ethical case for the sake of God's preferential option for the poor.[74]

The priority of the biblical subject matter (God of Israel, Liberator in exodus and in resurrection of Jesus Christ) is replaced by human experience in general for the sake of the ambiguous transcendental name of the Deity. Gustafson's ethics in the name of theocentricity eliminates the classic distinction between the teleological and the deontological types of ethics. These types are based partly on different perceptions and conceptions of the moral aspects of human experience. A theocentric perspective on ethics tends toward the subjectivist and situational, to the degree that we have no way that is free from social, cultural, and historical particularity in religion, moral theory, and theology.[75] Gustafson advocates for his theological type as the ideal-type, which can accept accountability for developing aspects of a tradition. This theological type is quite explicit about what is discarded from the theological tradition. It is also quite explicit about "how various theological doctrines and principles are recombined as a result of the selection of certain themes to be central." It gives "reasons for how one works with traditional materials and also reasons for the selection one makes from other ways of explaining and construing the significance of the 'world.'"[76] Human critical reason and experience function as a yardstick to judge, select, and shape the tradition, the biblical or classic text for construing the world.

The ethical way in which we construe the world stands for the ways in which we act in it. Gustafson undergirds Niebuhr's type of Christian ethics related to Augustine and Calvin. Niebuhr's construal of the world in a radically monotheistic way[77] remains congenial for Gustafson who is convinced that an alteration of the world occurs partly through the alteration of our visions of the world. This is undertaken by construing, interpreting, and understanding life in a theocentric focus.[78] This perspective remains a paralyzing element in undergirding God's mission through the reconciliation of Jesus Christ in terms of proclamation, dialogue, and prophetic *diakonia*. A theocentric ethics without recourse to reconcili-

---

74. Gustafson, *Examined Faith*, 104.
75. Gustafson, *Ethics*, 1:150.
76. Ibid., 154.
77. R. Niebuhr, *Radical Monotheism*, 49–89.
78. Gustafson, *Ethics*, 1:193.

ation and eschatology is not concerned with ethically and prophetically dealing with God's humanity in Christ for us. A radically monotheistic faith provides all moral laws with a universal form to which Kant's categorical imperative offers a testimony.[79]

---

79. R. Niebuhr, *Radical Monotheism*, 34.

15

Narrative Theology and a Community of Character

A Narrative Ethics Joins in a Critical Conversation with a Theocentric Ethics

STANLEY HAUERWAS, ONE OF the important representatives, proposes a narrative theology with a faith community of ethical virtue. His endeavor lies in his attempt to keep Christian ethics Christian. He seeks to affirm the narrative character of Christian social ethics. Recognizing narrative as a basic category for social ethics, Hauerwas insists that "the social significance of the gospel requires the recognition of the narrative structure of Christian conviction for the life of the church."[1] A faith community is narrative-dependent and social ethics is a correlative with the content of the narrative. Christians must learn what is going on in the cross and resurrection of Christ, then they may know what they should do. Therefore, the primary task of Christian social ethics is not to make the world better or more just, but to trust in God's promise of redemption.[2]

Thus, the church does not exist in order to provide an ethos for democracy or any other form of social organization. In this light, Hauerwas critiques liberalism on the grounds that the church should not reinforce liberal assumptions about freedom in the name of the gospel. He appreciates George Lindbeck and Hans Frei as the ones who direct his atten-

---

1. Hauerwas, *Community of Character*, 9.
2. Ibid., 10.

tion to the narrative character of existence. We are spoken in, with, and through narrative before we speak of ourselves.³

POSTLIBERAL NARRATIVE THEOLOGY

According to Lindbeck's postliberal theology in a cultural-linguistic mode, religion or culture, like language, can be understood only in the light of their own presuppositions and intratextual narratives. Doctrine functions as a communally authoritative rule or discourse.⁴ An anthropological notion of thick description (Clifford Geertz) is used only as an interpretive medium in order to critique the "hermetic" approach that runs the danger of blocking analysis from the proper object. Religion must be thickly described.

The interpretative task for postliberal narrative theology focuses only on how to interpret a text in terms of its immanent meaning inherent in the religious language for which the text is a paradigmatic instance. At last, according to Lindbeck, "it is the text, so to speak, which absorbs the world, rather than the world the text."⁵ Because the world of the scripture is able to absorb the universe, God's ongoing activity in the world of creation is discarded. Redescribing reality within the scriptural framework, intratextual theology undermines the translation and reinterpretation of Scripture into extra-scriptural categories. An intratextual theology advocates for the conformation of Jesus Christ only as depicted in the narrative. Thus, it ignores that Jesus Christ is also living as the Lord of the reconciled world.

A postliberal theology presents the Reformation theology of proclamation as having an emphasis on intratextuality (*scriptura sui ipsius interpres*). Scripture was interpreted by its use, by the *viva vox evangelii*. This emphasis on the living word in the intratextual context applies the scriptural language, concepts, and categories to contemporary realities.⁶ This postliberal aspect is framed in the cultural-linguistic character of religions and discards a freedom of the living Word of God in an extra-biblical manner. Only biblical narrative is maximized while God's act of

---

3. Hauerwas, *Performing the Faith*, 137.
4. Lindbeck, *Nature of Doctrine*, 18.
5. Ibid., 118.
6 Ibid., 118–19.

speech is undermined in its extrabiblical and creational dimensions. A postliberal theology is convinced of Barth's exegetical emphasis on narrative as a chief source for intratextual narrative theology, which Lindbeck deems as an appropriate way of doing theology in consistency with a cultural-linguistic understanding of religion and a regulative view of doctrine.[7] However, a postliberal theology completely sidesteps Barth's deliberation of the freedom of God's speech-act outside the walls of the Christian church.

Driven by postliberal narrative theology, some scholars also conceptualize a narrative theology in a cultural-linguistic formation by paying attention to the social and cultural use of the meanings of the Scripture in context. Insofar as the interaction between culture and language shapes and generates a new meaning for the text or biblical narrative, a possibility of shaping theology in a postmodern context[8] takes on a narrative theology of the Spirit's speaking act.

Theologians who attempt to shape a narrative theology in a postmodern context beyond foundationalism accept Scripture as the norming norm of theology (*norma normans*) in light of the speaking act of the Holy Spirit on the basis of the Calvinist doctrine of inspiration (2 Tim 3:16–17). They further develop the speech act of the Spirit in connection with speech-act theory of J. L. Austin. As the Spirit speaks through the Bible, they advocate an illocutionary act, not a locutionary act. The locutionary act is how a sentence is enunciated while the illocutionary act is what the speaker intended to do through this enunciation. The Spirit's illocutionary act is coupled with the Spirit's speech act of appropriating the biblical text itself and it is seen in terms of the original meaning of the text and the textual intentionality.[9]

In this narrative formulation the speech-act of the Spirit is also confined only to the biblical text. For the interaction between theology and culture, narrative theology again brings the Spirit's act of speaking through scripture in a contextual manner to the fore. The Spirit's act of speaking always comes to its hearers within a specific historical-cultural context. In this regard, a hermeneutical task is introduced in the elabora-

---

7. Ibid., 135.
8. Grenz and Franke, *Beyond Foundationalism*.
9. Ibid., 73–74.

tion of the specificity of the Spirit's speaking for the conversation with the cultural context.[10]

However, if the speech-act of the Spirit is only affirmed through Scripture for the reader, this pneumatic, narrative theology sidesteps Jesus Christ as the living Word of God as *norma normans* over and in relation with the text itself. Here the living voice of God in the narrative frame loses its freedom to speak to us in creation and in the reconciled world, as it is continually involved in human discourse and public affairs. Furthermore, according to Calvin, the Holy Spirit as the Spirit of creation entails a universal dimension, embracing the biblical text and the world. Within the pneumatic, narrative theology, we observe that a myopic confinement is obvious in its ignorance of God's ongoing act of speech under the universal activity of the Holy Spirit.

CHURCH AND WORLD

Following in the footsteps of postliberal narrative theology, Hauerwas transfers a theological relapse into the church. The church is the peaceable kingdom while the world is full of lies and violence. The church's primary task is to follow Jesus's way of life and teaching, by demonstrating to the world that it is "world." God becomes visible through the holiness of the church and the church must leave it to God to change the world. Christian ethics takes its bearings from the essential parts of the liturgy, because the heart of the church is worship. However, Moltmann argues that Hauerwas fails to cope with the world through the gospel of the kingdom of God. Hauerwas is not interested in disturbing the world, let alone in calling it into question.[11]

At any rate, to advance his constructive Christian ethic based on narrative and virtue, Hauerwas critically examines the philosophical and the theological tradition of morality. Kant dethroned the sacred narrative that is solely based on ecclesial faith, arguing that it has no influence upon the adoption of moral categories and maxims. True religion according to Kant consists in what we must do in order to become worthy of what God has done for our salvation. Thus, morality becomes the es-

---

10. Ibid., 161.
11. Moltmann, *Ethics of Hope*, 32.

sence of religion.¹² Jesus Christ is the cardinal prototype of humanity for all humanity. On the other hand, proponents of the Social Gospel were inspired by the prophetic tradition of Scripture and challenged the social structure of injustice and violence. For Walter Rauschenbusch, salvation is the voluntary socializing of the soul, participating in a divine organism of mutual service. God is the all-embracing source and exponent of the common life and good of humankind.¹³

According to Hauerwas, the Social Gospel movement, under the spell of the Protestant liberalism of Albrecht Ritschl, aims at mobilizing the energy and power of the church for social renewal. In the wake of the Social Gospel movement a term "Christian sociology" has come into the picture. Christian sociology brings a concern for social justice and the related analysis of the economic and social strategies. Christian ethics serves the end and purpose of sociology. The saved organization for the Social Gospel is democratic while the unsaved one is autocratic and competitive.¹⁴ Developing strategies for the realization of justice in the social realm, however, proponents of the Social Gospel had little interest in understanding how the concept of justice was derived from or informed by religious convictions. The reductionist assumptions sponsored by Protestant liberalism have come to the surface in this context.¹⁵

According to Hauerwas, Reinhold Niebuhr began his career as a Social Gospel advocate, but became its most powerful critic. Niebuhr's neo-orthodox critique of the Social Gospel is leveled at the optimistic view of the Social Gospel toward social institutions and change. An Augustinian notion of humanity's fallenness and its need for salvation keeps Niebuhr aloof from the grand idealistic vision of the Social Gospel. Rather, it helps him seek the possibility of forgiveness "only when morality is transcended in religion."¹⁶

In Niebuhr's critique of Social Gospel, Hauerwas insists that the forgiveness of sin is for Niebuhr the hallmark of Christian ethics, remaining central to the systematic display of Christian ethics.¹⁷ However, Niebuhr

12. Kant, *Religion within Limits of Reason Alone*, 123.

13. Rauschenbusch, *Theology for Social Gospel*, 98–99.

14. Hauerwas, "On Keeping Theological Ethics Theological (1983)," in Berkman and Cartwright, eds., *Hauerwas Reader*, 57.

15. Hauerwas, *Community of Character*, 90.

16. Niebuhr, *Interpretation of Christian Ethics*, 201.

17. Hauerwas, "On Keeping Theological Ethics Theological (1983)," in Berkman and

does not share Barth's rejection of liberalism. Despite Niebuhr's critique of America, according to Hauerwas, America was his church. This perspective distinguishes Niebuhr from Social Gospel proponents, notably Rauschenbusch who emphasizes the necessity for the church to speak out against American society.[18]

Hauerwas is under the influence of H. Richard Niebuhr, as he takes issue with theological problems that the Social Gospel movement raised. Hauerwas was suspicious of any attempt to use God to underwrite humanity's interests. He keeps a theological rationale for ethical reflection; ethical questions could only be answered adequately in theological terms. Hauerwas concurs with H. R. Niebuhr's basic statement: "God is acting in all actions upon you. So respond to all actions upon you as to respond to his action."[19] Hauerwas shares the legacy of H. R. Niebuhr with Gustafson, while moving in a direction of postliberal narrative theology.

ETHICS OF VIRTUE OR CHARACTER

Given ethical developments, however, Hauerwas's appreciation of ethics of virtue differentiates him from Gustafson. Hauerwas contends that ethics of virtue or character is not necessary in contrast to an ethic of obligation. MacIntyre's *After Virtue*[20] retrieves virtue and character, expressing renewed interest in the virtues among philosophers and theologians. The term virtue, *aretē*, indicates excellence, denoting the power of anything to fulfill its function. For instance, the virtue of the eye is seeing. Underlying accounts of virtue is a combination of excellence and power.[21] For Aristotle, virtue consists in observing the mean defined by a rational principle. A person of practical wisdom would use it to determine moral action. At issue in Hauerwas's ethics of virtue is *how* we do what we do rather than *what* one does or does not do. Virtue is associated with a more profound formation of the self.[22]

Cartwright, eds., *Hauerwas Reader*, 59.
  18. Ibid., 60.
  19. H. R. Niebuhr, *Responsible Self*, 126.
  20. MacIntyre, *After Virtue*.
  21. Hauerwas, *Community of Character*, 111.
  22. Ibid., 113.

In *After Virtue* narrative remains the crucial category in the account of the moral life. Narratives provide the link between our actions and human actions, and human actions are enacted narratives. Thus, agents are coauthors of their own narratives. The narrative of one's life is embedded within the story of one's community, which shapes one's identity.[23] A correlation between personal identity and practical reason is best displayed as the enactment of ongoing narratives. However, in *After Virtue* tradition has replaced narratives, and the former is understood as a historically extended, socially embodied entity. The tradition is used as an argument about the goods in constituting that tradition.[24]

For Hauerwas, an attempt to contrast an ethic of virtue with that of duty is misleading. The recognition and performance of duty becomes possible because we are virtuous. A person of virtue or character is also dutiful. Furthermore, Hauerwas contends that our capacity to be virtuous depends on the existence of communities formed by narratives, which are faithful to the character of reality.[25] In this light, Hauerwas critiques contemporary discussions of morality because they have neglected the virtues. Thus, ethical theory is not founded on a moral community or tradition. For Hauerwas, an ethic of virtue depends on the historical nature of human existence formed by narrative. The language of virtue and character is fruitful for providing moral expressions, which are appropriate to Christian convictions.[26]

JUSTIFICATION AND SANCTIFICATION

Two metaphors are important for Hauerwas to understand Christian life: journey and dialogue. Barth's christological section subtitled, "The Way of the Son of God into the Far Country," is guided by the image of God's journey and the invitation for us to be part of the journey. This perspective leads Hauerwas to reinterpret the theological acumen of justification and sanctification on character for the moral life. According to Hauerwas, justification and sanctification as secondary theological notions are subordinated to hearing and living the story of God as revealed through the life

23. MacIntyre, *After Virtue*, 218, 221.
24. Ibid., 222.
25. Hauerwas, *Community of Character*, 114, 116.
26. Ibid., 132.

and death of Jesus of Nazareth. The metaphor of the journey should be the primary one for articulating the shape of Christian existence and living. Hauerwas wants to help Protestants develop their insights from a rereading of Aristotle's *Ethics* and the *Summa Theologica* of St. Thomas Aquinas.[27]

A theological notion of justification and sanctification remains hollow without reference to the nature and significance of the church, which is crucial for sustaining the Christian journey. The theological language of justification and sanctification must not be separated from Jesus's life and death. In the inauguration of the kingdom in the Christian community, sanctification is a way of reminding us of the journey undertaken, making the story of Jesus our story. Justification is a reminder to the character of the story—thereby, what God has done for us, providing us with a path to follow.[28]

THE MORAL AUTHORITY OF SCRIPTURE

Hauerwas seeks to find the moral authority of Scripture in such a way that the presence of prophecy as an essential part of the canon makes it possible to remold the tradition as a source of life-giving power. This aspect is crucial for understanding how Scripture functions ethically. By the term "political" Hauerwas does not mean that Scripture should be used as an ideology for justifying the demands of the oppressed. Rather, constantly remembering and reinterpreting, Scripture can be read as a political task because there can be no community without tradition.[29] Scripture shapes a community, the bearer of the Word. Without such a community, a claim about the moral authority of Scripture does not make sense. Interpretation is the constant adjustment or change required, insofar as the current community stays in continuity with tradition. Interpretation of the Scripture reappropriates the tradition in terms of a greater depth of understanding. Scripture provides the means for the community to seek new life. The literature is to be read as a story with a beginning, a progression, and an end. It is certain that Scripture also contains material that is

---

27. Hauerwas, "A Retrospective Assessment of an 'Ethics of Character,'" in Berkman and Cartwright, eds., *Hauerwas Reader*, 88.

28. Hauerwas, "Jesus and Social Embodiment of Kingdom (1983)," in Berkman and Cartwright, eds., *Hauerwas Reader*, 141.

29. Hauerwas, *Community of Character*, 53.

non-narrative in form, for instance, the psalms, the wisdom literature, and the more discursive books of the New Testament. Hauerwas argues that those forms of literature in Scripture cannot be understood properly without a connection to the story of God's call and care of Israel and the life, death, and resurrection of Christ.[30]

Politics depends on tradition, since politics is a community's internal dialogue with itself regarding the various possibilities of understanding and self-extending.[31] The church's more profound political task is to challenge the moral presuppositions of our polity and society rather than engaging in politics to secure a more nearly just society. Genuine justice depends on more profound moral convictions.[32] Hauerwas tends to sidestep moral ambiguity and the human state of estrangement in the life of faith community, because the faith community represents the kingdom of God under the condition of imperfection and shortcomings. The faith community lives according to the grace that is expressed in an ethical form, rather than demonstrating and propagating moral virtuous character to the world.

JESUS' LIFE IN GOD'S KINGDOM

Driven by an ethics of virtue, Hauerwas emphasizes the centrality of Jesus' life, death, and resurrection for reflection on Christian ethics. He is influenced especially by John Howard Yoder's work, *The Politics of Jesus*. Yoder emphasizes Jesus as a model of radical political action for the possibility of a Messianic ethic. Jesus is portrayed as the one with significance for contemporary Christian social ethics.[33]

Yoder, an American Mennonite theologian, takes up the idea of Augustine that Christ is both sacrament and example. According to Yoder, a false understanding of Jesus as sacrament has developed within spiritual significance, undermining political, social, and ethical significance. Following Jesus is possible through a radical rejection of violent forces in light of the resurrection of Christ. Followers of Christ seek to live in radical political opposition to a violent empire. When threatened with violence, Christians may trust that God alone conquers enemies and

30. Hauerwas, *Performing the Faith*, 139.
31. Hauerwas, *Community of Character*, 61.
32. Ibid., 73–74.
33. Yoder, *Politics of Jesus*, 2, 11.

protects God's people. Christians must look to the crucifixion and resurrection of Christ as the divine example and promise, which is central to the peace of God's kingdom. The assertive, yet non-violent Christ found in the synoptic gospels opens new possibilities to the church through his example of life, death, and resurrection.

Sharing Yoder's interest, Hauerwas's concern is to make Jesus's life a more profound theological point with regard to the eschatological aspects of Jesus's message of the proclamation of the kingdom of God. Christological issues must be decisive in Jesus's life in the presence of God's kingdom in this world.[34]

Recovering the narrative dimension of Christology, Hauerwas argues that the story of Jesus is a social ethic. The form of the church must exemplify Jesus's ethics.[35] Attending to the narrative form of the gospels, Hauerwas insists that we learn to locate our lives within God's life, and thereby within the journey comprising God's kingdom. "The cross is not a symbol of God's kingdom; it is that kingdom come . . . It is only by God's grace that we are enabled to accept the invitation to be part of that kingdom . . . Thus, our true nature . . . is revealed in the story of this man in whose life, we believe, is to be found the truth. . . . The resurrection of Jesus is the absolute center of history."[36] The narrative character of the gospels is integral to the affirmation of Jesus' redemptive significance. Emphasis is given to a renewed sense of the significance of the kingdom of God in Jesus's preaching and ministry.[37] The story of Jesus creates a community in correspondence with the form of Jesus's life. The church is the center of any attempt to develop Christian ethics.

DIETRICH BONHOEFFER WITHIN NARRATIVE ETHICS

Hauerwas's reading of Bonhoeffer is motivated by the attempt to develop Bonhoeffer on issues of truth and politics, seeking a parallel between Bonhoeffer and Yoder for the sake of the interconnection between forgive-

---

34. Hauerwas, "A Retrospective Assessment of an 'Ethics of Character,'" in Berkman and Cartwright, eds., *Hauerwas Reader*, 119.

35. Hauerwas, *Community of Character*, 37, 40.

36. Hauerwas, "A Retrospective Assessment of an 'Ethics of Character,'" in Berkman and Cartwright, eds., *Hauerwas Reader*, 133, 136.

37. Hauerwas, *Community of Character*, 44.

ness, trustfulness, and nonviolence. According to Hauerwas, Bonhoeffer rightly understood the truthful proclamation of the gospel as the gift that the church gives to any politics. Bonhoeffer's notion of "telling the truth" is explored by Hauerwas under the premise that politics cannot be divorced from truth.[38] This aspect implies a shift from narrative ethics to discourse ethics in train of thought.

Hauerwas sees in Bonhoeffer's theological politics as stated in his *Discipleship* a parallel with Yoder's *The Politics of Jesus*. Bonhoeffer's critical account of the challenge that faces the church and its self-preservation is similar to Yoder's critical account of a Christian transmuted to inwardness.[39] Bonhoeffer's life is characterized as polyphony, while the other melodies of life provide the counterpoint to the *cantus firmus* (main melody).[40]

Hauerwas argues that Bonhoeffer attempts to rethink the Lutheran two-kingdom theology through his christological recovery of the significance of the visible church. Nevertheless, Hauerwas argues that Bonhoeffer failed to escape from the limits of the habits that shaped Lutheran thinking on the matters of theological politics. In his critical view of Bonhoeffer's mandate, Hauerwas concurs with Barth's critical remark of mandate as a hint of North German patriarchalism.[41] Hauerwas, siding with Karl Barth, is convinced that the character of a society and state should be judged by the willingness to have the gospel trustfully and freely.

However, Bonheoffer's ethics of the mandate must be seen in connection with his theological notion of the church's resistance and *status confessionis*. A political activity is endorsed "not just to bandage the victims under the wheel, but to jam a spoke in the wheel."[42]

Bonhoeffer's notion of confession and resistance does not undermine the concept of natural law espoused with the first function of the law in connection with the Decalogue. Exercise of reason in the political world is not discarded, but encouraged in Bonhoeffer's exposition of the dialectical relationship between the natural law and the gospel. Bonhoeffer's christological centering is imbued with his theological jus-

---

38. Hauerwas, *Performing the Faith*, 62–67.
39. Ibid., 35, 43.
40. Ibid., 37.
41. Ibid., 51.
42. Bonhoeffer, *Testament to Freedom*, 139.

tification of the teaching of the first function of the law as the just and unalterable will of God.[43]

The will of God takes effect in the *primus usus* or the *lex naturae*, which takes effect in reason and morality, standing in relation to the gospel.[44] When the government denies its civil and political function given by God and blasphemes God, the church testifies to the power of God, which is praised in the torments and martyrdoms of the congregation.[45] This perspective entails the church's political responsibility, that is, to summon the world to belief in Jesus Christ and his reconciliation.[46] In accordance with the signs of the times, the church's mission toward the world must be performed polemically against the apocalyptic proclamation (Rev 13).

Bonhoeffer's unique interpretation of the relationship between natural law and the gospel can be seen in his statement: "Concerned with the form of the secular order in accordance with the will of God, the *primus usus* is not concerned with the christinization of worldly institutions or with their incorporation in the church. Their genuine worldliness or naturalness is in obedience to God's word."[47] If Hauerwas retains a dimension of virtue ethics in the Aristotelian sense, his narrative and virtue ethics needs to have a more profound dialogue with Bonhoeffer's ethics concerning law-gospel hermeneutics, *theologia crucis*, and recognition of people in the world come of age.

DEBATE: NARRATIVE ETHICS AND REVISIONIST ETHICS

Epistemological priority of the church and the narrative of Jesus are criticized by James Gustafson as a form of sectarian retreat, ignorant of a civic and public responsibility. In *Resident Aliens*, Hauerwas and William Willimon present the church as a Christian colony that is a new polis focused on the gospel of Jesus against the world. They seek to retrieve the distinctiveness of Christian life in terms of deepening practices of communal and congregational discipleship. This entails the missional renewal of the faith community. However, their argument is that the political task

---

43. Bonhoeffer, *Ethics*, 300.
44. Ibid., 302.
45. Ibid., 343.
46. Ibid., 345.
47. Ibid., 312.

of Christians is to be the church rather than changing the world.[48] The connection between God, church, and world remains under-investigated, thus the church is isolated from the public and secular world. In envisioning the church as a separate and isolated colony, it is hard to comprehend congregational life embedded within the hybrid, fluid, and complex nature of culture today. Their approach to the church and the world in a postliberal fashion is not adequate to engage with the complexity of globalized cultural environment.

Gustafson takes issue with the Christian colony approach, arguing that it is a sectarian approach to ecclesiology.[49] For Gustafson, religion and science are rational activities. In principle, theological claims must be subject to correction and revision in light of the result and achievements undertaken through the social and physical sciences. This revisionist position urges theologians to relativize the Christian tradition in terms of other sources of knowledge; we may construe God's relation to the world through our modern knowledge.

Driven by a revisionist, correlation model, Gustafson argues that theological fideism is correlative to a sociological tribalism. A truncated ethic is incapable of dealing adequately with contemporary challenges. Narrative theology and sectarianism go hand in hand.[50] Contrary to Gustafson's characterization, however, Hauerwas insists that his stance is in the Catholic tradition. Hauerwas is based on his fidelity to the biblical narratives, notably the gospel narratives. The principal criterion for Christian behavior is in its conformity to the stories of Jesus. Hauerwas presents an alternative vision of peace rooted in God's action in Christ, which shapes and constitutes Christian character.[51]

This biblical narrative is remembered and reinterpreted within the church, whose identity is constituted by telling the story of God's peaceable dealing with humanity in Jesus Christ. The Christian memory of God's action in Christ is the theological grounds of valid moral claims. Interpretation and remembering in the faith community become political actions.[52] Hauerwas counters those who seek to create a universal ethics

---

48. Hauerwas and Willimon, *Resident Aliens*, 38.

49. Gustafson, "Sectarian Temptation."

50. Hauerwas, "Why the 'Sectarian Temptation' is a Misrepresentation," in Berkman and Cartwright, eds., *Hauerwas Reader*, 93.

51. Hauerwas, *Against the Nations*.

52. Schweiker, *Responsibility and Christian Ethics*, 91.

from a general metaphysical perspective. Rather, Christian moral existence is constructed by describing people through the world of biblical narrative and its memory of God's action in Christ. The biblical narrative shapes a community, which in turn enacts the scriptural vision of a life whose norm is peaceableness. The responsibility of the church is not grounded in general moral claims and principle. Hauerwas turns his previous concept of virtue ethics and faith community with character into a Shalom community.

Thus, Christian morality must be pacifistic because the gospel narratives are read as pacifistic. A sectarian charge made against Hauerwas means that the church, in the case of narrative ecclesiology, is socially and culturally isolable from the wider society and culture, making no contribution necessary in political and public life. Gustafson's revisionist correlation standpoint endorses the notion that other institutions in society and culture have to provide symbols and constructs; these interpret the same reality that Christian faith and theology provide for moral norm and ethical deliberation.

Gustafson chides Hauerwas for not offering the doctrine of creation as a basis for ethics. According to Gustafson, faithful witness to Jesus is not a sufficient theological and moral basis for engaging and addressing the moral and social problems of our century. Developing God's relation to all aspects of life in the world, Gustafson attempts to develop those public and secular relations not exclusively in a sectarian, the church-oriented form. Gustafson's controversial thesis reads: Jesus is not God.[53] Gustafson's theocentric ethics is in contradiction to the mission of the triune God in which Jesus Christ as the second person of the Trinity is God's self-interpretation in the presence of the Holy Spirit. A public ethic based on creation in a theocentric sense needs to be refined in the Trinitarian-hermeneutical sense, which includes the communicative sphere, plural fecundity of creation, and an emancipatory dimension.

It is certain that Hauerwas has emphasized the importance of the integrity of the church as an alternative political community. His advocacy for recovering the integrity of the church as integral to our political witness does not necessarily mean the withdrawal of the church from economic, cultural, legal, and political life. At this juncture, Hauerwas appreciates

---

53. Hauerwas, "Why the 'Sectarian Temptation' is a Misrepresentation," in Berkman and Cartwright, eds., *Hauerwas Reader*, 95.

Barth's insight into the creator as the redeemer.[54] However, unlike Barth, Hauerwas does not provide a doctrine of revelation or the revelatory power of the biblical material as confirmed in human experience. In order to clarify his ethical bone of contention, according to which the first task of the church is not to make the world more just but to make the world the word, Hauerwas emphasizes the church's engagement with the world. Hauerwas values Bonhoeffer's notion of the *sanctorum communion*, which is the Christian community of love as a sociological type, built on the word of God. This aspect finds its validity in narrative ethics.[55]

According to Hauerwas, Gustafson's ethics tends to abandon ethical faithfulness to the biblical narrative, notably the gospel message about the kingdom of God, because such faithfulness is attacked as a biblical tribalism in Gustafson's ethics. Behind Gustafson's charge of biblical faithfulness as tribalism is the Enlightenment presumption that tribes do not represent open and tolerant communities capable of acknowledging universal rights.[56]

H. R. NIEBUHR'S RESPONSIBLE SELF: THEOCENTRIC ETHICS AND NARRATIVE ETHICS

Concerning the debate between Hauerwas and Gustafson, H. R. Niebuhr's ethics of responsible self occupies an important place. For Gustafson, H. R. Niebuhr's ethics of response and responsibility provides an alternative model for understanding the moral aspects of human experience: "All life has the character of responsiveness, I maintain."[57] In H. R. Niebuhr's conviction, "God is acting in all actions upon you. So respond to all actions upon you as to respond to his action."[58] The task of ethics lies in aiding us to understand ourselves as moral agents rather than conceptualized in terms of model between responsibility and human response to God's command for renewal of the world. Narrative ethics is also grounded in

---

54. Hauerwas, *Community of Character*, 225.

55. Hauerwas, *Performing the Faith*, 14, 19.

56. Hauerwas, "Why the 'Sectarian Temptation' is a Misrepresentation," in Berkman and Cartwright, eds., *Hauerwas Reader*, 109.

57. H. R. Niebuhr, *Responsible Self*, 46.

58. Ibid., 126.

Niebuhr's general ethics while remaining open to moral tradition of virtue and political ethics of Yoder.

To know something of the characteristics of God's intentions is to be seen in human response to God's action in all actions upon us. The Christian turns to the biblical materials to gain some knowledge of God's intentions since the biblical message and symbols have revealed something of the reality of life in the world under God's rule. This can be used to interpret the meaning of general events. H. R. Niebuhr defines the idea of responsibility as the idea of an agent's action as response to an action upon him or her. This response is in accordance with the agent's interpretation of his or her action and also with his or her expectation of response to his or her response.[59]

Responsibility begins with receptivity, because the self knows itself in the presence of the other selves and lives in response to other selves. To be held morally accountable, all human responses are interpreted, mediated, and directed by our understanding of the world in which we live. Response to interpreted actions forms the second component of responsible action. As H. R. Niebuhr holds, "we interpret the things that force themselves upon us as parts of wholes, as related and as symbolic of larger meanings."[60]

H. R. Niebuhr's general use of Scripture does not seek correspondence between particular current events and particular biblical texts. Response to God's action is hopeful and trusting response. Responsibility is responsive action in accordance with interpretations and it seeks an answer to the question posed to us. We have to answer the question "what is going on?" Responsible action entails an answer to this question.

H. R. Niebuhr's prior question "What is going on?" differentiates his ethics of responsibility from other ethical terms, the good and the right. Teleological ethics is concerned with the highest good, to which the right is subordinated. In this ethics, the human being is envisioned as "man-the-maker." This imagery in teleological ethics asserts the moral demand in order to enhance some end in terms of which ends or goods to be pursued in human life. Deontological ethic is concerned with the right. This vision finds expression in the imagery "man-the-citizen," in which

---

59. Ibid., 65.
60. Ibid., 61–62.

the moral life is about rules for action and social existence. This ethics articulates the norms for life and the ground of that norm.[61]

However, H. R. Niebuhr prefers the fitting action for the ethics of responsibility. He develops an agent-relational account of the human action. In the imagery of "man-the-answerer," accountability plays an important role in addition to responsiveness and the response to interpreted action upon us. A moral agent is responsible for anticipated reactions to his or her actions. A consequentialist concern is expressed in the form of reaction and continued interaction.

The fitting action is conducive to the good and the right.[62] We respond to action upon us in a fitting way as we interpret the meaning of actions upon us. In accordance with the interpretation, H. R. Niebuhr seeks to answer the question: "What shall I do?" In responsible action accountability is also made in anticipation of reply because the agent anticipates the reactions to his or her action, in view of objections, confirmations, and corrections.[63]

H. R. Niebuhr's responsible self is grounded in the practical ends-and-means reasoning asking about the purpose. The rational reasoning of purposiveness and humanity[64] seeks only the fitting action to the question of "what is going on." H. R. Niebuhr is convinced that his ethics of responsible self is based on human moral life in general and it offers a key to the understanding of the biblical ethos which represents the historical norm of the Christian life.[65] H. R. Niebuhr's ethics underpins action fitted into the context of a universal, eternal life-giving action by God. What is right is a fitting response to others and it is framed within a relational theory of value and goodness, within the multidimensional domain of value. Value is present in the fittingness or unfittingness.[66]

An ethics as practical construal of the world in the sense of H. R. Niebuhr is undertaken and driven by purpose rationality in the fitting manner concerning what is going on in the world. H. R. Niebuhr's limitation does not see a negative consequence of purpose rationality connected

---

61. Schweiker, *Responsibility and Christian Ethics*, 101.
62. H. R. Niebuhr, *Responsible Self*, 61.
63. Ibid., 64.
64. Ibid., 50.
65. Ibid., 65.
66. H. R. Niebuhr, "The Center of Value," in *Radical Monotheism*, 103.

with the notion of responsibility in the Western process of disenchantment of the world. When purpose responsibility and rationality has become instrumentalized to serve the technological-fitting advancement to conquer the nature, it no longer functions as the responsible self but as irresponsible self. Responsible self must be in complementarity with ethics of conviction which is also responsible for the society, emphasizing value rationality, communicative solidarity, and liberating dimension of religious-moral reasoning.

H. R. Niebuhr is not convinced of the theological logic of describing Hitler as the rod of God's anger and UN as the instrument of God's judgment, because God is the universal judge of all sides in a conflict. All sides are called to fulfill their duties to God, because the universal is present in every particular. In H. R. Niebuhr's ethics of response, we find it difficult to find that God is on the side of the oppressed in human society. For H. R. Niebuhr God is judging the oppressors—the perpetrators as well as the oppressed—and the victims, without reservation.

In Niebuhr's general, ethical perspective underlying Hauerwas and Gustafson, there remains an underdevelopment in matters pertaining to the faith community as missional disciples, and biblically grounded prophetic ethics of reconciliation in the public sphere. Discipleship of God's mission remains neutral in fitting attitude of responsible self. *Being the church* under the mission of God cannot adequately be understood without the church's engagement with God's active involvement in creation and life arrangements. The church as missional community is driven by God's mission for the sake of reconciling movement, recognition, and renewal within human communities, institutions, and cultures in seeking to share the Good News and enhance the integrity of life.

16

Biblical Realism and a Global Public Theology

MacIntyre constructs a hypothesis about contemporary moral theology: "Either it will remain within the theological closed circle: in which case it will have no access to the public and shared moral criteria of our society. Or it will accept those criteria: in which case it may well have important things to say, but these will not be distinctively Christian."[1] Given this statement, John Howard Yoder centers his ethical writings on the teachings of Jesus in the gospel and on the call to discipleship of Jesus. Yoder calls this position "Biblical realism." In the *Politics of Jesus*, Yoder selects the Lukan account and develops his ethics of nonviolent resistance to evil in accordance with his Mennonite tradition. All throughout, he remains within MacIntyre's closed theological circle. However, an ethic of "Biblical realism" does not necessarily remain in a closed theological circle.

Reinhold Niebuhr was born in Wright City, Missouri and became the pastor of Bethel Evangelical Church in Detroit (1915–1928) and later professor of Christian Social Ethics and Theology at Union Theological Seminary in New York (1928–1960). His work had the most important impact on social thought and public policy among Christian thinkers and practitioners in our secular political world. Niebuhr's ethics of responsibility assumes a prophetic character in the tradition of Augustine's political realism. According to Niebuhr's strong conviction, "a realist conception of human nature should be made the servant of an ethic of pro-

1. MacIntyre, *Against Self-Image*, 23.

gressive justice and should not be made into a bastion of conservatism, particularly a conservatism which defends unjust privileges." Niebuhr defines his conviction as "the guiding principle of . . . relation of religious responsibility to political affairs"[2] against unjust privilege and unjustified usurpation. Niebuhr's ethical position as a Christian realist may be characterized within the confines of a biblical prophetic faith. Niebuhr's biblical realism is dialectical in light of love as an "impossible possibility" that remains central in his *Interpretation of Christian Ethics*.[3]

In *The Children of Light and the Children of Darkness*, Niebuhr argues that the human capacity for justice makes democracy possible, while the human inclination to injustice makes democracy necessary.[4] Democracy, which is a method of finding proximate solutions to insoluble problems, is the political system best adapted to the strengths and limitations of human nature.

Niebuhr's "pessimistic optimism" underlying his biblical prophetic realism stands in the Augustinian tradition, despite his disagreement with Augustine's neoplatonic elements. In Niebuhr's account, Augustine was the first great "realist" in Western history, a notion grounded in Augustine's biblical conception of human selfhood. Self-love, in modern terms, egotism, is the source of evil. The social effects of human egotism are contained in his definition of the life of the city of this world (the *civitas dei*) dominated by self-love, which is tied to self's abandonment of God.

Contrary to self-love, the love of God actuates the *civitas dei*, which is distinguished from the city of this world. Augustine was a consistent realist as he called attention to the fact that human community (the family, the commonwealth, and the world) is as full of dangers as the greater sea. Augustine's realism is contained in his analysis of the *civitas terra* in juxtaposition with the *civitas dei* that has to be commingled with the city of this world. *Civitas terra* should have the love of God as its guiding principle.[5] Common linguistic and ethnic forces are divisive on the ultimate level, thus *civitas dei* is beset by the tensions, frictions, competitions of interest, and conflicts to which every human community is exposed. Challenging Cicero's argument that a commonwealth is rooted in

2. R. Niebuhr, *Man's Nature and Communities*, 24–25.
3. R. Niebuhr, *Interpretation of Christian Ethics*.
4. R. Niebuhr, *Children of Light and Children of Darkness*, ix.
5. R. Niebuhr, "Augustine's Political Realism," in Brown, ed., *Essential Reinhold Niebuhr*, 130.

a compact of justice, Augustine contends that commonwealths are bound together by a common love rather than a sense of justice.[6]

AUGUSTINIAN REALIST POLITICS

Augustine's conception of the radical freedom of the human being, his formula for leavening the city of this world with the love of *civitas dei*, makes it impossible for Niebuhr to accept the idea of fixed forms of human behavior and social organization built upon Aristotelian foundations. The proponents of natural law introduce some historically contingent form or social structure into God's inflexible norm, identifying the individual reason with a universal reason. However, an Augustinian realist notion of the leavening influence corrects those who are myopically realistic in seeking only their own interests in violation of the interests of others.[7] The Augustinian option for the holy Jerusalem over against a river of Babylon is rooted in his reliance upon a biblical conception of selfhood; this aspect improves on limitations of medieval Christianity, which culminated in Thomist-Aristotelian thought.[8]

In this light, Niebuhr's distinction between the children of light and the children of darkness is of a dialectical and pragmatic, rather than a dualistic character. Humanity's capacity for justice has to be assessed in view of human inclination to injustice. The notion of children of light refers to those who seek to bring self-interest under the principle of a more universal law and in harmony with a more universal good. However, according to the Bible, the children of this world are in their generation wiser than the children of light. The children of the world, or the darkness, are those who know no law beyond the self. They are wise, although evil, because they understand the power of self-interest.[9] According to Niebuhr, Christian collaboration with the ideology of German Nazism is the example that uncovers the stupidity of the children of light more than the malice of the children of darkness.[10] Niebuhr's pragmatic attitude is

6. Ibid., 127.
7. Ibid., 134.
8. Ibid., 140.
9. R. Niebuhr, "Children of Light and Children of Darkness," in Brown, ed., *Essential Reinhold Niebuhr*, 166.
10. Ibid., 178.

seen in his argument that the preservation of a democratic civilization requires the wisdom of the serpent and the harmlessness of the dove. The children of light must be armed with the wisdom of the children of darkness while remaining free from their evil and malice.[11]

THEOLOGICAL LIBERALISM AND THE ORTHODOX POSITION

Niebuhr's ethical sense of responsibility can be read in this light. It is wrongly assumed to preach the gospel *sub specie aeternitatis* (under the standpoint of eternity) as if there is a way of transmuting the Christian gospel into a system of historical optimism without regard to different contexts and historical particularities. Christian life with a high sense of responsibility warns against degenerating into an intolerable otherworldliness. The awful responsibility of the people of God becomes visible in the world's cities of destruction in the account of Abraham's petition (Gen 19:22–23).

Recognizing the inadequacies of theological liberalism, Niebuhr finds his position in affinity with neo-orthodox theology, which represents a recovery of the classical Christian heritage. However, he has a theological reservation about Karl Barth. Niebuhr seeks to overcome the antithesis between the dogmatism of the Orthodox Church and the liberal church under the bushel of the culture of modernity.

Orthodox Christianity expresses its morality in dogmatic and authoritarian moral codes, deriving their authority from a sacred canon. In contrast, the liberal church is dominated by the desire to refuse the anachronistic ethics or the incredible myths of the orthodox religion. It has endeavored to reconcile religion and science, disavowing the incredible portion of its religious heritage and making the remainder amenable to the modern mind. It adjusts itself to the credos and prejudices of modernity while unfortunately running into the danger of obscuring the distinctiveness of the Christian message and the creativity of Christian morality.

According to Niebuhr, the limitation of orthodox Christianity lies in its premature identification of the transcendent will of God with canonical moral codes and their primitive social standards. It fails to derive any significance for political and moral principles from the law of love. It

11. Ibid., 181.

destroys a dynamic relationship between the ideal of love and principles of justice. There is the deeper pessimism underlying Christian orthodoxy. Insofar as the church claims the problem of politics to be irrelevant to the Christian life, it is an ally of the established social forces. On Niebuhr's account, the final sin is always committed in the name of religion. He considers Marx's critique in this regard: "The beginning of all criticism is the criticism of religion."[12]

The words of Jesus (Luke 22:25) demonstrate the critical attitude of a prophetic religion toward the perils of power and the uncritical acceptance of social power (Rom 13). In contrast to Luther's attitude during the peasant rebellion and the neo-Lutheran notion of *Schöfungsordung* (the order of creation), which was in collaboration with the Nazi ideology, Niebuhr is convinced of the Calvinist theory of resistance in the thought of Beza, Knox, the Dutch, and the American Calvinists, who laid the foundation for a dynamic relationship between Calvinism and the democratic movement.[13]

According to Niebuhr, liberal Christianity fails to secure the absolute and transcendent ethic of Jesus from the relative moral standards of a commercial age and the whole of modern secular liberal culture to which liberal Christianity is tied. Here, the transcendent ideals of Christian morality have become immanent possibilities in the process of history and nature. The transcendent impossibilities of the Christian ethic of love degenerated into the immanent and imminent possibilities of a historical process in which the experience of depth in life is completely dissipated.[14] Niebuhr deems both liberalism and Marxism as secularized and naturalized versions of the Hebrew prophetic movement and the Christian religion. The significant achievement of the prophetic movement in Hebraic religion lies in an ethico-religious passion.[15]

---

12. R. Niebuhr, "Christian Witness in Social and National Order," in Brown, ed., *Essential Reinhold Niebuhr*, 95.

13. R. Niebuhr, *Interpretation of Christian Ethics*, 98.

14. Ibid., 5–6.

15. Ibid., 16.

JESUS AND PROPHETIC ETHICS

In genuinely prophetic religion, Niebuhr argues, God transcends the created world and promises an ultimate redemption of the sinful world. Prophetic Christianity maintains its independence against naturalism and other-worldliness, but also preserves its purity against sacramental vitiations of its own basic prophetic mythology. The inclination of Christianity, which deviates from prophetic religion in terms of sacramental complacency and also mystic otherworldliness, is partly derived from a Greek influence. However, the religion of Jesus is a prophetic religion built on the moral ideal of love, vicarious suffering, and the kingdom of God. Niebuhr suggests that the kingdom of God is always a possibility in history, but also remains an impossibility in history, beyond every historical achievement. His conviction is expressed in the thesis: "Only a vital Christian faith, renewing its youth in its prophetic origin, is capable of dealing adequately with the moral and social problems of our age."[16]

For Niebuhr, the ethic of Jesus distinguishes itself from every naturalistic ethic (egoism imbedded in pre-established harmony according to Adam Smith) and prudential ethic (reason transmuting the anarchy of egoism into a higher harmony, as in the case of utilitarianism). Love as the quintessence of the character of God is regarded as axiomatic in the faith of prophetic religion. In dealing with the problem of political justice, the Christian church has to set all propositions of justice under the law of love, presenting the gospel to nations and to individuals as well, bringing them to the possibility of a new and whole life.[17]

The religious orientation of this ethic is expressed clearly in the statement: "You cannot serve God and mammon." Rather than undergirding an ascetic ethic, this saying is a test of complete devotion to the sovereignty of God. Wealth, in Jesus's estimation, is a source of distraction: "Where your treasure is there will be your heart be also." The ethic of Jesus for instance, in special cases (Mark 3:32–34; Luke 9:60; Matt 10:37) is not applicable to the problems of contemporary society.[18] The kingdom of God is always at hand in the sense that the impossibilities are really possible, leading to new actualities in given moments of history and soci-

---

16. Ibid., 21.

17. R. Niebuhr, "Christian Witness in Social and National Order," in Brown, ed., *Essential Reinhold Niebuhr*, 97.

18. R. Niebuhr, *Interpretation of Christian Ethics*, 31.

ety. Nevertheless, every actuality of history and society manifests itself as only an approximation of the ideal. The kingdom of God is in fact always coming, but never established here and now.[19]

In Niebuhr's analysis, the Kantian axiom, "I ought, therefore I can," is accepted as basic to all analyses of the moral situation. The role of reason and immortality from stoics to Kant has been assessed, but it is difficult to relate it to the dynamic aspects of life. Kantian ethical idealism upholds the assertion that the intelligible self is the lawgiver, imposing the law of rational consistency: Act so as to make thy action the basis of universal law. But what is it that persuades people to obey the law? The ambiguities of Kantian ethics and the failure of rationalistic ethics in general necessitate the importance of the Christian doctrine of love and faith.

In elaborating an adequate ethic for the social problems of human existence, there is tension between Christian love's perfectionism and its realism. Niebuhr's ethical project is grounded in his vision, according to which prophetic Christianity needs to develop a more adequate social ethic within the terms of its understanding of the total human situation. That is, with a stronger emphasis on its prophetic, and a lesser emphasis on its rationalistic, inheritance.[20] The prophetic faith in a God who is both the ground and the ultimate fulfillment of existence is thus involved in every moral situation. This creates a morality that implies an ultimate perfection of unity and harmony, although it is not realizable in any historical situation.

The universalism of prophetic ethics transcends the demands of rational universalism. It is unfortunate that historical Christianity has, in part, departed from the prophetic position. For instance, the theology of Thomas Aquinas is influenced by Aristotelian rationalism, considering a rational and mystical contemplation of the divine as previously superior to moral action. In Aristotelian ethics, the slave and women do not have the same rights as the freeman. In Stoicism the difference in the intelligence of human beings prompts Stoic doctrine to a certain aristocratic condescension toward fools. However, in prophetic religion the obligation is toward the loving will of God, a more transcendent source of unity than any discoverable source in the natural world. Christian universalism represents a more impossible possibility than the universalism of Stoicism.

---

19. Ibid., 36.
20. Ibid., 61.

Christian faith is a living and vital presupposition of life and conduct.[21] In prophetic ethics the transcendent unity of life is an article of faith. The law of love is an impossible possibility. The perspective that upholds the love commandment as a simple possibility, rather than an impossible possibility, is rooted in a faulty analysis of human nature (humans being creatures of finitude).[22] The crown of Christian ethics is the doctrine of forgiveness. The whole genius of prophetic religion is expressed in the grace of justification. Forgiveness is in the same relation to punitive justice as sacrificial love is to distributive justice. But forgiveness is finally in contrast to punitive justice, "morality beyond morality" (Berdyaev).[23] Forgiveness is purely in the realm of grace. Yet love is a possibility if the impossibility of love is recognized. An ethics culminating in an impossible possibility generates its choice in terms of the doctrine of forgiveness. Forgiveness is possible only when morality is transcended in religion. Luther's notion of justification finds its ethical culmination in Niebuhr's biblical realism. This is because we must be saved by the final form of love, that is, forgiveness.[24]

Niebuhr adopts the facts of experience as his starting point for Christian realism, seeing justice as a balance of power between groups in a state of flux—whether classes, races, or nations. Therefore, perfection is never achieved in history. Different from Barth, Niebuhr starts with self-interest and power, as deeply grounded in the cross—the heart of the Christian gospel. The term "transvaluation of values" is at the heart of Niebuhr's perspective on the cross, which is not simply the keystone of Christian faith but the very key to history itself.[25] However, in James Cone's account, Niebuhr's realism (based on facts of experience) and the theology of the cross do not manage to deal with the issue of race because of his call for gradualism, patience, and prudence. In his many essays about racial issues in America, Africa, and Asia, Niebuhr was not capable of making the problem of race one of his central theological and political concerns.[26]

---

21. Ibid., 132.
22. Ibid., 72.
23. R. Niebuhr, "Love and Law in Protestantism and Catholicism," in Brown, ed., *Essential Reinhold Niebuhr*, 153.
24. R. Niebuhr, *Irony of American History*, 63.
25. Cone, *The Cross and the Lynching Tree*, 30–35.
26. Ibid., 39–41.

PUBLIC THEOLOGY AND POLITICAL ECONOMY

Appreciating Niebuhr's ethics based on biblical realism, Max Stackhouse proposes a public ethic and Christian economic stewardship that affirms H. Richard Niebuhr's typology "Christ transforming culture."[27] The term public theology originated in Reinhold Niebuhr's article "Public Theology and the American Experience." Robert Bellah published his famous essay on "civil religion," drawing from Alexis de Tocqueville and also from Emil Durkheim's adoption of the term that can be traced through Rousseau's *Social Contract* to Cicero's *De Legibus*. In contrast to the term "civil religion," Martin Marty prefers "public theology."[28] Marty appreciates Reinhold Niebuhr, a Christian realist, who identifies the Augustinian understandings of human nature and sociopolitical developments in history. Marty also identifies Puritan theologian Jonathan Edwards, Christian educator Horace Buschnell, and Social Gospel leader, Walter Rauschenbusch, as influences upon the American public. They utilize theological language to interpret and guide the basic ordering and fabric of the common life in the public sphere and see the basic aspects of the human condition under God's reign.[29]

Stackhouse seeks a rationale for a public theology of political economy in developing a vision of economic stewardship for modern life. For this task, he values the tradition of Christian sociology, notably represented by Shailer Matthews's notion of Christian personalism and Walter Rauschenbusch's notion of social gospel. These movements claimed social relationships to be democratic not only on a political level but also applied to social and economic institutions and attitudes.[30]

In accordance with Scripture and the classical teachings of the tradition, Stackhouse is convinced that Jesus can be seen as the initiator of a new era of social relations, challenging the principalities and the powers. Jesus may give us a clue to new, constructive possibilities. The term "Christian sociology" is introduced as a major heading. Drawing upon the principle of tradition, reason, and experience in a quest for a public theology, Stackhouse finds it necessary to bring other ethical resources to the crises experienced in the contemporary context.

---

27. Stackhouse, *Public Theology and Political Economy*, 43.
28. Stackhouse, *Globalization and Grace*, 87.
29. Ibid., 88.
30. Stackhouse, *Public Theology and Political Economy*, 53.

THE BIBLICAL OUTLOOK ON GOD'S KINGDOM AND ECONOMIC ORDER

According to Stackhouse, the biblical texts reject the possessive individualism that is celebrated by the followers of Adam Smith. Such a picture of human being, which is based on individualism and selfish rationality in calculating costs and benefits, does not fit a biblical notion of human being as the image of God. It is not the providential laws of the market that produce good results for human life. Against this, public ethics accentuates the fact that God can bring about the transformation of human will, inclining people to see the importance of compassion. In this regard, the society can build an ethos that honors and actualizes vocation, covenant, and moral law.

In the discussion of the democratization of the economic order, Stackhouse articulates Rauschenbusch's prophetic biblical orientation. In Rauschenbusch's vision of Christian prophecy, emphasis is placed on the connection between Jesus' teaching and the Old Testament prophets. It is certain that Jesus' prophetic activity transcends the nationalistic features of the prophetic tradition and becomes universal in scope and horizon, including all humanity.[31] For Rauschenbusch, the apocalypticism in the New Testament implies the overthrow of the present world powers, seeking new possibilities in discernment of the signs of the times. However, such revolutionary aspects of the gospel have been relegated to the spiritual, individualistic, and otherworldly features of the New Testament witness. Supported by alliances between ecclesiasticism and privilege, and being cut off from the masses, Christianity has yielded to speculative reflection, disengagement, individualistic pietism, and sacramental ritualism. The historical consequences have resulted in the obfuscation of the social, ethical dimensions of Jesus' teachings. At issue is in the concept of the Social Gospel indirectly and diffusely influencing contemporary social and public life with the New Testament.

For Rauschenbusch, a biblical notion of the kingdom of God is a collective concept with political overtones and inspiration. It is notably marked by a transformed attitude toward the economic sphere in Jesus' teaching about God versus mammon.[32] Portraying Jesus as the explicit ally of the poor and working class, Rauschenbusch deemed class analy-

---

31. Ibid., 59, 60.
32. Ibid., 62.

sis a useful tool in biblical exegesis, applying Jesus' teachings as distinct guidelines for social arrangements and the command to love. Christian sociology, in the fashion of Rauschenbusch, runs in the direction of a democratization of the economic order in a socialist manner.[33]

Nevertheless, in Stackhouse's account, the founding figures of Christian sociology were patriotic while also sympathetic with the laboring classes. Most of them held collectivism to be a threat to truth and justice, to pluralism and democracy, and to humanity and the faith. They contend that it has little to do with the prudent stewardship of society or material creation.[34] Given this, Stackhouse avoids a way of individualistic, commercial capitalism as well as the collectivist political economy of communism. What is common in the concept of Christian sociology lies in the democratization of the economic order and provides ethical guidelines for public discussions of economic life. A basic principle envisioned in this regard is "persons in community," which means living under God's justice and toward God's kingdom. This principle embraces dimensions of personalism and communitarianism in the economic life and order. It is thusly connected with the transcendent point of reference: God's truth, justice, and love known in Jesus Christ. The transcendent point of reference plays as a yardstick to measure people and the institutions of the community.[35]

Stackhouse further holds that the principle, "persons in community," is presupposed and regarded as normative prior to economic activity. This is because it articulates the social nature of the human self and applies spiritual and moral principles to the structure and fabric of social relationships in community. We may find a clue to the transformation of human relationships and community structures in religion—a religion ethical in root and branch living in accordance with a vision of the kingdom of God.

The kingdom of God as the overriding biblical symbol for the future is a necessary conceptual norm to which all the eschatological motifs point. The fundamental shape of the future is indicated to be political transformation over and against both existential or spiritual and natural transformation. Under the root metaphor of the kingdom of God humanity and community are fulfilled and transformed first within a social, po-

---

33. Rauschenbusch, *Christianizing Social Order*.
34 Stackhouse, *Public Theology and Political Economy*, 48.
35. Ibid., 64.

litical sphere, embracing the forces of the cosmos and creation. The vision of the kingdom of God is broken only proleptically, only in a provisional way; expectation of the breaking of the possibilities of the future into the realities of the now.[36]

However, Stackhouse maintains that the church has continually fixed the vision of the kingdom of God on the spiritual in contradiction to its sociopolitical meanings. It needs to undertake prophetic articulation in the midst of the sociopolitical realm in which God's presence may be found.[37] Stackhouse's public theology seeks to offer reliable, warranted guidance about how we should believe in the face of social realities, emphasizing the specific responsibility of religious leadership and institutions.[38]

CHRISTIAN SOCIOLOGY AND A META-ETHICAL MODEL

In his project of "social theory and theological reconstruction" Stackhouse proposes a model of the meta-ethical theory by operating social analysis within the meta-ethical framework. Ethics plays a normative role in social analysis through the positing of three questions: what is right (intrinsic worth), what is good (the end and the consequences), and what is fit (applicability of the right and the good pertaining to the present conditions). A theological credo is shaped, weaving a supra-historical combination of right, good, and fit. The intrinsic meanings, ultimate purposes, and appropriate matrices of life and history can have some coherence in regard to what is and what ought to be. An analytical ethic may supply a credo that is capable of evoking recognition of theological-confessional assumptions to social analysts and their participation in the construction of meta-ethical models. A theological credo that can render a model of the right, good, and fit must be tested and confirmed according to its relationship to the structures, projections, and functions of human life and institutions in a given society.[39]

Stackhouse's meta-ethical model is of interpretive character because theological norms can only be grasped in terms of symbol, which is not

---

36. Stackhouse, *Ethics and Urban Ethics*, 103–4.
37. Ibid., 106.
38. Stackhouse, *Public Theology and Political Economy*, 92.
39. Stackhouse, *Ethics and Urban Ethics*, 66–67.

judgment over history. Rather, theological symbols are used to discriminate between better and worse within the historical perspective. His argument is best described: we transcend historically conditioned perspective by credo, while a theological credo unrelated to our present context loses the power to deal with the data of life.[40]

Furthermore in his public ethics, three modes of discourse correspond to the tasks of ethics. The first defines, analytically and ethnologically, the values and norms that dominate a social or cultural ethos. The second determines deontologically what values and norms are right or wrong or teleologically good or evil. The third is prescriptive and calls for the reconstruction of the social and cultural ethos. Thus, public ethics emphasizes these three focuses on contextual, deontological, and teleological analyses.[41]

TRINITY AS PUBLIC THEOLOGY AND PLURALISM

A meta-ethical model reinterprets the Trinitarian theological tradition in the direction of the kingdom of God. It demands pluralism in recognition of a transcendent unity, attending to the concrete powers and values of creative order; the new supernatural forms of identity overcoming alienation, and the quest for the Holy Spirit of community engenders cultural innovation.[42]

The metaphysical-moral notion of pluralism based on unity and coherence with diversity has given rise to the political notion of constitutional democracy. Pluralism can be accepted as a blessing in modern civilizations and religious communities, such as ecumenical churches. Leadership is given to groups whose voices were previously undermined and marginalized by the dominion of white, male elites. However, pluralism and its dynamism can also be a pitfall, as in when it becomes an idol with a universal normlessness. The metaphysical-moral vision, which Stackhouse establishes to give guidance of stewardship to the world, undergirds the Christian understanding of the triune God. In this framework pluralism is a normative theological belief including a social, ethical aspect. The metaphysical-moral grounds see pluralism in

40. Ibid., 68.
41. Stackhouse, *Globalization and Grace*, 231.
42. Stackhouse, *Ethics and Urban Ethics*, 140.

terms of persons in community and the community of persons. Such a theological-Trinitarian understanding of pluralism may be postbiblical Christian contributions regarding the relationship between Word and world. Constructing Christian stewards of the Word, Trinitarian language can be pertinent to public discourse, as it undergirds Christian sociology in the formation of modern political economies.[43]

A public theology can develop and refine biblical themes in new directions by incorporating the analysis of the intellectual and social realities of the current political and economic structure into a theological framework. The chief task of Christian stewardship lies in cultivating a new pubic theology and mission that is grounded in disciplined but diverse communities of faith and service. This public theology is sensitive to the need for a new birth of cross-cultural and historically informed Christian sociology. It elaborates a new sense of missional vocation for providing guidance to the lives of people and develops new covenantal ways for faith communities struggling with the complexities of modern life.[44] Thus, theology and ethics are key disciplines for Stackhouse to delve into the critical examination, refinement, and penetration of spheres of life such as politics, business, technology, and the guidance of religious conviction and social-ethical orientations in the public sphere.[45] Public theology shapes missional church to be socially engaged in these realms.

GLOBAL PUBLIC THEOLOGY AND ECONOMIC GLOBALIZATION

According to Stackhouse, a theory of globalization may be understood as an inevitable consequence of the technical advancement and economic transformation in 19th century Europe. Globalization takes hegemony in interaction with world economy, expanding its political, economic, military, and cultural lead. This refers to an inevitability of globalization based on expansion and penetration of capital movement beyond national boundaries to the global economy in pursuit of capital accumulation and world market. According to Stackhouse, globalization is best understood

---

43. Stackhouse, *Public Theology and Political Economy*, 174–76.
44. Ibid.,176.
45. Stackhouse, *Globalization and Grace*, 80.

"as a worldwide set of social, political, cultural, technological, ethical and ideological motifs."[46]

Supporting the relation of economic globalization to Christianity, Stackhouse argues that globalization forms an alternative to postmodernism, demanding the rediscovery of universalistic principles of anthropology, spirituality, morality, and law. Combining religious faith with globalization, Stackhouse insists that "the Christian faith is the most valid worldview or metaphysical moral vision available to humanity." In a globalizing Christian world, Stackhouse hopes to engage with people of other cultures and faiths and non-Christian religions. In his conviction, where a religion becomes widely shared, it shapes an ethos that gives identity to a particular culture. It tends to promote a social ethic fostering distinctive public institutions, thereby molding civilizations.[47]

Earlier on, Stackhouse's pubic theology was undertaken within Christian stewardship in modern society in terms of scripture, tradition, reason, and experience.[48] It represented a prophetic line of the Social Gospel in the American context. However, currently, his Christian public theology in a globalized fashion argues that globalization "rests on and evolves good, reconstructing and transforming Grace" in terms of God's providential grace. Thus, the civilization of globalization is accepted as an ultimate destiny that it anticipates as an inclusive heavenly city, the image of a complex and holy civilization which comes to us by grace.[49] However, in theological justification of globalization under the rubric of God's providential grace, we are aware that there is lack of considering the unprecedented levels of injustice, inequality, dominion, and violence generated by the free market principle. At issue in the providential public theology is the Christian sanction of natural law as universally valid, moral, rooted in God, and the baptism of globalizing civilization. It is unfortunate that Stackhouse's providential public theology accuses such biblical, prophetic perspective to be the business of liberationists who easily fall into the ideology of Marxist dialectics.[50]

---

46. Ibid.
47. Ibid., 8.
48. Stackhouse, *Public Theology and Political Economy*, 1–15.
49. Stackhouse, *Globalization and Grace*, 249.
50. Stackhouse, *Public Theology and Political Economy*, 22.

A PUBLIC THEOLOGY OF GRACE AND GLOBALIZATION

In his study of "globalization and grace," Stackhouse further develops his rationale for a Christian public theology in a globalizing world. He submits his public theology as a modest protest against political philosophy and political theology. It resists the arguments of political philosophy according to which religious believers must park their religious modes of discourse outside the public sphere. Otherwise, they must restate religious languages in a theologically neutral manner for rational and empirical arguments to be allowed. Against this trend, Stackhouse finds such political arguments fundamentally discriminatory, thereby agreeing with Nicholas Wolterstorff. According to Wolterstorff, religious convictions teach people to "strive for wholeness, integrity, integration, in their lives" through the Word of God, the teaching of the Torah, the commands and example of Jesus among others. Religion is about something other than social and political existence.[51]

Public theology is against political theology, although it is not an antipolitical view. This protest comes from the conviction that the public is prior to the republic and the moral and spiritual fabric of civil society. The public should be more determinative of politics than politics is for society and religion. In the fabric of civil society, religious faith and faith-based ethics and organizations are a decisive component.[52] However, Stackhouse does not undertake a conceptual clarity of civil society that retains diverse and different direction from Hobbes and John Locke on the one hand and from Rousseau, Hegel, and Habermas on the other hand.

According to Stackhouse, the meanings of theology are understood in confessional, contextual, and dogmatic senses. Although the pubic theology draws upon these diverse spectrums, its task is apologetic in terms of faithfulness to the classical sources of faith and their ecumenical or Catholic norms. Beyond that, public theology is willing to encounter secular, philosophical and non-Christian religious orientations to the world.[53]

Stackhouse's Christian sociology in a universalistic framework seeks to offer a more adequate basis for cross-cultural understanding since what is truly divine is the only truly universal reality. His vision

---

51. Audi, *Religion in Public Square*, 105; cf. Stackhouse, *Globalization and Grace*, 99–100.

52. Stackhouse, *Globalization and Grace*, 103.

53. Ibid., 107.

of the universalization of public theology leads him to a controversial argument according to which theology points toward what is necessary for all in ethics, law, and society in a global era. However, in this framework his project of a Christian public theological ethic for a globalizing world is vulnerable to the totalization of wisdom and insights of other faith communities into a Christian yardstick. This is because Stackhouse controversially advocates for a Christian public theology coupled with the globalization of ethics: Globalization is a form of creational and providential grace that comes to a catholic and ecumenical partial fulfillment pointing toward a salvific vision for humanity and the world.[54] It is unfortunate that Stackhouse reduces the prophetic message of God's reign and Jesus' liberating message to mere servants of the creational and providential grace of globalization. That is, a Catholic and ecumenical partial fulfillment in redeeming humanity and the world.

PUBLIC THEOLOGY AND THE SOCIOLOGY OF RELIGION

Driven in the ecumenical, global direction, Stackhouse values Max Weber as his mentor for the task of reconstructing a public theology as an alternative to the pathologies of laissez-faire capitalism and the tyrannies of Marxist collectivism. In the formation of a new "ecumene" on the Christian side of Christian sociology, Stackhouse integrates the social interpretation of political and economic life. Here Max Weber's historical, comparative sociology is regarded as a new resource to overcome the limitations of an anthropological concept of *homo economicus* as conceptualized in Adam Smith and Karl Marx.

The relation between the facts of a social phenomenon and its ethical or spiritual value and validity is of a dialectical character in an open-ended manner rather than being normatively fixed. Historical and comparative analysis reveals that each level of fact and value influences the other. Religious ideas play a normative role in forming specific constellations and configurations of political and economic life.

It is certain that Weber's sociological method is not unilaterally structured in an idealist explanation, but it finds a typology of selective affinity between religious ideas and material development. His sociological contribution lies in keen analysis of the process of Western modern-

---

54. Ibid., 249.

ization, that is, the disenchantment of the world in terms of sorting out purpose rationality and selective affinity between religious ideas and socio-economic ethos. A spirit of capitalism called for by Weber denotes the rationalizing attitude or basis for modernization.

In Weber's definition of capitalism, its ethos can be seen as a methodical, disciplined, social organization of human and material means of production in pursuit of the accumulation of increased capital; this is then rationally deployed to further efficient production. This has brought constant social change in the transformation of traditional rationality and value into the new pattern of a modern purpose rationality of capitalism.

Given this, Stackhouse argues that a political economy becomes an "iron cage" if there is no inner spiritual and ethical foundation. Those who debate economic issues with literatures of Adam Smith and Marx have been trapped in ideological cages by confusing things as they are with things as they ought to be.[55]

In contrast to Stackhouse's evaluation, however, Weber's theory of "iron cage" takes issue with the Calvinist's methodical ascetic ethics of calling in a paradoxical manner. The content of the Puritan worldly asceticism and mission was carried out of monastic cells into everyday life. Dominating worldly morality, it plays a normative role in building the tremendous cosmos of the modern economic order, which is bound to the technical and economic conditions of machine production. It determines the lives of all the individuals born into this mechanism with irresistible force. In Baxter's view, the care for external goods should only lie on the shoulders of the saint like a light cloak; it can be thrown aside at any moment. However, Weber sharply diagnoses that the cloak should become an iron cage—this is the fate of capitalism connected with the process of modernization, the disenchantment of the world.[56] In the last stage of this cultural development Weber's diagnosis sounds unfortunate or pessimistic: "Specialists without spirit, sensualists without heart; this nullity imagines that it has attained a level of civilization never before achieved."[57]

Weber, in his diagnosis, implies a dimension of the public ethic regarding the emergence of the new prophets or a great rebirth of old ideas

---

55. Ibid., 91.
56. M. Weber, *Protestant Ethic and Spirit of Capitalism*, 181.
57. Ibid., 182.

and ideals. This perspective is connected with his view of the ethics of responsibility and ethics of conviction as investigated and addressed in his 1919 lecture in the midst of social revolution in Germany. It is unfortunate that Stackhouse sidesteps Weber's complicated position regarding the limitations of Western civilization and his ethical position concerning the reality of polytheism and the iron cage. A theological-ethical reflection on God's mission and missional church does not need to be grounded in Weber's notion of purpose rationality related to its responsibility in matters of political economy. Weber's ethics of responsibility remains in an individual heroic manner without considering the responsibility of economic life in solidarity with those who are oppressed and marginalized for the sake of the common good.

A REFLECTION ON JUSTICE IN THE CONTEXT OF GLOBALIZATION

From a public ethical perspective, a theory of justice remains an important insight for the church's responsibility to society and globalization. Readjusting the law to distribute to each person his or her due remains an important task for the church's social responsibility in an ecumenical and global context. God's command of preservation must not be ideologically misused to sanctify the status quo in service of the powerful, as seen in the process of economic globalization. Human law is the distribution of what is due to each person (*suum cuique*). The Roman law dictum (*suum cuique*) expresses the multiplicity of the natural and the rights pertaining to it. However, this principle, which is for determination of rights, does not consider the conflict of rights inherent in the natural itself. The conflict demands the intervention of positive rights from outside, both divine and secular. Nonetheless, its relative correctness must not be deprived and due honor is rendered to the will and the gift of God the Creator. All rights are fulfilled in the reconciliation of Jesus Christ through the Holy Spirit who shall give to each his own.[58]

Distributive justice and the defense of freedom in the genuine sense of democracy may be regarded penultimate, that is, before the ultimate. The penultimate attitude in feeding the hungry, protecting natural rights of living creatures, and upholding economic justice must be respected

---

58. Bonhoeffer, *Ethics*, 152.

and validated in regard to the approaching ultimate. The individual comes into the world with a natural right of his or her own.[59]

The *suum cuique* in the sense of social justice and the defense of liberty in the democratic sense belong together. What matters in the domain of natural life is the preservation of the life of human beings as a species.[60] This theological, ethical reflection on social justice, the defense of freedom, and the natural rights of humanity takes issue with an optimistic sanction of economic globalization as God's grace in creation in a providential manner. In the global context, the universality of economic dependence is called interdependence, or mutual dependence. The material nature of injustice is defined by the exploitation, which is nonreciprocal social or worldwide relationship. The fundamental inequalities hinder the social-realization of the whole of society, failing to provide equitably to all its members what they materially need for the sustainability of their lives. Thus, the *suum cuique* is needed.

---

59. Ibid., 153.

60. Bonhoeffer, *Ethics*, 154. See further Gollwitzer, *An Introduction to Protestant Theology*, 196–200.

V

Postcolonial Public Theology and World Christianity

MISSIONAL CHURCH, PUBLIC THEOLOGY, and World Christianity constitute a coherent chapter to delve into, as we further develop the public ethical theology and discipleship of God's mission in postcolonial World Christianity. Along the process of globalization, life in many public spheres continues to be shaped and influenced by multiple cultures and religions in a pluralist fashion. A postcolonial claim for cultural hybridity and multicultural diversity within World Christianity emphasizes a necessity for reframing mission as constructive theology in a post-Western framework, recognizing difference and otherness in appreciation of a non-Western understanding of the living narrative of the divine salvific drama.

Part V is an endeavor to present postcolonial public theology in the comparative religious framework in the experience of World Christianity. As we previously stated, public ethical theology is primarily based on a hermeneutical deliberation of God as the infinite horizon of speech-event in an archeological search for those buried in history and society concerning the coming of God's kingdom. God as the Subject of speech underlines God's word-in-action in the Hebrew manner of *dabar* as obvious in the promise of God with Israel, while including God's universal covenant with Noah. In a biblical narrative, we read that God's covenant with Abraham includes God's blessing of Hagar and Ishmael. An interdisciplinary study of mission, moral theory, culture, ethnicity, gender, and religious ethics becomes an indispensable part in characterizing postcolonial public theology in a constructive notion of God's mission in an ethical-hermeneutical framework.[61]

Furthermore, a concept of God's act of speech in an extraordinary and irregular fashion undergirds public theology as a prophetic dialogue in interreligious context and in the comparative study of religious ethics. This perspective shapes a postcolonial horizon of public theology in critical-constructive deliberation of the relationship between biblical narrative and colonized narrative, in terms of the recognition of an irregularized and foreclosed narrative in light of God's act of speech. God may speak in the reconciled world as it takes place in every direction and all different courses, especially in special concern for those on the margins, the poor, and the innocent victims. It strengthens mission as prophetic dialogue in the comparative study.

Such a perspective brings home the importance of a thick description of the biblical narrative in dynamic interaction with culture, colonized discourse, ethical ethos, and religions for the sake of fusion of horizons and in promotion of the ethics of emancipation by confessing Jesus Christ in postcolonial World Christianity. Postcolonial public theology is thus driven by a hermeneutical reorientation toward the standpoint of those who are "the outcast, the suspects, the maltreated, the powerless, the oppressed, and the reviled"[62]—in short, the *massa perditionis* (the mass who are bound for perdition). The hermeneutical outlook from below is more deeply undertaken in a postcolonial perspective from the Other.

Chapter 17 is a study of postcolonial public Theology in terms of hermeneutical reorientation and comparative ethics. This study incorporates postcolonial theory to the theological theme of creation and reconciliation to promote a constructive side of postcolonial theology in challenging the overemphasis on deconstruction in postcolonial theory. A deliberation is given to characterizing postcolonial public theology.

---

61. Chung, *Public Theology in an Age of World Christianity*.
62. Bonhoeffer, LPP 17.

Chapter 18 attempts to read Bonhoeffer in the East Asian context. Hauerwas proposed his creative reading of Bonhoeffer's political theology to deepen his argument that the first task of the church is to make the world the world. Through Bonhoeffer's deliberation on politics and truth, Hauerwas contends that his narrative ethics is concerned with elaborating that we cannot and should not avoid engagement with the world.[63] Toward postcolonial public theology, I am more interested in undertaking a postcolonial reading of Bonhoeffer in dialogue with East Asian *minjung* theology and Confucian ethics of rectification.

Chapter 19 is an audacious interpretation of Barth by radicalizing his theology in dealing with a complex relationship between theology and religious pluralism, which is an integral part of his theology of God's mission and missional church.

Chapter 20 undertakes a comparative study of an eschatologically oriented ethics of emancipation by attending to the critical dialogue between European political theology and Liberation theology in Latin America.

---

63. Hauerwas, *Performing the Faith*, 14.

17

Postcolonial Public Theology

Hermeneutical Reorientation and Comparative Ethics

As previously examined, H. R. Niebuhr's ethics of responsibility takes a general, interpretative attitude as an onlooker. It has less to do with upholding the interpretive position to critically engage with sociocultural reality characterized by inequality, conflict, and hegemonic power. However, Hauerwas discerns a theological lack of the eschatological character of the Christian faith in H. R. Niebuhr's typology of Christ and culture. Transcendence becomes the hallmark of Niebuhr's understanding of God in a theocentric radical monotheism. Hence eschatology will succumb to a theocentrism.[1] Hauerwas's narrative ethics grounded in the gospel of Jesus in view of God's kingdom and Christian community offers a clue to uphold biblical narrative in dialogue with the different narratives of other faith communities on behalf of an interreligious ethic of virtue and character.

George Hunsberger, driven by a proposal by Hauerwas, Willimon, and Yoder, attempts to mediate the Christian identity as lived practice with an emphasis on the church's missional witness to the coming kingdom of God. A public configuration of the missional church emphasizes a spirit of companionship, a humble attitude that undergirds the truthtelling of the gospel. Such an aspect affirms particularity in Christian discourse, while underpinning courage in public action and keeping an eye on the eschatological horizon toward God's promised future.[2] This

---

1. Hauerwas, *Performing the Faith*, 17.
2. Hunsberger, "The Missional Voice and Posture of Public Theologizing."

combined approach finds its validity in Newbigin's idea of the congregation as a "hermeneutics of the gospel."[3]

Insofar as morality is socially and culturally constructed, moral reasoning and ethical attitude are shaped by social and cultural factors at large. A lifeworld in a sociohistorical setting and an ethnic background affects moral reasoning and ethical judgment. Thus it is important to examine social class, gender, and ethnic differences, different religious worldviews and narratives in moral judgment in light of God's act of speech in the otherness of the Other. A narrative ethic tends to neglect plural reality and discourses within the narrative world embedded within a sociohistorical context, because it describes peaceable people against the world, coded as the realm of non-peace.[4]

In contrast to Hauerwas, Gustafson's theocentric ethics and Tracy's correlational and revisionist model emphasizes public dialogue with the people of other cultures and faiths. God is in relation to all aspects of human life. If ethics is defined as the practical construal of the world, its task does not undermine a public dialogue with people of other religions. Rather its discourse undergirds the ethical commitment to social justice, peace among multireligious communities, and the sustainability of the globe.

HERMENEUTICAL REORIENTATION: RESPONSIBLE ETHICS AND GLOBAL PLURALISM

Regarding the debate between Hauerwas and Gustafson, I appreciate Schweiker's integrative ethics of responsibility for marking progress in its hermeneutical reorientation for an ethic of responsibility, integrity of life, and pluralism. A life lived in responsibility for the integrity of life is marked by another form of goodness, moral integrity, or the rectitude of conscience. Schweiker's imperative of responsibility is expressed in respecting and enhancing the integrity of life in all actions and relations.[5]

A pluralist approach to Scripture and ethics requires examining a construal of text and the moral outlook which infuses that construal. The Scripture as media space articulates the shape, intentionality, and task of conscience within a textual world. It presents a multidimensional vision

---

3. Newbigin, *Gospel in a Pluralist Society*, 222–33.
4. Schweiker, *Theological Ethics and Global Dynamics*, 140.
5. Ibid., xiv.

of reality within which historical/fictive characters live and act. This aspect insists on an important relation between text and interpreter. The semantic intentionality, what text "means," is related to the world of the interpreters in the Gadamerian sense of a fusion of horizons.

According to Paul Ricoeur, any text presents a world in front of itself in which one finds one's innermost possibility. The task of interpretation is to engage in the complexity of the text as a space of reasons. It is also to demonstrate individual or communal life. In the event of understanding, we see, evaluate, and live in specific and contextual ways.[6]

The aspect of the semantic power of a media space moves another step into configuring the relation between media worlds, actual life in all its complexity, and the moral intentionality of integrity. At issue here is to work on scriptural images within the moral imagination of cultures in order to respect and enhance life before God. The point of the hermeneutical reading is to provide a better grasp of the lived structure of experience which is embedded within historical and social life connections.[7]

Utilizing Gustafson's notion of theology as a way of construing the world, Schweiker is more interested in "emphasiz[ing] specific tasks of theological inquiry (analysis and articulation), its experiential and existential focus (the lived structures of reality)." It also accentuates "the practical intent of thinking."[8]

Importantly, Schweiker's contribution lies in conceptualizing comparative ethical thinking in morally pluralist context and in presenting theological humanism. A conviction aimed at respecting and enhancing the integrity of life is the claim of conscience which is the basic mode of human life as a moral being. In the global culture there is a compression of the world bringing an awareness of global interdependence and increasing conflict, as well. The idea of a "clash of civilizations" undermines a notion of global reflexivity which can be found in forms of interdependence and mutual influence through information coming from other cultures or civilizations. Globality is a space of reasons which is "marked by violence as much as creativity and discovery."[9]

---

6. Ibid., 143–44.
7. Ibid., xxi
8. Ibid., xxv.
9. Ibid., 7

Global reflexivity comes with massive moral challenges in our moral response to people of other cultures. It can be accepted as spaces of reasons in which we must foster reflexive interaction among religions. Religions as spaces of reasons must interact with other ways human beings are motivated to act, making sense of their lives in political, economic, cultural, and ecological realms. This comparative religious perspective improves on the inadequacy and poverty of ethics which is caused by the modern banishment of religious sources from moral thinking. Additionally, many religious thinkers wrongly assume that valid ethical arguments are confined to their respective community.[10]

For a shared moral framework in the Islamic, Christian, and Jewish traditions, hermeneutical realism is demanded, according to which complex and wild imaginative forms should be interpreted in order to understand the world. In this shared global ethical project, Levinas remains one of Schweiker's important mentors, who insists that "the trace of God is found in an encounter of responsibility for the other."[11]

The Christian ethics of responsibility, oriented toward respecting and enhancing the integrity of life, seeks to embrace others within the scope of moral concerns. It also upholds responsible existence for the lives of all involved, leading to a project of theological humanism. This aspect, inspired by Levinas, is refined in counter to the problem of overhumanization in the modern age (suppression of ecological life) as well as the postmodern deconstruction of humanism. A distinctive feature of a theological humanism takes into consideration hearing "the cry of mute things" that provides a deeper reason for presenting globality as a space of reasons.[12]

The moral space of life can be best understood through the metaphor of creation within which self and other exist. God's act of recognizing creation as good is that God blesses and then rests in its completion. God's blessing is the key metaphor to understanding the pluralist character of reality. Creation within the biblical narrative is an account of abundance and fecundity. The blessing backs the capacity to participate in bringing forth life in the interaction of natural and social cultural processes. This provides a depiction of reality to be analyzed as pluralistic in character. Thus, the notion of the integrity of life is a concept of moral goodness

---

10. Ibid., x.
11. Ibid., 162.
12. Ibid., 11.

which is apt for a pluralist age.¹³ God provides the bounty of life even to the enemy, the rebellious, and the ungrateful. Even they could make great moral achievements.

Creation as a pluralistic reality is linked to the concept of *creatio continua* which refers to God's creative activity in sustaining and enhancing natural life. According to Bonhoeffer, destruction of the natural means destruction of life while the unnatural is the enemy of life. Creation is directed toward reconciliation which prepares and fulfills it in expectation of God's kingdom of glory.¹⁴

CREATION, RECONCILIATION, AND ESCHATOLOGY

In Levinas's fashion, God as the infinite Saying continues to speak, address, and challenge our Christian self and consciousness toward an ethical responsibility and solidarity with the face of the others. In this light, the symbol of creation interpreted thus provokes reflection in responding to aspects of pluralism.¹⁵

Given this, I seek to advance a concept of public ethical theology in a linguistic-creational-emancipatory framework for the sake of postcolonial public theology. God's creation as goodness cannot be adequately comprehended by reflection on the emancipation of Israel from the Babylonian captivity (Gen 1). God's creation as goodness and emancipation is further linked to the stories of Jesus's ministry and mission in proclaiming the good news to the poor, healing the sick, and feeding the hungry—thereby the subaltern-minjung. The affirmation of creation upholds respect for life, regard for the enemy (forgiveness of sin), and grounds the struggle to enhance life beyond the logic of retribution toward restorative justice and responsible politics.

Here responsibility comes along with reconciliation. Creation as external environment for reconciliation is instituted, acknowledged, and healed in God's act of speech in Christ's reconciliation with the world. God's grace of reconciliation does not eradicate the right of the creation, but bolsters and sharpens it in terms of the discipleship of God's mission through the word-event in the coming of God's kingdom of glory.

13. Ibid., 33, 28.
14. Bonhoeffer, *Ethics*, 148.
15. Schweiker, *Theological Ethics and Global Dynamics*, 36.

Bonhoeffer's ethics of grace and reconciliation (in his distinction between cheap grace and costly grace) is a standard example of presenting an ethical project of God's mission as God's economy through word-event refering to the importance of restorative and distributive justice. Restorative justice as responsible forgiveness brings the healing of wounds and placates the memory of suffering together with the fundamental change and renewal in new creation.

Furthermore, Bonhoeffer's reflection of *suum cuique* which is the Roman law dictum: *to each his own* provides an insight into developing ethical reflection of natural rights in terms of the gift of God the Creator. A respect for the principle of *suum cuique* may be regarded as penultimate which is determined by the last thing. The natural rights of all individuals are given by God who guarantees these rights, continually making use of life itself. In this regard *creatio continua* may be comprehended as God's preservation of natural life connected with the preservation of the life of human beings as a species.[16] Creation as goodness and emancipation expresses that God intervenes effectively on behalf of the rights inherent in life. This perspective supports integration between restorative justice and distributive justice.

Driven by the integrative metaphor of creation and reconciliation, a theological archeologist becomes a practitioner of the hermeneutics of life and theological humanism in a hermeneutical-anamnestic sense. This challenges any attempt to deploy any one master narrative as sufficient to articulate the moral space of life given responsibility, freedom, and the integrity of life.

For a theological humanism it is crucial to incorporate a proleptic ethics in provolutionary character in terms of fusion of horizons between past, the present, and the future. A proleptically informed notion of the word-event correlates with the irregularity of God's act of speech from the Other. It underpins just political structures in the present and transforms those structures vitiated and violated by the neo-imperial system of politics, economics, and mass media under the spell of neo-liberal economic globalization. The propletic vision of God's future which is valued as the source and ground of theological humanism drives a set of provolutionary principles. The human being as *imago Dei* in a biblical context is inseparably connected with a notion of Jesus Christ, the second Adam. The

---

16. Bonhoeffer, *Ethics*, 154.

human being as the *imago Dei* is a new creature in Christ through the grace of justification and reconciliation. A notion of theological humanism is christologically grounded in God's humanity revealed in Christ. God's promise of new creatures in Christ, the prototype and ground of humanity as *imago Dei* qualifies and sharpens the whole enterprise of striving for justice, equality, and emancipation.[17]

COMPARATIVE THEOLOGY AND INTERRELIGIOUS EXCHANGE

A religious tradition, and also every human life, is more complex than one root metaphor: "Many metaphors are necessary and actually exist in a moral lexicon, while none alone exhausts the meaning of life and its worth."[18] This aspect provides a larger framework for undertaking a multidimensional theological-ethical analysis and response to global dynamics in the time of many worlds. Thus interreligious dialogue provides the crucial way to reflexivity and public debate. It is necessary for renewing the traditions and vitalizing ethical responsibility.

I observe that comparative religious ethics presents valuable opportunities for developing lived ethics in everyday life in the interreligious context of exchange and renewal. A public ethical discourse attempts to deal with theological meaning and discourse in connection with a wide matrix of human cultural and experiences of social world.

Based on the revisionist and correlation model, Tracy advocates a hermeneutics of plurality and ambiguity, arguing that the religions are exercises in resistance. Interpreting the religious classics means allowing ourselves to challenge them through every hermeneutic act of critique, retrieval, and suspicion. By understanding the religious classics, we must come into conversation with them. A genuine conversation is called for, appreciating the meaning and truth of the religious classics and testing their applicability or non-applicability in the strategy of resistance. Theological interpretation cannot avoid the plurality and ambiguity affecting all discourse. Ethical awareness and responsibility becomes crucial in comparative theology in interreligious engagement as it considers those who are buried and sacrificed in religious fanaticism and its de-

17. Peters, *God—The World's Future*, 388.
18. Schweiker, *Theological Ethics and Global Dynamics*, 214.

monic history of effects. Based on retrieval, critique, and suspicion, Tracy refines his notion of an analogical imagination in terms of a mystical-political model among all the religions.[19]

For Tracy, religious questions are questions of the nature of Ultimate Reality from which all comes and toward which all moves. Ultimate Reality, the origin and end of all reality, summons us to a shift from self-centeredness to Reality-centeredness. Tracy, in openness toward mutual transformation, considers Luther's saying: "Here I stand; I can do no other," and asks if anyone really wishes he had added *sotto voce*, "But if it really bothers you, I will move."[20] If the pluralists cannot learn from Luther's classic interpretation of Christianity, they can hardly learn from any interpretation of religion at all. Arguing for analogical language as the principal candidate for hermeneutics, which is characterized by similarities-in-difference, Tracy advocates for the unnerving place where one is willing to risk one's own position in attention to the Other.[21]

Tracy's mystical prophetic dialogue model tends to overemphasize *via negativa*, "God-beyond-God" (Meister Eckhart). Karl Barth's saying is used as one to support Tracy's negative dialectics of plurality and ambiguity: "The angels will laugh when they read my theology." This saying corresponds to Reinhold Niebuhr's argument that "our best acts of creation are the best examples of our ambiguity."[22] Tracy's analogous mystical-political theology remains an undercurrent in presenting its public-ethical guidance and prophetic radicalism in conversation with the other.

Tracy notices that comparative theology is used in two different ways. First, it refers to the comparison of doctrinal systems of two or more religious traditions. This is a non-theological enterprise, part of the general academic study of religions. On the other hand, a comparative theology as a confessional discipline maintains that one religious tradition (home tradition) is critically correlated with another religion. Theology in general should be included in religious studies, comprehending that comparative theology should be seen as a sub-discipline within comparative religion.[23]

---

19. Tracy, *Plurality and Ambiguity*, 93, 102.
20. Ibid., 91.
21. Ibid., 93
22. Ibid., 97.
23. Clooney, ed., *New Comparative Theology*, x–xiii.

Driven by Tracy's insight, however, Francis X. Clooney takes a step in a different way by maintaining that comparative theology entails an aspect of "faith seeking understanding." It is undertaken as normative, constructive, and revisionist procedure for the benefit of believers. Thus, it does not proceed from a religiously neutral starting point,[24] while taking an interest in the methods of comparison and the findings and results arising from the non-theological study of religion.[25] Clooney seeks a new model of comparative theology that entails a revisionist as well as a constructive project. Thus theologians interpret the meaning and truth of one tradition in terms of critical correlations with other religious traditions and their classic texts.

For a proposal of comparative theology, comparison begins with the critical study of another religion in the reading of classic texts and sometimes by virtue of personal conversation with the practitioners of the religious traditions. This conversation also leads to an internal conversation within the home tradition. This correlation reinterprets the classic texts, art, rituals, and ascetic practices in investigation of the other traditions. The critical correlations will recognize similarity, while sometimes holding difference. Both similarity and difference are of theological significance for the comparative theologians on account of the alterity of the Other.

Given this, comparative theology underscores that interreligious dialogue is an intrinsic aspect of the theological enterprise, not a supplementary reflection to Christian theology. As Clooney argues, "Comparison and the appropriation of the new and different now take place *within* Christian theology, *while* it is being formulated, *not* as an appendage or corollary to an already fully formed theology."[26] What differentiates comparative theology from the theology of religions lies in the soteriological questions which dominate theologies of religions. With excessive emphasis on the soteriological issue, a pluralist theology of religions tends to sidestep detailed studies of the specific and particular teachings of the other religious traditions.

Comparative theology requires the careful and detailed study of other religions with sensitivity and caution toward the domestication of difference. This comparative project is attentive to the postmodern

---

24. Ibid., xiii.
25. Ibid.
26. Cited in ibid., xi.

condition (Jean-Francois Lyotard) to avoid the threat of the Other while acknowledging its transformative power.[27] Comparative theology relies on limited experiments rather than religious experience in general. The correlation character of comparative theology qualifies a hermeneutical project in terms of a commitment to a home tradition while remaining in tension to the other. Understanding the Other is undertaken in a way that does not annul the Other's alterity nor mute its renewing power. It resists a temptation to escape the tension of rootedness and vulnerability. This is characterized by fidelity or commitment to a home tradition while remaining vulnerable to the Other.[28]

I find the place of comparative hermeneutics in postcolonial public theology in emphasizing solidarity, recognition, and emancipation for those burdened and oppressed in the world of religions. A comparative study of the texts can be strengthened by a sociobiographical practice of emphatic listening to the life stories of those on the margins within the religious traditions.

POSTCOLONIAL THEORY AND ITS CHARACTERIZATION

Post-colonialism in the hyphenated form describes a historical and chronological period with political independence. However, Postcolonialism (or postcoloniality) expresses that the consciousness of the subalterns is awakened in psychological, social-cultural, political, and economic realms.[29] In the once-colonized world beset by contradictions, confusions, hybridity, and liminalities, cultural hybridity and liminal consciousness mark the postcolonial condition. A concept of hegemony in the fashion of Antonio Gramsci plays an important role in the context of postcolonial theory. According to this concept, a dominant group exercises power over the subjected or subaltern group in terms of domination and intellectual and moral leadership. Rather than upholding control and dictatorship in a unilateral sense, hegemony performs itself by tacit assent.[30]

Michel Foucault remains one of important mentors for postcolonial theory. He undertakes a strategy for revealing political, cultural, and in-

27. Ibid., xv.
28. Ibid.
29. Gandhi, *Postcolonial Theory*, 8. See further Westhelle, *After Heresy*, xvi.
30. *Gramsci Reader*, 249.

stitutionalized discourse as power discourse through the analysis of the correlation between power and knowledge. Demonstrating the insurrection of subjugated knowledge, Foucault takes issue with the effects of centralizing power and institutionalized authority.[31]

Led by Foucault, Said's study of Orientalism seeks to demystify the intellectual and cultural representation of the Orient done by the Western authorities during the colonial period. Insofar as power and knowledge are interconnected, representation of the Orient is associated with the financial and institutional support of the colonial regimes. The orient was created, or Orientalized, as a colonial discourse underlying the two distinctive features of homogenization and essentialization of the Orient.[32]

However, If Foucault and Said aim to re-write the history of boundaries and subjugated knowledge, it is indispensable to take seriously discontinuity, rupture, and the threshold of the colonized world and create counter hegemony in search for freedom and emancipation. A hermeneutical reorientation toward the Other in comparative religious framework improve on the limitations of Foucault's genealogy and Said's extra-hermeneutical position.[33]

Homi Bhabha is concerned with the subaltern history of the margins of modernity, and he seeks to rename the postmodern from the position of postcolonial theory.[34] Power functions by imposing binary structures, totalizing and repressing the difference into sameness. However, differences are always expressed through mimicry, ambivalence, dissimulation, hybridization, and fractured identities. Hybridity is a problem of colonial representation. Dissimulation, or else mimicry, is a survival tactic on the part of the colonized. Dissimulation means being between and betwixt, or the Third Space as Bhabha calls it.[35] The resilience of the subaltern is practiced in dissimulation. Hybridity enters upon the dominant discourse while estranging its basis and authority.[36]

Bhabha's concept of hybridity is based on Fanon's image of black skin/white mask. The liminal problem of colonial identity and its vicissitudes

31. Foucault, *Power/Knowledge*, 84.
32. Said, *Orientalism*, 4–5, 104.
33. For my critical study of Foucault and Said, see Chung, *Hermeneutical Self and an Ethical Difference*, 264.
34. Bhabha, *Location of Culture*, 175.
35. Ibid., 37.
36. Ibid., 114.

emerges in the impossible object which is expressed in the White man's artifice inscribed on the Black man's body.[37] "Remembering Fanon . . . is a painful re-membering, a putting together of the dismembered past to make sense of the trauma of the present."[38] Nonetheless, Bhabha's notion of hybridity tends to generalize the colonial encounter, misusing Fanon's praxis of emancipation from mimicry.

In her study "Can the Subaltern Speak?" Spivak has contributed to clarifying Marx's notion of representation: Representation as speaking for in politics and representation as re-presentation in art or philosophy. Marx uses two different verbs such as *vertreten* (in the sense of proxy) and *darstellen* (in the sense of portrait). Re-presentation (*Darstellung*) is overwritten by representation (*Vertretung*) substituting re-presentation. Spivak avoids a discourse of victimization in which the subaltern is only helplessly inscribed into an essentialist, utopian politics.[39] Her argument—the subaltern cannot speak—is a prescriptive act of protecting the subaltern from being commodified or reified. It is difficult to find the politics of meaning and emancipation underlying hybridity and liminality.

However, Marx's own vision of re-presentation can be expressed in his real humanism concerning the reality of the subaltern. Unlike Spivak, political representation rather challenges a structure of political economy, which inscribes the subaltern into the exchange value, fetishism, and reification. A solidarity with the subaltern for emancipation remains central in Marx's political praxis. For Marx, a human is the highest being, "that is, with the categorical imperative to overthrow all circumstances in which man is humiliated, enslaved, abandoned, and despised."[40]

There is room between the colonizer and the colonized "only for forced labor, intimidation, pressure, the police, taxation, theft, rape, compulsory crops, contempt, mistrust, arrogance, self-complacency, swinishness, brainless élites, degraded masses."[41] In a discourse concerning "colonization=thingification," a socio-critical logic of reification

---

37. Bhabha, "Remembering Fanon," in Williams and Chrisman, eds., *Colonial Discourse and Post-colonial Theory*, 117.

38. Ibid.

39. Westhelle, *After Heresy*, 126.

40. Marx, 'Toward a Critique of Hegel's *Philosophy of Right*: Introduction," in McLellan, Karl Marx Selected Writings, 69.

41. Césaire, "Discourse on Colonialism," in Williams and Chrisman, eds., *Colonial Discourse and Post-colonial Theory*, 177.

can sharpen a concept of thingifiction, in a critical analysis of Western modernization under Empire.

POSTCOLONIAL PUBLIC THEOLOGY AND ITS CHARACTERIZATION

In distinction from postcolonial deconstructive theory, I am more interested in proposing a postcolonial public theology in a constructive, hermeneutical, and archeological manner in light of God's act of speech and the Other. A postcolonial public theology in the hermeneutical framework asserts that the Gospel as *viva vox evangelii* ought to be proclaimed with the spoken word, while opening a possibility for God to speak to us in the dynamic notion of *creatio continua*. This aspect provides an insight for a postcolonial reframing of God as the infinite horizon of speech-event which calls one to speak or communicate the gospel to another, opening a future by listening to God's act of speech in the otherness of the Other and the world.

The word of God is apprehended in concrete terms, when the relationship is understood between what it says and what it effects. Seen as an active and effective word in the presence of the Holy Spirit, the word of God can be interpreted in a more comprehensive sense of event. More than that, language-event must be comprehended in connection with history, tradition, culture, and society. Indeed, hermeneutical theology speaks out against the reduction of language to a technical instrument through which the human life can be manipulated (for instance, as seen in the case of the technique of commercial advertising and propaganda or ideology in politics).

Word as communication is promise contained in the gospel of Jesus Christ which backs up God's mission as translation in the postcolonial context of World Christianity. Here human linguistic participation is encouraged in interpreting the word of God and its communication in dialogue with people of other cultures is indispensable.

Moreover, analogical imagination (Tracy) provides an insight to develop an archeological re-writing of the history of the subaltern-minjung in terms of similarity-in-difference. If we see our current history and society in terms of *similarity*, it is also significant to undertake it in an archeological rewriting of *dissimilarity* or irregularity of the marginalized in history and society. A notion of hybridity can be met with fusion of horizons in relation to human existence in social location, which is embedded within knowledge-power-discourse (social cultural formation) and economic material formation (labor, capital, reification, and market).

Driven by hermeneutical reorientation in an archeological-anamnestic framework, I seek to conceptualize an ethical vision of God's mission through God's economy in a linguistic-creational-emancipatory aspect. For me "linguistic" means semantic, by way of combining a critical-dialectical notion of analogy with social discourse imbedded within the power-knowledge interplay. Language as social discourse is to be seen in terms of contextual issues such as ethnic stratification, social inequality, and political representation against misrepresentation of the dominant group. This aspect characterizes a notion of postcolonial hermeneutics of intertextuality in diachronic historical and social-synchronic correlation.[42]

At this juncture, I am indebted to Levinas's distinction of the said from the saying in relation to God's saying in the otherness of the Other, because the said tends to obscure the underlying saying activity. *Dabar* in Hebrew manner means speak, talk, and reveal related to the God of promise, transcendence, hope, and future. YHWH—"God will be that will be"—finds its locus in Paul's eschatological theology, which states that "God may be all in all" (1 Cor 15:28).

Enrique Dussel, driven by Levinas's ethics of the alterity, proposes an ana-lectical method and ethical hermeneutics. His critique of Levinas is that Levinas' Other is still Eurocentric. Thus, Dussel rethinks the discourse from Latin America and from "ana-logy." The Other according to Dussel should be an Indian, an Africa, and Asian.[43] Dussel develops his "ana-lectical" method in opposition to a dialectical method, by beginning with the Other and discovering the analogical character of the word of the Other. For Dussel, *Logos* is at the root of analogy which tends toward a univocity by subsuming and suppressing differences. But *dabar* in Hebrew manner entails ana-logy that assumes an attitude of trust in the obedience of a disciple toward the Other. Here Dussel thinks of *analogia verbi* or *analogia fidei* in difference from the Thomistic notion of analogy.[44] The ana-lectical method underlying a notion of *analogia verbi*

---

42. Chung, *Hermeneutical Self and an Ethical Difference*, 133.
43. Barber, *Ethical Hermeneutics*, 50.
44. Ibid., 51.

discloses the analogical word of the Other in critique of false universals and totalization.

A new analogical theology in Dussel's sense seeks to recognize differences within the dialogue of the periphery among Africa, Asia, and Latin America, or between the center and the periphery. Underlying the ana-lectical method is a preferential ethical option for the Other and the poor. It entails the ethos of liberation.[45] In relation to Marx's deliberation of the Other in the socioeconomic realm, Dussel's ethical hermeneutics in the ana-lectical method seeks to rewrite and decipher a history for a privileging of the standpoint of history's forgotten and foreclosed Other.

For me, analogy emerges from my understanding of Jesus's language of parables and analogies which stands in his sociobiographical solidarity with ochlos-minjung, as it concerns the message of the coming of kingdom of God. God's narrative in the gospel of Jesus is woven in secular and discursive style, because Jesus utilizes secular parable and social discourse to witness to the truth of the kingdom of God which wants to be practiced and established on earth in accordance to God's economy.

Analogy is a language for speaking about a God who has multiple visions in the human world in avoiding idolatry and supporting people's experience of God in a social concrete manner (Hos 12:10). What matters in analogical language is a protest to all forms of idolatry and absolutism. This perspective incorporates the social discourse of the dissimilarity of the life of those vulnerable, fragile, and victimized through whose face God continues to work and address the church.[46]

In an analysis of the correlation between theology and the origins of race, we find a postcolonial approach to Christian imagination concerning the Western theological act of displacement and colonialism. Such an aspect argues that geography matters for race as well as for place-centered identity. It is of special significance to locate a theological account of the colonialist moment and its discourse of representation and displacement in a conceptualization of place-identity. Many of the wretched of the earth have become Christians, which challenges Christian theology to reckon with its ramification of colonialism. A social imagination in a new theological framework paves a way to interdisciplinary dialogue be-

---

45. Ibid., 61, 68.
46. Chung, *Public Theology in an Age of World Christianity*, 134–37.

tween geography, theology, postcolonial theory, race theory, and Native American studies among others.[47]

A reflection of God in the otherness of the Other remains substantial in developing a postcolonial public theology in terms of Christ's prophetic *diakonia* of reconciliation which transcends a logic of the binary opposition caused by the colonial discourse of representation. This perspective stimulates a postcolonial strategy of a new reading of the texts represented and domesticated by the institutionalized authority and scholarship.

Given this, a postcolonial public theology further explores a comparative religious ethics, emphasizing archeological reasoning in connection with language as social discourse and ethical praxis of solidarity. Hence mission as translation is advanced in the act of interpretation, which is engaged with the past represented, colonized, and distorted. It implies a moment of emancipation of the interpreter toward solidarity with the Other, through whose face God continues to speak and address our society. Mission is blessing to the Other who stands in God's illeity in the act of speech.

---

47. Jennings, *The Christian Imagination*, 290–93.

18

Dietrich Bonhoeffer and Comparative Religious Ethics

Minjung and Confucian Ethics

A RENEWED INTEREST IN BONHOEFFER IN EAST ASIA

IN THE MIDST OF worldwide cultural polycentrism, we need theological works to break through the dominion of Western theology and its philosophical and cultural assumptions. This task is not deconstructive in the straightforward way, but entails an archeological recovery of new meaning in hermeneutical engagement. The reality of "global dynamics and world-making"[1] becomes an important factor in stimulating comparative ethical study for the sake of postcolonial moral reasoning in overcoming distance, tribalism, or ideology in the aftermath of colonialism and Auschwitz (Shoah). Comparative study articulates a multidimensional integrity of life expressing plurality and commonality of ethics underlying public ethical theology and discipleship of God's mission in comparative religious studies.

Bonhoeffer already occupied a special place in the first model of minjung theology and literature, which began in the 1980s in South Korea. Bonhoeffer remains an inspiring figure in the second model of postcolonial minjung theology in its irregular, archeological fashion,[2] which is a recent arrival. Furthermore, Bonhoeffer's works find a renewed interest in Christian-Confucian dialogue in China. In a study of *Dietrich Bonhoeffer*

---

1. Schweiker, *Theological Ethics and Global Dynamics*, 4–5.
2. Chung, *Constructing Irregular Theology*.

and Sino-Theology,[3] Chinese scholars in Taiwan and Hong Kong enter into a dialogue with Bonhoeffer in appreciating and contextualizing his theology for the development of Sino-Christian theology.[4]

Given this, my interest is in dealing with the significance of Dietrich Bonhoeffer for theology and church in East Asia. The purpose of this chapter is to revive and contextualize Bonhoeffer's ethical insight in the context of comparative religious studies and in the experience of World Christianity in a new direction of postcolonial minjung theology.

PICTURE OF BONHOEFFER IN MINJUNG THEOLOGY

Minjung theology developed in South Korea to challenge the aftermath of Japanese colonialism and later to confront indigenous military dictatorship allied with Japanese politics. The minjung theology situates the pain of God within the outcry of the victim (*Han*). Han is a determining metaphor in delving into the social existential mentality or collective feeling of the victimized. This focuses on engaging with social history of *han*-ridden people who cry out for freedom and emancipation. God's mission is defined as solidarity with minjung-subaltern.

In the minjung biblical exegesis of Mark's gospel, there is an emphasis on the term *ochlos* (public sinners and tax collectors—*massa perditionis*). The place of the *ochlos* in Mark's gospel focuses on people without religious identity and without ethnic coherence, which are in contrast to *laos* or *goyim*. The word *ochlos* describes people off the land (*amha'aretz*), without property.[5] Furthering this biblical exegesis, I also take into account a mixed crowd (*erev rav*) as minjung who accompanied the Israelites' journey from Rameses to Succoth (Exod 12:37). Minjung theology emphasizes God's embrace of a mixed crowd to God's promise and blessing.

Given such biblical exegesis, minjung theology appreciates Bonhoeffer's "minjung" experience in the prison which remains fundamental in understanding Bonhoeffer's academic theology moving toward

---

3. Green and Tseng, eds., *Dietrich Bonhoeffer and Sino-Theology*; further see Rachel Zhu's Chinese translation of Andreas Pangritz's essay, "Theological Motifs in "Bonhoeffer's Decision to Participate in Political Resistance."

4. Tang Sui-Keung, "An Ethical Case of 'The Son Concealing the Misconduct of the Father,'" in Green and Tseng, eds., *Dietrich Bonhoeffer and Sino-Theology*, 365–93.

5. Ahn, "Jesus and Ochlos in the Context of His Galilean Ministry," in Chung et al., *Asian Contextual Theology for the Third Millennium*, 36–37.

a post-Eurocentric theology. It is concerned with seeing how Bonhoeffer's social experience has shaped his theological reorientation toward "the perspective of the outcast, the suspect, the maltreated, the powerless, the oppressed, the reviled—in short, from the perspective of those who suffer."[6] This connection between hermeneutics from below and the ethical commitment to the subaltern-subject can unfold in a non-Western perspective on theology of God's suffering and the suffering of people.[7]

POSTCOLONIAL READING OF BONHOEFFER

Having considered this, I further advance the postcolonial minjung theology by way of archeological hermeneutics seeking to unearth the irregular side or underside of the history and the society threatened and violated by the neo-colonial authority and dominion. A correlation between public ethical theology and discipleship of God's mission is archeologically driven and social biographically enacted for the sake of telling the truth to society and history. Archeological hermeneutics in this light grounds postcolonial moral reasoning upon the remembrance of the suffering and victims who are founded upon our memory of Jesus in our anamnestic reason.[8]

A postcolonial minjung theology is interested in refining a sense of co-textuality or intertextuality while considering the confluence of two narratives, i.e., narrative of God's suffering, promise, and righteousness in the biblical context in correlation with the suffering of people in the extrabiblical and secular spectrum. This hermeneutics of intertextuality undergirds an emphatic listening to the narrative of the victim, pursuing a third place for a politics of new meaning and discourse which runs counter to the institutionalized and hierarchical discourse from the top down. Thus the hermeneutical strategy of intertextuality, with attention to God's act of weaving intertexture in history and society, notably focuses on the interstice where diverse cultures, pluralist ideas and concepts, and victimized narratives of those who are fragile and vulnerable encounter one another, collide, and fuse.

6. Bonhoeffer, LPP 17.

7. Chung et al., *Asian Contextual Theology for the Third Millennium*, 127–45.

8. Metz, *Passion For God*, 143. For Global-critical perspective, see Yip, *Capitalism as Religion?*, 130–38.

Driven by postcolonial hermeneutics, I am interested in rereading texts, including Bonhoeffer's oeuvre, to bring Western literature into dialogue with East Asian classic texts in view of possible shared and multiple horizons. In Bonhoeffer's relationship to Sino-theology and also his indelible influence on *minjung* theology in East Asia, I have the objective of interpreting Bonhoeffer constructively in view of a post-western theology that recognizes the importance of the Other. Bonhoeffer's prophetic theology is grounded in a hermeneutical perspective from below which implies learning from the Other.

Bohoeffer's *theologia crucis* in a non-religious fashion may reinforce this irregular side of hermeneutics in the archeological-irregular manner. As Bonhoeffer provocatively asks, "[W]hat does it mean when the proletariat says, in his world of distrust: 'Jesus was a good man'?" The discourse of the working class about Jesus is speaking more than the bourgeois saying that Jesus is God.[9] In his critical concern about the radicalism of the gospel Bonhoeffer takes issue with bourgeois self-satisfaction, or "a convenient reversal of the gospel."[10]

Bonhoeffer's ethics of reconciliation emphasizes the radical side of the gospel, seeing religious others positively. The godlessness of the world is in its stance against religion and the church, however, Bonhoeffer regards this world to be full of promise. The world is accepted to God's reconciliation in Christ, which is more important than the pious in religious and Christian clothing.[11] This perspective shapes Bonhoeffer's concept of the church for others, because "the church is the church only when it exists for others."[12] Bonhoeffer's view on Jesus' "being there for others" stands in effect on the masses in light of God's reconciliation with the world. Thus Bonhoeffer argues that the "church should give away all its property to those in need," and "take the field against the vices of hubris, power-worship, envy, and humbug, as the roots of all evil."[13]

Bonhoeffer urges the church's solidarity with the Jewish victims, who are "the weakest and most defenseless brothers and [sisters] of

---

9. Bonhoeffer, *Christ the Center*, 35.
10. Bonhoeffer, *Ethics*, 64.
11. Ibid., 104.
12. LPP 382.
13. Ibid., 383.

Jesus Christ."[14] The experience of the catastrophe in the Jewish persecution drives Bonhoeffer to transcend the European framework of the Enlightenment and the self-preserving church. A notion of alterity, which is the dignity of the Other in their otherness, may break into Bonhoeffer's understanding of God in the *diakonia* of Christ's reconciliation which underlies the inseparable relationship between God and the Other in suffering. This aspect calls into question an excessive attachment to the power of God in the religious sense of *deus ex machina*. In some ancient Greek dramas a god is used to solve an unsolvable crisis by intervention, often brought on stage by an elaborate device and equipment.

In contrast, Bonhoeffer insists that "only the suffering God can help."[15] God allows God's self to be driven out of the world onto the cross. This notion of *theologia crucis* entails a critique of modernist notions of God according to onto-theo-logy which is implicitly connected with the Greek notion of *deus ex machina*. For Bonhoeffer, "there is no God who 'is there,'"[16] that is to say, "the Crucified, the man who lives out of the transcendent."[17] Thus we must live in the world as if there is no God.[18] The authentic meaning of God's transcendence must be found in God in human form for others underlying the horizon of reconciliation as recognition of the Other.

RESISTANCE IN STATUS CONFESSIONIS

Bonhoefer's concept of resistance was expressed in his challenge to the so-called Aryan clause. Bonhoeffer's April 1933 address on "The Church and the Jewish Question" is the important statement of political resistance.[19] For Bonhoeffer, the church is summoned to act responsibly when the state does not serve to maintain law and order in a legitimate and rightful manner. In the case of too much law and order, the state develops its

---

14. *Ethics*, 114.
15. LPP 361.
16. Bonhoeffer, *Act and Being*, 115.
17. LPP 382.
18. Ibid., 360.
19. Bonhoeffer, "The Church and the Jewish Question," 361–70.

excessive power and seeks to threaten Christian preaching and Christian faith. The church must stand against the encroachment of the state.[20]

According to Bonhoeffer, three proposals are possible for the church's responsible action. Firstly, the church asks whether the actions of the state are legitimate and exist in accordance with its own character. Secondly, the church must help those who are victimized by state action, standing under an unconditional obligation to the victims, whether they are Christians or non-Christians. Thirdly, the church should not just bind up the wounds of the victims beneath the wheel but seize the wheel itself.[21] At this point, the church finds itself in *status confessionis*.[22]

Ethical resistance to the dictatorship of the state becomes possible from God's presence in the suffering of people, awakening our mandate to sustain and enhance life arrangements given by God. The hermeneutical endeavor integrating biblical narrative with extra-biblical narrative perpetuates self-critical reflection on the Christian self as graced, ethical self, validating an attitude of engagement and solidarity for the integrity of life before the mystery of God in the presence of the suffering other.

POLITICS OF MARTYRDOM AND REALITY OF RESTRAINER

Regarding Bonhoeffer's politics of martyrdom, Karl Barth implies a possibility of tyrannicide within the Lutheran tradition by following in the footsteps of Calvin, Theodore Beza, and John Knox, while rejecting tyrannicide as a general possibility.[23] However, Bonhoeffer does not theologically conceptualize an issue of tyrannicide. For the sake of the politics of martyrdom, Bonhoeffer considers the reality of the restrainer (2 Thess 2:7) which takes effect and receives control under God's governance in preserving the world from destruction.

---

20. Ibid., 365.

21. Ibid.

22. Ibid., 366. The term *status confessionis* was used by the Reformers in the sixteenth century in the struggle against Roman Catholicism. According to "Formula of Concord," "The confirmation of open idolatry, as well as the protection of the weak in faith from offense, is at stake. In such matters we can make no concessions but must offer an unequivocal confession and suffer whatever God sends and permits the enemies of his Word to inflict on us" ("Formula of Concord," BC, 516).

23. Barth, *Church Dogmatics*, 3/4:450.

Bonhoeffer's concern was about the reality of victims, implying an active and direct political resistance within the concrete resistance of the church. This aspect supports our compassion and responsible action by the suffering of the brothers and sisters for whose sake Christ suffered. As instruments in the hand of the Lord of history, we share in Christ's large-heartedness by acting with responsibility and in freedom as the hour of danger comes. The Christian is called to sympathy and action[24]—thereby politics of martyrdom. This politics of martyrdom can be seen especially in reference to the reality of the restrainer.

In a chapter titled "Inheritance and Decay" in a fragment of his *Ethics*, Bonhoeffer considers the restrainer (2 Thess 2:7), who, equipped with great physical strength, effectively blocks those who can plunge everything into the abyss. The restrainer sets due limits to evil, used by God to preserve the world from destruction. The restrainer as such under God's governance of the world is not God, nor without guilt. Church and the restrainer are entirely different in nature, but in close alliance facing imminent chaos.[25]

Already in February 1938, Bonhoeffer was in contact with the emerging resistance movement among high-ranking officers and generals through his brother-in-law Hans von Dohnanyi, taking a special mission for the resistance movement. Bonhoeffer's role in the resistance movement was in ecumenical connection with leaders, notably Visser't Hooft, the first General Secretary of the World Council of Churches and Bishop Bell in Sigtuna, Sweden. Before Bonhoeffer was taken away for his execution, Bonhoeffer's last words for Bishop Bell (as reported by Payne Best): "Tell him . . . that for me this is the end but also the beginning. With him, I believe in the principle of our universal Christian brotherhood which rises above all national interests, and that our victory is certain—tell him, too, that I have never forgotten his words [our act of repentance toward God] at our last meeting."[26]

In fact, Bonhoeffer did not support the right to revolution,[27] because the intention of the preacher is to summon the world to belief in Jesus Christ bearing witness to the reconciliation. The theme of the proclama-

---

24. LPP 14.
25. Bonhoeffer, *Ethics*, 108.
26. Cited in Bethge, *Dietrich Bonhoeffer*, 1037n54.
27. Bonhoeffer, *Ethics*, 346.

tion is the grace of Jesus Christ and what is needed in Christian proclamation is concrete instruction in the concrete situation.[28]

Furthermore, the reality of the restrainer seen within the context of the *primus usus* stands in relation to the gospel, because the will of God takes effect in the *primus usus* or the *lex naturae*.[29] Because natural law in opposition to the Decalogue can never claim divine authority, the church proclaims the *primus usus* in the service of the gospel.[30]

Bonhoeffer's notion of *status confessionis* has remained an undercurrent in the church's confession of guilt in his theology of reconciliation. "The Church confesses that she has witnessed in silence the spoliation and exploitation of the poor and the enrichment and corruption of the strong."[31]

The politics of martyrdom underlying *status confessionis* is seen and comprehended by a hermeneutical view from below; that is "from the perspective of the outcast, the suspects, the maltreated, the powerless, the oppressed, the revived."[32] The world come of age in the reconciled world undergirds the perspective from below, which provides an insight into breaking through the European Enlightenment modernity for the sake of a postcolonial theology which can be further conceptualized from the perspective of the irregular side of history and society.

RECONCILIATION IN SOLIDAITY WITH THE VICTIM

In light of the reconciling love of God in Jesus Christ, Bonhoeffer further develops his ethical view from the Other because the godless world bears the mark of reconciliation as the free ordinance of God.[33] Bonhoeffer finds God and the world reconciled in Christ: "In the body of Jesus Christ God is united with humanity, the whole of humanity is accepted by God and the world is reconciled with God."[34] Bonhoeffer retains a keen sense for the integrity of natural life on the basis of the distinction between the ultimate and the penultimate. An ethical evaluation of the penultimate

28. Ibid., 349.
29. Ibid., 302, 304
30. Ibid., 308.
31. Ibid., 115.
32. LPP 17.
33. Bonhoeffer, *Ethics*, 292.
34. Ibid., 202.

and its significance for human historical, social and material existence is positively undertaken in the light of the ultimate message of the gospel.

Existence for others in participation in the being of Jesus implies that Christ is identified with the life and sufferings of his people. Bonhoeffer implies a Christology of solidarity in the messianic event of Isaiah 53, which is now being fulfilled in the representative suffering of the Jews for the nations.[35] Bonhoeffer's statement that "God consents to be pushed out of the world onto the cross"[36] reflects on the concrete event of the Jews being pushed out of the Eurocentric world into the place of deportation and destruction. The victim becomes an interlocutor for theology, because a theme of reconciliation in solidarity with the Other upholds remembering the irregular side of history, while supporting an archeological sense of digging through the social reality embedded within the contradiction between the perpetrator and the victimized and challenges.

God's reconciling love "encompasses even the most abysmal godlessness of the world."[37] Bonhoeffer takes the godlessness of the world more seriously than the pious in religious and Christian clothing. This characterizes an irregular dimension of Luther's theology in its prophetic radicalism. Luther's provocative statement—"God would rather hear the curses of the ungodly than the alleluia of the pious"[38]—finds its consonance in Bonhoeffer's ethics as formation in conformity to Jesus Christ in terms of the "below" and the "Other." This aspect underscores *theologia crucis* from below and the hermeneutics of the Other seen from the perspective of those on the margin and innocent victims, which paves a way toward listening both to the gospel and to the cultural and religious others in light of reconciliation.

As Walter Benjamin prophetically notes concerning junking history of European fascism, "Only that historian will have the gift of fanning the spark of hope in the past who is firmly convinced that *even the dead* will not be safe from the enemy if he wins. And this enemy has not ceased to be victorious."[39] An archeological reason in the remembrance of the mass suffering of the victims takes issue with a semiotic discourse of difference, deferral, and trace, which undermines the place of victimized history.

35. Pangritz, "Sharing destiny of His People," in De Gruchy, ed., *Bonhoeffer*, 273.
36. LPP 360.
37. Bonhoeffer, *Ethics*, 72.
38. Ibid., 104.
39. Benjamin, *Illuminations*, 247.

THE ETHICAL AND THE CONCRETENESS

A Biblical statement—in historical human existence everything has its time (Eccl 3)—is central to Bonhoeffer's deliberation of the ethical.[40] Since human activity lies in the center and in the fullness of everyday life, Bonhoeffer argues that ethical discourse cannot be undertaken in a vacuum; rather it stands only in a concrete context, linked with particular persons, times, and places—thereby ethical engagement with social topography. Bonhoeffer's ethical position contradicts the interpretation of the ethical as a universally valid rational principle. This principle, according to Bonhoeffer, has no element of concretion, and ends in unlimited subjectivism and individualism.[41] The ethical is destroyed when it is detached from its concrete relations. God's commandment is the speech of God coming to us, embodying concrete speech to the concrete person, as it is revealed and manifested in Jesus Christ, coming to us in the church, the family, labor and government.[42]

The commandment as the theme of a Christian ethic is concerned with sharing in life; thus the commandments of God comprise the ethical, not vice versa. The commandment of God found in the divine mandates becomes concrete in the revelation of Christ coupled with the reconciling love of God. Mandate is understood as the concrete divine commission built upon the revelation of Christ as it is evidenced and attested in the Scripture.[43] God's grace of justification, in its belonging to the ultimate, is expressed in our discipleship by promoting justice within the realm of the penultimate.

The Word of God as "word-event" in Bonhoeffer's sense means God's freedom and solidarity as heard in the extra-ecclesial sphere in light of God's reconciliation in Christ, especially in the event of life of those undermined and suppressed. Bonhoeffer's non-religious interpretation must be seen in light of his theology of reconciliation which appreciates and recognizes those outside the church in the sense of the below and the other. Bonhoeffer's prophetic ethics underlines God's reconciliation in the humanity of Jesus Christ and his solidarity with suffering Jews and calls into question a dichotomy that draws lines between "us" and "them."

40. Bonhoeffer, *Ethics*, 261.
41. Ibid., 268.
42. Ibid., 273–74.
43. Ibid., 282.

Bonhoeffer listens to God's irregular voice in the profound faithfulness of the Jews to the Torah. This aspect may have been willing to forfeit the stronghold of Eurocentric theology, creating a larger space for embracing other humanist sources of religions in terms of faithful moral integrity. It encourages other responsible religious people to join God's reconciliation and theological humanism on behalf of the subaltern in our midst.

COMPARATIVE ETHICAL STUDY: RESPONSIBILITY AND OTHER

According to Eberhard Bethge, Bonhoeffer in a letter (written in February 1928) showed an interest in Gandhi and the world of the Buddha. Gandhi became an example, posing a question for Bonhoeffer: why Christianity had its origin in the East. Bonhoeffer took interest in Gandhi's pacifistic method and nonviolent struggle. In another letter (May 22, 1934), Bonhoeffer contends that there is more Christianity in the world of the "heathens" than in the whole state church of Germany.[44]

Concerning a comparative religious ethics, challenging the violence, injustice, dominion against people's actual dignity and human rights should be central in light of God's reconciliation in solidarity with the subaltern-minjung. A responsibility in a genuine sense pushes to solidarity, risking life fearlessly and audaciously for the sake of the vulnerable ones in the social cultural context. The God of the victims is not only the Lord of the Church, but also the Lord of the world of many cultures and religions. Responsibility ethics is not confined to ends and consequences, nor based on a universal, categorical obligation in the sense of deontological moral theory. Human beings are primarily responders to others, participants in complex patterns of communicative interaction. According to R. H. Niebuhr, the diversity of cultural beliefs challenges the radical monotheism of Christian faith. An ethics of responsibility offers an alternative to the mainstreams of moral theory, teleological as well as deontological. However, in William Schweiker's account, Niebuhr still remains underdeveloped because he does not manage to incorporate the possible validity of other moral beliefs into his ethics of responsibility.[45]

---

44. Bethge, *Dietrich Bonhoeffer*, 138, 184, 379.
45. Schweiker, *Responsibility and Christian Ethics*, 24.

Schweiker considers Bonhoeffer, insisting that grace in a genuine sense becomes foundational for an ethics of responsibility defining the relationship between the church and the state. Jesus Christ bore responsibility and deputyship for humanity, thus he is the foundation for responsibility ethics. Accordingly, Bonhoeffer states that "responsibility for oneself is in truth responsibility with respect to the man, and that means responsibility with respect to mankind."[46] Bonhoeffer emphasized the meaning of responsibility as representative action for others in Christian ethics.[47] Bonhoeffer advocates a biblically informed notion of reconciliation in contrast to the ethical form of a general principle and a form of secularism. Both Christian and secular are recognized, with their special qualities and with their unity, only in the concrete responsibility of action springing from the reconciliation effected in Jesus Christ.[48]

Responsibility recognizes the Other as a responsible agent. The ethical in Bonhoeffer's sense is tied always to a definite time and a definite place, because we are historically existent in-the-place. For Bonhoeffer, the ethical in the sense of the universally valid and the rational resolves itself into individual atoms of reason. Formal reason is not a socially constructive principle, but a principle of atomization.

In an interdisciplinary and cross-cultural manner, Elias Bongmba makes a comparative study of Bonhoeffer and Levinas to propose a public ethics in the African context with the priority of the Other.[49] Embedded within the experience of the barbarianism and genocide of National Socialism, Levinas and Bonhoeffer remain pioneers who prioritize the face of the Other in the ethical-hermeneutical realm. In both cases, we perceive that recognition of otherness is defined as a presupposition for ethics. Ethics as first philosophy (Levinas) becomes a dialogue partner with theological ethics of reconciliation from the perspective from below and the Other (Bonhoeffer). Following in the footsteps of Levinas, Ricoeur notes that "the face of the other raises itself before me, above me, it is not an appearance that I can include within the sphere of my representations. To be sure, the other appears, his face makes him appear,

---

46. Bonhoeffer, *Ethics*, 222.
47. Schweiker, *Responsibility and Christian Ethics*, 57.
48. Bonhoeffer, *Ethics*, 229.
49. Bongmba, "Priority of the Other," in De Gruchy, ed., *Bonhoeffer*, 190–208.

but the face is not a spectacle; it is a voice. The voice tells us, 'Thou shall not kill.' Each face is a Sinai that prohibits murder."[50]

What brings Levinas and Bonhoeffer to ethical solidarity and humanism lies in their respective notions of the word of God (God's Saying or Jesus Christ) embedded within the life of those who are vulnerable and fragile through whose face God continues to speak to human consciousness and the church. Their face shall not kill. To see the Other is to recognize the gaze of the stranger, the widow, and the orphan:[51] "In the ethical relation, the other is presented at the same time as being absolutely other, but this radical alterity in relation to me does not destroy or deny my freedom."[52]

In the history of dehumanization reaching its apotheosis during the twelve year reign of Nazi terror, the irreducible dignity of humans was deeply wounded and a belief in efficacy, human freedom and responsibility became questionable. The God of the German Christians attacked the God of Israel, who is revealed in Jesus Christ, a Jew. Dehumanization is not merely found in the political arena, but also perpetrated by the social sciences in seeking to explain human subjectivity in the name of intelligible structure, or to announce anti-humanism in the slogan of the demise of the subject. Heidegger's fundamental ontology submerges human subjectivity into the impersonal historical terrain of being, succumbing to the Being of German *Volk*.[53]

According to Bonhoeffer, Heidegger's ontology of *Da-sein* is always directed upon itself in self-decision.[54] *Da-sein* as a way of appropriating itself into its own wholeness is built on the ontological care of the radical individual, resulting in the totalization of otherness; the Other is reduced to becoming a chimera for the self.

Existence under the rubric of *Da-sein* is characterized by its care likened to Odysseus's journey of homecoming. *Da-sein* is a way of appropriating the Other for its own sake. *Da-sein*'s project built on care is radically individualistic, resulting in appropriation or reduction of otherness into the self, in which the Other remains a chimera or a hostage for the self.

50. Ricoeur, *Oneself as Another*, 336.
51. Ibid., 77.
52. Levinas, *Difficult Freedom*, 16.
53. Levinas, *Humanism of the Other*, ix.
54. Bonhoeffer, *Act and Being*, 64.

According to Bonhoeffer, God's transcendence in Jesus Christ is drifted and lost, vulnerable to fundamental, ontological philosophy which has brought the loss of God's revelation and eliminated ethics for the Other in the public realm. The recognition of an Other as a precondition for the possibility of ethics begins with God's revelation in Jesus Christ which is a counter proposal to the modernist notion of onto-theo-logy. God's freedom creates a bond of communion with humanity through Word and the Spirit. Sociality and appreciation of the Other occur in faith community, Christ existing as community.

BONHOEFFER AND CONFUCIAN ETHICS OF RECTIFICATION

Sharing Bongmba's cross-cultural and comparative concern, I further undertake Bonhoeffer's legacy for the appreciation and sharing of ethical compassion in interreligious exchange. Elsewhere, I developed an intercultural reading of Bonhoeffer by taking socially engaged Buddhism as the dialogue partner.[55] My concern here is an introduction of Mencius's people's ethics in terms of the rectification of names. Bonhoeffer's ethics of resistance helps us to advance a comparative study of the Confucian notion of political resistance. In *Dietrich Bonhoeffer and Sino-Theology*, as was mentioned, Tang actualizes ethical self-cultivation in the Confucian context while considering Mencius' theory of four germinations or beginnings of the four basic human feelings or dispositions: commiseration, shame and dislike, deference and compliance, and right and wrong. However, I insist that Mencius's self-cultivation based on the theory of four beginnings is bound to his ethical consideration of people's rights in terms of the rectification of names.[56]

Mencius (371–289 BCE) continued to perpetuate the teaching of Confucius by giving a new outlook on an existing system. Mencius had established his political and social philosophy on behalf of the people. According to Mencius, the ruler must be in office to serve the interest and well-being of people. Heaven's mandate, unfathomable and incompre-

---

55. Chung, "Bonhoeffer Seen from Asian Minjung Theology," in Chung et al., *Asian Contextual Theology*, 127–45.

56. For a study of Mencius's ethics of rectification in comparative religious framework, see Chung, *The Hermeneutical Self and an Ethical Difference*, 118–22.

hensible, is known through the lives and voices of the people. The ruler must establish and organize all economic and political measures on behalf of the rights and dignity of people. For Mencius, "the people are the most important element (in a state); the spirits of the land and grain are secondary; and the sovereign is the least. Therefore to gain the peasantry is the way to become Emperor."[57]

Mencius's notion of the benevolent government argues that land is public property which the people cultivate in a condition of liberty. The role of institution lies in undergirding the people to nourish their living, ensuring a constant livelihood, establishing organizations for the education of the people. It enables the people to bury their dead without any dissatisfaction.[58]

In light of the Confucian principle of rectification of names, the voice of the people is the voice of God, thus the master becomes a private citizen to serve the voice of the people. When the ruler violates and does not rectify the name as the benevolent ruler, people have a right of resistance even implying the possibility of tyrannicide. Confucian ethics did not create a hierarchical system of patriarchy per se, rather it was developed in such a system and was considerably misused to serve only the interest of the powerful in the social, cultural, political system. Mencius' political idea has the limitations of feudal society, but it was shaped in accordance with a revolutionary reevaluation of everything. They challenge a sovereign break with all traditional or rational norms.[59]

Mencius argued that there were no just wars in the Confucian political ethics within the empire. The master becomes a simple private citizen, once he is no longer recognized by the people. Fung Yu-lan insists that Mencius's economic position retains socialist implications, in which the existing social system gains a new interpretation in the Confucian sense of creative transmitting and critical interpretation.[60]

A comparative, ethical study, seen in light of God's infinite horizon of speech-event within the reconciled world, incorporates pluralistic metaphors and discourses in undertaking an archeological deciphering of the forgotten side of the history and in promoting an emphatic lis-

---

57. Fung, *History of Chinese Philosophy*, 1:113.

58. *Mencius* 7.

59. M. Weber, "The Nature of Charismatic Domination," in *Selections in Translation*, 230.

60. Fung, *History of Chinese Philosophy*, 1:118–19.

tening to the social biography of those on the underside of history and society. In order to articulate the moral space of life in a cross-cultural perspective, we consider undertaking a pluralistic idea of freedom, responsibility, or integrity of life in rich religious traditions and history. This ethical pluralism supports many metaphors in a diverse moral lexicon. A multidimensional theory of moral value can be presented by using a range of metaphors about freedom, responsibility, and rectification in the globalized world embedded with many cultures and religions.[61]

Accordingly, the theological theme of "reconciliation" is the driving force underpinning the prophetic, humanist notion of commitment in complementarity between "responsibility for" and commitment to those suffering. It contains the intersection of the God of Israel, the victim, and Jesus as the Jew, paving the way for us to reconsider ethics of recognition in a comparative study. Thus I emphasize that Bonhoeffer's insight could break through Shoah or beyond Auschwitz as an example for a pluralistic configuration of ethics in our own time.[62]

Biblical Israel drives Bonhoeffer to discern the traces of God in the experience of the Other. Ethical maturity of humanistic atheism or moral wisdoms of other religions may find their justification in Bonhoeffer's hermeneutics of recognition in acknowledging the mystery of the God of Israel who embraces the otherness of innocent victims in light of Christ's reconciliation. Thus a hermeneutic of recognition of the Other forms a new horizon of prophetic hermeneutics which promotes the culture of the recognition of others in their uniqueness and difference.[63]

Comparative religious ethics in this regard becomes possible and meaningful, in respecting and enhancing the integrity of life, living responsibly in relation to others. *Fides quaerens intellectum* advocates faith which is imbued with anamnestic, subversive memory upon Jesus Christ and his suffering people.

This aspect may incorporate the Confucian notion of rectification of names in the moral lexicon for the sake of people's dignity and right. In contrast to modernist exaggerated optimism and postmodern nihilism,

---

61. Schweiker, *Theological Ethics and Global Dynamics*, 214.

62. The Shoah in terms of extermination of the Jews started in 1941. Bonhoeffer was (in his latest writings) contemporaneous to the Shoah, including some knowledge of the crimes against the Jews.

63. Metz, "1492—Through the Eyes of a European Theologian," in Metz and Moltmann, *Faith and the Future*, 70.

I take into account a prophetic legacy of Bonhoeffer for ethical humanism in dialogue with Mencius's people-oriented ethics. This comparative, religious configuration upholds Mencius's ethics of rectification, which implies a structural transformation of what is beset by injustice and violence to the life of people. An ethics of social rectification improves on the limitation of virtue ethics in an Aristotelian-Thomist sense. It underpins ethical commitment to the actual lives of people burdened in the history of dominion and power. Insofar as we discern *Dao*-truth through the face of the people, the outcry in their social discourse and their predicament can be a catalyst in guiding and fueling our ethical reorientation and commitment. The Confucian ethics of rectification comes together with Bonhoeffer's ethics, constituting a potential for developing an ethical humanism in the comparative religious context.

PARRHESIA AND *THEOLOGIA CRUCIS*

Bonhoeffer presents a reflection on *parrhesia*, asking, "what is meant by telling the truth?"[64] "Telling the truth," truthful speech of others, is different in one's relationships at each particular time and in the particular situation. Trustful speech is indebted to God, since the living God has set us within the context of living life. Trustful speech of God in relation to the Other challenges the notion of God as a metaphysical principle. According to Bonhoeffer, *parrhesia* entails a hermeneutical character, because it is "a matter of correct appreciation of real situations and of serious reflections upon them."[65]

I find Bonhoeffer's ethics of *parrhesia* to be a fulcrum of discourse ethics underlying postcolonial public theology and the discipleship of God's mission. Bonhoeffer's theological humanism, biblically, prophetically informed, promotes anamnestic reason founded upon the sociobiographical sharing of the victimized lives, and upholds an ethics of *parrhessia*, speaking the truth audaciously for those who are fragile, silenced, and vulnerable. The word of the cross, which entails a discursive form of *parrhesia,* is "as much alive as life itself."[66] It challenges us to interpret God in a new and fresh manner in terms of the standpoint of the sub-

---

64. Bonhoeffer, *Ethics,* 358.
65. Ibid., 359.
66. Ibid., 360.

jugated and subalterized. The exposed flesh of the crucified one reveals a secret of self and brings it to God's exposure in the face of Jesus Christ. "God's truth has become flesh in the world and is alive in the real . . . The concept of living truth is dangerous."[67]

Furthermore, Jesus' discourse of *parrhesia* (Mark 8:32) is made in his vocation of reconciliation for God's sake and the world. A *parrhesia* form of discourse demonstrates a spirit of resistance, calling into question the institutionalized authority in the religious and political realm. *Parrhesia*, speaking to each other frankly, finds political-religious meaning and discourse for the sake of the life of the marginalized, the victim, and the voiceless.[68]

This discourse ethics of *parrhesia* characterizes the irregular side of *theologia crucis*, in a passion for seeking the time lost for paving a space for them to speak for themselves. In the deliberation of *theologia crucis*, an archeological hermeneutics sets about to deciphering the discourses of the excluded and the subaltern on the irregularized side of the history and world. This perspective challenges a symbol of *theologia crucis* as tainted with colonial images of assimilation, sacrificial image, crusade, violence.

When *theologia crucis* in light of reconciliation comes along with the discourse ethics of *parrhesia*, the non-Christian people are recognized and appreciated in bringing their religious, moral reasoning and contribution to ethics of responsibility, compassion, and rectification. This comparative religious sharing supplements and renews a concept of communicative reason, in an endeavor to emphasize anamnestic reason and the sociobiographical practice of emphatically listening to life story of the vulnerable ones and the innocent victims.

The living word of God shapes the language of faith as seeking understanding of and communication with the Other, while faith is active and engaged in our praxis of love, compassion, and rectification. If theological ethics is based on "faith seeking moral understanding" (*fides quarens intellectum moralem*),[69] faith and moral reasoning find their justification in the living word of God, which comes to us as word-event in the embodiment of the physical face of Jesus in sociobiographical solidarity with the subaltern-minjung.

67. Ibid., 361.
68 Foucault, *Fearless Speech*.
69. Schweiker, *Responsibility and Christian Ethics*, 5.

BONHOEFFER: PEACE MOVEMENT AND WORLD CHRISTIANITY

In my postcolonial reading of Bonhoeffer in the East Asian context, I have attempted to review Bonhoeffer's prophetic legacy for postcolonial *minjung* theology and also his relevance in comparative religious study of Confucian ethics. The wisdom and moral reasoning of non-Christian religions is not meant to be a domestication of the gospel narrative into an indigenous cultural status quo or backwardness. But, interpretation of the gospel narrative in East Asia undergirds an audacious hermeneutics in retrieval of God's humanity in Jesus Christ in dialogue with the ethical humanism of people of other religions. This hermeneutics helps Christian existence embrace prophetic faithfulness to the God who was executed in the realm of social reality and to *minjung's* life rather than the realm of metaphysical ideas. God enters all human reality in order to change it materially and spiritually.[70]

In this light, Bonhoeffer's theology entails a strong missional implication for taking seriously postcolonial challenge and World Christianity. His theology, in deep conversation with the world, is imbued with God's reconciliation in Christ. Creation and reconciliation come together, while penultimate and natural life is appreciated and valued. Bonhoeffer's concept of church for others becomes a missional ecclesiology in terms of discipleship, resistance, solidarity, and recognition of the others. His theology of reconciliation is embodied in Jesus's solidarity with those who are fragile and vulnerable, underpinning mission as prophetic dialogue for the sake of ethical humanism and peace in acknowledging the maturity and dignity of those in the world under God's universal reign.

Given this, I am concerned with Bonhoeffer's contribution to the peace movement. Any order of creation is not an unchangeable order of creation, but at best an order of preservation for the sake of Christ. Accepting the reality of struggle and conflict must not lead to the affirmation of war, because war cannot be understood as one of God's orders of preservation. When the proclamation of the gospel ("your sins are forgiven") becomes concrete and alive in the life of the hearer, it implies articulating the concrete commandment by discovering God's order of preservation for today. For Bonhoeffer, God's commandment for today

---

70. Pangritz, *Barth in Theology of Bonhoeffer*, 33.

is the order of international peace.[71] If the order of international peace is God's commandment, it should be realized and fulfilled in international politics as well as among faith communities of religions. This perspective leads to a radical interpretation of the meaning of the gospel for God's shalom, articulating how moral identity is constituted and renewed in an act of understanding and interpretation, in the context of World Christianity.

Sharing Bonhoeffer's concern for the peace movement, Helmut Gollwitzer, a friend of Bonhoeffer, maintains that

> the man whom I accuse, is the real user of violence; all who, on the right or the left, outrage justice and stand in the way of peace; I myself believe that I must take the way of a pilgrim for peace; personally I would a thousand times rather be murdered, than kill others myself.[72]

Ethical integrity is rooted in God in Christ who emptied himself and took the form of a servant (Phil 1–11). The Sprit empowers us to be responsible agents. Bonhoeffer integrates his sense of God's self-limitation as a way of creating the space for human responsibility for the Other. The divine transcendence which is the self-limitation of God in Jesus Christ creates the space for the church to enhance freedom, responsibility, and solidarity in the sphere of the integrity and the coherence of all of life before God, notably with respect to suffering people.

Christian ethics of reconciliation appeals to scripture, revelation, and tradition and also upholds a dialectical act of reasoning which involves the linguistically created intersubjectivity of mutual understanding between the Christian self and the Other. Integration of responsibility and a communicative reason can be found in respect for the others in moral inquiry through: openness to the position of others, trustfulness in the presentation of all views, appeal to generally accessible evidence in making arguments, and finally in willingness to acknowledge the force of the better argument. These criteria help to guide moral actions in respecting and enhancing the integrity of life[73] for the sake of God's shalom.

---

71. Konrad Raiser, "Bonhoeffer and the Ecumenical Movement," in De Gruchy, ed., *Bonhoeffer for a New Day*, 329.

72. Gollwitzer, *Rich Christians and Poor Lazarus*, 65.

73. Schweiker, *Responsibility and Christian Ethics*, 218.

Bonhoeffer's dictum—only the suffering God can help—is a counter memory to the hegemonic history of the powerful, awakening us to an anamnestic reason founded upon Jesus, an innocent victim and his people in mass suffering. As James Cone maintains, a painful memory of an unspeakable crime against disfigured black bodies done in the lynching tree needs to be remembered; such a memory reminds us of the cost of discipleship in reference to the crucified people of history.[74] The experience of the Other as expressed in the lynching tree or the crucified minjung in history could help break through colonial dominion by healing the deep wounds of racial and structural violence. The cross placed alongside the lynching tree can help people to see Jesus in a new light in contrast to the violent crosses of the crusade and the Ku Klux Klan and empower his followers to take a stand against every kind of racial supremacy, injustice, dominion, and structural violence.

In terms of dialogue between the gospel and natural law written into the hearts of all, I acknowledge that people of other faiths bring Christian faith home to realize the important place of others in their moral character, standing notably in God's reconciliation in Christ with the world. The integration of biblical narrative with extra-biblical narrative fosters self-critical reflection on Christian self-understanding and calls for a humble attitude and prophetic audacity for self-renewal before the mystery of God and in appreciation of the Other. Responsibility, moral integrity, and rectification uphold a postcolonial sense of ethical reorientation in a direction of creating more space for the subaltern to speak for themselves. The very act of reading, writing, thinking, and interpreting must be built on a perilously critical frankness and audacity, doing something courageous for the sake of God's shalom and those who are deviant, unfit, and voiceless. Given this, Bonhoeffer can find his new meaning and voice for postcolonial public theology in confession of Jesus Christ as the representative of innocent victims in the midst of World Christianity.

---

74. Cone, *Cross and the Lynching Tree*, xiv–xv, xix, 42.

19

Karl Barth

Religion, Pluralism, and World Christianity

BARTH'S THEOLOGY OF GOD'S mission begins with God's established covenant with Israel and culminates in the reconciling work of Jesus Christ with the world. The gospel as the living voice of God can be heard in the reconciled world through which God may speak to the church in an unexpected and provocative manner. This theological perspective on God's mission of reconciliation leads to a critical examination of the hermeneutical dimension of Barth's theology of mission, which provides a wider spectrum of dialogue in the context of religious pluralism.

In the history of interpretation, Karl Barth has long been accused as the representative of neo-orthodox theology through his negative attitude toward religion. Theologians of religion, such as Paul Knitter, chide that Barth's theology is inappropriate in upholding engagement with the reality of religious pluralism because of Barth's strong critique of a point of contact and natural theology.[1]

Despite this charge, I notice that Barth's theology presents a structure of recognition of the Other in light of God's act of speech underlying a radical openness toward the world. When this aspect is overlooked, his Christocentrism has been misrepresented as a theological way of upholding an anti-religious and anti-cultural stronghold.

In contrast to Barth, Paul Tillich receives full sympathy from those committed to developing theology in the context of interreligous dialogue, notably in a Buddhist-Christian context. It is certain that Tillich's

---

1. Knitter, *No Other Name?*, 80–96.

contribution to a theology of culture is remarkable and paves the way for a new venture of Christian theology in the encounter with world religions. Given Tilllich's preferred position in the interreligious exchange, it is illuminating to explore a prophetic undercurrent in Barth's theology for interreligious dialogue, which has been little attended in the studies of God's mission and the missional church conversation.

THE EFFECTIVENESS OF GOD'S WORD IN UNIVERSAL HORIZON

Hendrik Kraemer, in his publication *The Christian Message in a Non-Christian World*, pictures Barth's theology one-sidedly as impeding Christian dialogue with other religions.[2] Since then, Barth's theology has received little sympathy in the context of wider ecumenism and World Christianity. However, the internal structure of Barth's theology challenges such a generalization. In his deliberation on the Word of God Barth conceptualizes the Word in a threefold sense (written, proclaimed, and revealed), in which he stresses the priority of the revealed Word over the other two forms of the Word of God. Barth's reflection on revelation in this regard is imbued with God's universal voice coming from the world.

Thus, Barth argues that God can speak to us in a completely different way than we would expect in the church (proclaimed) or from the scriptures (written). According to Barth, God can speak to us through a pagan or an atheist. God may be pleased to bless Abraham through Melchizedek, or Israel through Balaam, or help God's people through Cyrus. When God does speak in actuality through the face of the Other, we have to listen attentively to God.[3] Since God can speak to us in strange and profane forms, we must adopt a humble attitude and openness to other voices through which God continues to uphold God's own speech act in an irregular and unexpected fashion.

This perspective characterizes the freedom of God's act of speech underlying Barth's theology of the Word of God in a universal horizon. Barth seeks to develop his insight into the irregular and strange voices coming from the freedom of God's act of speech in relation to his later

---

2. Kraemer, *Christian Message in Non-Christian World*.
3. CD 1/1:55–60.

doctrine of lights within the framework of reconciliation. That is, true words *extra muros ecclesiae* (outside of churchly walls).

His early reflection on God's speech-act is culminated in his concept of secular parables in *Church Dogmatics* 4/3.1.§69, in terms of the continuous deepening and actualization of his previous concept of God's alien and extraordinary act of speech. In his inquiry into secular parables of truth in the world, Barth hermeneutically mediates the Word of Jesus Christ with various truth claims in a pluralistic context. God cannot abandon any secular sphere in the world that is reconciled in Jesus Christ. Even from the mouth of Balaam we recognize the well-known voice of the Good Shepherd. It must not be ignored or despised regardless of its sinister origin.[4]

However, Barth does not follow in the footsteps of Zwingli; he remains reluctant to canonize or give dogmatic status to such extraordinary ways and free communications of Jesus Christ.[5] Barth does not leave the ground of Christology, insisting that the church is given the task of how to examinine and investigate closely whether these profane words and lights are in agreement or correspondence with Scripture, church tradition, or dogma. The church further asks whether the fruits of these words outside Christianity are good and complementary, and whether their effect in the community is positive and productive. Barth calls this hermeneutical task a supplementary and auxiliary criterion. That is, "the fruits which such true words . . . seem to bear in the outside world."[6]

KARL BARTH, RELIGION, AND PURE LAND BUDDHISM

In the deliberation of revelation and religions, Barth undertakes a reading of Amida Buddhism. In his theological evaluation of religions,[7] Barth has already articulated the significance of the name of Jesus Christ in inter-religious context. Barth carefully examines Pure Land Buddhism in affinity to the grace religion of the Reformation. In his reading of this Buddhism,

---

4. CD 4/3.1:119.
5. CD 4/3.1:133.
6. CD 4/3.1:127.
7. CD 1/2 § 17.

Barth acknowledges that there is "a wholly providential disposition"[8] in the faith of Amida Buddha.

Barth, later in his doctrine of lights, is convinced that there is a positive evaluation of religions concerning secular parables of God's kingdom: "We may think of the radicalness of the need of redemption or the fullness of what is meant by redemption if it is to meet this need."[9] If we recognize the radicalism of the human desire for redemption in other religions, we meet the desire for grace or completeness of redemption in them. Thus, we can hear and recognize the true words of Jesus Christ in the reconciled world, especially coming from world religions.

In his definition of revelation as *Aufhebung* of religion,[10] Barth assigns a messianic parabolic character and dynamism to religions in light of the reconciling prophecy of Jesus Christ. The English translation of *Aufhebung* as "abolition" is seriously misleading and even wrongheaded. In the affirmative sense of *Aufhebung*, Barth contends that religions are kept and reserved and transformed in light of God's coming kingdom. They must not be totally denied, superseded, and destroyed. In Barth's use of *Aufhebung* in a dialectical sense, his evaluation of religion becomes obvious in both a negative and an affirmative sense. The negation of religion by revelation does not necessarily mean its abolition, but rather "religion can just as well be exalted in revelation."[11]

On the other hand, Barth's critique of religion is primarily given to Christianity as a religion, rather than being a polemic against people of non-Christian religions. Barth's theological approach to religions supports a tolerance, that is informed by the forbearance of Christ, and derived from the grace of God's reconciliation.[12] Barth's intention is to put the priority of revelation over religions, while he does not exhaust or totalize other religions into Christian sphere. It is certain that Barth affirms the Christian religion as the locus of true religion. However it does not mean that Christian religion fulfills human religion by becoming a superior or absolute religion in relation to non-Christian religions.[13]

8. CD 1/2:340.
9. CD 4/3.1:125.
10. CD 1/2 § 17.
11. CD 1/2:326.
12. CD 1/2:299.
13. CD 1/2:298.

According to Barth, Christian religion lives in coexistence with many other religions. "In His revelation God is present in the world of human religion."[14] Barth argues that we discern God's work in "a sphere in which His own reality and possibility are encompassed by a sea of more or less adequate . . . parallels and analogies in human realities and possibilities."[15] Christians should not become "iconoclasts in face of human greatness as it meets [them] so strikingly in the sphere of religion."[16] Thus Barth expresses a Christian attitude toward world religions in terms of self-criticism, spiritual poverty before God, and openness toward the Other. As Barth provocatively argues,

> [T]he Veda to the Indians, the Avesta to the Persians, the Tripitaka to the Buddhists, the Koran to its believers: are they not all 'bibles' in exactly the same way as the Old and New Testaments?[17]

In his appreciation of Amida Buddhism, Barth prefers Shinran's position to Honen's. Shinran (1173-1263) was a Japanese philosopher and religious reformer, founder of the JōdoShinshū school of Japanese Buddhism. Honen, a teacher of Shinran, once stated: "Even sinners will enter into life; how much more the righteous." If a sinner enters into the world of redemption and bliss through the grace of Amida, it goes without saying that the righteous enter into the bliss through their good deed and merit. However, Shinran radically reversed this statement: "If the righteous enter into life, how much more in the case of sinners."[18] The righteous must enter into the world of blessed life through the grace of Amida; the sinner does so also on the same basis. Barth sees the radicalism of justification by the power of Amida in Shinran's Pure Land Buddhism in comparison with the Reformation theology of grace and justification. We should be grateful for the lesson and teaching coming from such Buddhism.[19]

---

14. CD 1/2:297.
15. CD 1/2:282.
16. CD 1/2:300.
17. CD 1/2:282.
18. CD 1/2:341.
19. CD 1/2:342.

A COMPARATIVE NOTE: KARL BARTH AND PAUL TILLICH

Barth's reading of Amida Buddhism seen within the framework of parables of the kingdom of God helps us to compare Barth with Tillich's method of correlation. According to Tillich, the religious aspect points to that which is ultimate, infinite, and unconditional in human spiritual life. He defines religion as the ultimate concern that is manifest in all creative functions of the human spirit.[20] Thus religion is the all-determining substance, ground, and depth of human spiritual life. Religion as ultimate concern is the meaning-giving substance of culture, and culture is the totality of forms in which the basic concern of religion expresses itself. "Religion is the substance of culture, culture is the form of religion."[21] This spiritual and experiential definition of religion contradicts Barth's definition of religion as unbelief.

In his *Systematic Theology*, Tillich's approach is that of correlation. In this approach, theology should have a mutual working relationship with philosophy: philosophy asks the relevant questions and theology provides the answers from the perspective of Christian faith.[22] However, a theocentric perspective comes to the fore in Tillich's final speech by allowing for significant lights in other religions. In this speech, Tillich called for Christian theology to adopt a new approach to the history of religions and consequently to other religions. Tillich's way of accounting for this dynamism is through the use of the Greek term for time: *kairos*, a specifically appointed time. The *kairos* in Christ denotes a central event in the history of religions. There are, however, other *kairoi* in the history of religions. The *kairos* is unique, and *kairoi* are symbolic moments. Together they determine the dynamics of religious history.[23] Thus, according to Tillich, a claim of Christianity as the absolute religion and other religions as a progressive approximation to Christianity is excluded.[24]

In *Christianity and Encounter of World Religions*, Tillich calls his approach to the history of religions a dynamic-typological one. For Tillich, revelatory experiences are universally human because there are revealing and saving powers in all religions. Nonetheless, revelation is received by

---

20. Tillich, *Theology of Culture*, 8.
21. Ibid., 42.
22. Tillich, *Systematic Theology*, 1:60.
23. Tillich, *Christianity and Encounter of World Religions*, 73.
24. Tillich, *Systematic Theology*, 3:338.

a human being conditioned in a finite human situation and under the conditions of a human estranged character. A revelatory process brings the limits of adaptation and the failures of distortion to criticism.[25]

Tillich draws upon Rudolf Otto's *The Idea of the Holy*, in which Otto claims that the root of all religions is the experience of the Holy in contrast to the secular. Tillich further maintains that there are three main elements in the human experience of the Holy: the sacramental, the mystical, and the prophetic. The history of religions in its essential nature says that the sacred does not lie beside the secular, but in the depth of the secular. The sacred is the creative ground while at the same time it is a critical judge of the secular. Insofar as the Holy, or the Ultimate, is within the secular realm, this central event makes possible a concrete theology that has universal significance.

Tillich describes the unity of these three elements in a religion as the religion of the concrete spirit.[26] We cannot identify this religion of the concrete spirit with any actual religion, not even Christianity. Theonomy, from *theous* (God) and *nomos* (law), appears in the religion of the concrete spirit in fragments, never fully. Tillich's dynamic-typological approach assumes a theocentric and eschatological character in dealing with the history of religions,[27] while entailing existential and ontological analysis.

Tillich came to see Buddhism as a dynamic religion. It is impossible for Tillich to take Christianity as the absolute religion. The religions can be regarded as complementary rather than as exclusive of each other. Tillich issues a call for dialogue rather than conversion. True dialogue is possible only when both sides acknowledge the significance and revelatory character of the other's position. Tillich affirms a universal revelation of God, which is the source of religious experience.

The only possible solution to conflict in the interreligious context would be coexistence of different types without a universal claim.[28] This aspect leads Tillich to reject the exclusive claim of Christianity as the absolute religion and the other religions as preparatory ways to the Christian religion. The absolute is the event of Jesus as the Christ by which Christianity is created and judged to the same extent as any other

---

25. Tillich, *Christianity and Encounter of World Religions*, 64–65.
26. Ibid., 72.
27. Ibid., 74.
28. Tillich, *Systematic Theology*, 3:337.

religion. The revelatory character of Christ in Tillich's sense is closer to Barth's understanding of revelation from above.

In the Buddhist-Christian conversation Tillich endorses the dialogical-personal way by making inroads into Buddhist spirituality. An interreligious dialogue first presupposes that both partners acknowledge the value of the other's religious convictions, which are also ultimately based on a revelatory experience. Second, it presupposes that each dialogue partner is able to represent his or her own religious basis with commitment and conviction; thus dialogue is a serious confrontation. Third, it presupposes a common ground in which both dialogue and conflicts are made possible. Fourth, it presupposes that the openness of both sides to criticism is also directed against their own religious basis and prejudices.[29]

In the dialogue between Christianity and Buddhism, however, Tillich argues that a fusion of the Christian and Buddhist ideas of God would not be feasible.[30] Tillich's method of correlation entails an analogical imagination in terms of similarity-in-*difference*.

Tillich tries to draw some ethical consequences in terms of the principle of participation and identity. His comparative study of the Christian symbol of the kingdom of God and the Buddhist symbol of Nirvana remains a foundation for furthering mission as prophetic dialogue in the area of comparative religious study. According to Tillich, the kingdom of God is political in the dynamics of history, referring to a transformed heaven and earth in a new period of history. It is social, including the ideas of peace and justice with a political quality. It is of personal character, providing eternal meaning to the individual. The symbol of the kingdom of God emphasizes the fulfillment of humanity in every human individual. It is universal in character, embracing the fulfillment of creaturely life under all dimensions as expressed in St. Paul's vision: God being all in all.[31]

One participates in the kingdom of God in the Christian context, while in the Buddhist context one is identical with everything in Nirvana. Under the principle of identity, the sympathetic identification with nature is powerfully expressed in Buddhism. Nonetheless, in the history of Christian nature-mysticism the principle of participation becomes

---

29. Tillich, *Christianity and Encounter of World Religions*, 39.
30. Ibid., 42.
31. Tillich, *Systematic Theology*, 3:358–59.

influential (for instance, in the case of Francis of Assisi or in Luther's sacramental thinking of the real presence of Christ within bread and wine). The Christian notion of participation leads to agape, while the Buddhist notion of identity leads to compassion. Compassion, in the Buddhist sense, implies a state in which anyone who does not suffer the human condition (one who is in Enlightenment) may suffer by identification with another who does suffer.[32]

In a comparison of Tillich with Barth, George Hunsinger explains Barth's position in terms of Tillich's categories of autonomy, heteronomy, and theonomy. Other lights of religions are neither self-contained nor self-sufficient nor simply autonomous in comparison with the great light. These other lights are not conceived to be in competition with the great light or existing as the external, alien, and heteronymous outside it. True human words or secular parables are conceived of as coexistent with Jesus Christ, the Word of God that may be regarded as the theonomous principle in Tillich's sense. In a theonomous situation, the periphery is fully ruled by the truth of the center, rather than violated or superseded by it.[33]

In comparing Barth and Tillich, Hunsinger summarizes Barth's position in terms of "exclusivism without triumphalism or inclusivism without compromise."[34] This characterization tends to lose sight of Barth's deep theology concerning the irregular grace of God that expresses openness to the world of religious pluralism. Rather, Barth's exclusivity must be held together with Luther's teaching of justification *extra nos*. It characterizes self-critique of Christian exclusivism, spiritual poverty before God's mystery and the humble attitude of Christians toward God's irregular work in the reconciled world.

Barth's reflection on other religions as extraordinary instruments of the communication of God undergirds the idea that all human words are true words, genuine witnesses, and attestations of the one true Word. In other words, they are real parables of the kingdom of Heaven. This perspective implies a hermeneutical notion of the fusion of horizon between the ecclesial narrative and the extra-biblical communication event in light of God's living discourse.

---

32. Tillich, *Christianity and Encounter of World Religions*, 43–45.
33. Hunsinger, *How to Read Barth*, 263.
34. Ibid., 278.

Tillich's practical guidance in interreligious dialogue and the triadic deliberation of religion (sacramental, mystical, ethical) embedded within an eschatological framework may complement Barth's stance toward Buddhism as an analogical witness to the kingdom of God. Barth's analogical-dialectical theology based on similarity-in-difference comes to terms with Tillich's theocentric theology of religions in eschatological openness. According to Tillich, all missionary activity must use the religious consciousness that is present or can be evoked in all religions and cultures. It must follow the Old Testament's prophetic purification of the religious consciousness. Missional activity moves toward the central manifestation of the kingdom of God.[35]

The universal center of the manifestations of the kingdom of God in history is the claim which is an expression of the daring courage of the Christian faith. More than that, Christian claims must have a logos-determined explanation of faith for a theology that calls Jesus as the Christ the central manifestation of the divine Logos.[36] The Spiritual Community always lives in the churches and the churches confess their foundation in the Christ, who is the central manifestation of the kingdom of God in history.[37] Obviously, the kingdom of God and the Spiritual Presence are never absent in any moment of time.[38] Tillich's position is located in his dialectical understanding of viewing eternal punishment in reference to the doctrine of *apokatastasis*.[39]

GOD'S WORD IN MULTIPLE HORIZONS AND *THEOLOGIA NATURALIS*

As Barth states,

> while man may deny God, according to the Word of reconciliation God does not deny man . . . No Prometheanism can be effectively maintained against Jesus Christ . . . [For God], neither the militant godlessness of the outer periphery of the community,

---

35. Tillich, *Systematic Theology*, 3:365.
36. Ibid., 367.
37. Ibid., 378.
38. Ibid., 371.
39. Ibid., 416.

nor the intricate heathenism of the inner, is an insurmountable barrier.[40]

In light of God's reconciliation, Barth boldly affirms "dangerous modern expressions like the revelation of creation or primal revelations."[41] At this juncture, Hans Küng affirms that Barth corrects his previous position about natural theology, accusing Barth of not admitting it publicly.[42] However, in his early stage, Barth already accepted Söhngen's thesis: there has to be an *assumptio* of the *analogia entis* (analogy of being) by the *analogia fidei* (analogy of faith)—"the *analogia fidei* is *sanans et elevens analogia entis*"—namely, through Jesus Christ.[43] Barth's theology of reconciliation actually critically incorporates a dimension of natural theology into the freedom of God's act of speech. According to Barth, there is no point of tearing asunder "the original connection between creaturely *esse* [being] and creaturely *nosse* [knowing]."[44] Secular parables as "free communications of the will of [the] Lord"[45] become a central motif in Barth's theology of true words *extra muros ecclesiae*. If there are such words and lights, namely parables of the kingdom of God at a very different level in the secular world, "should it [the Christian community] not be grateful to receive it also from without, in very different human words, in a secular parable?"[46]

However, Barth does not intend to talk about words and lights in the world by appealing to the sorry hypothesis of natural theology. Earlier on, Barth developed his reflection on the freedom of God's act of speech through worldly affairs and in the otherness of the Other in the universal horizon of reconciliation. As Barth states,

> [I]n the world reconciled by God in Jesus Christ there is no secular sphere abandoned by Him . . . even where . . . it seems to approximate most dangerously to the pure and absolute form of utter godlessness.

---

40. CD 4/3.1:119–21.
41. CD 4/3.1:140.
42. Küng, *Does God Exist?*, 527.
43. CD 2/1:82.
44. CD 4/3.1:139.
45. CD 4/3.1:130.
46. CD 4/3.1:115.

Further, in light of the resurrection of Jesus Christ, Barth argues that we must "be prepared at any time for true words even from what seems to be the darkest places."[47] After all, "there is no refusal on the part of non-Christians [that] will be strong enough to resist the fulfillment of the promise of the Spirit which is pronounced over them too . . . or to hinder the overthrow of their ignorance of Christ."[48]

In relativizing, critically integrating, and constructively renewing "natural theology" socially, materially, and culturally by means of "universal" reconciliation in Jesus Christ,[49] Barth gives some indication that the true words may be heard even from "openly pagan" worldliness:

> We may think of the mystery of God, which we Christians so easily talk away in a proper concern for God's own cause. . . . We may think of the lack of fear in the face of death which Christians to their shame often display far less readily than non-Christians far and near. . . . Especially we may think of a humanity which does not ask or weigh too long with whom we are dealing in others, but in which we find a simple solidarity with them and unreservedly take up their cause.[50]

At this juncture, we observe that there are Judaism, socialism, and practical forms of humanness without faith and world religions next to the great light of Jesus Christ.[51] According to Barth, there are in the secular world a more distant (the express and unequivocal secularism of militant godlessness) and a closer periphery (the mixed and relative secularism) of the biblical-ecclesial sphere.[52] Barth expresses a preference for a secularism of militant godlessness over a mixed and relative secularism. Secular truth claims can be revealed to have "their final origin and meaning in the awakening power of the universal prophecy of Jesus Christ Himself."[53]

This aspect upholds a dialectical unity between Christ above and Christ from below which transcends a charge of positivism of revelation. In Jesus Christ the *humanum* of all humans exists and is exalted as such

---

47. CD 4/3.1:119.
48. CD 4/3.1:355.
49. Marquardt, *Theologie und Sozialismus*, 264.
50. CD 4/3.1:125.
51. Marquardt, *Theologie und Sozialismus*, 254.
52. CD 4/3.1:118.
53. CD 4/3.1:128–29.

to unity with God.⁵⁴ In exploring the inclusive horizon of the humanity of Jesus Christ as the *totus Christus*, Barth again maintains that the human nature elected by Him and assumed into unity with His existence is implicitly that of all humanity. In His being as a human, God has implicitly assumed the human being of all humanity. We all are in Him not only as *hominess* (human being), but our *humanitas* as such—for it is both His and ours—exists in and with God.⁵⁵

BARTH AND WORLD RELIGIONS

In the light of God's reconciliation, Barth has doubts about any attempt at Christianizing ideologies, cultures, and other religions in the name of Christian religion. Barth refers to the uniqueness of Christianity in encounter with other religions: "The religion of revelation is indeed bound up with the revelation of God: but the revelation of God is not bound up with the religion of revelation."⁵⁶

Markus Barth, a son of Karl Barth, reported on his father (provided by Bertold Klappert at the Leuenberg conference of 1992), that Karl Barth wanted to devote himself to the history of religion. In consideration of Barth's plan concerning the history of world religions, Klappert introduces Barth's research plan in terms of: the relation between Christianity and Judaism, the relation between Judaism and Islam and the relation between Buddhism and Hinduism.⁵⁷

Scrutinizing Markus Barth's authorized text on Barth's research plan, Eberhard Busch, an important biographer of Karl Barth, shared his idea with Klappert (on 12 December, 1992) that Markus' text would reveal Barth's own interest in exploring Christian relation to world religions in the context of the Second Vatican council. Busch is certain to characterize the title of Barth's planned text as "the ecumenical theology of the Holy Spirit."

Barth's ecumenical theology of the Holy Spirit underlines the universal horizon of the Holy Spirit in view of a doctrine of *apokatastasis*. "To be more explicit, there is no good reason why we should not be open

---

54. CD 4/2:49.
55. CD 4/2:59.
56. CD 1/2:329.
57. Chung, *Public Theology in An Age of World Christianity*, 119.

to this possibility . . . of an *apokatastasis* or universal reconciliation."[58] This refers to Barth's confession of hope in matters of a possibility of universal salvation, because God is reconciled in Christ with the world and the universal promise of the Holy Spirit was done. In this sense, Jesus Christ is the hope even for those of other faiths.[59]

The messianic prophecy of Jesus Christ has already happened upon all flesh: the Spirit is promised. Barth distinguishes between the resurrection, the outpouring of the Spirit, and the final return of Jesus Christ.[60] Christ's coming in the promise of the Spirit is the hope of all, to the extent that no aversion, rebellion, or resistance on the part of non-Christians will be strong enough to resist the fulfillment of the promise of the Spirit. The Spirit is pronounced over them, hindering the overthrow of their ignorance in the knowledge of Jesus Christ.[61]

Barth made a response to an interview question when it comes to the hidden Christ in the Indian context. He said, "The wind blows where it wills (John 3:8): Break-through (revelation) of the hidden Christ is always and everywhere possible: Inside and outside the church; even in the life and work and message of strangers (Melchizedek! [Gen 14:18; Heb 7:1–4]), heathens, atheists!"[62]

WIDER ECUMENISM AND WORLD CHRISTIANITY

Eberhard Busch reports on Barth's interest in the Second Vatican Council. During the Spring and Summer of 1966 Barth undertook a serious study of the sixteen Latin texts that were "produced by the council and of at least some specimens of the abundant literature devoted to the council."[63] After reviewing the documents of Vatican II and visiting the Vatican, Barth demonstrated a friendly attitude toward Catholic theology and its remarkable openness to the reality of religious pluralism. Delighted in the renewal movement of the Catholic Church after the council, Barth expressed a hope for this movement to unfold further. In his visit to the

58. CD 4/3.1:478.
59. CD 4/3.1:355–56.
60. CD 4/3.1:294.
61. CD 4/3.1:355.
62. Barth, *Gespräche: 1964–1968*, 565.
63. Busch, *Karl Barth*, 481.

Vatican Barth observed that "the church and theology over there are more on the move than [he] had imagined."[64] However, Barth did not overestimate the renewal movement within the Roman Catholic Church.

It is substantial to mention Barth's openness to dialogue with the Islamic community. We notice Barth's concern about Islam in his dialogue with J. Bouman from Lebanon. In his letter to H. Berkhof in Leiden (1968), Barth reported on his conversation with J. Bouman: "In theological appreciation of the situation there [in Lebanon] . . . we were but completely in agreement" that "a new communication about the relation between the Bible and the Koran is an urgent task for us."[65] A new communication about the relationship between Christianity and Islam demonstrates the important task of expanding a universal horizon of Barth's theology of words and lights[66] toward God's mission and religious pluralism.

Furthermore, "a new communication about the relation between the Bible and the Koran" refers to Barth's argument for a confession of guilt regarding "the deplorable role of the Church in the so-called crusades."[67] In the context of the ministry of the church, Barth views Islam's achievements positively, both in the primitive forms and in the higher forms. Islam's constructs are both interesting and imposing in their own way—psychological, sociological, aesthetic and ethical—as well as from the general human standpoint. From a missional perspective Barth maintains that they should be valued and taken seriously without the crass arrogance of the white Christian people.[68]

Given the result of Vatican II, Barth retracts his earlier hostile attitude concerning *analogia entis*, insisting that "we are in unity about what can be meant by it."[69] Barth's lifelong critical engagement with natural theology and *analogia entis* sharpened his political theology in protest to National Socialism. It leads him to ground the universal dimension of revelation and God's act of speech more deeply in the freedom of God who embraces cultural diversity and multireligious reality. Thus, we notice that later in his life Barth made a reconciling gesture toward Emil Brunner: "If he is still

---

64. Ibid., 484.
65. Barth, *Briefe 1961–1968*, 504. Klappert, *Versöhnung und Befreiung*, 50.
66. CD 4/3.1 § 69.
67. Barth, *Ad Limina Apostolorum*, 37.
68. CD 4/3.2:875.
69. Ibid., 337.

alive and it is possible, tell him again, 'commended to our God,' even by me. And tell him yes, that the time when I thought that I had to say 'No' to him is now long past, since we all live only by virtue of the fact that a great and merciful God says his gracious Yes to all of us."[70]

Given this, Barth's provocative thesis of God's revolution in terms of *"alles in allem real verändernde Tatsache dass Gott ist"*[71] is of special significance for the Christian church in relationship with the world of non-Christian religions. Jesus Christ as the "partisan of the poor"[72] endorses Barth's stance toward Judaism and other religions for the sake of mutual peace, respect, and social justice. At this juncture, it is vital to consider Barth's concept of Christ's standing for *massa perditionis* (the lost mass: *ochlos-minjung*).[73]

The church should learn to listen to those religions, in which there are unknown yet revealed lights from God's kingdom. Barth's theology seen in light of God's act of speech may find its validity and inspiration for upholding theology of World Christianity concerning emancipation from colonial Christendom and inculturation of the biblical message. Barth expressed his expectation in a lecture which was delivered for three hundred students. Most of them came from developing countries, staying as guests of the Mustermesse in Basle:

> There may be a religious West, but there is not a Christian West . . . It could well be that one day true Christianity will be understood and lived better in Asia and in Africa than in our aged Europe.[74]

For Barth, the theological task concentrates on the subject matter as interpreted in different times and places. A theological audacity can be best expressed in doing Christian theology for God's sake, responsibly and concretely with one's own language and thoughts, concepts and ways. Barth, in his response to South East Asian theologians, advocates for "no boring theology." Barth definitely discourages theologians in Asia from following any kind of Barthianism or emulating the Western dominant

70. Busch, *Karl Barth*, 476–77.

71. "The fact that not only sheds new light on, but materially changes, all things and everything in all things—the fact that God is." CD 2/1:258.

72. CD 4/2:180.

73. CD 4/3.2:587. For study about Karl Barth and minjung theology, see Chung *Karl Barth*, 479.

74. Busch, *Karl Barth*, 468.

form of theology. The religions, the dominant ideologies and realities in Asia, should become the life-setting, which theologians in Asia take seriously in audaciously doing their own theology for God's sake and the living dynamism of the gospel.[75]

---

75. "No Boring Theology!" *South East Asian Journal of Theology*, 4–5.

EXCURSUS
A Dialogue with Karl Barth and Beyond

THIS EXCURSUS IS A constructive dialogue with Barth's theology in terms of appreciation, critical distance, and further development breaking through him concerning emancipation and inculturation in the postcolonial context of World Christianity. Since Kraemer's book, *The Christian Message in a Non-Christian World,* Barth's theology has been misused as a theology of anti-religion. However, based on what I have examined in Barth's theological structure (II. God's Mission, Public Ethics, and Israel: Karl Barth Revisited) in connection with Barth and religious pluralism, all of his critics and followers, including neo-orthodox apologetic of Barth's theology, are revealed as ill-grounded. In Barth's uncompromising "No" to natural theology we simultaneously affirm his "Yes" to Israel and his approach to the reality of pluralism in the world in terms of the freedom of God's act of speech through the reconciling work of Christ.

A postcolonial reading of Barth in the context of World Christianity seeks to elaborate his multidimensional horizons within his theological thought in matters of emancipation and recognition of cultural or religious others. Barth's public-prophetic theology set within the doctrine of reconciliation marks a major contribution in the wider spectrum of ecumenism and public church in a globalized world. His deliberation of words and lights in the reconciled world can be understood as his creative appropriation of Calvin's teaching of the Holy Spirit in the universal horizon, while Barth incorporates Luther's theology of creation and word-event in the sense of *viva vox evangelii* to his theology of God's act of speech.

In the doctrine of reconciliation God's prevenient grace in creation is accepted, instituted, and integrated into Barth's theological way of actualizing God's word in love, reconciliation, and transformation. As Eberhard

Jüngel argues, Barth's theology can be seen as a Protestant counterpart to Karl Rahner's doctrine of the anonymous Christian, although on very different grounds and paths.[1]

APPRECIATION

As Craig Nessan rightly observes, in my previous study of *Karl Barth: God's Word in Action*,[2] I have attempted to interpret Barth in terms of his social biography, undertaking a reading strategy of his thorough-going socio-economic, political, and historical settings. This approach is a refreshing corrective to those interpretations of Barth as a representative of neo-orthodoxy in which Barth's theological subject matter is dissociated from God's word to social, political, and cultural location. As Paul D. Jones rightly notices,[3] my contextual-hermeneutical and historical-genetic approach to Barth follows in the footsteps of F. W. Marquardt who presents this approach in his book *Theologie und Sozialismus: Das Beispiel Karl Barths*. I have sought to clarify and deepen what Marquardt expressed in his ground thesis on God's Being in Revolution in terms of *alles in allem real verändernde Tatsache, dass Gott ist* (God's Being means the reality of really changing and transforming all in all).

Jones's interest in Barth's rhetoric and its intended political effects is differentiated from my socially engaged hermeneutical strategy in contextualizing and undertaking Barth. It is certain that Jones' rhetoric approach is valued as it engages with the political dimensions of Barth's Christology in appropriating the Calvinist notion of *munus triplex*, which needs to be related to a politically vibrant theological anthropology and ecclesiology.[4]

Following the School of Berlin in Germany (coupled with the prophetic-emancipatory legacy of Helmut Gollwitzer and Friedrich-Wilhelm Marquardt), I argue that one can understand neither the political writings of the young Barth nor the *Church Dogmatics* without careful attention to Barth's social critical commitments. These commitments were defined already when Barth served as a pastor in Safenwil (1910–1918), as he developed his own form of dialectical-theological socialism in his critical and

---

1. Jüngel, *God's Being is in Becoming*, 138.
2. Nessan, Review of *Karl Barth: God's Word in Action*, 386–88.
3. Jones, Review of *Karl Barth: God's Word in Action*, 474–77.
4. Ibid., 476.

constructive interaction with Leonhard Ragaz and religious socialism, notably coming from the elder Johann and younger Christoph Blumhardt.

For the sake of a social-biographical reading of Barth, an emancipatory hermeneutic is concerned with interpreting Barth in his exposition of the Tambach Lecture (1919), in relation to the first and second editions of the *Römerbrief* (1919/1922), and finally concerning all the way through the *Church Dogmatics*. God's revolution in Jesus Christ is constantly in pursuit of new social justice and order in light of the breakthrough and irruption of the kingdom of God *socially-analogically* in our midst. This dialectical-analogical approach becomes one of the defining characteristics of the second edition of the Romans commentary in continuity with his lesser known first edition of Romans (1919). Barth's emphasis (in the fashion of Kierkegaard) on the infinite qualitative distinction between eternity and time needs to be benchmarked only against his social, political context embedded within the October Revolution in Russia and General Strikes in Switzerland 1918. His dialectical-analogical theology recurs at key junctures in shaping and characterizing his *Church Dogmatics* as a form of political and emancipatory theology.

Joerg Rieger in his review of my study of Karl Barth[5] also acknowledges that a politico-theological hermeneutics underlines the term Jesus Christ as "partisan of the poor" in mediating the early Barth and the later Barth as a common thread. This observation hits the mark in my study of Barth as a political and publicly responsible theologian from the beginning to the end.

Furthermore, I read Barth's theology of Israel as the point of departure for developing a model of interreligious theology less travelled so far. I detect significant direction for the elaboration of such a theology in Barth's insight into recognizing an irregular voice of God stemming outside the walls of Christianity. Barth deeply considers a prophetic-hermeneutical way for God's act of speech through parables of the kingdom, especially through the face of the other. God's light in Christ's reconciliation may choose to shine through the Scriptures and teachings of other religions.

---

5. Rieger's review, in *Religious Studies Review* (September 2010), 211.

PROBLEM AND DEBATE: BARTH, NATURAL LAW, AND *CREATIO CONTINUA*

Appreciating three reviewers of my previous study of Barth, I do not sidestep Barth's problem with natural law and a classic doctrine of *creatio continua*. Barth challenges God's universal reign coupled with natural law which is grounded in the first function of the law. Barth's critique of natural law replaces God's preservation in the realm of creation by christocentric universalism.

Provocatively, Barth in his later stage wins back a clear and unequivocal sense for the concept of primal or original revelation (Paul Althaus) or creation revelation (Emil Brunner). However, his position is differentiated from Althaus's notion of primordial revelation or creation of order. Althaus conceptualizes his doctrine of law in terms of the contrast between God's primordial revelation and God's revelation in Jesus Christ. A distinction between law and gospel relies on the distinction between God's primordial form and christological form. The gospel prior to the law refers to the primal condition in which humanity knows God's will, even apart from the historical revelation in Christ. The function of the gospel is to restore an antecedent and primal condition, pointing to already existing orders and laws. Christ does not alter this condition of natural law. The gospel is restricted to the forgiveness of individual sins in a spiritual manner while the law became a system of autonomous orders of creation and history. As Althaus argues, "It is valid through itself; it shines on its own light; it is not essentially bound to faith in Jesus Christ and to his Gospel."[6]

It is unfortunate to see that Althaus's theology of original revelation led to the *Ansbacher Ratschlag* (Ansbach Recommendation) against the *Barmen Theological Declaration* of the Confessing Church. The Ansbach document, imbued with anti-Semitism, thanks God for the fact that God has given the *Führer*, Adolf Hitler, as a pious and faithful supreme pastor to the German people in the form of the National Socialist State.[7] Accordingly, the National Socialist order of the state is hailed as a good government. This theological setback continues to resurge in bolstering antithetical dualism between law and gospel to defend or conceal the inherent injustice of apartheid in South Africa or elsewhere.

---

6. Althaus, *Christliche Wahrheit*, 61–62. See Knitter, *No Other Name?*, 98.

7. For Duchrow's critique of Neo-Lutheranism during the period of National Socialism, see Duchrow, *Global Economy*, 12.

In contrast to Althaus and his political error, Barth incorporates the place of creation into christocentric lordship. Thus on the basis of Christ's reconciling work, God may preserve the creation as a good work and speak only on this basis. Creation has for Barth its meaning as the external basis of the reconciliation (covenant), which is the internal basis of creation. Although God's covenant or God's gracious election (reconciliation) in Barthian sense embraces the whole of created reality, a possibility of creation's participation in the covenant comes out because of Jesus Christ as its ontic reality. This perspective makes Barth open toward conceptualizing the realm of creation positively in light of Christ's reconciliation which incorporates God's universal reign in the sense of *creatio continua* to his own theology of God's act of speech.

Barth further discovers language first through God's self-revelation in Jesus Christ, because revelation grasps the language. Jüngel advocates that the language for Barth is not silenced by the language of revelation, but in a limited sense revelations of the *creatura* or *xtisis* itself may occur in the language.[8] In the world reconciled by God in Jesus Christ, no secular sphere is abandoned or withdrawn by God's control. The secular sphere speaks of God because God speaks to it and so allows it to speak of God. This capacity of language is, however, based on the capacity of Jesus Christ which goes beyond the sphere of the Scripture and the church. Parables of the kingdom of heaven are qualified as service to the free communications of Jesus Christ.

Nonetheless, in Barth's theology of creation, I do not find a biblical perspective on creation as emancipation. In the context of Genesis, creation, comprehended as emancipation, entails socio-historical experience of Israel about God's promise (or covenant) in the Babylonian captivity. Creation is experience, confirmation, and actualization of God's promise as it is inscribed in the memory of Israel regarding God's act of emancipation.

GOD KNOWN AND UNKNOWN

In his further development within the context of a posthumous writing about Christian life, Barth paves a way to the distinction between the known and unknown God. God is both a known and yet also an unknown God.[9] Barth considers the objective knowledge of God as the Creator of human

---

8. Jüngel, *God's Being is in Becoming*, 20.
9. Barth, *Christian Life*, 115.

nature on the part of those outside Christianity, because "the non-Christian world also knows the one, true, and living God very well objectively."[10] If a subjective knowledge of God on human side does not correspond to God's objective knowledge, it is at human fault. In his posthumously published work, a so-called 14th volume of *Church Dogmatics*, Barth writes:

> God is both a known and yet also an unknown God to the world and his community, to men in general and Christians in particular, to all of us.... We are referring to the objective knowledge of God as the Creator of human nature ... Man, not God, is at fault if a subjective knowledge of God on man's side does not correspond to God's objective knowledge.[11]

In his early reflection on the hiddenness of God (CD 2/1. § 27.1), Barth affirms that God is known by God alone. This perspective over-emphasizes the transcendence of the knowledge of God only in the grace of God's revelation and as visible only to faith and attested only by faith. He completely prevents natural theology or general revelation in the teaching of church fathers who advocated the relative viewability and conceivability of God.[12] However, in a different direction from his early statement, Barth provocatively argues in the posthumous writing that

> God's name, then, is already holy in the world that he created good long before Christianity begins to pray for its hallowing or to be zealous for the honor of God. Is not his name holy in every blade of grass and every snowflake?[13]

Barth's reflection of "unknown God" can be compared with Luther's distinction between the hidden God and the revealed God or Calvin's theology of the Holy Spirit in a universal horizon. Luther made distinction between God hidden and God revealed in light of the crucified Christ in contrast to Erasmus who ignores this distinction. God's unfathomable being in self is the *terminus a quo* from which God is presented in God's Word. God's being for us is the miracle of grace revealed in the gospel and grounded in the freedom of God.[14]

---

10. Ibid., 196.
11. Ibid., 121.
12. CD 2/1, 200.
13. Ibid., 121.
14. Gollwitzer, *Existence of God*, 221.

CRITIQUE:
LANGUAGE AND SOCIAL CONNECTION WITH LIFE

Theological-critical hermeneutics of the word of God needs to seek to develop a deeper penetration in order to understand the word of God in terms of human language embedded within social, cultural, political, and emancipatory realm. Such hermeneutics employs critical analysis of language as social discourse imbued with the mutual dependence between knowledge, interest, dominion, and power. The word springs up in the processes of life and a living and life-giving word issues forth life in an eschatologically open-ended manner, entailing the ideology-critical force to distortion, dominion, and propaganda. Barth's political hermeneutics and God's act of speech in creation may help a theological-critical hermeneutics to be more socially engaged and liberatively guided.

Indeed, Barth's language of social analogy provides an insight into integrating social political discourse to the gospel concerning the kingdom of God. A hermeneutical dimension of analogy as similarity-in-difference may incorporate a dimension of social discourse embedded within life connection—thereby the sociocultural and material-economic condition of human language for the sake of a prophetic hermeneutics of suspicion and solidarity. Such an aspect further utilizes cultural anthropological analysis of language which includes ethnic stratification, social inequalities, and sociopolitical representation. An analysis of language as social discourse and cultural stratification emphasizes language and culture in mutual interaction concerning change, context, and power.

Given this, Barth's dialectical-analogical theology grounded in his political experience of his time needs to be furthered in the linkage of word with life connection concerning diversity, plurality, and difference. God's relationship with us and the world cannot be merely comprehended in dialectical-analogical fashion, which tends to perpetuate a hierarchical notion of mimesis, copy, and correspondence. Barth's dialectical and analogical theology presents a correspondence theory of truth in the classical thought of mimesis or imitation concerning the relation of the ideal and the real (Plato). According to this Western tradition, what appears is mere appearance, a deficiency. The copy never equals its prototype.

Barth's theological "above" is concerned with the *Sache*, the subject matter of God's act of speech in creation, but his hermeneutical reflection of theological *Sache* in the sense of living reality of revelation takes a path of analogy only in terms of theory of correspondence in seeking to break through the ontological difference between God and creatures through revelation from above, which definitely includes the aspect from below. Obviously, a charge of positivism of revelation does not fit Barth in this regard. Yet, an aspect of hermeneutical underdevelopment of language as social discourse brings Barth to commit the forgetfulness of the difference and plurality between beings and beings in historical life setting and social location. This perspective argues that theological understanding of revelation is also influenced, circumscribed, and refracted under historical effectiveness and within social location.

Barth's theology grounded on God's act of speech can acknowledge the plurality and difference of historical and social ontology, which is undertaken in more egalitarian, more democratic, and more pluralistic manner. This prophetic and socially engaged form of emancipatory hermeneutics must arise from God's word-in-action itself, beginning with *Dabar* in a Hebrew manner, which means that in which a thing shows itself as grace, dialogue, judge, and emancipation. *Dabar* mediates dynamically and linguistically God-in-self (the immanent Trinity) with God-for-us (the economic Trinity). God-in-dialogue prevents the theology of correspondence from running into a hierarchical direction. In the beginning the Word was in dialogue with God of Israel.

BREAKTHROUGH BEYOND BARTH

Barth's initial hermeneutical impulse on the path of his *Church Dogmatics* includes an indirect answer to the hermeneutic problem. Barth brings out the unity of hermeneutics by claiming general validity for the hermeneutics by means of Scripture. For Barth the general and only valid hermeneutic must be learned from the Scripture as the testimony to revelation. This Scripture-oriented or narrative hermeneutics or narrative theology remains, however, in tension with his later notion of the freedom of God's act of speech in the creational realm and reconciliation. Barth does not manage to overcome this tension and left an unresolved question inherent within his dogmatic-analogical framework concerning God's act of speech, revelation, creation, and reconciliation.

According to Barth, if God comes to speech as God, revelation takes place as *Dei loquentis persona* (God speaking in person). The aspect of God's speaking act does not necessarily eliminate general hermeneutical significance, because God may speak through the Other in a completely different manner. It is certain that Barth encourages the church to examine closely whether the profane words and lights are in agreement with the Scripture, church tradition, or dogma.

However, this perspective, which is unilaterally oriented toward Christian dogmatic tradition, tends to marginalize an emic standpoint, which articulates the unique understanding of those who receive the gospel in non-Western culture. Cultures, through which God continues to speak, are internally diverse, always in flux and impacted by social stratification and power relations. All people, all religions exist within cultures laden with power relationships and social stratification.

Given this, I redefine the theological-critical hermeneutics in light of God as the infinite horizon of speech-event, that is, a postcolonial notion of intertextuality underlying the encounter and interaction between biblical narrative and extrabiblical realm for the sake of fusion of horizons underlying and sharpening an anthropological notion of thick description. The word of God in the sense of *viva vox evangelii* through God's act of speech (or God's Saying in the sense of Emmanuel Levinas) allows for a conjunction with the idea of hermeneutic coupled with the Hebrew concept of God's self-manifestation through the Word and the Greek concept of the Logos, particularly for postcolonial constructive direction. We may stand aside critically from the tradition in order to examine it critically and constructively; then we return to it to interpret it and recover its new meaning for our present time. This perspective finds theological-critical hermeneutics in agreement with non-theological, general hermeneutics through the analysis of language as social discourse in interdependence between knowledge, power, dominion, and institution.

Indeed, Barth's deliberation of language as social analogy in the sociopolitical context retains a potential to break through the limitation of a mimetic hermeneutics within itself. Barth facilitates my project to undertake a postcolonial concept of living and emancipatory word of God by incorporating theology from below (God's reconciliation) and the Other (God's Otherness in the life of subaltern-minjung). We must acknowledge that our understanding of the revelation is refracted and prejudiced in the plurality and difference of the world, in which hermeneutical reflection of historical, social ontology seeks to understand that which is different, particular, and local. The horizon of biblical narrative can be understood insofar as it is related to our present-day experience in life connection with the other, through whose face God continues to address to the church. This perspective implies that a Christian understanding or approach to other religions can be fashioned in terms of a dynamic interaction between the gospel, God's ongoing activity in the world of religions, and human expressions of ultimate reality in open-ended step and approximation. Christian tradition (scripture and its living interpretation through history) and its social discourse in contemporary life context come to terms with human experience in social location, as these Christian sources are melted into our current horizons of meaning.

God cannot be spoken of in theology apart from the world. Likewise, the world cannot be spoken of in theology apart from God. Certain foreshortenings and distortions in the process of translation are exculpated in terms of accommodation. This process is interpreted as analogous to the incarnation and reconciliation which stands in expectation of the final consummation. God's coming in the life, death, and resurrection of Jesus Christ strengthens hermeneutical theology of speech-event in dialogue with the Other and undergirds the sociocutural and political realm for prophetic ethical solidarity with those who are burdened and foreclosed on the irregular side of history.

CONFESSING JESUS CHRIST IN POSTCOLONIAL WORLD CHRISTIANITY

Barth's analogical featuring of God's word-act in a christocentric manner is grounded in God's gracious predestination as the sum of the gospel, and further deepened in his doctrine of reconciliation. A theological correlation between election and reconciliation appreciates the difference and plurality of human lives in diverse and different contexts.

Gospel does not replace the word of creation, but integrates it into God's universal reign and drives it in an eschatological light through conversation, recognition, and prophetic *diakonia*. A theology of creation must be more positively seen in light of God's universal reign and reconciliation, granting language, reason, wisdom, and religions to people of other cultures. The creation remains a text to be readable and deciphered within the hermeneutical framework. The creation stands in God's word of trustworthiness, address, and promise in an eschatological light: reconciliation and the advent of Jesus Christ.

If Jesus Christ as "partisan of the poor" (Karl Barth) is in solidarity with the *massa perditionis*, it is important to explore Jesus's public discourse coupled with *ochlos-minjung* and incorporate it into his message about the kingdom of God. In God's act of speech, God may represent the face of the subaltern through Jesus as the partisan of the poor. Thus the subaltern can speak by occupying its place in doing something audacious for God's sake. An analysis of Jesus' discourse form of *parrhesia* which articulates and conditions *theologia crusis* could help us to reveal to what extent the interplay between theological knowledge system and institutionalized power structure plays a significant role in sustaining Western theological metadiscourse still in the postcolonial context of World Christianity.

Insofar as Barth's political analogy is articulated in connection with socio-historical dialectics, his theology is more explicitly capable of demonstrating an emancipatory hermeneutics from below and the other, which emphasizes God's act of speech from the perspective of the outcast, the suspects, the maltreated, the powerless, the oppressed, the reviled—in short, from the perspective of *massa perditionis*.[15] This refers to confessing Jesus Christ in postcolonial World Christianity.

However, in his response to Eberhard Bethge's Bonhoeffer biography I hear that Barth wanted to further develop his theological direction and trajectory in the following direction: ethical discipleship–democratic socialism –the peace movement–political *diakonia* of the church: all in all political responsibility of Christian theology and church for the world.[16] More than that, as Marquardt sharply discerns a limitation in Barth's theology of Israel, Israel's self-understanding or human understanding of God, world, and humanity must not be dismissed as a *quantité négligeable*. If God has not thrown away God's people, Israel and people of other cultures must be seen in light of God's ongoing activity in them, so they are not degraded merely to a puppet figure. Israel represents the eschatological proviso of God, God's freedom and transcendence, allowing God to be God in all of God's freedom; it resists the Christian pathos about the end of time, considering the eschatological subjection of Jesus Christ until God might be all in all (1 Cor 15:28).[17]

---

15. Bonhoeffer, LPP 17.
16. Barth, *Fragments*, 119.
17. Marquardt, *Theological Audacities*, 28–29.

In my dialogue by breaking through Barth's theology, Barth still is honored as one of the church fathers and a great theologian who encourages me to move beyond Western Christianity toward World Christianity in a postcolonial relief. A critical dialogue with Barth and beyond should be understood with sincere gratitude and respect, yet with a theological audacity in seeking to break through Barth's theological achievements and inspiration for postcolonial public theology. Barth's dictum in warning his students is central in this regard: Don't become Barthians!

20

Eschatology, Political Ethics, and Liberation

A THEOLOGICAL JUSTIFICATION OF ETHICS has been presented in the concept of kingdom of God underlying public ethical theology as ethics of discipleship. Eschatology in the New Testament is deemed decisive in basic orientation of the proclamation of Jesus and of the early church. Theologians who are politically oriented toward liberation seek to justify the coming of the kingdom of God as the theological goal of Christian ethics in a European context of political theology and in a Latin American context of liberation theology. The symbol of the kingdom of God provides a point of reference that includes both world and the ethical issues. This chapter explores a discipleship ethics as public ethics concerning eschatology, political responsibility, and emancipation.

ESCHATOLOGICAL GROUND FOR POLITICAL ETHICS

For Moltmann, eschatology takes on normative significance such that the eschatological orientation of faith seeks fulfillment against the existing world. Not *presentia Christi* but *adventus Christi* forms the fundamental category of hope and expectation as it relates to the God of hope, a God with the future as God's essential nature (Ernst Bloch). For Moltmann, presentative eschatology means creative expectation in Bloch's sense, because hope sets about critiquing and changing the present reality by opening toward the universal future of the kingdom of God.[1] Moltmann's

---

1. Moltmann, *Theology of Hope*, 335.

eschatological Christology in messianic dimensions maintains that the beginning of the coming consummation of salvation has already taken place in the coming of Christ. This messianic Christology must be followed by a messianic ethics in a way that the present has been already gripped and determined by the eschatological future. Eschatological future becomes present without ceasing to be future by making the present a present future.[2] The present order is profoundly challenged by the promise which is the basis of one's hope in the resurrected Christ. The event of promise is the beginning of the critique of everything that is. Ethics of the kingdom of God are discipleship-ethics while the ethics of the discipleship of Jesus are the anticipation-ethics of his future. This eschatologically open Christology is carried out by the outpouring of the Holy Spirit which is the beginning of Christ's parousia, because the Spirit is the pledge of glory (2 Cor 1:22; Eph 1:14). What begins in the Spirit will be completed in the kingdom of glory. The kingdom of God's glory has its beginning in the coming of Christ (the kingdom of Christ) and is already heralded in the kingdom of the Spirit. In the Spirit the kingdom of glory lays hold of the present.[3]

Pannenberg introduces eschatology and the concept of the kingdom of God into the discussion of ethics. Eschatology is accorded a metaethical status, because Jesus' message speaks of the political kingdom of God and its coming. Pannenberg's ethical reflection is based on eschatological expectation of a better community in the future, because only the future realization of justice will correspond to the will of God. Given this, Pannenberg appreciates Ernst Bloch's philosophy of hope which interprets the teaching of natural law as anticipation of a better future. This aspect comes from the Jewish expectation of the kingdom of God. Pannenberg's proleptic ethics is driven in the framework of the eschatological hope for justice in relation to the teaching of natural law.[4] God's future lordship is already present as the prolepsis in the life and message of Jesus through God's love. The creative imagination of love is the mainspring for rational and moral behavior. For Pannenberg, Christian ethics takes its point of departure in the creative imagination of love which overcomes the limitation of situation ethics. Theology

---

2. Moltmann, *Ethics of Hope*, 38.
3. Ibid., 38.
4. Pannenberg, *Ethics*, 50.

and its subject matter should not be demonstrated in terms of ethical relevance or some ethical standard, but the reality of God and God's revelation must first be established for the ethical relevance.[5] This is Pannenberg's attempt at a new theological basis for ethics.

Ted Peters, driven by Pannenberg and Moltamnn, proposes a proleptic ethics in provolutionary character in which a propletic understanding of the Christian faith is called the life of beatitude. Faith in Jesus Christ is rooted in God's future and also in the future redemption of the entire creation. The future and promise of God is confirmed in the proleptic revelation of the future in Jesus Christ. Projecting such vision creates "advent shock" to the present aeon which is experiencing the reality of lordless powers. That is the brokenness and fragmentation of a fallen world yearning for wholeness in final consummation.[6] As God raised Jesus from the dead on Easter, so will God bring the whole of creation to its fulfillment and consummation in the new creation. The future-oriented category of the pro- replaces the category of *re-* (for example, revolution, return, renewal, revival, reformation) with *pro-*volution.[7]

The life resulting from beatitude is a life lived now with the future new creation in, with, and under our present faith. This is a life of hope releasing into our daily activity the power of a Spirit-inspired love.[8] The propletic ethics begins with eschatology and works back to ethics because a strong eschatology stimulates and upholds a strong ethics. Marx's critique of religion in a dialectical sense is accepted into proleptic ethics, because Marx sees the eschatological element within religion which underpins consciousness of the need for change, in terms of the sigh of the oppressed and the protest against real distress.[9] Eschatological prolepsis is the very foundation of ethics, seeking to incarnate God's future proleptically in present day reality.

---

5. Ibid., 55, 65, 67
6. Peters, *God—The World's Future*, 381.
7. Ibid., 380.
8. Ibid., 392.
9. Ibid., 378.

CRITICS OF PAN-ESCHATOLOGICAL THEOLOGY

Eschatology provides orientation and encouragement for ethics. God's future announced in the promise is not in contrast to the existing structure of the world, because promise entails a positive relationship concerning the announced future to the present reality. It is certain that eschatology cannot replace ethics, nor it is separated from ethical praxis and orientation.

However, it is Karl Barth who cautions a pan-eschatological direction in theological conceptualization of hope as Christian expectation of God's future which covers and explains the transcendental character of all theological subjects, contents, and discussion. In this pan-eschatological project, everything—the crucifixion, the resurrection, faith, love, the kerygma, the Church, baptism, the Lord's Supper, the Christian ethos and even God—is eschatologically comprehended as "my future." Taking issue with the pan-eschatological framework, Barth argues that "little importance can now be attached to a particularly eschatological sphere of hope as Christian expectation of the future, or to hope itself as a particular dimension of Christian existence."[10] Barth asserts faith, love, and hope—in accordance with St. Paul (1 Thess 1:3; 1 Cor 13:13)—as particular dimensions of Christian existence. Faith includes and gives rise to hope in the fulfillment of the promise of God (Heb 11:9), because faith is described as the basis and presupposition of hope and promise. Faith believes that God is true and hope expects that God will manifest God's truth in the future. Faith expects that eternal life has been given to us while hope nourishes and sustains faith. No one can expect anything from God without previously believing God's promise and future. The weakness of our faith must be supported and cherished by hope and expectation.[11]

According to Barth, not the Christian awaiting his or her future, but God in Jesus Christ creates Christian expectation of God's future. This perspective places Barth in contradiction with Moltmann who argues that "*spes quaerens intellectum—spero, ut intelligam.*"[12] Moltmann holds that Barth's understanding of the future of Christ is grounded merely in the revelation, the revelation of that which is and the Church remembers. For Moltmann, Christ's future revelation is not unveiling of the same thing in

---

10. Barth, *Church Dogmatics*, 4/3.2:912.
11. Ibid., 912–13.
12. Moltmann, *Theology of Hope*, 33.

the past, but it must be conceived as an event taking place in promise and final fulfillment. The Christian expectation awaits the fulfillment of the promised righteousness of God in all things, the fulfillment of the resurrection of the dead that is promised in the resurrection of Christ. In faith in Christ Christian hope has the primacy,[13] because all the knowledge of faith will be an anticipatory, fragmentary knowledge in establishing a prelude to the promised future.[14]

A theology of hope in Moltmann's fashion, driven by the future promise of God, reveals that all knowledge and thinking in history is eschatologically oriented and stamped as provisional and fragmentary.[15] Barth's notion of the eschatological reservation is replaced by eschatological anticipation and hope which emphasizes God's final future in our midst through the resurrection of Jesus Christ.

However, for Barth, God as the source and ground of faith, love, and hope is the one who changes everything and all in a transformative and revolutionary manner. Thus Jesus is the partisan of the poor in this light. Christian existence in hope, deriving from God, is existence in movement and action, that is a prophetic existence characterized by the liberation of the Christian.[16] According to Barth, there is "a periphery with its own apparently independent facts and factors and problems," necessary to human life: "the material, spiritual, technical, civilizing or cultural goods, contrivances, machines and gadgets"[17] that the Christian should not ignore. A sincere and zealous collaboration is obviously demanded on this periphery of human existence. When we lose this periphery we would definitely lose the center. It is not things, but "the lordship, the tyranny, the fatal dominion over man of things both great and small, the autonomous, abstract and absolute estimation and worship of things, of institutions, machines and furniture, even of ideas as such, the reversal of the order that they are to serve man and not man to serve them."[18]

---

13. Ibid., 229.
14. Ibid., 33.
15. Ibid.
16. Barth, *Church Dogmatics*, 4/3.2.939.
17. Ibid., 666.
18. Ibid., 667.

ESCHATOLOGICAL IRRUPTION AND LIBERATION IN DEBATE AND NEW DIRECTION

From the perspective of liberation theology in Latin America, European eschatological theology is critiqued, because it relegates secular history to a secondary role, sidestepping a critical analysis of concrete sociopolitical realities. Such a notion of eschatology fails to connect the action of God with action of human participants in human concrete historical and social terms and experience. The hope based on the death and resurrection of Jesus must be rooted in the heart of historical praxis in our oppressed and exploited present. A theology of hope grounded in the transcendental future would be a futuristic illusion.[19]

Liberation theologians value Bloch's contribution of philosophy of hope which assumes a concrete utopic function, mobilizing human action in history and society. A *docta spes* (teaching of hope) transforms the present, because what is real is an open-ended process, not-yet-conscious. This perspective of hope which subverts the existing order corresponds to Marx's philosophy of praxis which is characterized by eyes on the future and with real action in the present toward classless society. This is articulated in Marx's thesis of Feuerbach: "Philosophers have only *interpreted the world*, in various ways; the point, however, is *to change it*."[20]

At any rate, this implies a hermeneutics of suspicion in Marx's sense, because the texts of classical English economics, tradition of utopian socialism, and sources of idealism of German philosophy provide a horizon for Marx's philosophy of praxis and critique of political economy. Marx's theory of interpretation is undertaken through the scientific-dialectical analysis of correlation between institutional superstructure and material basis and it is driven for appropriation of new meaning and discourse in solidarity with the laborers.[21]

In an ethics of liberation eschatology plays a central role in emphasizing the saving event in everyday events of history. God's proclamation in Jesus Christ addresses the reality of human historical existence.[22] God's kingdom is the standard of justice. The kingdom of God is more actively present in the midst of people. In constructing a new, free, and just so-

---

19. Gutiérrez, *Theology of Liberation*, 124.
20. Ibid., 123.
21. Chung, *Cave and the Butterfly*, 206.
22. Bonino, *Toward a Christian Political Ethics*, 33.

ciety, human beings contribute to the work of the kingdom of God. The growth of the kingdom occurs historically in liberation and liberation as great human achievement is rooted in God's love.[23]

Moltmann already emphasizes that God's kingdom relates to the political world and Christian hope is symbolized in the resurrection of Jesus Christ. Hope inspires people to transform the political reality, aware of the danger of ignoring the present life.[24] In Moltmann's theology of the cross, God is identified with the poor, the estranged, and the forsaken through the suffering of Jesus Christ. Every eschatological theology must become a political theology, in other words, a socio-critical theology.[25] Moltmann develops his political hermeneutics of liberation in the vicious circles of death: (1) the vicious circle of poverty in the economic dimension; (2) the vicious circle of force in the political dimension; (3) the vicious circle of racial and cultural alienation; (4) the vicious circle of the industrial pollution of nature; (5) the vicious circle of senselessness and god-forsakenness. Ways toward liberation include the economic dimension of life (social justice), the political dimension of life (democratic human rights), the cultural dimension of life (identity in recognition), and the ecological dimension of society and nature (peace with nature), and the meaning of life (courage to be or faith).[26]

Furthermore, Moltmann challenges, if praxis in Latin American liberation theology is the criterion, what is the criterion of praxis?[27] Theological reflection must be the first act rather than the second act visible in liberation theology, because faith in Christ has its own praxis in terms of the discipleship of Christ crucified. However, a fideism in Moltmann needs to be sharpened in matters pertaining to the way to understand the meaning and reality of Christ crucified in sociocritical analysis of the correlation between the message of Christ crucified and his people in contemporary wretchedness.

Bonino acknowledges that Jesus in his experience of crucifixion demonstrates his solidarity with those abandoned and victimized in their own suffering. Christ's promise of resurrected life leads a suffer-

23. Gutiérrez, *Theology of Liberation*, 104.
24. Moltmann, *Theology of Hope*, 26–32.
25. Moltmann, *Crucified God*, 326.
26. Ibid., 329–37.
27. Moltmann, *Experiences in Theology*, 294.

ing people to a resistance to and denunciation of social evils.[28] Despite his sympathy to Moltmann, Bonino argues that Moltmann's ethics of hope describes contemporary social evils in an abstract and superficial manner. Thus political ethics in eschatological fashion fails to dismantle the roots of poverty, racism, and the structural violence. Moltmann's theology of hope is not capable of finding a language adequate to cope with human life rooted and oppressed in sociohistorical context for the possibilities of liberation.[29]

Moltmann expresses a critique of several Latin American theologians, complaining that the Latin American theology does not present its own face, but uses the frame of European thinkers (Kant, Hegel, Marx, among others). In Moltmann's critique, Bonino does not manage to advance beyond what Barth, Bonhoeffer, Metz and Moltmann himself had already undertaken.[30]

Segundo asks in return whether Moltmann wants the Latin American theology to be an exotic for him to appropriate for his universal theology. Segundo argues that Moltmann wants the Latin American theology to be a native product so that Moltmann processes and barters in the theological market of the North Atlantic world. In it Moltmann is a dominant figure.[31]

The ethics of liberation begin with the people's praxis. Differences of social status and self-understanding produce diversity and plurality in moral practices which, in turn, shape and condition ethical and moral theory. Míguez Bonino's work *Toward a Christian Political Ethics* articulates the importance of ethical reflection as a resource for social transformation aimed at challenging existing structure and constructing a new societal order.

Bonino speaks of the praxis of Christians as anticipating God's reign while human participation in God's initiative is defined as the work of the kingdom (Gutiérrez) or as building the kingdom (Leonardo Boff). For Gutiérrez, the option for the poor is based on God's own choosing to be with the poor (thus solidarity with the poor is a religious experience), while Bonino grounds the potion for the poor on the obedience of faith to a God

---

28. Bonino, *Doing Theology in a Revolutionary Situation*, 145.
29. Gutiérrez, *Theology of Liberation*, 124.
30. Moltmann, "An Open Letter to José Míguez Bonino," 58.
31. Westhelle, *After Heresy*, 128.

Eschatology, Political Ethics, and Liberation

of love and justice.[32] God's kingdom relates to all sociopolitical activity without being reduced to human liberation achieved within history.

According to Gutiérrez, the levels of praxis entail (1) a socio-political-economic dimension breaking from oppressive social, political, and economic structures; (2) a historical-utopian dimension in assuming people's responsibility for their own destiny; (3) Christian faith in interpretation of liberation as freedom from sin and communion with God and neighbor.[33] All three forms of liberation are taken together as a liberating praxis moving toward an integral freedom for the exploited.

The theological-ethical method operates in a process of hermeneutical circle and by means of multiple sources. According to Segundo, the hermeneutical circle is defined as "the continuing change in our interpretation of the Bible which is dictated by the continuing changes in our present-day reality, both individual and societal."[34] The hermeneutical circle moves from praxis in terms of ideological suspicion of prevailing ideology in society and church toward a phenomenological analysis of superstructure and theology. Next it undertakes exegetical suspicion of the prevailing interpretation of the Scripture by leading to constructing a new way of interpreting the Scripture (new hermeneutics). Finally, the new way of reading the Scripture illumines the historical situation and thereby creating a new pastoral practice with the church.[35]

Christian praxis, based on the gospel, uses social scientific theory and research to critically analyze institutions and their policies. Social analysis becomes a constitutive moment within theological-ethical method which facilitates our understanding of the political and economic world. The liberation project is summarized as "socialist in the organization of its economy, democratic in terms of the political participation of the people, and open in the sense of insuring the conditions for personal realization, cultural freedom and opportunity, and the mechanisms for self-correction."[36] His basic ethical criterion is the maximizing of universal human possibilities which means the realization of distinctively human goods and the minimizing of human costs which includes the

---

32. Schubeck, *Liberation Ethics*, 211.
33. Gutiérrez, *Theology of Liberation*, 24–25, 135–40.
34. Segundo, *Liberation of Theology*, 8–9.
35. Schubeck, *Liberation Ethics*, 67.
36. Bonino, *Toward a Christian Political Ethics*, 77.

loss of human goods, material conditions, and human rights. The first principle (maximizing universal human possibilities) establishes a priority of justice over order while the second principle examines the appropriateness of the means in regard to social change.[37] This principle of justice relates to revolutionary struggle and to everyday political actions in a conviction of preferential option for the poor.

Gutiérrez gives a missional contour of his theology of liberation in terms of the church's metanoia, denunciation, and annunciation. The mission of the church needs to be articulated in its historical and social coordinates and its present reality. This concrete historical and social reality and condition should be at the center of undertaking theological reflection on the mission of the church. The primary task of the mission in the Latin American context is to make the prophetic denunciation of every situation which is dehumanizing, oppressing, and alienating. It should challenge every sacralization of oppressive structures of the prevailing system to which church is tied. This prophetic denunciation entails public character because the church is in public society. A prophetic denunciation including church's self-renewal and *metanoia* is achieved by annunciation of the gospel. The love of God calls all of us in Christ and through the action of the Spirit for union among themselves and communion with God.

To announce the gospel is to announce the coming of the kingdom of God, because gospel message reveals what is rooted and hidden in social injustice and violence. Evangelization is a powerful factor in personalization which is stimulated by the annunciation of the gospel. The liberating word of God which announces the coming of the kingdom of God reveals a situation of injustice and oppression which is incompatible with this coming. From within a commitment to liberation, proclamation of the gospel entails a conscienticizing, or policitizing function in concrete, effective solidarity with people and exploited social classes.[38]

In contrast to the position that the church civilizes by evangelization, Gutiérrez argues that the church should politicize by evangelizing in the struggle against institutionalized violence. Underlying the mission of the church is a hermeneutical praxis of denunciation and annunciation which opens human history to the future promised by God and reveals God's present work.[39] In the liberation context ethics becomes ethics of

---

37. Schubeck, *Liberation Ethics*, 227–28.
38. Gutiérrez, *Theology of Liberation*, 152–53.
39. Ibid., 154–55.

discipleship in reproducing the Spirit of Jesus in proclaiming the kingdom of God, translating it into practice, engaging in corporate moral discernment and the promotion of justice for the poor.[40]

Given Liberation theology's commitment to the poor, Craig L. Nessan, a confessional-prophetic theologian in the U.S. appreciates a contribution of liberation theology concerning eschatology and social problem, in which liberation theology underscores the significance of eschatology as the core of liberation ethics of discipleship for the present. It has the concrete relevance and application in refined hermeneutical-ethical manner and contextualizes the message of the coming of the kingdom of God for the present struggle against poverty, social oppression, and institutionalized structure of violence. It is certain that liberation theology does not claim that the kingdom of God can be achieved by mere human endeavor struggling for justice and liberation.[41] Furthermore, Nessan argues that liberation theology is faithful to the living legacy of the Word of God as it brings its liberating aspect to contemporary situation of extreme poverty in Latin America and across globe. It challenges and awakens the churches of the North to a new commitment and active engagement in solidarity with the poor at home and abroad.[42] Nessan maintains that liberation theology persists with vigor into the twenty-first century and shows its vitality, which will be appreciated as an important moment in theological history by the generation to come.[43]

A theology of liberation, together with a black theology of liberation (James Cone), finds the way and the voices of the subaltern in theological skill of the word of God and its liberating eschatology. Vítor Westhelle gives a postcolonial contour for liberation theology. A postcolonial concept of hybridity is heard in such phrases as the option for the poor or evangelization by the poor in an unconscious act of dissimulation (Leonard Boff). Westhelle is convinced that the hybridity of a liberating theology takes seriously God's presence in a human going into depravity as to encompass the whole of creation by breaking through national and ethnic frontiers.[44]

40. Schubeck, *Liberation Ethics*, 77.
41. Nessan, *Vitality of Liberation Theology*, 4–5.
42. Ibid., 6.
43. Ibid., 150.
44. Westhelle, *After Heresy*, 157.

Segundo also conceptualizes Chalcedon's notion of *communicatio idiomatum* as hitting the very mark of the dimension of hybridity. This classic language of hybridity results from the move between a language ruled by strict logic of literal statements and another in symbolic and metaphorically elusive manner. This hybrid semantics is characterized by the mingling of the sublime with the lowly. In Segundo's view, Chalcedon's formulation of *vere Deus et vere homo* does not show a metaphysics of exchange of abstract attributes. As Segundo argues, "Jesus, in his *limited* human history, interpreted from a secular tradition in search of the meaning of human existence, reveals to us the Absolute, the ultimate reality, the transcendent datum par excellence."[45]

For Segundo, the gospel is not a closed book but a living text which is in need of being proclaimed alive and anew in the sense of *viva vox evangelii* in every course and all ways. This liberation configuration of word-event means, beyond ecclesial proclamation, an ethics of discipleship in faithfulness to Jesus when the gospel is identified with the particular contexts and life giveness, in which human life is socially, economically, politically religiously shaped and conditioned.[46]

Gospel narrative will have the hybrid form for communication and translation as it continues to be told and retold in indigenous language in Latin America, Africa, and Asia. Liberation theology as a subaltern theology in postcolonial context undertakes the universal act of rendering the gospel as *viva vox Dei* in its manifold particularities in all times and places. Irregularity of God's speech-event enables a postcolonial strategy of hybridity in the act of fusion of horizons by emphatic listening to life stories of those subalternized. According to Westhelle, the task of liberation theology calls for heeding the voices of the voiceless, bringing the invisible to sight, and lifting the downtrodden. This is the hybrid task of a subaltern and liberation theology in postcolonial context of World Christianity. Walter Benjamin, a Jewish thinker, and St. Paul remain important mentors in this direction: "Only for the sake of the hopeless ones have we have been given hope."[47] "Hoping against hope, he believed that he would become the father of many nations." (Rom 4:18).

---

45. Cited in ibid., 160.
46. Ibid., 161–63.
47. Benjamin, *Illuminations*, 17, cited in Westhelle, *After Heresy*, 163.

Epilogue

THIS EPILOGUE IS A further reflection on what has been discussed in public theology and discipleship of God's mission in the postcolonial context of World Christianity. Globalization, world religions, and theological education are interwoven in a way that dialogue across religious boundaries and increased engagement with world religions become critical and instrumental. Advancing mutual understanding and appreciating relationships across faith traditions has become an arbiter in pedagogical issues in American institutions.[1] The United States has become the most religiously diverse nation on earth, running in a direction of "the marbling of civilization and peoples."[2]

Coupled with the reality of multiculturalism, postcolonial challenge and the voice of World Christianity are raised against Western Christianity as a tool of colonialism or global hegemony, along with economic globalization. As we hear in the words of one black South African, "When the white man came to our country, he had the Bible and we had the land. The white man said to us 'let us pray.' After the prayer, the white man had the land and we had the Bible."[3] The cultural assumptions of Western missionaries and empire-builders become questionable and suspicious in the rise of the new post-western Christianity. Western cultural imperialism begins to dissipate, as the vernacular principle is applied in translation of the biblical narrative.[4]

1. This aspect challenges to make a discourse of God's mission and Trinitarian theology more relevant to postcolonial World Christianity.

---

1. Roozen and Hadsell, eds., *Changing The Way Seminaries Teach*, 3–5.
2. Eck, *New Religious America*, 4.
3. Mofokeng, "Black Christians, the Bible and Liberation."
4. Jenkins, *Next Christendom*, 113.

According to the Prologue of John, the inner being of God (*perichoresis*) implies togetherness between God and the Word in the presence of the Holy Spirit. This biblical aspect is differentiated from Greek ontological understanding of *perichoresis* which paves the way to Trinitarian onto-theo-logy. The inner being of the triune God is called *perichoresis*, a term coined by John of Damascus in the eighth century.

Since Damascus the inner being of God has been conceptualized in an ontological manner. An ontological concept of *perichroresis* continues to be communally conceptualized and mutually conditioned in the model of social doctrine of the Trinity. The economic Trinity also has a retroactive effect on the immanent Trinity, and creation is conceptualized as God's self-limitation, the withdrawal of God's self.[5] The cross of Christ is the content of the doctrine of the Trinity.[6]

It is certain that Jesus, the crucified, allows us to believe in God as omnipotent in impotence. However, God of Israel as Lord of the church and the world must not be venerated in God's own small corner. A Trinitarian reflection needs to be sought in God as God-in-dialogue in the life of *perichoresis* underlying God's act of speech. The person and word of the God who speaks signify that we are such creatures as God's dialogue partners.[7] This aspect characterizes the sociality of God in an original and relational sense, emphasizing the vitality and liveliness of the triune God in terms of *verbum relationis* (word of relation).

The Trinitarian life in *perichoresis* and the classic notion of relations of origin contain a historical implication for a biblically related concept of *toledot* in the life of Israel (production, creation, and history). The triune God creates the world through the Word. This implies the coming communion with Israel in the spiritual power of Torah.[8] God-in-dialogue shapes an important aspect of God's mission in developing God's word in Israel in connection with *Logos*.

Within the linguistically constituted experience of the Trinitarian salvific drama, the subject matter of the Trinity comes into language, whose character is that of an event opening up a completely new dimension of life and future. Language has its true being only in dialogue, in

---

5. Moltmann, *Trinity and the Kingdom*, 59.
6. Moltmann, *Crucified God*, 246.
7. Gollwitzer, *Existence of God*, 190.
8. Marquardt, *Was dürfen wir hoffen, wenn wir hoffen dürften?*, 3:222.

coming to understanding.[9] The unity of God the Father and God the Son in the presence of the Holy Spirit is reflected in the phenomenon of dialogue and promise, while the mystery of the Trinity remains ultimately incomprehensible in terms of human thought and word. Nonetheless, the mystery of the Trinity revealed in the gospel presents itself as self-revealing in human language enclosed within the world horizon of communication. This aspect breaks though a notion of language as a mere tool or a copy, which is constructed and judged by the original. The Greek notion of *perichoresis* as the original tends to conceive of the God's word in ontological and hierarchical manner in which human language remains a mere tool or a copy.

However, God's being for us is undertaken by envisaging God's unfathomable being in self as the *terminus a quo* (the resource). From this side out, God is presented in God's Word. God's being for us is defined as the miracle of grace which is revealed in the gospel and grounded in the freedom of God.[10] *Theologia crucis* in the gospel of Jesus Christ, namely the heart of God-in-dialogue, is in deep relation with the freedom and irregularity of God in universal and reconciling reign of the world. God's existence confessed by faith is a call of promise awakening joy and fear, summoning us to fulfillment of life for proclamation and communication. In the year of jubilee (Luke 4:19) God comes to light. We exist, blessed by grace, as God exists eternally blessed in God's self.[11] God's Word comes to us as God's act of speech (*Dei loquentis persona*: God speaking in person) in historical and missional context. The historical-relational manifestation of the triune God as the Subject of speech takes place in creation, incarnation, and Pentecost (Spirit of communication of God's act of speech).

2. Driven by a Trinitarian hermeneutic of God-in-dialogue, I seek to reframe a theology of God's universal reign in terms of three life arrangements (*ecclesia, politia,* and *economia*). Craig Nessan makes an important and creative study of Luther's two kingdoms in terms of God's two strategies for Christian political responsibility. In this interpretation, one kingdom of God is undertaken through two distinct, yet complementary strategies:[12] a right-hand strategy (the kingdom of gospel) and a left-hand

---

9. Gadamer, *Truth and Method*, 446.
10. Gollwitzer, *Existence of God*, 221.
11. Ibid., 245.
12. Nessan, "Christian Political Responsibility," 52.

strategy (involving the establishment of just order in society through the state, economy, law, education, family, and church).

Given this, it is important to refine a metaphor for God as the householder of political economy in relation to social justice, solidarity, and emancipation. God's own economy in Trinitarian life is the ground of the human political economy for the integrity of life in sustaining and enhancing people and earth. In the horizon of God's economy which applies to the life of the church, the term *oikos* refers to a way of correlating God and economy, while it denotes access to livelihood in relation to family, institution, state, market, nature, and finally God. The God-*oikos* relationship, which makes it possible to underscore God-economy correlation, sharpens God's mission through God's economic and salvific activity, in the Trinitarian sense, on behalf of the just structure of the world economy as an alternative to global capitalism. This aspect is grounded in a life-giving economy which is central in the socio-economic and political-ideological context of the biblical tradition imbued with Israel's experience of the God Yahweh.[13]

Seen in light of the Torah and the Gospel, a biblical notion of *diakonia* involves the way the household, livelihood, and social economic structure are organized concerning the lending of money and taking interest (Lev 25:35–38), on which Torah put strict regulations on the use and abuse of surety for loans (Exod 22:26–27). Jesus as the circumcised deacon overcomes human mastery by becoming a slave. He emptied himself, taking the form of a household slave (Phil 2:6–7). God's economy has become obvious in Jesus's existence as deacon and household slave, which provides a conceptual basis for articulating God's economy in terms of integrating social economic reality into theological reflection. Public missional theology is inspired by choosing life (Deut 30:19), following in the footsteps of Jesus as the image of the invisible God, the firstborn of all creation (Col 1:15). John's statement, that "I came that they might have life, and have it in all its fullness" (John 10:10), includes not merely the theme of choosing life, but of the Torah and the prophets.[14]

Faith is active in love seeking God's righteousness, solidarity, and shalom in the world. The promise, hope, and anticipation of the coming of God are presented to us as God's gift which is deeply connected with

---

13. Meeks, *God the Economist*, 33. Duchrow, *Alternatives to Global Capitalism*, 145.
14. Gorringe, *Capital and the Kingdom*, 12.

faith active in love—thereby through the kingdom of grace. The kingdom of gospel is in deep conversation with the kingdom of nature expecting of the coming of kingdom of God (*regnum gloriae*), which, as a principle of critique and transformation of the world, will come finally *extra nos*. The reign of Christ (in the kingdom of grace) will be fulfilled by God's kingdom of glory (1 Cor 15:28).

God appears to be place-provider, which sharpens a meaning of the triune God in dialogue for historical engagement, solidarity, and enhancement of the integrity of life. The lifeworld of natural law should be kept intact and protected from a reality of lordless powers, that is, powers and principalities entangled within the colonization of the lifeworld.

A twofold sense of eschatology is important in the presentative one (in the kingdom of grace) and eschatological coming one (in the kingdom of glory). The presentative eschatology in the grace of justification, reconciliation, and justice mobilizes the church's ethics of discipleship and solidarity to set about criticizing and renewing the present status quo, moving forward the universal future of the kingdom of glory. It leads to critical distance from a reifying politics of system which vitiates and penetrates life arrangements in the public sphere, controlling and misusing them for the sake of the powerful. The system of the reifying politics is under deconstructive critique in light of God's irruption as God's mission in those life arrangements. God the infinite horizon of speech-event cannot be properly understood apart from a critical-constructive reflection of God the place-provider which underlies a theology of social *topos* set within a socio-critical and hermeneutical reframing of kingdom of God.

Non-Christian people who live out their stations in life arrangements have a responsibility to enhance the integrity of life, shaping institutions that are just and equitable. There are dialogue and solidarity between Christians and non-Christians, underpinning the common endeavor for the common good in expectation for God's reign in just, equitable, and reconciled society. An emancipatory ethics of solidarity and resistance occupies a special place in the Trinitarian-eschatological framework, promoting discourse ethics of *parhessia* for the sake of lifeworld (reconciled) against the unredeemed reality of the world under the spell of commodity fetishism, social reification, and hyperreality.

3. This perspective offers an insight for me to undertake God as the infinite horizon of speech-event in relation to God the *topos* of the

world.¹⁵ A notion of *Deum justificare* in Psalm 51 connects the active and emancipatory of word-event with a theological reflection of God the Provider of life arrangements in the world. From Ps 90:1 ("Lord, Thou hast been our dwelling-place"), it follows that God is the dwelling place of the world. The broad place (Job 36:16) implies the living-space is the safe stronghold enclosed by God. God becomes utopian ("no-place"), which implies that God does not find any place in the world. "There was no place for them in the inn" (Luke 2:7). Jesus Christ goes to prepare a place for the disciples: "In my Father's house there are many dwelling places." (John 14:2–3).

In the body of Christ, a penultimate-eschatological embodiment of God's *topos,* the least, the fragile, and the voiceless are ascribed and granted a special place in God's concern and care. God as the *topos* of the world expedites the faith community to become Shalom Church in the quest for distributive justice, reconciliation, and mutual recognition (Acts 4:32–35). In the context of Revelation, John describes a vision of the New Jerusalem (Rev 21:24), a city in which culture and cultural diversity will not be wiped away, but redeemed. Cultural diversity in God's place is not a problem to be transcended, but a blessing. God as the *topos* of world refers to a new heaven and earth, coming from God's eschatological glory *extra nos.*

Diakonia-discipleship should be articulated in accordance with God's *topos* in God's political economy central to ethics of solidarity. It seeks more people-based forms of *diakonia* in a prophetic and emancipatory framework, calling for a paradigm shift from patronizing interventions toward the eschatological hope of a new heaven and earth. This perspective helps organize social, ecological, and democratic structure and guide economic process at the national level which is of crucial importance to global conditions for the future of life.¹⁶

4. The biblical ground term of the living Word of God is identical with the word of deed, that is, identification between word and event in the Hebrew manner. God's word is *dabar* in self-speaking and action, interacting with people's lives and genealogy in the past, present, and

---

15. I am indebted to the conception of God the *topos* of the world from F. W. Marquardt, while developing it in my own distinctive manner concerning the ethical and practical relationship between speech-event and social topography in socially engaged context. See Marquardt, *Eia, wärn wir da,* 24–37.

16. Duchrow, *Alternatives to Global capitalism,* 306.

future. God's speaking is identical with God's action of economy in self-manifestation through Torah, prophecy, and the life of Israel as attested in the Hebrew Bible. In this history of Israel God is living and emancipatory.[17] The living and active Word of God which also gives us ground for hope is the word which speaks and promises: Jesus Christ is *Dabar-Logos* of our hope.[18] The gospel according to form and content is about the eschatological message of the Christian proclamation. We regard the eschatological presence as a linguistic-creational-emancipatory form coming out of the power of the Easter event. Eschatological presence is the linguistic-emancipatory basis for a new hermeneutics to read the gospel as transformative narrative about Jesus, the future person.[19] Jesus in the gospel is connected with apocalyptic, futuristic, and eschatological views of Jesus as the new creator.

Furthermore, *theologia crucis* in eschatological form is presented in Jesus the slain Lamb in an apocalyptic framework, which is related to the suffering of all victims in world history. Jesus the slain Lamb becomes the representative of all victims.[20] The biblical witness to presentative eschatology retains its reality from the messianic-apocalyptic eschatology. The futuristic eschatology must be also comprehended in reference to presentative eschatology in the kingdom of grace which motivates the church to take part in God's shalom and emancipatory mission of life-enhancing. The two senses of biblical eschatology are not played off against each other.[21]

The gospel is the hope which is the source of all promises and ground for all religions and wisdom. The faith can be interpreted as hope. The entire gospel as the living Word of God entails promise. The self-promise of God in Jesus Christ is full of promise and blessing for all. In this light, a concept of the promise has a definite category of revelation.[22] Within this perspective, gospel proclaimed in a living voice (*viva vox evangelii*) is full of hope and promise characterizing the biblical and eschatological notion of revelation. This perspective entails the eschatological character of

---

17. Marquardt, *Das christliche Bekenntnis*, 1:170.
18. Marquardt, *Was dürfen wir hoffen, wenn wir hoffen dürften?*, 1:53.
19. Ibid., 1:365.
20. Ibid., 1:387.
21. Marquardt, *Was dürfen wir hoffen, wenn wir hoffen dürften?*, 3:424.
22. Ibid., 1:155.

the word of God, *promissio Dei,* entailing God's present involvement and irruption in the public sphere through the power of the Holy Spirit. The creation waits with eager longing for the eschatological revealing of God's children, thus in this hope and promise the creation itself will obtain the freedom of the glory of the children of God (Rom 8:20–21).

Promissio Dei in the life of Israel comes to us as *missio Dei* in the gospel of Jesus Christ in the presence of the Holy Spirit, which implies God the Subject of speech continuing to work, emancipate, and address in the sense of *creatio continua* in expectation of God's final coming. The eschatological form of God's kingdom (glory) remains a hope for the church. "Behold I make all things new." All new things can and must happen in our earthly relationships, thus the church's mission is in the service of agape.[23]

5. A theological theory of language within a comprehensive hermeneutical framework underpins the cause of Christian faith in public forum in the whole experience of the world. In a dialogue between Christian faith and the whole experience of the world, what is specific to Christian faith, is made distinctive and more obvious.[24] The specific task of a theological theory of language concerns explanation and clarification of the language of faith in constant reference to the figure of Jesus. The Scripture imbued with the incomparable power of the gospel is deeply grounded in the language of the world, not something distilled out of or separated from the ordinary language of the world.[25]

A notion of the language of faith takes a critical stance against secularism and religionism. Religionism means the formal establishment of a religious attitude as though it were self-sufficient in isolation from the experience of the world. In the attitude of religionism the language of religion becomes a provincial dialect.[26] A theological theory of languages makes the constant reference of the language of faith to Jesus of Nazareth for the sake of the dialogue of faith in relation to the experience of the world. A theology of the language of faith warns against taking the gospel as a timeless entity estranged from the experience of the world, in which the gospel turns into a pseudo-law. All the while, it eschews an attempt

---

23. Gollwitzer, *Rich Christians and Poor Lazarus*, 14.
24. Ebeling, *Introduction to Language*, 183.
25. Ibid., 189.
26. Ibid., 194.

to apply the divine law literally to the present experience of the world, in which the law turns into a pseudo-gospel.[27]

A theological theory of language breaks through the descriptive representation or the misunderstanding of revelation as information about an outside reality, because God is not comprehended as an object of scientific investigation and human discovery. Nevertheless, a theological theory of language tends to reduce God to a linguistic event and ignore a word of discipleship, emancipation, and solidarity in connection with sociohistorical life connection, which also refracts and conditions theological language in an ideologically distorted manner. This emphasizes a theology of *viva vox evangelii* in active and emancipatory horizon which takes place between human beings and the world. This living dynamism of the Word of God which is central in a theological-emancipatory hermeneutic transcends the limitation of word-event theology which tends to under-develop a horizon of God's act of speech through the world. An emancipatory theology of the active and living Word of God emphasizes the primacy of the spoken gospel against the primacy of the written revelation (narrative understanding of the written revelation as the real form of revelation).[28] The emancipatory Word of God is connected with the God of promise in Israel, the gospel of Jesus Christ concerning the kingdom of God in which the word of God retains socio-political connection to the public realm.

6. A strong critique of theology of word-event comes from a theology of hope in the eschatological framework. Moltmann argues against a theology of word-event because it is existential, unhistorical, and un-eschatological.[29] For Moltmann, the proclamation and pronouncement summon us to a path toward an eschatological promise, thus the word has an inner transcendence regarding its future.[30] The revelation of God in the eschatological event of Christ's promise reveals, affects, and provokes that open history is grasped in the mission of hope.[31] Thus, Moltmann upholds Hoekendijk's mission-in-hope for God's eschatological Shalom. The purpose of mission is the realization of the eschatological hope of

27. Ibid., 204.
28. Gollwitzer, *Existence of God*, 230–31.
29. Moltmann, *Theology of Hope*, 281.
30. Ibid., 326.
31. Ibid.

justice, the humanizing of people, the socializing of humanity, peace for all creation, which can be anticipated in the faith community.[32]

Critics of the word-event theology also argue that the preached word of law and gospel intellectualizes the distinction between law and gospel as the event of justification, leaving little space for the Spirit. The Spirit is merely understood as a hermeneutical status in bridging the individual's reception of the shift from law to gospel.[33]

Unlike critics of word-event theology, Pannenberg employs and appreciates a theology of word-event. All talk about the word of God is related to human linguisticality. First, God is not known except through the world in which God reveals God's self by word-events—that is to say, the God who speaks is not received as any special, supernatural Word alongside human speech. Speaking about God means speaking about the all-determining reality as conceived of as present and active in every event. Every human word owes its existence in the final analysis to an unthematic, hidden presence of God in the depth dimension of linguistic consciousness. However, human speech that really does carry the divine word is vulnerable to distortions. Given this possibility of the distortion of language, Pannenberg argues that there is still an element of positivity in the theology of word-event because of his focus on a revelatory authority.[34]

Pannenberg's position is induced by Gadamer's and Dilthey's hermeneutics. Gadamer's expression "the fusion of horizons" describes the meeting between the horizon of the past text and the present horizon of the interpreter. Such a horizon presupposes the totality of history as its ultimate frame of reference.[35] Gadamer speaks of the texts in terms of words alone (the linguisticality of reality) in which tradition is linguistically mediated. Against this direction, Pannenberg argues that the fusing of the horizon of the past and the present is not an accomplishment of language alone. Rather, it is historically mediated. For his concept of universal history as the totality of history, Pannenberg incorporates into the framework of universal history Dilthey's concept of experienced meaning in the historical life context. The meaning is accessible only in the anticipation of a future which has not yet appeared. In broadening

---

32. Ibid., 329.
33. For the critique of theology of word-event, see Helmer, "Trinity and Luther," 266.
34. Pannenberg, *Theology and Philosophy of Science*, 281–82.
35. Ibid., 284.

hermeneutics into a universal-historical perspective, Pannenberg argues that the historian can know the future goal and end of history because it has proleptically occurred in the resurrection of Jesus of Nazareth. This universal significance of the gospel also serves as the basis of Christian ethics in connection with God's mission.

A proleptic eschatology modifies and complements the linguistic existence of human life in terms of universal history via Dilthey's philosophy of history. History as effect in Gadamerian sense is reformulated in light of the proleptic history of God in Jesus Christ for the sake of horizons between the general history and the proleptic history. However, Dilthey's critique of historical reason runs counter to Hegelian notion of absolute knowledge in the sense of universal history. Dilthey always starts from the reality of life in a given network of manifestations of life, which has nothing to do with a proleptic understanding of the present reality. Furthermore, a history of effect in Dilthey's sense, despite its limitation, anticipates Gadamer's notion of history of effect. For Dilthey, a human being is a historical being, and he or she becomes creative historically and linguistically, having freedom to realize themselves as newly and creatively in the future. Because Dilthey locates a human being in and through history, we are not in a position to judge which world view has superiority over another.[36]

7. Our debate of word-event and eschatological theology facilitates an understanding of translation in the act of interpretation which is eschatologically driven and undertaken in open-ended manner. Mission in the postcolonial context is always inculturation and emancipation, expressing translation of the message in the sense of indigenization as a commentary on interpolation. In translation work, languages at the periphery are allowed to express their insights into the gospel in their own way. Traditional and popular religious symbols in the act of translation concern themselves against colonial annexation and subjugation and indigenous belief systems resurge and persist with strength and cultural conviction.

Western Christianity in an age of discovery is accused of assimilating the pattern of displacement, in which displaced slave bodies, not just slave bodies, come to represent a natural state. The displaced slave bodies are conceptualized to represent slave bodies as natural ones. A linguistic

---

36. For my study of Dilthey, see Chung, *Hermeneutical Self and an Ethical Difference*, 43–44.

deployment alters reality in the designation of convert and heretic, believer and unbeliever. The European is the key to the theological act of displacement, pursuing a soteriological motive for mission and colonialism. Body differences are articulated through white and black, extending to all peoples. This colonial Christianity indicated a profound theological distortion, operating displacement in the expansion of European Christendom.[37]

The multicultural nature of the gospel is emphasized with its power of translatability. The Christian religion began to resound, full of the idioms and styles of new converts, becoming multilingual and multicultural.[38] World Christianity is thus defined and "interpreted by a plurality of models of inculturation in line with the variety of local idioms and practices."[39]

Mission as translation appreciates the recipient culture as the true and final focus of proclamation, articulating that an inevitable stage is involved in the process of reception and adaptation. This project of translation implies a theological relativism, yielding one language system to alteration or eradication which necessitates a form of alienation or estrangement from the original. A peripheral role is more importantly assigned in view of the original mode, because the latter is deemed as inadequate, or defective, or inappropriate. Translation challenges an affirmation of the primacy of the biblical message and narrative over the cultural underpinnings of the recipient.[40]

However, a shortcoming in the project of mission as translation can be seen in the modernist assumption of translating all of biblical narratives and languages into indigenous language. In early Christianity we perceive that translatability entails commensurability concerning the contextual equivalences sought for establishing points of encounter with the wisdom of non-Christian societies (for instance, Greek notion of Logos concerning Jesus Christ).[41] Nevertheless, there are also zones of untranslatability between different traditions and languages. In translating a kerygmatic thought in the Bible to a Totemic system of thought or multireligiously

---

37. Jennings, *Christian Imagination*, 22, 31, 37.
38. Sanneh, *Disciples of All Nations*, 27.
39. Sanneh, *Whose Religion is Christianity?*, 35.
40. Jennings, *Christian Imagination*, 156.
41. Berling, *Syncretic Religion of Lin Chao-en*, 11.

fused reality in Asia, the untranslatability of central expressions and idioms still remains because of the incommensurability of language.[42]

Culture is a context within which cultural linguistic systems of construable signs and symbols are interworked. These linguistic, symbolic systems within the culture should be interpreted in a meaningful and understandable manner. If culture is taken to be those webs, the analysis of it is therefore an interpretative one in search of meaning.[43]

In the anthropological study of culture and language, social discourse entails an analogical-metaphorical horizon which is not reduced to narrative or textuality. In the structural anthropology of Lévi Strauss, savage thought extends its grasp in terms of *imagines mundi*, working like a kaleidoscope. When one says that the members of one's clan descend from bears or one's neighbor from eagles, this utterance implies the relationship between one's clan and one's neighbors in a concrete metaphorical way.[44]

When this metaphorical aspect of commensurability-in-difference is ignored, a syncretic model of transposition or translation accommodates borrowed elements to the world view of the home tradition. The ethnocentric self-centeredness, dominion of the dialogue partner, self-conscious pattern of selectivity and unqualified form of translation are guided by assimilation, accommodation, and one-sided conversion.

In order to avoid a syncretic notion of translation as accommodation, it is important to consider a notion of fusion of horizons in an eschatologically driven and open-ended manner in an encounter between biblical witness to God and indigenous lifeworld. The context-constitutive and constituted horizons of the linguistically structured lifeworld shape and guide the process of translation in the act of interpretation in terms of dialectical interplay between equivalent and non-equivalent elements in metaphorical-analogical manner. Translation as hermeneutical conversation between the living Word of God and one's cultural reality is in ongoing journey and companionship with the Other. In translation metaphorically-analogically undertaken, we listen to life expressions of the gospel recipient, their social discourse, and cultural ethos in terms of similarity-in-difference underlying a hermeneutical step: appropriation, critique, self-exposure, and creative construction of a new horizon of

42. MacIntyre, *Whose Justice?*, 375. Chung, *Reclaiming Mission as Constructive Theology*, 94–95.

43. Geertz, *Interpretation of Culture*, 5.

44. Ibid., 353. Chung, *Reclaiming Mission as Constructive Theology*, 97.

meaning. This aspect keeps translation from a crude notion of translation as syncretic phenomenon.

8. A postcolonial reframing of public theology and discipleship of God's mission emphasizes a radical dimension of God's act of speech embracing the church and the world, attending issues of power, neo-colonial hegemonic legacy in previously colonized countries, and sociohistorical reality. Historical-linguistic tradition influences and affects human social existence and understanding, but ever-changing circumstances of life, culture and historicized society makes the effect of history incomplete, limited, and also open-ended. History as effect is not dictating its power from top down. Rather it is socialized in the public location imbued within organizations, processes, and institutions, thereby in social life connections.[45]

Given this, a postcolonial public theology seeks to develop an analogical-discursive formation, archeologically envisioning a reconstruction of the lifeworld of the subaltern against the universal history and civilization. It pursues a sought-after thick description in ethically engaging with people of other cultures and religions in light of the living voice of God who speaks to us through the zones of untranslatability, that is, the face of those downtrodden and buried on the underside of history. This public ethical aspect driven in solidarity with the other audaciously risks for a transformation of the self into the graced self in becoming blessing to the other in light of God's Saying. The epiphany of the face is ethical, so the bond between expression and responsibility remains the essence of language.[46]

A postcolonial public theology does not romanticize the center of gravity in shift from the countries of the northern and western hemispheres toward the southern and eastern ones called the Global South. Talking about a shift of power or gravity tends to exaggerate the reality of World Christianity only through membership numbers. Rather, a postcolonial public theology engages in mutual interaction, encouragement, and edification between the churches of global North and global South,[47] sharing and witnessing to the living Word of God. Their churches recognize, appreciate, and participate in God's mission in the multicultural life horizon by promoting the dynamism of God's speech-event continually involved in the interaction of the fusion of horizons between biblical narrative and

---

45. Chung, *Public Theology in World Christianity*, 145–46.
46. Levinas, *Totality and Infinity*, 200.
47. Wuthnow, *Boundless Faith*, 61.

cultural expression of it in eschatological expectation of the coming of God. It retains a task of thick description of the biblical narrative.

Faith community as shalom church finds its validity as a community of hermeneutical conversation in publicizing and contextualizing faith in conformity to Jesus' life of sociobiography with those on the margin in the sense of *parrhesia,* denouncing the structure of injustice and violence, while announcing the Good News for everybody. It also expresses a protest against the process of colonization of lifeworld under the spell of global economy, political mechanism, ideology of mass media, and hyperreality of simulation. This colonization process has become obvious in producing the regime of sign-value. Commodity becomes a sign-value replete with meaning, forming our everyday life. Social reproduction beyond mere production appears to be the organizing and simulating principle of society. Because of the proliferation of media and its ability to simulate reality with film, television, photographs and the like, we live in a simulated reality. When simulation creates reality itself through images, Baudrillard calls this hyperreality.

The reality of commodification also reifies our language and discourse affixed to the achievement brought by the system of social production and reproduction in the field of informative technologies, internet, TV, and mass media. A hyperreality creates a media-saturated consciousness incarcerated and beguiled by codes, models, and signs which are central for the society of simulation.[48] A hyperreality built on a metadiscourse is mobilized by the dynamic interplay between religious knowledge and institutionalized power saturating the human body. The human body is a place beguiled by greed, dominion, and power related to a hyperreality that the regime of sign value generates. A notion of biopower may retain a particular truth in a critical view of association, institution, and the society ruled by a mechanism of violence and injustice. It claims a place of the Other to become pivotal in the context of public ethics and interreligious dialogue for the sake of praxis of *parrhesia* in solidarity with the subaltern.

---

48. *Baudrillard: A Critical Reader,* ed. Kellner, 8.

Bibliography

Abe, Masao. *Divine Emptiness and Historical Fullness: A Buddhist Jewish Christian Conversation with Masao Abe.* Edited by Christopher Ives. Valley Forge, PA: Trinity, 1995.
Adams William Y. *The Philosophical Roots of Anthropology.* Stanford, CA: CSLI, 1998.
Ahn Byung-Mu, *Draussen vor dem Tor: Kirche und Minjung in Korea.* Edited by Winfried Glüer. Göttingen: Vandenhoeck & Ruprecht, 1986.
Althaus, Paul. *The Theology of Martin Luther.* Translated by Robert C. Schultz. Philadelphia: Fortress, 1966.
———. *The Ethics of Martin Luther.* Translated by Robert C. Schultz. Philadelphia: Fortress, 1972.
———. *Die christliche Wahrheit.* 7th ed. Gütersloh: Gütersloher, 1966.
Amin, Samir. *Capitalism in the Age of Globalization: The Management of Contemporary Society.* London: Zed, 1998.
Andersen, W. F. W. Kantzenbach, and G. F. Vicedom. *Lutherische Stimmen zur Frage der Atomwaffen.* Theologische Existenz Heute 67. Munich: Kaiser, 1958.
Anderson, Gerald H, editor. *Biographical Dictionary of Christian Missions.* Grand Rapids: Eerdmans, 1998.
Aquinas, Thomas. *Summa Theologica.* New York: Benzinger, 1947.
Asvaghosa, *The Awakening of Faith: The Classic Exposition of Mahayana Buddhism.* Translated by Teitaro Suzuki. Mineola: Dover, 2003.
Audi, Robert. *Religion in the Public Square: The Place of Religious Convictions in Political Debate.* Lanham, MD: Rowman & Littlefield, 1997.
Auerbach, Erich. *Mimesis: The Representation of Reality in Western Literature.* Princeton: Princeton University Press, 2003.
Barber, Michael D. *Ethical Hermeneutics: Rationalism in Enrique Düssel's Philosophy of Liberation.* New York: Fordham University Press, 1998.
Barth, Karl. *Ad Limina Apostolorum.* Translated by Keith R. Crim. Edinburgh: St. Andrew's, 1969.
———. *Against The Stream: Shorter Post-War Writings 1946–52.* Translated by E. M. Delacour. Edited by Ronald Gregor Smith. London: SCM, 1954.
———. *Anselm: Fides quaerens intellectum.* Translated by Ian W. Robertson. London: SCM, 1960.
———. *Briefe 1961–1968.* Edited by J. Fangmeier and H. Stoevesandt. Karl Barth Gesamtausgabe 6. Zurich: TVZ, 1975.

———. *Christ and Adam: Man and Humanity in Romans 5.* Translated by T. A. Smail. Edinburgh: Oliver & Boyd, 1956.

———. "The Christian Community and the Civil Community." In *Karl Barth: Theologian of Freedom*, edited by Clifford J. Green, 265–95. Minneapolis: Fortress, 1991.

———. *The Christian Life: Church Dogmatics, vol. IV, pt. 4. Lecture Fragments.* Translated by Geoffrey W. Bromiley. Grand Rapids: Eerdmans, 1981.

———. "Church and Culture." Translated by Louise Pettibone Smith. In *Theology and Church: Shorter Writings, 1920-1928*, 334–54. Preacher's Library. London: SCM, 1962.

———. *Church Dogmatics. 1/1: The Doctrine of the Word of God.* 2nd ed. Translated by G. W. Bromiley. Edited by G. W. Bromiley and T. F. Torrance. London: T. & T. Clark, 1975.

———. *Church Dogmatics. 2/1: The Doctrine of God.* Translated by T. H. L. Parker et al. Edited by G. W. Bromiley and T. F. Torrance. London: T. & T. Clark, 1957.

———. *Church Dogmatics. 3/3: The Doctrine of Creation.* Translated by G. W. Bromiley and R. J. Ehrlich. Edited by G. W. Bromiley and T. F. Torrance. London: T. & T. Clark, 1960.

———. *Church Dogmatics. 3/4: The Doctrine of Creation.* Translated by A. T. MacKay et al. Edited by G. W. Bromiley and T. F. Torrance. London: T. & T. Clark, 1961.

———. *Church Dogmatics. 4/1: The Doctrine of Reconciliation.* Translated by G. W. Bromiley. Edited by G. W. Bromiley and T. F. Torrance. London: T. & T. Clark, 1956.

———. *Church Dogmatics. 4/2: The Doctrine of Reconciliation.* Translated by G. W. Bromiley. Edited by G. W. Bromiley and T. F. Torrance. London: T. & T. Clark, 1958.

———. *Church Dogmatics. 4/3.1: The Doctrine of Reconciliation.* Translated by G. W. Bromiley. Edited by G. W. Bromiley and T. F. Torrance. London: T. & T. Clark, 1961.

———. *Church Dogmatics. 4/3.2: The Doctrine of Reconciliation.* Translated by G. W. Bromiley. Edited by G. W. Bromiley and T. F. Torrance. London: T. & T. Clark, 1961.

———. *Die Christliche Dogmatik im Entwurf.* Vol. 1. Ed. Gerhard Sauter. Zurich: TVZ, 1982.

———. *Die Kirchliche Dogmatik. 2/1: Die Lehre von Gott.* Zurich: TVZ, 1940.

———. "Die Theologie und die Mission in der Gegenwart." *Zwischen den Zeiten* 10/3 (1932) 189–215. Reprinted in Karl Barth, *Theologische Fragen und Antworten*, 100–126. Zollikon: Evangelischer, 1957.

———. *Dogmatics in Outline.* Translated and edited by Colin E. Gunton. London: SCM, 2001.

———. *Eine Schweizer Stimme, 1938–1945.* Zurich: TVZ, 1985.

———. *The Epistle to the Romans.* 6th ed. Translated by Edwyn Hoskyns. London: Oxford University Press, 1968.

———. *Fragments Grave and Gay.* Edited by Martin Rumscheidt. Translated by Eric Mosbacher. London, Collins, 1971.

———. *Gespräche 1964–1968.* Edited by E. Busch. Karl Barth Gesamtausgabe 28. Zurich: TVZ, 1997.

———. "Letter to F.-W. Marquardt, September 5, 1967." In *Letters: 1961-1968*, translated and edited by Geoffrey W. Bromiley, 262–63. Edinburgh: T. & T. Clark, 1981.

———. *Modern Theology 1: Karl Barth. Selections from Twentieth Century Theologians.* Edited by E. J. Tinsley. London: Epworth, 1973.

———. "No Boring Theology! A Letter from Karl Barth." *The South East Asian Journal of Theology* (1969) 4–5.

———. *The Theology of Schleiermacher. Lectures at Goettingen 1923-24*. Edinburgh: T. & T. Clark, 1982.

———. *The Word of God and the Word of Man*. Translated by Douglas Horton. New York: Harper, 1957.

Baudrillard, Jean. *Baudrillard: A Critical Reader*. Edited by Douglas Kellner. Oxford: Blackwell,1994.

Bayer, Oswald. *Martin Luther's Theology: A Contemporary Interpretation*. Translated by Thomas H. Trapp. Grand Rapids: Eerdmans, 2008.

Bellah, Robert, et al. *The Good Society*. New York: Knopf, 1991.

Benjamin, Walter. *Illuminations*. London: Pimlico, 1999.

Berger, Peter L. *The Sacred Canopy: Elements of a Sociological Theory of Religion*. New York: Doubleday, 1967.

Berger, Peter L., and Thomas Luckmann. *The Social Construction of Reality*: A Treatise in the Sociology of Knowledge. New York: Doubleday, 1966.

Berling, Judith A. *The Syncretic Religion of Lin Chao-en*. New York: Columbia University Press, 1980.

Berkman, John, and Michael Cartwright, editors. *The Hauerwas Reader*. Durham, NC: Duke University Press, 2001.

Bethge, Eberhard. *Dietrich Bonhoeffer, Theologe, Christ, Zeitgenosse*. Munich: Kaiser, 1967.

———. "Dietrich Bonhoeffer und die Juden." In *Die Juden und Martin Luther–Martin Luther und die Juden: Geschichte, Wirkungsgeschichte, Herausforderung*, edited by Heinz Kremers et al., 211-48. Neukirchen: Neukirchener, 1985.

Bevans, Stephen B., and Roger P. Schroeder. *Constants in Context: A Theology of Mission for Today*. Maryknoll, NY: Orbis, 2004.

Bhabha, Homi K. *The Location of Culture*. London: Routledge, 1994.

Biéler, André. *La Pensée Économique et Sociale de Calvin*. Paris: Edition Albin Michel, 1961.

———. *The Social Humanism of Calvin*. Translated by Paul T. Furhman. Richmond, VA: Knox, 1964.

Bonhoeffer, Dietrich. *Act and Being*. Edited by Wayne W. Floyd Jr. Translated by H. Martin Rumscheidt. Minneapolis: Fortress, 1996.

———. *Christ the Center*. New York: Harper & Row, 1978.

———. "The Church and the Jewish Question." In *Berlin: 1932-1933*, edited by Larry L. Rasmussen, translated by Isabel Best and David Higgins, 361-70. *Dietrich Bonhoeffer Works* 12. Minneapolis: Fortress, 2009.

———. *The Cost of Discipleship*. New York: Simon & Schuster, 1959.

———. *Ethics*. New York: Simon & Schuster, 1995.

———. *Illegale Theologenausbildung: Finkenwalde 1935-1937*. Vol. 14 of *Dietrich Bonhoeffer Werke*. Gütersloh: Gütersloher, 1996.

———. *Letters & Papers from Prison*. Edited by Eberhard Bethge. New York: Macmillan, 1971.

———. *Life Together/Prayerbook of the Bible*. Translated by Daniel W. Bloesch and James H. Burtness. Edited by Geffrey B. Kelly. Vol. 5 of *Dietrich Bonhoeffer Works*. Minneapolis: Fortress, 1996.

———. *No Rusty Swords: Letters, Lectures and Notes, 1928-1936*. Vol. 1 of *Collected Works of Dietrich Bonhoeffer*. London: Colins, 1965.

———. *Sanctorum Communio: A Theological Study of the Sociology of the Church.* Edited by Clifford J. Green. Translated by Reinhard Krauss and Nancy Lukens. Minneapolis: Fortress, 1996.

———. *Testament to Freedom: The Essential Writings of Dietrich Bonhoeffer.* Edited by Geffrey B. Kelly and Burton Nelson. San Francisco: HarperSanFrancisco, 1990.

Bonino, J. Míguez. *Doing Theology in a Revolutionary Situation.* Philadelphia: Fortress, 1975.

———. *Toward a Christian Political Ethics.* Minneapolis: Fortress, 2007.

Bosch, David J. *Transforming Mission: Paradigm Shifts in Theology of Mission.* Maryknoll, NY: Orbis, 2004.

Bouwsma, William J. *John Calvin: A Sixteenth Century Portrait.* Oxford: Oxford University Press, 1988.

Braaten, Carl, and Robert Jenson, editors. *Union with Christ: The New Finish Interpretation of Luther.* Grand Rapids: Erdmans, 1988.

Brandenburg, Ingrid, and Klaus Brandenburg. *Hugenotten, Geschichte eines Martyrium.* Leipizig: Leizig, 1990.

Brandt, James M. *All Things New: Reform of Church and Society in Schleiermacher's Christian Ethics.* Louisville: Westminster John Knox Press, 2001.

Brandt, Walther I., editor. *Luther's Works: American Edition.* Vol. 45. Philadelphia: Muhlenberg, 1962.

Brookfield D. Stephen, and Stephen Preskill. *Discussion As a Way of Teaching: Tools and Techniques for Democratic Classrooms.* 2nd ed. San Francisco: Jossey-Bass, 2005.

Brown, R. McAfee, editor. *The Essential Reinhold Niebuhr: Selected Essays and Addresses.* New Haven: Yale University Press, 1986.

Browning, Don S., and Francis S. Fiorenza, editors. *Habermas, Modernity, and Public Theology.* New York: Crossroad, 1992.

Brubaker, Pamela, and Rogate Mshana, editors. *Justice Not Greed.* Geneva: WCC, 2010.

Busch, Eberhard. *Karl Barth: His Life from Letters and Autobiographical Texts.* Translated by John Bowden. Grand Rapids: Eerdmans, 1994.

———. *Unter dem Bogen des einen Bundes: Karl Barth und die Juden 1933–1945.* Neukirchen-Vluyn: Neukirchener, 1996.

Cady, Linell E. *Religion, Theology, and American Public Life.* Albany, NY: SUNY, 1993.

Cahill, Lisa Sowle. *Sex, Gender and Christian Ethics.* Cambridge: Cambridge University Press, 1996.

Calvin, John. *Commentaries on Galatians, Ephesians, Philippians, Colossians, I & II Timothy, Titus, Philemon.* Translated by William Pringle. Reprint, Grand Rapids: Baker, 1993.

———. *Commentaries on the Book of the Prophet Ezekiel.* Translated by Thomas Myers. Reprint, Grand Rapids: Baker, 1993.

———. *Commentary on the Epistles of Paul the Apostle to the Corinthians.* Translated by John Pringle. Reprint, Grand Rapids: Baker, 1993.

———. *Institutes of the Christian Religion.* Vol. 1. Edited by John T. McNeil. Translated by Ford Lewis Battles. Library of Christian Classics 20. Philadelphia: Westminster, 1960.

Chapman, Mark D. *Ernst Troeltsch and Liberal Theology: Religion and Cultural Synthesis in Wilhelmine Germany.* Oxford: Oxford University Press, 2001.

Chung, Paul S. *The Cave and the Butterfly: An Intercultural Theory of Interpretation and Religion in the Public Sphere.* Eugene, OR: Cascade, 2011.

———. *Christian Mission and a Diakonia of Reconciliation: Justification and Justice.* 3rd ed Minneapolis: Lutheran University Press, 2010.

———. *Constructing Irregular Theology: Bamboo and Minjung in East Asian Perspective.* Leiden: Brill, 2010.

———. *The Hermeneutical Self and an Ethical Difference: Intercivilizational Engagement.* Cambridge: Clarke, 2012.

———. *Karl Barth: God's Word in Action.* Eugene, OR: Cascade, 2008.

———. *Martin Luther and Buddhism: Aesthetics of Suffering.* 2nd ed. Eugene, OR: Pickwick, 2008.

———. *Public Theology in an Age of World Christianity: God's Mission as Word-Event.* New York: Palgrave Macmillan, 2010.

———. *Reclaiming Mission as Constructive Theology: Missional Church and World Christianity.* Eugene, OR: Cascade, 2012.

Chung, Paul S., Ulrich Duchrow, and Craig L. Nessan. *Liberating Lutheran Theology: Freedom for Justice and Solidarity in a Global Context.* Minneapolis: Fortress, 2011.

Chung, Paul S., Veli-Matti Kärkkäinen, and Kim Kyoung-Jae, editors. *Asian Contextual Theology for the Third Millennium: Theology of Minjung in Fourth-Eye Formation.* Eugene, OR: Pickwick: 2007.

Clements, Keith W., editor. *Friedrich Schleiermacher: Pioneer of Modern Theology.* Minneapolis: Fortress, 1991.

Clifford Geertz. *The Interpretation of Cultures.* New York: Basic, 1973.

Clooney, Francis X., editor. *The New Comparative Theology: Interreligious Insights from the Next Generation.* New York: T. & T. Clark, 2010.

Coates, Harper H., and Ryugaku Ishizuka. *Honen: The Buddhist Saint.* 1925. Reprint, New York: Garland, 1981.

Cobb, John B. Jr. *Beyond Dialogue: Toward a Mutual Transformation of Christianity and Buddhism.* Eugene, OR: Wipf & Stocks, 1988.

Cone, James H. *The Cross and the Lynching Tree.* Maryknoll, NY: Orbis, 2011.

Cortese, Anthony. *Ethnic Ethics: The Restructuring of Moral Theory.* Albany: SUNY, 1990.

Crowner, David, and Gerald Christianson, editors. *The Spirituality of the German Awakening,* New York: Paulist, 2003.

De Gruchy, John W., editor. *Bonhoeffer for a New Day: Theology in a Time of Transition.* Grand Rapids: Eerdmans, 1997.

Diamond, Irene, and Lee Quinby. *Feminism and Foucault: Reflections on Resistance.* Boston: Northeastern University Press, 1988.

Di Leonardo, Micaela, editor. *Gender at the Crossroads of Knowledge: Feminist Anthropology in the Postmodern Era.* Berkeley, CA: University of California Press, 1991.

Dillenberger, John, editor. *Martin Luther: Selections from His Writings.* Garden City, NY: Anchor, 1961.

Dorrien, Gary. *Social Ethics in the Making: Interpreting an American Tradition.* London: Wiley-Blackwell, 2011.

Duchrow, Ulrich. *Alternatives to Global Capitalism: Drawn from Biblical History, Designed for Political Action.* Utrecht: International, 1998.

———. *Global Economy: A Confessional Issue for the Churches?* Translated by David Lewis. Geneva: WCC, 1987.

———. *Two Kingdoms: The Use and Misuse of a Lutheran Theological Concept.* Geneva: LWF Department of Studies, 1977.

———, editor. *Colloquium 2000: Faith Communities and Social Movements Facing Globalization*. Geneva: WARC, 2002.
Duchrow, Ulrich, and Franz J. Hinkelammert. *Property for People, Not for Profit: Alternatives to the Global Tyranny of Capital*. London: Zed, 2004.
Durkheim, Emile. *The Elementary Forms of Religious Life*. Translated by Karen E. Fields. New York: Free, 1995.
Eade, Diana. *Courtroom Talk and Neocolonial Control*. New York: de Gruyter, 2008.
Ebeling, Gerhard. *Dogmatik des Christlichen Glaubens*. Vol. 3. Mohr: Tubingen, 1979.
———. *Introduction to a Theological Theory of Language*. Translated by R. A. Wilson. Philadelphia: Fortress, 1973.
———. *Luther: An Introduction to His Thought*. Minneapolis: Fortress, 2007.
———. *Lutherstudien*. Vol. 1. Tübingen: Mohr, 1971.
———. *Word and Faith*. Translated by James W. Leitch. Philadelphia: Fortress, 1963.
Fabiunke, Gűnter. *Martin Luther als Nationalöknom*. Berlin: Akademie, 1963.
Feuerbach, Ludwig. *The Essence of Christianity*. Translated by George Eliot. New York: Harper & Row, 1957.
Fashing, Darrell J., and Dell Dechant. *Comparative Religious Ethics: A Narrative Approach*. Oxford: Blackwell, 2001.
Flett, John. *The Witness of God: The Trinity, Missio Dei, Karl Barth, and the Nature of Christian Community*. Grand Rapids: Eerdmans, 2010.
Forde, Gerhard O. *Theology for Proclamation*. Minneapolis: Fortress Press, 1990.
Foucault, Michel. *The Archeology of Knowledge and the Discourse on Language*. New York: Random House, 1982.
———. *Fearless Speech*. Los Angeles: Semiotexte, 2001.
———. *Power/Knowledge*. Edited by Colin Gordon. New York: Pantheon, 1980.
Freytag, Walter, editor. *Mission zwischen gestern und morgen: vom Gestaltwandel der Weltmission der Christenheit im Licht der Konferenz des Internationalen Missionsrats in Willingen*. Stuttgart: Evang. Missionsverl, 1952.
Frymer-Kensky, Tikva, et al. *Christianity in Jewish Terms*. Oxford: Westview, 2000.
Fukuyama, *The End of History and The Last Man*. New York: Free, 1992.
Fung Yu-lan. *A History of Chinese Philosophy, 1: The Period of the Philosophers*. Translated by Derk Bodde. Princeton: Princeton University Press, 1983.
Gadamer, Hans-Georg. *Truth and Method*. 2nd rev. ed. Edited by Joel Weinscheimer and Donald G. Marshall. New York: Continuum, 2004.
Gayhart, Bryce A. *The Ethics of Ernst Troeltsch: a Commitment to Relevancy*. N.Y.: Lewiston: E. Mellen Press, 1990.
Geis, R. R. *Leiden an der Unerlöstheit der Welt: Briefe, Reden, Aufsätze*. Edited by D. Goldschmidt and I. Übershär. Munich: Kaiser 1984.
Geertz, Clifford. *The Interpretation of Cultures*. New York: Basic, 1973.
Gollwitzer, Helmut. *Auch das Denken darf dienen: Aufsätze zu Theologie und Geistesgeschichte*. Vol. 1. Munich: Kaiser, 1988.
———. *Die Kapitalistische Revolution*. Munich: Kaiser, 1974.
———. *The Existence of God As Confessed by Faith*. Translated by James W. Leitch. London: SCM, 1965.
———. *An Introduction to Protestant Theology*. Translated by David Cairns. Philadelphia: Westminster, 1978.
———. *Krummes Holz-Aufrechter Gang: Zur Frage nach dem Sinn des Lebens*. Munich: Kaiser, 1985.

———. *The Rich Christians and Poor Lazarus*. Translated by David Cairns. New York: Macmillan, 1970.
Gorringe, Timothy J. *Capital and the Kingdom: Theological Ethics and Economic Order*. Maryknoll, NY: Orbis, 1994.
Graham, W. Fred. *The Constructive Revolutionary: John Calvin and His Socio-Economic Impact*. Lansing, MI: Michigan State University Press, 1987.
Gramsci, Antonio. *The Antonio Gramsci Reader: Selected Writings 1916–1935*. Edited by David Forgas. New York: New York University Press, 1988.
Green, Clifford. *Karl Barth: Theologian of Freedom*. Minneapolis: Fortress, 1991.
Green, Clifford, and Thomas Tseng, editors. *Dietrich Bonhoeffer and Sino-Theology*. Taiwan: Chung Yuan Christian University, 2008.
Gregersen, Niels H., et al., editors. *The Gift of Grace: The Future of Lutheran Theology*. Minneapolis: Fortress, 2005.
Gregory, Peter N. *Tsung-mi and the Sinification of Buddhism*. Princeton: Princeton University Press, 1991.
Grenz Stanley, and John Franke. *Beyond Foundationalism: Shaping Theology in a Postmodern Context*. Louisville: Westminster John Knox, 2001.
Gruchy, John W. de, editor. *Bonhoeffer for a New Day: Theology in a Time of Transition*. Grand Rapids: Eerdmans, 1997.
Guder, Darrell L., editor. *Missional Church: A Vision for the Sending of the Church in North America*. Grand Rapids: Eerdmans, 1998.
Gustafson, James M. *Ethics from a Theocentric Perspective 1.Theology and Ethics*. Chicago: The University of Chicago Press, 1981.
———. *An Examined Faith: The Grace of Self-Doubt*. Minneapolis: Fortress, 2004.
———. "The Sectarian Temptation: Reflections on Theology, the Church, and the University." *Proceedings of the Catholic Theological Society* 40 (1985) 83–94.
Gutiérrez, Gustavo. *A Theology of Liberation*. Maryknoll, NY: Orbis, 1999.
Habermas, Jürgen. *Justification and Application: Remarks on Discourse Ethics*. Translated by Ciaran P. Cronin. Cambridge, MA: MIT Press, 1993.
———. *The Theory of Communicative Action*. Vol. 2, *Lifeworld and System: A Critique of Functional Reason*. Translated by Thomas McCarthy. Boston: Beacon, 1987.
Harnack, Adolf von. *Marcion: Das Evangelium vom fremden Gott*. Darmstadt: Wissenschaftliche Buchgesellschaft, 1960.
Harvey, Peter. *An Introduction to Buddhist Ethics*. Cambridge: Cambridge University Press, 2000.
Hauerwas, Stanley. *Against the Nations*. Minneapolis: Winston, 1985.
———. *Character and the Christian Life: A Study in Theological Ethics*. San Antonio: Trinity University Press, 1975.
———. *A Community of Character: Toward a Constructive Christian Social Ethic*. Notre Dame: University of Notre Dame Press, 1981.
———. *Performing the Faith: Bonhoeffer and the Practice of Nonviolence*. Grand Rapids: Brazos, 2004.
Hauerwas S., and William H. Willimon. *Resident Aliens: Life in the Christian Colony*. Nashville: Abingdon, 1989.
Haynes, Stephen R. *The Bonhoeffer Phenomenon: Portraits of a Protestant Saint*. Minneapolis: Fortress, 2004.

Helmer, Christine M. "The Trinity and Martin Luther: A Study on the Relationship between Genre, Language and the Trinity in Luther's Late Works (1523–1546)." PhD diss., Yale University, 1997.

Hinkelammert, Franz J. *The Ideological Weapons of Death: A Theological Critique of Capitalism*. Maryknoll, NY: Orbis, 1986.

Hodgson, Peter C. *Winds of the Spirit: A Constructive Christian Theology*. Louisville: Westminster John Knox, 1994.

Hoekendijk, J. C. *The Church Inside Out*. Philadelphia: Westminster, 1966.

Howell, Brian M., and Jenell W. Paris. *Introducing Cultural Anthropology: A Christian Perspective*. Grand Rapids: Baker Academic, 2011.

Hunsberger, George R. "The Missional Voice and Posture of Public Theologizing." *Missiology* 34/1 (2006) 15–28.

Hunsinger, George. *How to Read Karl Barth: The Shape of His Theology*. New York: Oxford University Press, 1991.

———, editor and translator. *Karl Barth and Radical Politics*. Philadelphia: Westminster, 1976.

Hyon Gak Sunim, editor. *Zen Master Seung Sahn: The Compass of Zen*. Boston: Shambhala, 1997.

Ingleby, Jonathan. *Beyond Empire: Postcolonialism and Mission in a Global Context*. Milton Keynes: Author House, 2010.

Irigaray, Luce. *An Ethics of Sexual Difference*. Translated by Carolyn Burke and Gillian C. Gill. Ithaca, NY: Cornell University Press, 1993.

Iwand, Hans J. *Glauben und Wissen*. Edited by Helmut Gollwitzer. Nachgelassene Werke 1. Munich: Kaiser, 1962.

———. *The Righteousness of Faith* According to Luther. Edited by Virgil F. Thompson. Translated by Randi H. Lundell. Eugene, OR: Wipf & Stock, 2008.

Jansen, Reiner. *Studien zu Luthers Trinitätslehre*. Bern: Lang, 1976.

Jenkins, Philip. *The Next Christendom: The Coming of Global Christianity*. Oxford: Oxford University Press, 2002.

Jennings J. Willie. *The Christian Imagination: Theology and the Origins of Race*. New Haven: Yale University Press, 2010.

Jones, Paul D. Review of *Karl Barth: God's Word in Action*, by Paul S. Chung. *Scottish Journal of Theology* 63/4 (2010), 474–77.

Jüngel, Eberhard. *God as The Mystery of the World: On the Foundation of the Theology of the Crucified One in the Dispute between Theism and Atheism*. Translated by Darrell L. Guder. Grand Rapids: Eerdmans, 1983.

———. *God's Being is in Becoming: The Trinitarian Being of God in the Theology of Karl Barth*. Translated by John Webster. Grand Rapids: Eerdmans, 2001.

Kant, I. *Basic Writings of Kant*. Edited by Allen W. Wood. New York: Modern Library, 2001.

———. *Fundamental Principles of the Metaphysics of Morals*. Translated by Thomas K. Abbot. New York: Liberal Arts, 1949.

———. *Religion within the Limits of Reason Alone*. Translated by T. M. Green and Hoyt H. Hudson. New York: Harper, 1960.

Kärkkäinen, Veli-Matti. *Christ and Reconciliation*. Grand Rapids: Eerdmans, 2013.

Kaufman, Gordon D. *In Face of Mystery: A Constructive Theology*. Cambridge, MA: Harvard University Press, 1993.

Kelley, G. B., and F. B. Nelson, editors. *A Testament to Freedom*. San Francisco: HarperSanFranciso, 1990.
King, Ursula, editor. *Religion and Gender*. Oxford: Blackwell, 2005.
Kitamori, Kazoh. *The Theology of the Pain of God*. 1965. Reprint, Eugene, OR: Wipf & Stock, 2005.
Klappert, Bertold. *Israel und die Kirche: Erwägungen zur Israellehre Karl Barths*. Munich: Kaiser, 1980.
———. *Miterben der Verheißung. Beiträge zum jüdisch-christlichen Dialog*. Neukirchen: Neukirchener, 2000.
———. *Versöhnung und Befreiung: Versuche, Karl Barth kontextuell zu verstehen*. Neukirchen-Vluyn: Neukirchener, 1994.
Knitter, Paul F. *No Other Name? A Critical Survey of Christian Attitudes toward World Religions*. Maryknoll, NY: Orbis, 1996.
Kogen, Mizuno. *Essentials of Buddhism: Basic Terminology and concepts of Buddhist Philosophy and Practice*. Tokyo: Kosei, 1996.
Kolb, Robert, and Timothy J. Wengert, editors. *The Book of Concord. The Confessions of the Evangelical Lutheran Church*. Minneapolis: Fortress, 2000.
Kraemer, H. *The Christian Message in a Non-Christian World*. New York: Harper & Row, 1938.
Krusche, Werner. *Das Wirken des Heiligen Geistes nach Calvin*. Göttingen: Vandenhoeck & Ruprecht, 1957.
Küng, Hans. *Does God Exist? An Answer for Today*. New York: Vintage, 1981.
———. *Global Responsibility: In Search of a New World Ethic*. Translated by John Bowden. Eugene, OR: Wipf & Stock, 2004.
Kwok Pui-Lan et al. *Off the Menu: Asian and Asian North American Women's Religion and Theology*. Louisville: Westminster John Knox, 2007.
Lehming, Hanna, et al., editors. *Wendung nach Jerusalem. Friedrich-Wilhelm Marquardts Theologie im Gespräch*. Munich: Kaiser.
Levinas, Emmanuel. *Basic Philosophical Writings*. Edited by Adriaan T. Peperzak, Simon Critchley, and Robert Bernasconi. Bloomington, IN: Indiana University Press, 1996.
———. *Difficult Freedom: Essays on Judaism*. Translated by Sean Hand. Baltimore: Johns Hopkins University Press, 1990.
———. *Humanism of the Other*. Translated by Nidra Poller. Urbana, IL: University of Illinois Press, 2006.
———. *Totality and Infinity: An Essay on Exteriority*. Translated by Alphonso Lingis. Pittsburgh: Duquesne University Press, 2007.
Lewis, Gordon R., and Bruce A. Demarest. *Integrative Theology: Historical, Biblical, Systematic, Apologetic, Practical*. Vol.1. Grand Rapids: Zondervan, 1996.
Lindbeck, George A. *The Nature of Doctrine: Religion and Theology in a Postliberal Age*. Louisville: Westminster John Knox, 1984.
Linbeck, Carter. *Beyond Charity: Reformation Initiative for the Poor*. Minneapolis: Fortress, 1993.
Lohse, Bernhard. *Martin Luther's Theology: Its Historical and Systematic Development*. Minneapolis: Fortress, 1999.
Lull, Timothy, editor. *Martin Luther's Basic Theological Writings*. Minneapolis: Fortress, 1989.
Lull, Timothy, and William R. Russell, editors. *Martin Luther's Basic Theological Writings*. 2nd ed. Minneapolis: Fortress, 2005.

Luther, Martin. *D. Martin Luthers Werke: Kritische Gesamtausgabe* [WA]. Vol. 2 Weimar: Bohlaus Nachfolger, 1884.

———. *D. Martin Luthers Werke: Kritische Gesamtausgabe.* Vol. 57. Weimar: Bohlaus Nachfolger, 1939.

———. *D. Martin Luthers Tischreden: 1531-46* [WATr]. Vol. 1 of *D. Martin Luthers Werke: Kritsiche Gesamtausgabe. Tischreden.* Weimar: Bohlaus Nachfolger, 1912.

The Lutheran World Federation. "A Call to Participate in Transforming Economic Globalization." Lutheran World Federation Tenth Assembly, Winnipeg, Canada, 21–23 July 2003.

Lutz, Charles P., editor. *Church Roots: Stories of Nine Immigrant Groups That Became The American Lutheran Church,* Minneapolis: Augsburg, 1985.

MacIntyre, Alasdair C. *After Virtue: A Study in Moral Theory.* 2nd ed. Notre Dame: University of Notre Dame Press, 1984.

Marquardt, F.-W. *Das christliche Bekentnis zu Jesus dem Juden.* Vol. 1, *Eine Christologie.* Munich: Kaiser, 1990.

———. *Die Entdeckung des Judentums für die christliche Theologie: Israel im Denken Karl Barths.* Munich: Kaiser, 1967.

———. *Eia, wärn wir da—eine theologische Utopie.* Munich: Kaiser, 1997.

———. *Theologie und Sozialismus: Das Beispiel Karl Barths.* Munich: Kaiser, 1972.

———. *Verwegenheiten: Theologische Stücke aus Berlin.* Munich: Chr. Kaiser Verlag, 1981.

———. *Von Elend und Heimsuchung der Theologie: Prolegomena zur Dogmatik.* Munich: Kaiser, 1998.

———. *Was dürfen wir hoffen, wenn wir hoffen dürften? Eine Eschatologie.* Vol. 1. Munich: Kaiser, 1993.

———. *Was dürfen wir hoffen, wenn wir hoffen dürften? Eine Eschatologie.* Vol. 3. Munich: Kaiser, 1996.

Marty, Martin. *The Public Church.* New York: Crossroad, 1981.

———. "Reinhold Niebuhr: Public Theology and the American Experience." *Journal of Religion* 54/4 (1974) 332–59.

McCormack, Bruce L. *Karl Barth's Critically Realistic Dialectical Theology: Its Genesis and Development, 1909–1936.* Oxford: Clarendon, 1995.

McLellan, David, editor. *Karl Marx Selected Writings.* Oxford: Oxford University Press, 1988.

McNeill, John T. *The History and Character of Calvinism.* Oxford: Oxford University Press, 1954.

Mead, Margaret. *Male and Female: A Study of the Sexes in a Changing World.* New York: Morrow, 1949.

Meeks, M. Douglas, *God The Economist: The Doctrine of God and Political Economy.* Minneapolis: Fortress, 1989.

Mencius. Translated by Zhao Zhentao, Zhang Wenting, and Zhou Dingzhi. Hunan, China: Hunan People's, 1999.

Meneses, Eloise Hiebert. "Science and the Myth of Biological Race." In *This Side of Heaven: Race, Ethnicity, and the Christian Faith,* edited by Alvaro Nieves and Robert J. Priest, 33–46. New York: Oxford University Press, 2007.

Metz, John Baptist. *A Passion For God: The Mystical-Political Dimension of Christianity.* Edited and translated by J. Matthew Ashley. New York: Paulist, 1998.

Metz J. Baptist, and Jürgen Moltmann. *Faith and the Future: Essays on Theology, Solidarity, and Modernity.* Maryknoll, NY: Orbis, 1995,

Minjung Theology: People as the Subjects of History. Edited by Commission on Theological Concerns of the Christian Conference of Asia. Maryknoll, NY: Orbis, 1981.

Mofokeng, Takatso. "Black Christians, the Bible and Liberation." *Journal of Black Theology in South Africa* 2/34 (1988) 34–42.

Moltmann, Jürgen. *The Coming of God: Christian Eschatology.* Translated by Margaret Kohl. Minneapolis: Fortress, 1996.

———. *The Crucified God: The Cross of Christ as the Foundation and Criticism of Christian Theology.* Translated by Margaret Kohl. Minneapolis: Fortress, 1993.

———. *Ethics of Hope.* Translated by Margaret Kohl. Minneapolis: Fortress, 2012.

———. *Experiences in Theology: Ways and Forms of Christian Theology.* Translated by Margaret Kohl. Minneapolis: Fortress, 2000.

———. "Open Letter to José Míguez Bonino." *Christianity and Crisis* 36 (1976) 57–63.

———. *The Spirit of Life: A Universal Affirmation.* Translated by Margaret Kohl. Minneapolis: Fortress, 1993.

———. *Theology of Hope: On the Ground and the Implications of a Christian Eschatology.* Translated by James W. Leitch. Minneapolis: Fortress, 1993.

———. *The Trinity and the Kingdom: The Doctrine of God.* Translated by Margaret Kohl. Minneapolis: Fortress, 1993.

Nessan, Craig L. "Christian Political Responsibility: Reappropriating Luther's Two Kingdoms." In Paul S. Chung, Ulrich Duchrow, and Craig L. Nessan, *Liberating Lutheran Theology: Freedom for Justice and Solidarity in a Global Context,* 46–52. Minneapolis: Fortress, 2011

———. "Missionary Theology and Wartburg Theological Seminary."*Currents in Theology and Mission* 31/2 (2004) 85–95.

———. Review of *Karl Barth: God's Word in Action,* by Paul S. Chung. *Dialog: A Journal of Theology* 50/4 (2011) 386–88.

———. *Shalom Church: The Body of Christ as Ministering Community.* Minneapolis: Fortress, 2010.

———. *The Vitality of Liberation Theology.* Oregon, Eugene, OR: Pickwick, 2012.

Newbigin, Lesslie. *Gospel in a Pluralist Society.* Grand Rapids: Eerdmans, 1989.

Nhat Hanh, Thich. *The Diamond that Cuts Through Illusion: Commentaries on the Prajnaparamita Diamond Sutra.* Berkeley: Parallax, 1992.

———. *The Heart of Understanding: Commentaries on the Prajnaparamita Heart Sutra.* Edited by Peter Levitt. Berkeley: Parallax, 1988.

———. *Zen Keys.* Translated by Albert and Jean Low. Garden City, NY: Anchor, 1974.

Niebuhr, H. Richard. *Christ and Culture.* New York: Harper & Row, 1951.

———. *Experiential Religion.* New York: Harper & Row, 1972.

———. *H. Richard Niebuhr. Theology, History, and Culture: Major Unpublished Writings.* Edited by William Stacy Johnson. New Haven: Yale University Press, 1996.

———. *Radical Monotheism and Western Culture: With supplementary essays.* New York, Harper, 1960.

———. *The Responsible Self.* New York: Harper & Row, 1963.

———. *Schleiermacher on Christ and Religion.* New York: Scribner's, 1964.

Niebuhr, Reinhold. *The Children of Light and the Children of Darkness.* New York: Scribner's, 1944.

———. *An Interpretation of Christian Ethics.* New York: Harper & Row, 1963.

———. *Irony of American History.* New York: Scribner's Sons, 1952.

———. *Man's Nature and His Communities.* New York: Scribner's Sons, 1965.

Niesel, Wilhelm. *The Theology of Calvin*. Translated by Harold Knight. Grand Rapids: Baker, 1980.

Noel James A., and Matthew V. Johnson, editors. *The Passion of the Lord: African American Reflections*. Minneapolis: Fortress, 2005.

Oberman, Heiko A. "Die Juden in Luthers Sicht." In *Die Juden und Martin Luther–Martin Luther und die Juden: Geschichte, Wirkungsgeschichte, Herausforderung*, edited by Heinz Kremers et al., 136–62. Neukirchen: Neukirchener, 1985.

Ong, Aihwa. *Flexible Citizenship: The Cultural Logics of Transnationality*. Durham, NC: Duke University Press, 1999.

Palmer, Martin. *The Jesus Sutras: Rediscovering the Last Scrolls of Taoist Christianity*. New York: Ballantine, 2001.

Pangritz, Andreas. *Karl Barth in the Theology of Dietrich Bonhoeffer*. Translated by Barbara and Martin Rumscheidt. Grand Rapids: Eerdmans, 2000.

———. "Sharing the Destiny of His People." In *Bonhoeffer for a New Day: Theology in a Time of Transition*, edited by John W. De Gruchy, 258-277. Grand Rapids: Eerdmans, 1997.

———. "Theological Motifs in Bonhoeffer's Decision to Participate in Political Resistance." Translated into Chinese by Rachel Zhu as "PengHuoFei'Er Lun li Xue de Shen Xue Dong Ji." *Regent Review of Christian Thoughts* 2/2 (2005), 257–68.

———. "Umkehr und Erneuerung. Helmut Gollwitzers Beitrag zur Veränderung des christlich-jüdische Verhältnisses." *Berliner Theologische Zeitschrift* 12/2 (1995) 269–84.

Pangritz, Andreas, and Paul S. Chung, editors. *Theological Audacities: Selected Essays of Friedrich-Wilhelm Marquardt*. Eugene, OR Pickwick, 2010.

Pannenberg, W. *Ethics*. Translated by Keith Crim. Philadelphia: Westminster, 1981.

———. *Jesus, God and Man*. 2nd ed. Translated by Lewis L. Wilkins and Duane A. Priebe. Philadelphia, Westminster, 1968.

———. *Systematic Theology* Vol. 1. Translated by Geoffrey W. Bromiley. Grand Rapids: Eerdmans, 1991.

———. *Systematic Theology* Vol. 3. Translated by Geoffrey W. Bromiley. Grand Rapids: Eerdmans, 1998.

———. *Theology and the Philosophy of Science*. Translated by Francis McDonagh. Philadelphia: Westminster, 1976.

Paulson, Steven, D. *Lutheran Theology*. New York: T. & T. Clark, 2011.

———. *Luther for Armchair Theologians*. Louisville: Westminster John Knox, 2004.

———. "Luther on the Hidden God." *Word & World* 19/4 (1999) 363–71.

Pelikan, Jaroslav, editor. *Luther's Works: American Edition*. Vol. 1. St. Louis: Concordia, 1958.

———. *Luther's Works: American Edition*. Vol. 4. St. Louis: Concordia, 1964.

Peters, Ted. *God—The World's Future: Systematic Theology for a New Era*. 2nd. ed. Minneapolis: Fortress, 2000.

Pieris, Aloysius. *Love Meets Wisdom: A Christian Experience of Buddhism*. Maryknoll, NY: Orbis, 1988.

Peura, Simo. "Gott und Mensch in der Unio: Die Unterschiede im Rechtfertigungsverständnis bei Osiander und Luther." In *Unio: Gott und Mensch in der nachreformatorische Theologie*, edited by Matti Repo und Rainer Vinke, 31–61. Helsinki: Luther-Agricola-Gesellschaft, 1996.

Plaskow, Judith. *Standing Again at Sinai: Judaism from a Feminist Perspective.* New York: HarperCollins, 1990.
Polanyi, Karl. *The Great Transformation.* Boston: Beacon, 1957.
———. *The Livelihood of Man.* Edited by Harry W. Pearson. New York: Academic, 1977.
Reist, Benjamin A. *Toward a Theology of Involvement: The Thought of Ernst Troeltsch.* Philadelphia: Westminster, 1966.
Riaser, Konrad. "Bonhoeffer and the Ecumenical Movement." In *Bonhoeffer for a New Day: Theology in a Time of Transition*, edited by John W. de Gruchy, 319–39. Grand Rapids: Eerdmans, 1997.
Ratke, David C. *Confession and Mission, Word and Sacrament: The Ecclesial Theology of Wilhelm Loehe.* St. Louis: Concordia, 2001.
Rauschenbusch, W. *Christianizing the Social Order.* New York: Macmillan, 1912.
———. *A Theology for the Social Gospel.* Nashville: Abingdon, 1945.
Rendtorff, Trutz. *Ethics.* Vol. 1, *Basic Elements and Methodology in an Ethical Theology.* Translated by Keith Crim. Minneapolis: Fortress, 1986.
———. *Ethics.* Vol. 2, *Applications of an Ethical Theology.* Translated by Keith Crim. Minneapolis: Fortress, 1989.
Ricoeur, Paul. *The Conflict of Interpretations.* Edited by Don Ihde. Evanston, IL: Northwestern University Press, 1974.
———. *Essays on Biblical Interpretation.* Edited by Lewis S. Mudge. Philadelphia: Fortress, 1980.
———. *Oneself as Another.* Translated by Kathleen Blamey. University of Chicago Press, 1992.
Rieger, Joerg. Review of *Karl Barth: God's Word in Action*, by Paul S. Chung. *Religions Studies Review* 36/3 (2010) 211.
Rieth, Ricardo. *"Habsucht" bei Martin Luther: Ökonomisches und theologisches Denken. Traditionen und soziale Wirklichkeit im Zeitalter der Reformation.* Weimar: Böhlaus Nachfolger, 1996.
Robinson, James M., and John B. Cobb Jr., editors. *The New Hermeneutics*, vol. 2 of *New Frontiers in Theology: Discussions among Continental and American Theologians.* London: Harper & Row, 1964.
Roozen, David A., and Heidi Hadsell, editors. *Changing The Way Seminaries Teach: Pedagogies for Interfaith Dialogue.* Hartford, CT: Hartford Institute for Religious Research, 2009.
Rumscheidt, H. Martin, editor. *Fragments Grave and Gay.* London: Collin, 1971.
Rupp, E. Gordon, and Philip S. Watson, editors. *Luther and Erasmus: Free Will and Salvation.* Philadelphia: Westminster, 1969.
Said. Edward. *Orientalism.* London: Routledge, 1978.
Sanneh, Lamin. *Disciples of All Nations: Pillars of World Christianity.* New York: Oxford University Press, 2008.
———. *Translating the Message: The Missionary Impact on Culture.* Maryknoll, NY: Orbis, 1989.
———. *Whose Religion Is Christianity? The Gospel beyond the West.* Grand Rapids: Eerdmans, 2003.
Santmire, H. Paul. *The Travail of Nature: The Ambiguous Ecological Promise of Christian Theology.* Minneapolis: Fortress, 2000.
Schattauer, Thomas H. "The Löhe Alternative for Worship, Then and Now." *Word & World* 24/2 (2004) 145–56.

———. "'Sung, Spoken, Lived': Worship as Communion and Mission in the Work of Wilhelm Loehe." *Currents in Theology and Mission* 33/2 (2006) 113–21.

Schleiermacher, Friedrich. *Brief Outline on the Study of Theology*. Translated by Terrence N. Tice. Richmond, VA: Knox, 1966.

———. *The Christian Faith*. Edited and translated by H. R. Mackintosh and J. S. Stewart. New York, Harper & Row, 1963.

———. *Hermeneutics and Criticism and Other Writings*. Translated and edited by Andrew Bowie. Cambridge: Cambridge University Press, 1998.

———. *Hermeneutics: The Handwritten Manuscripts*. Edited by Heinz Kimmerle. Translated by James Duke and Jack Forstman. Missoula: Scholars, 1977.

———. *Introduction to Christian Ethics*. Translated by John C. Shelley. Nashville: Abingdon, 1989.

———. *Lectures on Philosophical Ethics*. Edited by Robert B. Louden. Translated by Louise Adey Huish. Cambridge: Cambridge University Press, 2002.

Schmid, H. *The Doctrinal Theology of the Evangelical Lutheran Church*. Philadelphia: Lutheran Publication Society, 1899.

Scholl, Hans. *Reformation und Politik: Politische Ethik bei Luther, Calvin und den Frühhugenotten*. Stuttgart: Kohlhammer, 1976.

Schottroff, Luise, and Wolfgang Stegemann. *Jesus von Nazareth. Hoffnung der Armen*. Stuttgart: Kohlhammer, 1990.

Schüssler-Fiorenza, Elisabeth. *In Memory of Her: A Feminist Theological Reconstruction of Christian Origins*. Crossroads, New York, 1992.

Schwarz, Hans. *True Faith in the True God: An Introduction to Luther's Life and Thought*. Minneapolis: Augsburg, 1996.

———. "Wilhelm Loehe in the Context of the Nineteenth Century." *Currents in Theology and Mission* (2006) 93–104.

Schweiker, William. *Responsibility and Christian Ethics*. Cambridge: Cambridge University Press, 1995.

———. *Theological Ethics and Global Dynamics: In the Time of Many Worlds*. Malden, MA: Blackwell, 2004.

Segundo, J. Luis. *Liberation of Theology*. Translated by John Drury. Maryknoll, NY: Orbis, 1976.

Simpson, Gary M. *Critical Social Theory: Prophetic Reason, Civil Society, and Christian Imagination*. Minneapolis: Fortress, 2002.

———. "'Written on their hearts': Thinking with Luther about Scripture, Natural Law, and the Moral Life." *Word & World* 30/4 (2010) 419–28.

Sonderegger, Kristine. *That Jesus Christ Was Born a Jew: Karl Barth's "Doctrine of Israel."* University Park, PA: Pennsylvania State University Press, 1992.

Soulen, R. Kendall. *The God of Israel and Christian Theology*. Minneapolis: Fortress, 1996.

Stackhouse, Max L. *Ethics and the Urban Ethics: An Essay in Social Theory and Theological Reconstruction*. Boston: Beacon, 1972.

———. *Globalization and Grace*. New York: Continuum, 2007.

———. *Public Theology and Political Economy: Christian Stewardship in Modern Society*. Grand Rapids: Eerdmans, 1987.

Stankiewicz, W. J. *Politics & Religion in Seventeenth-Century France: A Study of Political Ideas from the Monarchomachs to Bayle, as Reflected in the Toleration Controversy*. Berkeley, CA: University of California Press, 1960.

Stolle, Volker. *Luther Texts on Mission. The Church Comes from All Nations*. Translated by Klaus D. Schultz and Daniel Thies. Saint Louis: Concordia, 2003.
Tamburello, Dennis E. *Union with Christ: John Calvin and the Mysticism of St. Bernard*. Louisville: Westminster John Knox, 1994.
Taylor, Charles. *Sources of the Self: The Making of the Modern Identity*. Cambridge, MA: Harvard University Press, 1989.
Thiemann, Ronald F. *Constructing a Public Theology: The Church in a Pluralistic Culture*. Louisville: Westminster John Knox, 1991.
———. *Revelation and Theology: The Gospel as Narrated Promise*. Notre Dame: University of Notre Dame Press, 1985.
Tillich, Paul. *Christianity and the Encounter of World Religions*. Minneapolis: Fortress, 1994.
———. *Love, Power, and Justice: Ontological Analyses and Ethical Application*. Oxford: Oxford University Press, 1954.
———. *Morality and Beyond*. New York: Harper, 1963.
———. *Systematic Theology*. 3 vols. Chicago: University of Chicago Press, 1951–1963.
———. *Theology of Culture*. Edited by Robert C. Kimball. Oxford: Oxford University Press, 1959.
Torrance, T. F. *Karl Barth, Biblical and Evangelical Theologian*. Edinburgh: T. & T. Clark, 1990.
Tracy, David. *The Analogical Imagination: Christian Theology and the Culture of Pluralism*. New York: Crossroad, 2000.
———. *Blessed Rage for Order: The New Pluralism in Theology*. Chicago: University of Chicago Press, 1996.
———. *Plurality and Ambiguity: Hermeneutics, Religion, Hope*. Chicago: University of Chicago Press, 1987.
———. "Theology, Critical Social Theory, and the Public Realm." In *Habermas, Modernity, and Public Theology*, edited by, Don S. Browning and Francis Schüssler Fiorenza, 19-42. New York: Crossroad, 1992.
Tracy, David, and John B. Cobb Jr., *Talking About God*. New York: Seabury, 1983.
Troeltsch, Ernst. *The Absoluteness of Christianity and the History of Religions*. Translated by David Reid. Richmond, VA: Knox, 1971.
———. *The Social Teaching of the Christian Churches*, Vol. 2. Translated by Olive Wyon. Louisville: Westminster John Knox, 1992.
Valentin, Benjamin. *Mapping Public Theology: Beyond Culture, Identity, and Difference*. Harrisburg, PA: Trinity, 2002.
Van Gelder, Craig, and Dwight J. Zscheile. *The Missional Church in Perspective: Mapping Trends and Shaping the Conversation*. Grand Rapids: Baker Academic, 2011.
Vicedom, Georg F. *Actio Dei: Mission und Reich Gottes*. Munich: Kaiser, 1975.
———. *The Challenge of the World Religions*. Translated by Barbara and Karl Hertz. Philadelphia: Fortress, 1963.
———. *Church and People in New Guinea*. New York: Association, 1961.
———. *Die Mission der Weltreligionenen*. Munich: Kaiser, 1959.
———. *Mission im ökumenischen Zeitalter*. Gerd: Gütersloher, 1967.
———. *The Mission of God: An Introduction to a Theology of Mission*. Translated by Gilbert A. Thiele and Dennis Hilgendorf. Saint Louis: Concordia, 1965.
———. *Myths and Legends from Mount Hagen*. Translated by Andrew Strathern. Port Moresby: Institute of Papua New Guinea Studies, 1977.

———, editor. *Christ and the Younger Churches*. London: SPCK, 1972.

Wallace, Ronald S. *Calvin, Geneva and Reformation: A Study of Calvin as Social Worker, Churchman, Pastor and Theologian.* Grand Rapids: Baker Book House, 1988.

Weber, Max. *Essays in Sociology*, trans. and ed. H. H. Gerth and C. Wright Mills. New York: Oxford University Press, 1958.

———. *The Protestant Ethic and the Spirit of Capitalism*, trans. Talcott Parsons. Mineola, NY: Dover, 2003.

———. *Selections in Translation*. Edited by W. G. Runciman. Translated by Eric Matthews. Cambridge: Cambridge University Press, 1978.

Weber, Otto. *Grundlagen der Dogmatik*. Vol. 2. Neukirchen-Vluyn: Neukirchener, 1987.

Welch, Claude. *Protestant Thought in the Nineteenth Century.* Vol. 1, *1799–1870*. New Haven: Yale University Press, 1972.

———. *Protestant Thought in the Nineteenth Century*. Vol. 2, *1870–1914*. New Haven: Yale University Press, 1985.

Wendel, Francois. *Calvin: Origins and Development of His Religious Thought*. Translated by Philip Mairet. Durham, NC: Labyrinth, 1987.

Westhelle, Vítor. *After Heresy: Colonial Practices and Post-colonial Theologies*. Eugene, OR: Cascade, 2010.

William, Paul. *Mahayana Buddhism: The Doctrinal Foundations*. London: Routledge, 1989.

Williams, Patrick, and Laura Chrisman, editors. *Colonial Discourse and Post-colonial Theory: A Reader*. New York: Columbia University Press, 1994.

Wind, Renate. *Dietrich Bonhoeffer: A Spoke in the Wheel*. Translated by John Bowden. Grand Rapids: Eerdmans, 1991.

Wuthnow, Robert. *Boundless Faith: The Global Outreach of American Churches*. Berkeley, CA: University of California Press, 2009.

Yip, Francis. *Capitalism as Religion? A Study of Paul Tillich's Interpretation of Modernity*. Cambridge, MA: Harvard University Press, 2010.

Yoder, John Howard. *Karl Barth and the Problem of War and Other Essays on Barth*. Edited by Mark Thiessen Nation. Eugene, OR: Cascade, 2003.

———. *The Politics of Jesus: Vicit Agnus Noster*. 2nd ed. Grand Rapids: Eerdmans, 1972.

Zimmermann, W.-D. *Begegnung mit Dietrich Bonhoeffer: Ein Almanach*. Munich: Kaiser, 1964.

Index

Ad Limina Apostolorum, 149, 326
Agential theory of responsibility, 199, 217, 221
Analogans, 100, 103
Analogatum, 100, 101, 103
Analogia attributionis, 99, 100
Analogia entis, 322, 326
Analogia fidei, 100, 101, 103, 104, 121, 288, 322
Analogia inaequalitatis, 100
Analogia relationis, 76, 78, 79, 100
Analogia verbi, 288
Analogical hermeneutics, 101
Analogical imagination, xxvii, 228, 282, 287, 319
Androcentricity, 189
Anfechtungen, 13
Apokatastasis, 321, 324, 325
Arcana virtus Dei, 29
Archeological hermeneutics, 185, 293, 308
Archeological methodology, xxxiv
Aristotelian rationalism, 256
Ascetic Protestantism, 166
Asian *minjung* theology, 72, 273, 304
Aufhebung, 315
Augsburg confession, 4, 60, 68, 84
Augustinian rule, 5

Bakla, 190
Barmen Theological Declaration, 38, 40, 332
Barth, Karl, x, xix, xx, xxi, xxvi, xxiv, xxx, 15, 25, 26, 28, 36, 38, 44, 45, 46, 56, 57, 73–151, 153, 215, 242, 246, 253, 257, 273, 296, 309, 312–40, 344, 345, 348, 369, 370, 372–77, 379–81, 383, 384
Barth's analogical politics, 122, 130
Barth's model of correspondence, 123
Benjamin, Walter, 299, 352
Beruf, 6, 32
Bhabha, Homi, 285, 286
Biblical realism, xx, 250, 251, 253, 255, 257, 258, 259, 261, 263, 265, 267, 269
Binary opposition, xxxiv, 290
Bonhoeffer, Dietrich, x, xi, xx, 38, 39–55, 118, 153, 241–43, 269, 272, 273, 279, 280, 291–311, 339, 348
Bonino, Miguez, 346–49

Calvin, Jean, x, xi, 20–36, 83, 98, 118, 153, 157, 216, 224, 226, 227, 230, 235, 296
Canon within the canon, 7, 96
Cantus firmus, 242
Capitalist spirit, 31
Categorical imperative, 179, 198, 199, 231, 286
Causa Dei, 110
Christian sociology, 236, 258, 260, 261, 263, 266
Chthonic powers, 131
Church-sect-mysticism, 166, 168
Circulus vertitatis Dei, 102,
Circumincessio, 81
Civil society, xxiii, xxv, xxviii, 178, 265
Civitas dei, 251, 252
Civitas terra, 251

386 Index

Colonization of the lifeworld, xxix, 130, 357
Communicatio idiomatum, 82
Communio sanctorum, 87, 118
Commercialization, 112
Commodification, 367
Cone, James, 311, 351
Confucian ethics, ix, 273, 291, 304, 305, 307, 309
Creatio continua, xvii, 16, 17, 65, 68, 162, 180, 279, 280, 287, 332, 333, 360
Creatio ex nihilo, 9
Credo ut intelligam, 121
Crystal Night, 41
Cultural Protestantism, 201
Communicative rationality, xi, 174, 177, 178

Dabar, 7, 49, 79, 148, 151, 171, 272, 288, 336, 358, 359
Dabru emet, 133
Deconstruction, xxxiii, 44, 132, 191, 192, 272, 278
Dei loquentis persona, 77, 98, 105, 106, 336, 355
Deum justificare, 13, 358
Deus ex machina, 295
Dialectical predestination, 44, 138
Discourse ethics, 154, 172, 174, 175, 177, 179, 181, 183, 195, 242, 307, 308, 357
Disenchantment of the world, 249, 267
Distributive justice, 257, 268, 280, 358
Docta spes, 346
Dreieinigkeit, 80
Durkheim, Emile., 185
Dussel, Enrique, 288

Economic Trinity, 4, 13, 77, 159, 336, 354
Ebeling, Gerhard, xxxvi, 8, 11, 13, 14, 18, 53, 94, 184, 206, 208, 223, 360
Ecclesia invisibilis, 85
Ecclesia visibilis, 85
Ecclesia semper reformanda, 86, 112
Empire, xxxiii, xxxiv, xxxviii, 36, 130, 171, 172, 240, 287, 305, 353
Ethics of conviction, 249, 268

Ethics of virtue, 209, 237, 240
Ethnic ethic, 185
Erev rav, 292
Eudaimonia, 204
Extra muros ecclesiae, 314, 322

Faith seeking understanding, 283
Fanon, Frantz, 286
Foucault, Michel, 130, 177, 191, 192, 284, 285
French Calvinism, 21, 22
Fung Yu-lan., 305
Fusion of horizons, xii, xiv, xvii, xxxv, 18, 161, 176, 177, 180, 272, 277, 280, 288, 337, 352, 362, 365, 366

Gadamer, Hans-Georg, 6, 18, 96, 174, 175, 176, 177, 180, 195, 355, 362
Geertz, Clifford., 114, 233, 365
Global civil society, xxiii
Global pluralism, 276
Global public theology, 195, 250, 251, 253, 255, 257, 259, 261, 263, 265, 267, 269
God against God, 82
God as *ganz ändernde*, 113
God-beyond-God, 282
God in self, 4, 101, 336
God's ecology, 162
God's economy, xii, xiii, xv, xviii, xix, xxxvii, 11, 12, 159, 160, 161, 184, 195, 280, 288, 289, 356
God's illeity, 290
God's irregular voice, xxxvii, 18, 301
God's *oikos*, xxxvii, 159
God's two strategies, 66, 355
Gollwitzer, Helmut, x, xi, 4, 10, 14, 64, 65, 66, 106, 109, 126, 269, 310, 330, 334, 354, 355, 360, 361
Goyim-wisdom, 142
Grenzfall, 117, 118
Gutiérrez, Gustavo, 346–50
Habermas, Jürgen, xxvi, xxvii, xxviii, 130, 154, 177, 178, 265
Halakha, 189
Heidelberg Disputation, 13
Hermeneutical circle, 78, 102, 106, 185, 203, 205, 349

Hermeneutical reorientation, xx, 195, 272, 275, 276, 285, 288
Hermeneutics of the gospel, 276
Historical relativism, 167, 168–70, 172, 181
History of effect, xvii, 363
Hoekendijk, J. C., xxxi, 60, 69, 70,
Homo economicus, 266
Homo incurvatus in se, 89
Hyperreality, 357, 367

Id quo maius nihil cogitari nequit, 121
Ideal type, 165, 230
Imagines mundi, 365
Immanent Trinity, 4, 13, 57, 77, 78, 336, 354
Interpolation, xxxiv, 363
Intratextuality, 233
Invisible hand, 159, 172
Iron cage, 130, 267, 268

Kant, Immanuel, 174, 175, 197, 198, 199, 201, 207, 225, 235, 236, 256, 348
Klappert, Bertold, 43, 47, 140, 149, 324, 326
Knowledge-power-discourse, 288
Küng, Hans, 322

Late Judaism, 45
Larva dei, 16
Legis amatores, 50
Leviathan, 130, 131
Levinas, Emmanuel, 278, 288, 302, 303, 337, 366
Lex naturae, 243, 298
LGBTQ, 191
Lindbeck, George, xxviii, 232–34
Locke, John, 160, 265
Lordless powers, xviii, 65, 116, 128, 130–32, 156, 171, 343, 357
Luther, Martin, x,xi, 3–19, 25, 32, 38, 48–55, 59, 67, 88, 93, 96, 97, 118, 153, 223, 334, 362

Malkuth YHWH, 65
Marquardt. F. W., x,xi, 7, 8, 55, 119, 120, 140, 141, 146, 148–50, 323, 330, 339, 354, 358, 359

Massa perditionis, ix, 127, 272, 292, 327, 339
Mencius, 304, 305
Method of correlation, 214–19, 221, 223, 225, 227, 229, 231, 317, 319
Mimicry, xxxiv, xxxv, 285, 286
Minjung, ix, xxxv, xxxvii, 72, 127, 273, 279, 287, 289, 291, 292, 293, 294, 301, 304, 308, 309, 311, 327, 337, 339
Ministerium Verbi Divini, 88, 91, 107
Moltmann, Jürgen, xi, xxx, 9, 27, 82, 123, 147, 157, 209, 235, 306, 341, 342, 344, 347, 348, 354, 361
Monotheistic piety, 226
Mysterium trinitatis, 81

Narrative ethics, 232, 241–43, 246, 273, 275
Natural theology, 312, 322, 323, 326, 329, 334
Neo-Augustinian theology, 155
Neoliberal globalization, 171
Nessan, Craig L., xii, xxi, 330, 351, 355,
Niebuhr, Reinhold, xi, xxiv, 236, 251, 252, 254, 255, 257, 258
Niebuhr, H. R., 301
Norma normans, 57, 234, 235

Oikonomia, xxiv, xxxvii, 127, 159, 160
Ontological ethics, 219
Onto-theo-logy, 295, 304
Orientalism, xxxiii, xxxiv, 285

Palimpsest, xxxiv, xxxv
Panentheism, 80
Pannenberg, Wolfhart, xi, 342, 343, 362, 363
Paranesis, 65
Parrhesia, xi, 102, 128, 307, 308, 339, 367
Pelagianism, 134
Perichoresis xxx, 5, 78, 80, 81, 82, 354, 355
Phenomenology of involvement, 168
Phronēsis, 154, 175, 177, 195
Pietism, 62, 259
Possessive individualism, 127, 160, 259

Postcolonial public theology, xx, xxi, 271–73, 275, 277, 279, 281, 283, 284, 285, 287, 289, 290, 307, 311, 340, 366
Postcoloniality, 284
Postliberal narrative theology, 233–35, 237
Praeparatio evangelica, 70
Praedestinatio dialectica, 138
Praedestinatio gemina, 138
Predestination, 20, 23, 24, 26, 27, 28, 29, 31, 32, 44, 60, 137, 138, 157, 338
Primus usus, 243, 298
Profanum vulgus, 128
Prolepsis, 84, 342, 343
Public ethical epistemology, xvi
Pure Land Buddhism, ix, 314, 316
Puritan Calvinism, 166
Purpose rationality, 248, 267, 268

Radical monotheism, 215, 216, 230, 231, 248
Ratio veritatis, 121
Rauschenbusch, Walter, 122, 211, 236, 237, 258, 259, 260
Rectification of names, 304–6
Regnum gloriae, xxxv, 65, 357
Regnum naturae, xxxv, xxxvi, 65
Revisionist correlation model, xxiii, xxv, 244
Ritschl, Albrecht, xi, 199, 200, 201, 236

Sabellian modalism, 77
Schleiermacher, F. D. E., xi, xx, 195, 197, 201, 202–14, 227
Schöfungsordung, 254
Schweiker, William, xvi, 182, 199, 217, 220, 244, 248, 276, 277, 279, 281, 291, 301, 302, 306, 308, 310
Segundo, Juan, 348, 349, 352,
Sensus divinitatis, 29, 30
Sexual dimorphism, 190
Simul peccator et justus, 210
Smith, Adam, 160, 255, 259, 266, 267
Social gospel, 62, 63, 122, 123, 155, 211, 236, 237, 258, 259, 264
Social humanism, 33
Special ethics, 115, 117, 119, 128, 129,

Spivak, Gayatri Chakravorty, 286
Stalinism, 130
State socialism, 126, 129
Status confessionis, 12, 295, 296, 298
Stoicism, 256
Sub specie aeternitatis, 253
Summum bonum, 161
Suum cuique, 268, 269, 280

Theocentrism, 226, 275
Theologia crucis, 4, 9, 13, 14, 45–47, 82, 243, 294, 295, 299, 307, 308, 355, 359
Theological humanism, 277, 278, 280, 281, 301, 307
Theonomous ethics, 216, 218
Thick description, xvii, 18, 114, 171, 233, 272, 337, 366, 367
Thingification, 286
Tillich, Paul, 227, 228, 312, 317–21
Totus Christus, 84, 324
Tracy, David, xxvi, xxvii, 132, 214, 227, 228, 229, 281, 282, 287
Troeltsch, Ernst, 14, 164–70, 180, 181, 199, 200, 201
Tyrannicide, 118, 296, 305

Union with Christ, 23–26, 28, 226
Universalismus verus, 209

Verbum relationis, 79, 354
Vere Deus et vere homo, 352
Vertretung, 286
Visio Dei, 226
Viva vox evangelii, x, xvii, 6, 7, 54, 66, 97, 105, 107, 194, 233, 287, 329, 337, 352, 359, 361

Weber, Max, 11, 31, 32, 165, 172, 266, 267, 305
Western humanism, 192
Westminster confession, 30
Willingen conference, xxix, 57, 62, 73
Witness-people myth, 39, 41
Yoder, John Howard, 117, 240, 241, 247, 250, 275

Zwingli, Ulrich, 16, 25, 314

www.ingramcontent.com/pod-product-compliance
Lightning Source LLC
Chambersburg PA
CBHW071228290426
44108CB00013B/1322